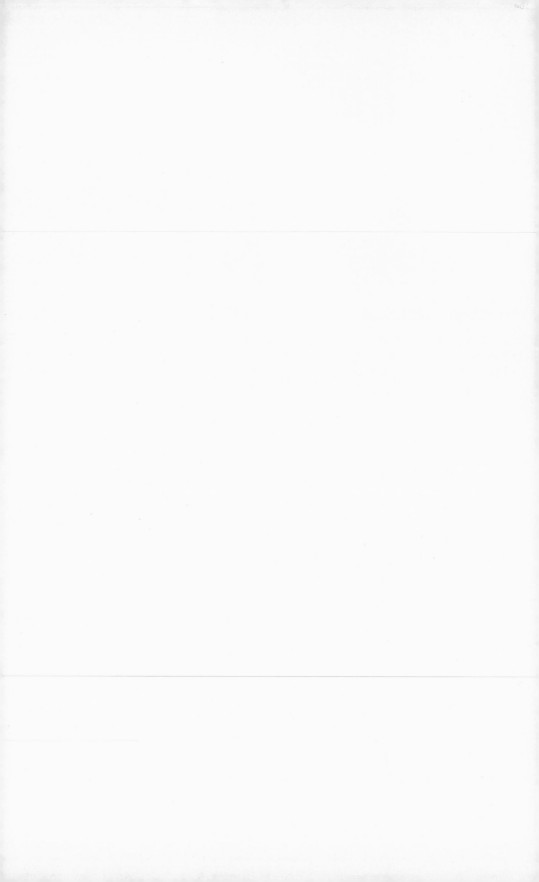

America Confronts Terrorism

AMERICA CONFRONTS TERRORISM

Understanding the Danger and
How to Think About It

A Documentary Record

EDITED WITH AN INTRODUCTION BY

John Prados

Ivan R. Dee

CHICAGO 2002

ISBN 1-56663-444-x

LC 2002141102

Contents

America Confronts Terrorism

Introduction

A SERIES OF terrorist attacks in the United States on New York City and Washington, D.C., on September 11, 2001, was rapidly followed by an attack using anthrax spores in the mail to U.S. senators, media figures, and journalists. A war on terrorism ensued, accompanied by stringent internal security measures within the United States and an unhealthy degree of public hysteria. The anthrax incidents, at first also attributed to foreign terrorists, are almost certainly the work of a disaffected American or small group. But the entire set of events has already assumed an importance greater than anything since the end of the cold war. In terms of American society, democracy, and the polity, the potential consequences riding on current events are enormous. It is vital to understand not only the events taking place but their contexts, not just what is happening but what led up to it, and not just what pundits are interpreting for us but what the U.S. government has concluded and observed. That is the purpose of this book.

Until September 11 there was little public interest in programs aimed at countering terrorism. The demands for action afterward reflect feverish desires to strike at the enemy—a diffuse, mostly hidden array of ethnic, political, and religious groups with widely varied agendas. Until September 11 there was little public knowledge of the terrorist enterprise. The rush to respond afterward is still based on a paucity of information, even though a great deal of this material is available in the United States and routinely circulated by the U.S. government, as the contents of this volume will reveal. Effective action should be based upon accurate appreciation, and the need for public scrutiny of executive actions requires that Americans (and citizens of all other nations involved in this war on terrorism) have a better understanding of the problem. Many of the documents reproduced in this collection can be tools to that end.

Part of the difficulty in improving awareness of the terrorist threat is that much of the earlier violence had occurred elsewhere and had not been aimed directly at Americans. Over the decades of the 1980s and 1990s, only 871 Americans died in the thousands of terrorist incidents that were recorded. Roughly 20 percent of those victims perished in a single incident, a purely home-grown plot

in which an American blew up the Alfred P. Murrah Federal Building in Oklahoma City on April 19, 1995. The vast majority of deaths caused by terrorists
have been of foreign citizens in their own lands. Averaging the number of
Americans killed in terrorist attacks over the number of years of data, typical
formulations have it that a chicken bone stuck in the throat is deadlier, or that
one has a higher probability of being struck twice by lightning. Americans did
not focus on the issue until the tragedy of September 11 brought the terrorism
question home to so many so personally.

Symptomatic of the problem are the reports of the review boards that have
examined individual catastrophic incidents and commissions that have looked
at larger issues in the terrorist arena. Again and again these bodies have reached
the same or analogous conclusions and have recommended logical countermeasures, only to see further disasters occur in very similar ways. Inability to
implement various recommendations has been closely related to the lack of
public demand before September 11. In the famine or feast cycle so typical of
democracy, now the danger is one of going too far in the direction of draconian
measures. Before proceeding down that road, it is worth pausing to view the
playing field and see where we have already been.

This collection consists primarily of U.S. government documents, some
from the executive departments, others from Congress. The documents represent authoritative collations of data; reports on groups, incidents, or individual
terrorists; official statements and orders; analyses of government activity or opti-
mal courses of action; field manuals; recommendations by expert panels; and
advisories to Congress commenting upon executive-branch data or actions.
Each section of the collection is introduced by commentary designed to place
the documents in context or supply an overview of the subjects to which the
material pertains. In their original form, many of the documents included here
are massive compendiums that cover many subjects. In almost all cases the documents have been edited in order to distill the main points of interest, to avoid
length, to eliminate extraneous items or introductory comments, or to concentrate on the topic in each section. A few of the documents are not of U.S. origin
but are statements, orders, or manuals put out by terrorist groups, primarily the
Al Qaeda network of Osama bin Laden. In some cases the documents or public
statements excerpted simply demonstrate the state of U.S. knowledge at given
points in time while the introductory passages furnish the main substantive
content.

In two instances articles are included among the selections, both of which
contribute to the understanding of special features of the problem of terrorism.
One illuminates the practical difficulties involved in a terrorist organization
adopting new technologies; the second represents the additional commentary
of an individual who headed a review board examining a particular bombing

incident. My original intention had been to select articles more widely, but a survey of recent periodical literature turned out to be much less useful than anticipated. In a few subject areas, especially on the danger of terrorist use of nuclear, chemical, and biological weapons, there were many articles to choose from. But on the overall problem of terrorism and the best course to take in response, the literature proved noticeably thin. This seems to follow from the general lack of public interest in terrorism before September 11, and from the inclination of experts and the media to concentrate on the fixations of the moment. Precisely because the issue of terrorist use of these weapons of mass destruction—exotic weapons, to be sure—has received so much attention both inside and outside government, it is avoided here. September 11 was high concept, low technology. Mass destruction that day was achieved by box cutters, not nuclear weapons.

The collection opens with a brief reconstruction of the attacks on September 11 and the plotting that preceded them. This demonstrates that the attacks were carefully prepared over a long period of time and coordinated by an organization. Osama bin Laden and Al Qaeda are introduced in that section, which includes the text of the declaration that bin Laden issued on October 7, 2001, part threat and part exhortation for followers. Statements by intelligence agencies and officials follow in the next segment, which delineates the expectations the U.S. government chose to reveal to the public in the months before the attacks.

In Part II the lens turns to the analysis of and recommendations by a national commission formed by Congress to examine the problem of terrorism and potential U.S. responses. The next section contains a compendium of the statistics of terrorist attacks as presented in annual reviews by the State Department during the 1990s, along with the most recent report as well as a paper commenting on that material. Osama bin Laden's background is the subject of Part IV, in which the documents excerpt what the Central Intelligence Agency and the State Department revealed about bin Laden at various points in the late 1990s. The next segment of the collection turns to terrorists and their methods with a set of profiles of groups assembled by an experienced analyst (and former CIA officer) at the Congressional Research Service, the paper already mentioned on terrorist acquisition of technology, and a primer by terrorists on techniques for various kinds of activities necessary to carrying out operations.

Major terrorist incidents of the late 1990s are examined in detail in Part VI. Documents here include summaries of the incidents, reports of review panels that searched for intelligence failures or security weaknesses, and commentaries by government analysts. The documents show differences in the incidents but also some remarkable similarities. Terrorists succeeded repeatedly even where intelligence failure did not occur, while the security measures that tightened constantly were never sufficient. The same kind of pattern exists in the September 11 attacks themselves. Any inquiry into whether intelligence failed to detect the September 11 plot ought really to be extended more widely, while Americans should avoid overoptimistic expectations as to the ability of security to prevent terrorism.

Finally, Part VII moves to discuss government programs to counter terrorism. The documents include executive orders freezing terrorist funds, Treasury Department reports on frozen assets, the reports of congressional committees authorizing intelligence budgets, legal commentary on the assassination ban that exists in government regulations, and military manuals for the planning of special warfare activities. Comments introducing this segment examine government programs in this area overall, recent developments such as initiatives for homeland security, budget levels, the Bush administration's war on terrorism, and other aspects of response strategy. No authoritative document could be excerpted that formulates, advocates, or even comments upon a political program to reduce the attractions of the terrorist life for potential militants—a troublesome finding that shows the narrow confines of the current strategy against terrorism.

I wish to acknowledge the assistance of many individuals and institutions in assembling this volume. The staffs of the libraries at New York University, Columbia University, and the University of Maryland were helpful and efficient. Their collections contained a number of the items selected here. Colleagues at the National Security Archive, in Washington, D.C., tireless compilers of the record of the U.S. government, provided vital assistance and again were sources for documents in this collection. Institutional support vital to the production of the manuscript was provided by the International Center for Advanced Studies of New York University. Individuals in these and other places helped the author with discussions that sharpened themes and issues. Finally, the victims of September 11 deserve credit they never solicited, for they have energized us all.

JOHN PRADOS

Washington, D.C.
January 2002

The Horror on September 11

It does not sit right to use superlatives in describing the terrorist attacks that took place in the United States on September 11, 2001. They were the most violent foreign attacks on American soil since Japan struck Pearl Harbor in December 1941. Like the Pearl Harbor raid, it now appears the adversary was not prepared for or capable of an immediate follow-up assault or a sustained campaign. Unlike Pearl Harbor, the adversary was a group of private individuals united in an organization with a mixture of religious and political motives rather than a nation embarking on war. The perpetrators were terrorists, not some military establishment carrying out a national policy. The goals of the terrorists were to destroy a mix of civilian and military targets in Washington, D.C., and New York City. The forces used were four small cells totaling nineteen men who succeeded in inflicting massive destruction.

Also unlike Pearl Harbor, September 11 took place in the age of television. Many Americans, and indeed people all around the world, watched live as three large jet airliners crashed into their targets—one as it was happening. The immediate impact seemed devastating; the outpouring of commentary that began virtually instantaneously further seared the events into memory. Police action, forensic investigation, and media reporting quickly established the broad details of terrorist acts which were not apparent in the instant of the events. Many in-depth accounts of these events will further cement the memories of all who witnessed desperate victims trying to escape or jumping to their deaths, or emergency workers trapped under collapsing buildings. But as yet there is no official account of the events of that fateful day, particularly one that concentrates on sketching in the plotting and preparation that led to the attacks. As America responds to terrorism, a measured response requires a sharper understanding than is permitted by a focus on the events of the attacks. This need to appreciate the methods of the adversary requires a description of the September 11 attacks and their antecedents.

Between 8:00 and 8:42 a.m. on September 11, four scheduled airliners departed on their routine trips, unknowingly bearing teams of hijackers. Two left from Logan Airport in Boston, both bound for Los Angeles: American Airlines

Flight 11 (at 8:00) with ninety-two persons aboard, and United Airlines Flight 175 (at 8:14) with fifty-six passengers and nine crew. Both were Boeing 767 aircraft, not quite of the huge 747 jumbo jet variety but very large planes. Also bound for Los Angeles, but leaving Washington's Dulles Airport (at 8:20) was American Airlines Flight 77 carrying sixty-four travelers and crew. This plane was a Boeing 757, a somewhat smaller predecessor of the 767. Last off the ground was United Airlines Flight 93 from Newark, bound for San Francisco with thirty-eight people on board, also a Boeing 757. Each of these planes was taken over by groups of hijackers between about twenty and forty-five minutes into their journeys. The planes were then diverted from their courses, hijackers at the controls.

Three of the four aircraft were flown into landmark buildings in New York City and Washington. Flight 11 smashed into the North Tower of the World Trade Center in New York at 8:47 a.m. Fire weakened structural supports, and the building collapsed at 10:30. The Trade Center's South Tower, hit lower down the side of the building by Flight 175 at 9:03, fell at 9:50 a.m. President George W. Bush authorized military countermeasures shortly after the second crash, and F-16 interceptor jets were launched from Langley Air Force Base in eastern Virginia, but these were still roughly a dozen minutes away when a third aircraft, Flight 77, struck the Pentagon at 9:43 a.m. Hijackers aboard the fourth plane were overpowered by passengers, and that aircraft crashed in the countryside in southwestern Pennsylvania.

The September 11 attacks were well planned and closely coordinated. It is now estimated that the perpetrators spent half a million dollars to place their teams of hijackers aboard the aircraft with weapons and the skills needed to fly the planes. There were four teams, three of them with five hijackers and the last with four, leading to the inference that one person did not make the plane (in this case Flight 93, aboard which the passengers successfully overpowered their captors). Almost half the hijackers had trained to fly large commercial aircraft. All were men. All were Muslims and Middle Eastern nationals, mostly from Saudi Arabia but also from Egypt, Lebanon, and the United Arab Emirates. They arrived in the United States separately, in ones and twos over an extended period. Many of the pilots had been in the United States for a long time—some of their aviation schooling dated to 1996. Several, thought to have been group leaders or the most senior, had been in and out of the United States. Those thought to have been soldiers, the strong-arm men who would hold back the passengers, arrived beginning in the spring of 2001. Apparently only the team leaders knew that the purpose of their effort was to use the planes themselves as weapons; the soldiers thought they were merely carrying out a conventional hijacking. A couple of the Boston hijackers crossed the Canadian border just before the attacks, catching a feeder flight at Portland, Maine, that deposited them at Logan in time for the main act. The others lived quietly across America, in places like Florida, California, and New Jersey. They were either near their points of departure or immediately before the attacks traveled to them.

Far apart geographically, the future hijackers kept in close touch by electronic mail. But they avoided using personal computers for communication, instead relying upon public facilities such as the Internet-wired computers in libraries. Face-to-face meetings were preferred to telephonic contact (see Part V for a terrorist manual that instructs in precisely these kinds of measures). In an encounter that has gained some notoriety, in Florida a few days before September 11 one of the militants argued with a waitress over the bar tab he had run up with several comrades. Alcohol is forbidden to devout Muslims. So is solicitation of sex, though a couple of the hijackers spent one of their last nights in Boston dialing up dating services. The pilots used some of their time to pore over aviation maps and watch videotapes illustrating the features of Boeing cockpits. Everyone, but especially the soldiers, worked out in gyms near where they lived.

Mohammed Atta, the man with the liquor bill, was the leader of the September 11 plot. He had gone to flight school in Florida—instructors found him humorless—and he bragged about being a pilot in that argument at the bar. But Atta was much more than that. Living in Hamburg, Germany, and studying at the Technical University there, this Egyptian citizen earned a degree in urban planning, writing a thesis on rebuilding Beirut after the destruction there in the 1970s and '80s. Atta may have had the ability to calculate force and load factors in an impact analysis of airplane crashes into the World Trade Center. Son of a lawyer, raised in an affluent family who insist that their Mohammed could not have had anything to do with a plot like September 11, Atta nevertheless roomed in Hamburg with two others who were among the hijackers. Another roommate has been linked to cash transfers to the hijackers in America. German authorities have associated Atta with the formation of a cell in Hamburg connected to the Al Qaeda terrorist network. He first entered the United States at Newark International Airport on a tourist visa in June 2000, beginning flight classes sometime later, and was involved with another of the eventual hijackers, also a flight student, in a safety violation that December 26 at the Miami airport. In the months before September 11, Atta traveled widely from his base in Florida, including to Germany, twice to Spain, to the Czech Republic, and within the United States. He maintained this affluence, renting cars, staying at good hotels, and so forth. Cell phone records show that Atta made hundreds of calls, including to other hijackers who then called others among their group. Atta left behind a five-page handwritten note, sometimes described as a will, plus flight training materials, found in a car in a Logan airport parking lot. Along with devotional phrases and tips for one's last night, the paper contained a reminder to check knives and ID and "make sure that nobody is fol-lowing." Mohammed Atta boarded Flight 11 and led the hijack team on that air-plane.

September 11 is attributed to the Al Qaeda network. One of the strongest pieces of evidence is a videotape of Osama bin Laden, the leader of Al Qaeda, in a conversation recalling the day of the attacks. On that tape bin Laden speaks of "Brother Mohammed" running the operation and shepherding the Muslim militants. Bin Laden also talks of calculations of expected damage to the World Trade Center buildings.

Two senior Al Qaeda representatives, Tawfiq bin Atash and Fahad al-Quso, both of whom have been linked to the suicide boat attack in Yemen on the U.S. destroyer *Cole* (see Part VI), met with two of the hijackers in Malaysia in Janu-ary 2000. One of the hijackers meeting those operatives would be associated by both British and American investigators with two other terrorist incidents, the *Cole* attack and the truck bombings of American embassies in Africa in August 1998, both of which are credited to bin Laden's Al Qaeda.

Anti-terrorist security missed some opportunities to apprehend individual hijackers during the months before September 11. One chance was lost when the CIA asked the State Department to place the visitors to Malaysia on its watch list on August 21—they had already entered the United States six weeks earlier. Another chance was lost with Zaid Samir Jarrah, detained in Dubai for questioning on his arrival from two months in Pakistan (and Afghanistan) at the end of January 2001. Jarrah satisfied his questioners but was later put on a U.S. watch list, again after he had entered the country. Jarrah was aboard Flight 93 on September 11. On September 11 nine of the nineteen hijackers were in the United States on valid visas, three had visas that had expired, and immigration could find no record of the other seven.

The plotters did what they could to prepare specifics for September 11. Mo-hammed Atta's rental car was spotted in the vicinity of Logan airport, at points where flight operations could be observed, at least five times. Some of the flights hijacked, or similar ones on the same routes, were traveled on other days in a sort of dry run. The hijackers used box-cutting knives in the expectation these would more easily get past airport security, though the question of how ex-actly these weapons *did* get on the airplanes is as yet unresolved. If nineteen people had each smuggled a knife onto a plane, the chance of exposure would have been maximized, and the planes would have been delayed with some risk of a renewed search of passengers. If four persons had each carried five or more knives onto the planes a different set of risks would have applied. Lying to the crew and passengers about weapons, a single weapon, only a handful of weapons, or no weapons at all are each a plausible scenario. Because of in-flight danger to passengers and the general experience that people hijack planes to get somewhere, air crews have traditionally been instructed to cooperate with declared hijackers. A number of the airplane tickets for September 11 were booked online, and the hijackers flew business class to be close to the cockpits and ahead of most other passengers on the planes.

Despite the care and preparation that evidently went into the September 11 plot, America benefited somewhat from bravery, luck, and good fortune. The bravery of the passengers on Flight 93 who fought their band of hijackers robbed the terrorist enemy of one weapon. Luck was a lady at the Pentagon, where the face of the building hit by Flight 77 had just finished a renovation that strengthened its structure and improved its fireproofing. The dead there were held to 189 where the toll could have been much higher, to include many of the hundreds of injured. Long cross-country nonstop flights, which the terrorists chose in order to gain the benefit of large aircraft fully loaded with fuel, struck the World Trade Center relatively early in the morning, before all employees had arrived for work. The twin towers also stood up long enough to permit thousands of people to escape from them. The death toll in New York, originally estimated at 6,000 or more (and ultimately indeterminate), at this writing stands at 2,890 souls and may yet go lower. All the people on the four airplanes perished. The overall toll currently numbers 3,114 persons. On September 11 the world received a shocking introduction to the realities of modern terrorism.

Bin Laden Statement, October 7, 2001: "The Sword Fell"

Here is America struck by God Almighty in one of its vital organs, so that its greatest buildings are destroyed. Grace and gratitude to God. America has been filled with horror from north to south and east to west, and thanks be to God. What America is tasting now is only a copy of we have tasted.

Our Islamic nation has been tasting the same for more 80 years, of humiliation and disgrace, its sons killed and their blood spilled, its sanctities desecrated.

God has blessed a group of vanguard Muslims, the forefront of Islam, to destroy America. May God bless them and allot them a supreme place in heaven, for he is the only one capable and entitled to do so. When those have stood in defense of their weak children, their brothers and sisters in Palestine and other Muslim nations, the whole world went into an uproar, the infidels followed by the hypocrites.

A million innocent children are dying at this time as we speak, killed in Iraq without any guilt. We hear no denunciation, we hear no edict from the hereditary rulers. In these days, Israeli tanks rampage across Palestine, in Ramallah, Rafah and Beit Jala and many other parts of the land of Islam, and we do not hear anyone raising his voice or reacting. But when the sword fell upon America after 80 years, hypocrisy raised its head up high bemoaning those killers who toyed with the blood, honor and sanctities of Muslims.

The least that can be said about those hypocrites is that they are apostates who followed the wrong path. They backed the butcher against the victim, the oppressor against the innocent child. I seek refuge in God against them and ask him to let us see them in what they deserve.

I say that the matter is very clear. Every Muslim, after this event, after the senior officials in the United States of America starting with the head of international infidels, Bush and his staff who went on a display of vanity with their men and horses, those who turned even the countries that believe in Islam against us — the group that resorted to God, the Almighty, the group that refuses to be subdued in its religion.

They have been telling the world falsehoods that they are fighting terrorism. In a nation at the far end of the world, Japan, hundreds of thousands, young and old, were killed and this is not a world crime. To them it is not a clear issue. A million children in Iraq, to them this is not a clear issue.

But when a few more than 10 were killed in Nairobi and Dar es Salaam [capitals of Kenya and Tanzania, where the American Embassies were bombed in 1998], Afghanistan and Iraq were bombed and hypocrisy stood behind the head of international infidels: the modern world's symbol of paganism, America, and its allies.

I tell them that these events have divided the world into two camps, the camp of the faithful and the camp of infidels. May God shield us and you from them.

Every Muslim must rise to defend his religion. The wind of faith is blowing and the wind of change is blowing to remove evil from the Peninsula of Muhammad, peace be upon him.

As to America, I say to it and its people a few words: I swear to God that America will not live in peace before peace reigns in Palestine, and before all the army of infidels depart the land of Muhammad, peace be upon him.

God is the greatest and glory be to Islam.

PART I

Appreciations of the Threat of Terrorism

PREDICTING THREATS to the United States is the function of the intelligence community. A shorthand term for the full panoply of organizations that engage in this work, the intelligence community consists of more than a dozen key entities, though offices in many other federal agencies have some degree of involvement in this area. Best known among these entities is the Central Intelligence Agency (CIA). Its chief, the director of Central Intelligence (DCI) is simultaneously the head of the community as a whole and the principal intelligence officer of the United States. Most community members are components of the Department of Defense (DOD), or Pentagon. These include the organizations best known next to CIA, which are the National Security Agency (NSA) and the National Reconnaissance Office (NRO). Since the mid-1990s the National Imagery and Mapping Agency (NIMA) has been added to the mix, and Pentagon participants in the community include the intelligence staffs of the army, navy, air force, and Marine Corps. The Federal Bureau of Investigation (FBI), Department of the Treasury (which includes the Secret Service and Customs Service), and Department of Energy have major intelligence functions. The Department of State also has a small version of the CIA's analytical component in its Bureau of Intelligence and Research (INR). All of these units are members of a sort of community board of directors called the National Intelligence Council (NIC), chaired by the director of Central Intelligence.*

The intelligence community has monitored terrorism for close to three decades, issuing both secret reports and public, unclassified analyses. The highest level of secret reports, called national intelligence estimates or special national intelligence estimates, are drafted by an office which serves the DCI and are approved by the National Intelligence Council. Other reports are crafted by the analytical unit of the CIA, called the Directorate of Intelligence, by the DCI's Counterterrorism Center, and by DIA or INR. Under the system of congressional oversight that exists today, the DCI, the director of DIA, and the State Department INR director each testify publicly every year—on the current global situation and foreseeable threats—to intelligence committees of the Senate and House of Representatives. These congressional committees are also briefed on and have access to national intelligence estimates and other intelligence reports.

This section excerpts testimony presented in 2001 by Director of Central Intelligence George Tenet, DIA director Vice Admiral Thomas R. Wilson, and INR director Thomas Fingar. All three officials discussed terrorism in their presentations. Admiral Wilson probably came closest to the contours of what occurred on September 11 with his declaration that a key near-term (within twelve to twenty-four months) concern of DIA was a major terrorist attack against U.S. interests, either at home or abroad and possibly with a weapon designed to inflict mass casualties. Director Tenet termed Osama bin Laden "the most immediate and serious threat" and saw the bin Laden organization as capable of multiple attacks with little or no warning. Nevertheless the CIA chief was silent on the threat of a direct attack along the lines of September 11.

To provide more depth on the matter of intelligence predictions, this section also features portions of several more CIA documents. All are unclassified texts, meaning they contain only information the CIA deemed suitable for public view. None was produced for the specific purpose of predicting terrorist activity. Rather, "Global Trends 2015" sought to foresee the leading international concerns a decade and a half hence. This report was an official product of the National Intelligence Council in December 2000. It anticipated terrorist incidents designed to produce mass casualties but reserved its greatest concern for the danger that nations will sponsor terrorism. The "Strategic Intent" document represents CIA's effort to fashion a business plan of sorts for guiding the

*Certain organizations with clear roles in homeland defense, the wars against drugs and terrorism, or other security functions are not NIC members. This includes the Coast Guard, which forms part of the Department of Transportation; the U.S. import-export control offices, parts of the Department of Commerce; and the Border Patrol, which belongs to the Department of Justice.

management of intelligence resources. A March 1999 paper released by Director Tenet's own office, "Strategic Intent" identified five major trends challenging the United States over the next decade, one of which is "Increasing Threats to U.S. Citizens and Infrastructures." The specific elements of threat embodied in the paper, however, are electronic, chemical, and biological attack. The last item in this section, CIA's "Terrorism: Frequently Asked Questions," is a fact sheet from early October 2001, after the New York and Washington attacks, which stipulates that the agency had no role in the rise of Osama bin Laden, and that it has the authority necessary to recruit spies and root out terrorist networks. This document is included to show a CIA perspective after the attacks.

Evident in these documents is intelligence concern with an old issue—state sponsorship of terrorism—as well as the set of questions surrounding weapons of mass destruction, which has been a U.S. government preoccupation over the past several years. There is little sense that terrorists might resort to the kind of high-concept, low-technology attack that actually happened on September 11. In these offerings intelligence appears to be reactive rather than predictive, responding to themes current in government and the wider national security community, not acting on the basis of a close analysis of terrorist proclivities and capabilities.

Beyond the open record is a secret one of classified analyses and national intelligence estimates, to which this study has had no access, but it is not likely that the secret record contains more accurate predictions than those shown here, if only because in the controversy following the September 11 attacks such a prediction surely would have boiled to the surface.

A survey of Director Tenet's past testimony to Congress further illustrates the slow development of intelligence community perceptions on terrorism. The name Osama bin Laden did not appear in CIA testimony until 1999, after the truck bombings of two U.S. embassies in Africa (see Part VI). Tenet's January 1998 statement noted an increased risk that individuals or groups would attack U.S. interests; growing terrorist interest in acquiring chemical, biological, or nuclear weapons (Part V excerpts a useful analysis of the difficulties involved in a terrorist organization actually adopting new technology); and state support of terrorist organizations. Exotic weapons feature again in Director Tenet's February 1999 statement, which expresses concern that bin Laden's is only one among about a dozen groups that have sought or expressed interest in these kinds of arms. Further bin Laden attacks were anticipated at any time, though here the express concern was bombings with conventional explosives, along with possible kidnappings and assassinations. Tenet singled out Iran as a state sponsor of terror. That continued to be true in his February 2000 annual testimony, possibly the CIA's most extensive recent commentary on terrorism. Tenet again repeated his concern about exotic weapons, again linked bin

Laden with them, and noted, "We are aware of several instances in which terrorists have contemplated using these materials." The testimony also observed that "terrorists also are embracing the opportunities offered by recent leaps in information technology," using computerized files, e-mail, and encryption to support their activities. While noting success in bringing more than two dozen foreign terrorists to justice since July 1998, Tenet commented that efforts at security could not overcome the fundamental causes of the phenomenon, in his words, "poverty, alienation, disaffection, and ethnic hatreds deeply rooted in history." This point is missing from the 2001 report reprinted here. Of security by itself, Tenet noted in 2000, "I must be frank in saying that this has only succeeded in buying time against an increasingly dangerous threat."

The reader should keep these materials in mind as the nation approaches the investigations to be made of the September 11 attacks. The consequences of the attacks have been so horrendous that they almost beg the question of whether some intelligence failure was involved. Indeed, September 11, 2001, is often compared to the disastrous 1941 attack on Pearl Harbor, a case in which there has been a fierce debate over intelligence failure ever since.

Like Pearl Harbor, in the case of September 11 a number of pieces of information have emerged that suggest a prediction could have been made. In both the 1998 embassy bombings and the 1999–2000 millennium plot (broken up by security services in the United States, Canada, Jordan, and France), bin Laden's organization demonstrated a capability to make coordinated multiple attacks. In both the embassy bombings and the 2000 attack in Yemen on the American destroyer *Cole* (see Part VI), vehicles were used as the mechanism of attack, in one case trucks, in the other a boat. Conceptually, using an airplane represented only an extension of that logic. It also emerged in the trial of defendants involved in the embassy bombings that bin Laden had bought an executive jet and was interested in pilot training for some of his militants. An extraneous development (depending on the degree to which Iraq is thought to have been involved in this plot, which is disputed) is that an Iraqi defector in 2000 brought information that persons were being taught to hijack aircraft at an Iraqi special services center. An analyst could have taken such an indicator and used it to develop a scenario for something like what actually happened. It also emerged that the FBI had made inquiries at some of the flight schools that bin Laden militants used in learning to fly large commercial aircraft, starting several years ago. In addition the United States, probably from NSA or from liaison with foreign intelligence organizations, had knowledge that one of the terrorists of September 11 had met in Malaysia early in 2001 with a known lieutenant of Osama bin Laden. A few of the terrorists who entered the United States to carry out the attacks were known to the CIA, which was slow to pass the information along to the FBI for its onward transmission, and the data did not reach the

U.S. Customs until after the individuals had entered the country. Finally, a videotape of bin Laden circulated in the spring of 2001 that mentioned hard blows to be struck, and somewhere the word "Hiroshima" was used. The CIA evidently thought incidents around U.S. embassies were involved and that the timing was for about the 4th of July. The U.S. embassy in Rome was in fact closed due to a terror warning. This much is already in the public record.

On the other hand, it is in the nature of special operations—in terrorism as in regular or unconventional warfare—that sensitive plans are closely held. It is most likely that only bin Laden, his chief planner for this plot, the chief go-between coordinating between the planners and the terrorist strike group, and the chief of the strike group (Mohammed Atta) knew the full details of the plan. To have had proper warning would have meant recruiting one of those four individuals as a CIA spy. A lower-level agent reporting merely that some effort was afoot could have led to little more than something like the Rome embassy closing. In a videotape of a November 2001 conversation that was filmed privately and captured in Afghanistan, bin Laden comments on the September 11 attacks. The transcript of that discussion appears to confirm both that Atta organized the attacks and that others on the hit teams were unaware their real purpose was to crash planes into buildings.

Meanwhile, mention of Hiroshima played directly into existing intelligence concerns about terrorist acquisition of weapons of mass destruction. An analyst would have had to get past the type of weapon used at Hiroshima to the notion of large-scale civilian destruction to put that piece of the puzzle into a more correct context. As for jets and pilots, bin Laden was a rich man from a family long accustomed to private jets and pilots (see Part IV). Proper context would have required an understanding of how large was the bin Laden effort to train pilots; it is not clear that authorities possessed that amount of knowledge. The actual hijacking of aircraft for weapons was conceptually difficult since hijackings had almost always been for the purpose of going somewhere, not for self-destruction. In several earlier instances plotters had conceived of using planes in attacks, but none had ever come to fruition. The Secret Service was aware of a case in which a man had speculated about hijacking a plane to crash into the White House, and the CIA was aware that a terrorist apprehended in connection with the 1993 World Trade Center bombing had plotted with a confederate to crash a plane into CIA headquarters. Some terrorists in France had also plotted to crash a plane into the Eiffel Tower in Paris. Because no such incident had ever occurred, this eventuality remained hypothetical.

An intelligence analyst might conceivably have assembled the jigsaw puzzle of terrorist intentions into an appreciation of the real threat of September 11. But even then he would have had no more than a scenario. The initial problem would have been to convince his superiors, and the intelligence community as a whole, with its focus on weapons of mass destruction, that this represented a more concrete near-term threat. Equally important, even at that point the CIA and FBI would have had only a scenario, not the bin Laden plan or a specific warning. It is not evident that September 11 could have been avoided or that an intelligence failure occurred.

On the other hand, as with Pearl Harbor the antecedents to September 11 seem to contain the stuff of a potential intelligence failure, and a classic dispute over what happened or did not. Given the dimensions of the events of that day, an assessment of the intelligence is inevitable. The CIA cannot remain credible if it is perceived as a colossal bungler of intelligence. The community as a whole faces a broad challenge from terrorism, and if there is a better way to organize in response to that challenge, the time to find it is sooner rather than later. The key questions in search of answers are whether an intelligence failure occurred; whether responsibility lies with the CIA, the FBI, or elsewhere; and what form the intelligence community should take to cope with the problems of the modern world.

The Worldwide Threat 2001: National Security in a Changing World

Statement by CIA Director George Tenet Before the Senate Select Committee on Intelligence, February 7, 2001

The threat from terrorism is real, it is immediate, and it is evolving. State sponsored terrorism appears to have declined over the past years, but transnational groups—with decentralized leadership that makes them harder to identify and disrupt—are emerging. We are seeing fewer centrally controlled operations, and more acts initiated and executed at lower levels.

Terrorists are also becoming more operationally adept and more technically sophisticated in order to defeat counterterrorism measures. For example, as we have increased security around government and military facilities, *terrorists are seeking out "softer" targets that provide opportunities for mass casualties.*

Employing increasingly advanced devices and using *strategies such as simultaneous attacks,* the number of people killed or injured in international terrorist attacks rose dramatically in the 1990s, despite a general decline in the number of incidents. Approximately one-third of these incidents involved US interests.

Usama bin Ladin and his global network of lieutenants and associates remain the most immediate and serious threat. Since 1998, Bin Ladin has declared all US citizens legitimate targets of attack. As shown by the bombing of our Embassies in Africa in 1998 and his Millennium plots last year, *he is capable of planning multiple attacks with little or no warning.*

His organization is continuing to place emphasis on developing surrogates to carry out attacks in an effort to avoid detection, blame, and retaliation. As a result it is often difficult to attribute terrorist incidents to his group, Al Qa'ida.

Nevertheless, we and our Allies have scored some important successes against terrorist groups and their plans, which I would like to discuss with you in closed session later today. Here, in an open session, *let me assure you that the Intelligence Community has designed a robust counterterrorism program that has preempted, disrupted, and defeated international terrorists and their activities.* In most instances, we have kept terrorists off-balance, forcing them to worry about their own security and degrading their ability to plan and conduct operations.

The Taliban shows no sign of relinquishing terrorist Usama Bin Ladin, despite strengthened UN sanctions and prospects that Bin Ladin's terrorist operations could lead to retaliatory strikes against Afghanistan. The Taliban and Bin Ladin have a symbiotic relationship—Bin Ladin gets safe haven and in return, he gives the Taliban help in fighting its civil war.

Global Trends 2015

Central Intelligence Agency, National Intelligence Council

The following items are terrorism-related items from the National Intelligence Council's "Global Trends 2015: A Dialogue About the Future With Nongovernment Experts" report (December 2000).

TRANSNATIONAL TERRORISM

States with poor governance; ethnic, cultural, or religious tensions; weak economies; and porous borders will be prime breeding grounds for terrorism. In such states, domestic groups will challenge the entrenched government, and transnational networks seeking safehavens.

At the same time, the trend away from state-supported political terrorism and toward more diverse, free-wheeling, transnational networks—enabled by information technology—will continue. Some of the states that actively sponsor terrorism or terrorist groups today may decrease or even cease their support by 2015 as a result of regime changes, rapprochement with neighbors, or the conclusion that terrorism has become counterproductive. But weak states also could drift toward cooperation with terrorists, creating de facto new state supporters.

Between now and 2015 terrorist tactics will become increasingly sophisticated and designed to achieve mass casualties.

We expect the trend toward greater lethality in terrorist attacks to continue.

REACTING TO US MILITARY SUPERIORITY

Experts agree that the United States, with its decisive edge in both information and weapons technology, will remain the dominant military power during the next 15 years. Further bolstering the strong position of the United States are its unparalleled economic power, its university system, and its investment in research and development—half of the total spent annually by the advanced industrial world. Many potential adversaries, as reflected in doctrinal writings and statements, see US military concepts, together with technology, as giving the United States the ability to expand its lead in conventional warfighting capabilities.

This perception among present and potential adversaries will continue to generate the pursuit of asymmetric capabilities against US forces and interests abroad as well as the territory of the United States. US opponents—state and such nonstate actors as drug lords, terrorists, and foreign insurgents—will not want to engage the US military on its terms. They will choose instead political and military strategies designed to dissuade the United States from using force, or, if the United States does use force, to exhaust American will, circumvent or minimize US strengths, and *exploit perceived US weaknesses. Asymmetric challenges can arise across the spectrum of conflict that will confront US forces in a theater of operations or on US soil.*

THREATS TO CRITICAL INFRASTRUCTURE

Some potential adversaries will seek ways to threaten the US homeland. The US national infrastructure—communications, *transportation,* financial transactions, energy networks—*is vulnerable to disruption by physical* and electronic *attack* because of its interdependent nature and by cyber attacks because of their dependence on computer networks. *Foreign governments and groups will seek to exploit such vulnerabilities using conventional munitions,* information operations, and even WMD.

TERRORISM

Much of the terrorism noted earlier will be directed at the United States and its overseas interests. Most anti-US terrorism will be based on perceived ethnic, religious or cultural grievances. Terrorist groups will continue to find ways to attack US military and diplomatic facilities abroad. Such attacks are likely to expand increasingly to include US companies and American citizens. *Middle East and Southwest Asian-based terrorists are the most likely to threaten the United States.*

Strategic Intent for the United States Intelligence Community

Director of Central Intelligence

OUR VISION

A unified Intelligence Community optimized to provide a decisive information advantage to the President, the military, diplomats, the law enforcement community and the Congress.

The intent of this vision is to bring together our extraordinary intelligence capabilities to provide the nation a decisive information advantage. . . .

This Strategic Intent serves as the DCI's foundation for a new Intelligence Community strategic planning process. This process will be jointly managed by the DCI and the Department of Defense and will provide linkages between Service, Agency, and Departmental assets. In addition to incorporating the strategic plans of individual intelligence entities, we are developing key functional plans that cut across the Community covering a range of intelligence business areas . . .

The first section of this Strategic Intent addresses the external environment in which we will be expected to perform our mission. . . .

Five major trends will challenge us over the next decade.

GREATER COMPLEXITY IN NATIONAL SECURITY CHALLENGES

With the demise of the bipolar world has come a range of second-order effects: less cohesive alliances, arms control regimes that are more difficult to maintain, and weapons-related technologies that are more difficult to control. Some regional powers may move to assert their interests, often with destructive effects.

Hostile states such as North Korea, Iraq, and Iran will not want to provoke a conventional challenge to the US but are more likely to develop asymmetric strategies to pursue regional ambitions. These will range from subversion of US regional partners and the threatened use of Weapons of Mass Destruction to attacks on US civil infrastructure and the adoption of unique and unexpected forms of warfare or weapons.

As our dependence on technology increases, so will our vulnerabilities, and the threat from foreign intelligence services will become more difficult to counter. US military, diplomatic, and commercial activities will be targeted by both traditional and nontraditional intelligence adversaries. In addition, adversaries will increasingly seek to deny or misrepresent national security information.

GREATER GLOBAL INTEGRATION AND INTERDEPENDENCE

The forces behind global interdependence—international trade and finance, information flows, and technology transfers—make nations less insular and less self-reliant, but some states will lose a degree of control over their domestic agendas. In other cases, the erosion of state authority may occur at the same time that population growth, economic expansion, and urbanization increase demands on government infrastructures.

Terrorists and organized crime groups will take advantage of advanced information technologies to undermine government efforts to stop them. At the same time, drug trafficking, illicit arms flows, uncontrolled refugee migrations, and environmental damage will threaten regional stability. This will require unprecedented interagency and international cooperation in law enforcement and humanitarian relief efforts.

A RAPIDLY CHANGING TECHNOLOGICAL ENVIRONMENT

The exponential growth of technology presents both opportunities and challenges. Leveraging new technologies will alter war fighting concepts and place greater demands on intelligence, requiring greater flexibility in our intelligence, surveillance, and reconnaissance systems. The pace, volume and fidelity of these information demands will create unprecedented challenges in our efforts to attain information superiority.

Technologies such as overhead imagery and encryption are becoming widely available, and it will be just as easy for our adversaries to move information quickly and hide or encrypt their secrets. Protecting our data from corruption or theft will be a challenge.

INCREASING THREATS TO US CITIZENS AND INFRASTRUCTURES

The terrorist bombings of US troops in Saudi Arabia and civilians in the World Trade Center and the Dar Es Salaam and Nairobi embassies portend a growing threat to Americans. The evolving technology provides terrorists new and more damaging tools against our security. As recently recognized by the President's Commission on Critical Infrastructure Protection, ". . . our security, economy, way of life, and perhaps even survival, are now dependent on the interrelated trio of electrical energy, communications, and computers."

Over the next decade we will be vulnerable to electronic, chemical, and biological attacks against critical infrastructures, such as information and communications; banking and finance; electrical power, oil, and gas; distribution of food and goods; and vital human needs such as medical services.

CIVIL AND ENVIRONMENTAL PRECURSORS TO CONFLICT

Bosnia, Haiti, and Rwanda have demonstrated that internal conflicts threaten regional peace because of displaced populations and the humanitarian crises they engender. Growing populations and the increased competition for resources will be a source of national and regional conflict and US policy makers and military commanders will require early warning of these problems and assessments of how best to contain their impacts on US interests.

Natural disasters will require the commitment of US resources and humanitarian support. The US public and the government increasingly expect that intelligence resources will contribute to warning and help in ways that will require new and different intelligence support.

WHAT THE GLOBAL TRENDS IMPLY FOR INTELLIGENCE

As the boundaries between foreign and domestic threats become increasingly blurred and transnational threats pose new challenges, we will be called upon to perform new roles, take on new missions, and adapt our capabilities.

Terrorism: Frequently Asked Questions

Central Intelligence Agency

HAS THE CIA EVER PROVIDED FUNDING, TRAINING, OR OTHER SUPPORT TO USAMA BIN LADEN?

No. Numerous comments in the media recently have reiterated a widely circulated but incorrect notion that the CIA once had a relationship with Usama Bin Laden. For the record, you should know that the CIA never employed, paid, or maintained any relationship whatsoever with Bin Laden.

AREN'T THERE RESTRICTIONS ON CIA'S RECRUITMENT OF CRIMINALS AND OTHER UNSAVORY CHARACTERS?

The guidelines at issue simply require field officers to obtain prior CIA Headquarters approval before establishing a relationship with an individual who has committed serious crimes, human rights abuses, or other repugnant acts. We have never turned down a field request to recruit an asset in a terrorist organization. Furthermore, we do not avoid contact with individuals—regardless of their past—who may have information about terrorist activities.

There seems to be a misunderstanding regarding whether CIA has been prevented from dealing with "unsavory" characters who might be able to provide information on terrorism and other threats to US national security. A number of commentators have stated that the CIA is banned by regulations from doing so and now only gathers intelligence from individuals of high personal integrity—individuals who do not have access to the type of information our country needs. This perception is wrong.

Internal CIA regulations governing the recruitment of such individuals were issued in 1995 in response to Congressional calls for greater notification when the Agency has a relationship with an "unsavory" individual. This was generated by a concern that CIA was dealing with people in Central America in the early 1990's who were involved in human rights abuses.

It is understandable that people are now examining ways to give the Intelligence Community greater authority to deal with the terrorist threat, and it is possible that modifications of the Agency's current guidelines will result from this examination. But make no mistake, the CIA has been working relentlessly against the terrorist target, and the Agency is not constrained from recruiting individuals with unsavory backgrounds.

The greatest challenge is to penetrate the terrorist networks themselves. This effort requires an extensive analytic effort to understand shadowy terrorist organizations, train CIA officers in their language, deploy them among their culture, and support them in the dangerous and enormously difficult mission of penetrating these groups. These challenges are the focus of our efforts.

HOW DO YOU DEFINE TERRORISM?

The Intelligence Community is guided by the definition of terrorism contained in Title 22 of the US Code, Section 2656(d):

—The term "terrorism" means premeditated, politically motivated violence perpetrated against noncombatant targets by subnational groups or clandestine agents, usually intended to influence an audience.

—The term "international terrorism" means terrorism involving the territory or the citizens of more than one country.

—The term "terrorist group" means any group that practices, or has significant subgroups that practice, international terrorism.

Global Threats and Challenges Through 2015

Vice Admiral Thomas R. Wilson
Director, Defense Intelligence Agency
(Statement for the Record, Senate Select Committee on
Intelligence, February 7, 2001)

THE EMERGING GLOBAL SECURITY ENVIRONMENT

"What's past is prologue" Shakespeare wrote. Those words have relevance today with respect to the recent and future global security environment. The 1990s were a time of transition and turmoil as familiar Cold War issues, precepts, structures, and strategies gave way to new security paradigms and problems. That transition continues, with the end nowhere in sight. In fact, I expect the next 10 to 15 years to be at least as turbulent, if not more so. The basic forces bringing stress and change to the international order—some of them outlined below—will remain largely at work, and no power, circumstance, or condition is likely to emerge capable of overcoming these and creating a more stable global environment. Within this environment, the 'Big C' issues—especially counter drug, counter intelligence, counter proliferation, counter terrorism—that have been a focal point of this Committee's efforts will remain key challenges for the United States. I will discuss each of these in some detail.

Globalization—defined here as the increasing (and increasingly less restricted) flow of money, people, information, technology, ideas, etc. throughout the world—remains an important, and perhaps even the dominant, influence. Globalization is generally a positive force that will leave most of the world's people better off. But in some ways, globalization will exacerbate local and regional tensions, increase the prospects and capabilities for conflict, and empower those who would do us harm. For instance, the globalization of technology and information—especially regarding weapons of mass destruction (WMD) and advanced conventional weapons—will increasingly accord smaller states, groups, and individuals destructive capabilities previously limited to major world powers. Encouraging and consolidating the positive aspects of globalization, while managing and containing its 'downsides,' will be a continuing challenge.

Globalization is independent of any national policy and can weaken the power of governments to control events within and beyond their borders. Nevertheless, many individuals, groups, and states equate globalization to 'Americanization' . . . that is, the expansion, consolidation, and perceived dominance of US power, values, ideals, culture, and institutions. This dynamic—in which the US is seen as both a principal proponent for and key benefactor of globalization—and the global reaction to it, will underpin many of the security challenges we face during the first two decades of the 21st century.

Not everyone shares our particular view of the future and *disaffected states, groups, and individuals* will remain an important factor and a key challenge for US policy.

- Some (e.g. Iran, various terrorists, and other criminal groups) simply reject or fear our values and goals. They will continue to exploit certain aspects of globalization, even as they try to fend off some of its consequences (like openness and increased global connectivity). They will frequently engage in violence—targeting our policies, facilities, interests, and personnel—to advance their interests and undermine ours.
- Others, either unable or unwilling to share in the benefits of globalization, will face deepening economic stagnation, political instability, and cultural alienation. These conditions will create fertile ground for political, ethnic, ideological, and religious extremism. For many of those 'left behind,' the US will be viewed as a primary source of their troubles and a primary target of their frustration.
- Still others will, at times, simply resent (or be envious of) US power and perceived hegemony, and will engage in 'milder' forms of anti-US rhetoric and behavior. As a consequence, we are likely to confront temporary anti-US 'coalitions' organized or spontaneously forming to combat or rally against a specific US policy initiative or action.

Global demographic trends remain a factor. World population will increase by more than a billion by 2015, with 95 percent of that growth occurring in the developing world. Meanwhile developing-world urbanization will continue, with some 20–30 million of the world's poorest people migrating to urban areas each year. These trends will have profound implications that will vary by country and region. Poorer states, or those with weak governance, will experience additional strains on their resources, infrastructures, and leadership. Many will struggle to cope, some will undoubtedly fail. At the same time, some advanced and emerging market states—including key European and Asian allies—will be forced to reexamine longstanding political, social, and cultural precepts as they attempt to overcome the challenges of rapidly aging populations and declining workforce cohorts. In these and other cases, demographic pressures will remain a potential source of stress and instability. . . .

The complex integration of these factors with other 'second and third order' trends and consequences—including the frequency, intensity, and brutality of ethnic conflict, local resource shortages, natural disasters, epidemics, mass migrations, and limited global response capabilities—portend an extremely dynamic, complex, and uncertain global future. Consider for instance the significant doubts we face today concerning the likely directions of Russia, China, Europe, the Middle East, and the Korean peninsula. Developments in each of these key states and regions will go a long way toward defining the 21st century security environment, but outcomes are simply too tough to call. This complexity humbles those of us charged with making judgments about the future and makes specific 'point-projections' of the future threat less meaningful. It is perhaps more useful for us to identify some of the more troubling potential circumstances, and broadly define the kinds of challenges we are most likely to encounter.

KEY NEAR TERM CONCERNS

While specific threats are impossible to predict, and new threats and challenges can arise almost without warning in today's environment, over the next 12–24 months, I am most concerned about the following potential situations.

- A *major terrorist* attack against United States interests, either here or abroad, perhaps with a weapon designed to produce mass casualties. Terrorism remains the 'asymmetric approach of choice' and many terrorist groups have both the capability and desire to harm us. Terrorism is the most likely direct threat to US interests worldwide. I will discuss the terrorist threat in more detail a little later on.
- *Worsening conditions in the Middle East.* An expansion of Israeli-Palestinian violence and the complete collapse of the Middle East peace process would have numerous troubling implications:

  - An increased risk of anti-American violence—particularly terrorism.
  - An increased risk of a wider regional conflict.

- Intensified Iraqi efforts to exploit the conflict to gain relief from sanctions.
- An increased chance that Iraq will be successful in gaining widespread support for lifting UN sanctions . . . a development that would likely strain our relations with regional and European allies, allow Iraq to rearm more rapidly, and ultimately, threaten the foundation of our Middle Eastern policy.

Current and Projected National Security Threats to the United States

Statement by Thomas Fingar,
Acting Assistant Secretary of State for
Intelligence and Research,
Before the Senate Select Committee on Intelligence,
February 7, 2001

. . . Happily, the severity of specific threats to our nation, our values, our system of government, and our way of life are low and likely to remain so for the fore-seeable future. Unfortunately, that is not the case with respect to threats to individual Americans and other national interests. Indeed, there appears to be a perversely inverse relationship between the diminution of threats to the United States homeland and the increasing magnitude and variety of threats to American citizens and interests.

The dramatic decline in the mega-threat symbolized by the end of the Cold War and the growing preponderance of our military capabilities make it increasingly difficult and irrational for any adversary to threaten our national existence. This makes resort to asymmetric threats more tempting. A variety of national and non-state actors are seeking both means and opportunities to achieve their goals by threatening Americans at home and abroad.

Americans abroad (residents, tourists, diplomats, business people, members of our Armed Forces, etc.) are a special target for many groups who oppose us and our values, resent our prosperity and power, or believe that Washington holds the key to achieving their own political, economic, or other goals. We become aware daily of threats to US businesses, military facilities, embassies, and individual citizens. Recent examples include the seizure of an American relief worker in Chechnya (since freed), the execution of an American oil worker seized in Ecuador, and the terrorist attack on the USS Cole.

Unconventional threats are the most worrisome because they are harder to detect, deter, and defend against. Misguided individuals, religious fanatics, self-styled crusaders, and agents of national or rebel groups can—and do—operate everywhere and are capable of striking almost anywhere, anytime. Their most common weapons are bullets and bombs, but some in the catchall category of "terrorists" clearly seek to obtain chemical or biological weapons. Others appear capable of inflicting isolated damage through attacks on our information infrastructure. The magnitude of each individual threat is small, but, in aggregate, unconventional threats probably pose a more immediate danger to Americans than do foreign armies, nuclear weapons, long-range missiles, or the proliferation of WMD and delivery systems.

Terrorism. The United States remains a number one target of international terrorism. As in previous years, close to one-third of all incidents worldwide in 2000 were directed against Americans. The most devastating attack was the October 12 bombing of the USS Cole in Yemen that killed 17 sailors and injured many more.

The locus of attacks can be, and increasingly is, far removed from the geographic origin of the threat. Usama bin Ladin (UBL) is based in Afghanistan but his reach extends far beyond the subcontinent. Plausible, if not always credible, threats linked to his organization target Americans and America's friends or interests on almost every continent. His organization remains a leading suspect in the Cole investigation, and he and several members of his organization have been indicted for the 1998 embassy bombings in Kenya and Tanzania. Had it not been for vigilant Jordanian security, UBL operatives would have conducted attacks in that country to disrupt Millennium celebrations. Members of his network and other like-minded radical Mujahedin are active globally. Bin Ladin funds training camps and participates in a loose worldwide terrorist network that includes groups such as the Egyptian Islamic Jihad and the Kashmiri Harakat al Mujahedin. The UBL network is analogous to a multinational corporation. Bin Ladin, as CEO, provides guidance, funding, and logistical support, but his henchmen, like regional directors or affiliates, have broad latitude and sometimes pursue their own agendas.

Some terrorists, including bin Ladin, have evinced interest in acquiring weapons of mass destruction. Thus far, however, only Aum Shinrikyo, the group responsible for the 1995 subway gas attack in Tokyo, has actually used such a weapon. There has been no repetition or credible threat of such an attack in the last five years, but the problem clearly has not gone away. There will be another attack; what we do not, and possibly cannot, know is when, where, by whom, and why.

State sponsorship of terrorism has declined, but it has not disappeared. Iran still supports groups such as the Palestine Islamic Jihad dedicated to the disruption of the Middle Easy Peace Process. Iraq also harbors terrorists and may be rebuilding its intelligence networks to support terrorism. Afghanistan's Taliban, though not a national government, does provide crucial safe haven to UBL.

PART II

Countering the Changing Threat

IN THE 1990s a number of initiatives in the United States, among the Group of Seven developed countries, and at the United Nations attempted to create law and international agreements that would allow for action against terrorist groups and movements. These measures, along with the behind-the-scenes activities of the Central Intelligence Agency and the Federal Bureau of Investigation, nevertheless failed to prevent several quite serious terrorist attacks. Even before the tragedy of September 11, 2001, bloody and destructive bombings occurred on August 7, 1998, aimed at the American embassies in two African cities, Nairobi, Kenya, and Dar es Salaam, Tanzania. Quite apart from the role of specific terrorist groups in these incidents, the events of 1998 called into question the adequacy of the general policy against terrorism. The United States Congress determined to mandate a policy review on the entire issue.

In 1999 the 105th Congress created a panel called the National Commission on Terrorism. It was established by a section of the appropriations act authorizing U.S. government foreign operations and export financing. The legislation establishing the study placed it entirely under congressional auspices, with a ten-member board selected by congressional leaders (three each were appointed by the majority leader of the Senate and the speaker of the House of Representatives, and two each by the minority leaders of those bodies). Chairing the panel was L. Paul Bremer, a former State Department official. The commissioners included a former head of the CIA, R. James Woolsey; General Wayne A. Downing, who had headed an investigation of the 1996 terrorist bombing of an American barracks in Saudi Arabia; Fred C. Ikle, a senior Pentagon official during the Reagan administration; John F. Lewis, Jr., a retired director of FBI counter-terror efforts; and an array of business executives and academic experts in the field.

The commission looked at data on terrorism (see the next section of this collection), reviewed the entire panoply of U.S. laws, regulations, directives, and practices as well as policy in the area of terrorism, and interviewed more than 130 officials, advisers, scientists, and others. Both CIA director George J. Tenet and FBI chief Louis J. Freeh testified before the commission, as did officers of the Central Intelligence Agency, special agents of the Federal Bureau of Investigation, analysts of the State Department's Bureau of Intelligence and Research and Office of the Coordinator for Counter-Terrorism, staff of the National Security Council, and officials of the Department of Defense. Individual commissioners or small groups met with officials of the governments of Canada, Egypt, France, Israel, Jordan, Poland, and the United Kingdom, addressing issues of intelligence sharing and cooperation with the United States. In fourteen plenary sessions, commissioners collected testimony from the experts.

The commission reported on June 7, 2000, issuing a study titled *Countering the Changing Threat of International Terrorism*. The document observed a terrorist trend toward seeking to inflict mass casualties and away from state sponsorship of terror, but warned of attacks both overseas and on American soil. The commission supported a more aggressive strategy against terrorists, commitment of greater resources, improvement of human intelligence collection, measures for what is now being called "homeland defense," immigration and border control actions, and improved executive and legislative review of counter-terrorist activities. The group also devoted considerable attention to the question of terrorist use of weapons of mass destruction. The recommendations and much of the data gathered by the commission appear in its report below.

Despite its extensive study, the recommendations of this national commission received little attention or formal action after the appearance of the report. In part this may be due to the fact that the executive branch had not been part of the commission and had little stake in the result. The report also appeared during a presidential election year in which foreign policy, including issues of terrorism, played only a small role. Terrorism also seemed to have receded as a policy issue as time passed after the 1998 embassy bombings. A Congressional Research Service commentary on the report which appears here, "Background and Issues for Congress," predicted that the commission report was likely to "spur strong congressional interest in counter-terrorism policy" in the 2001 session—but in fact this did not materialize in advance of the September 11 attacks. The commission report nevertheless provides a road map to many of the measures taken by the United States since those bombings.

Countering the Changing Threat of International Terrorism

Report of the National Commission on Terrorism, June 7, 2000

FOREWORD

. . . Throughout our deliberations, we were mindful of several important points:

- The imperative to find terrorists and prevent their attacks requires energetic use of all the legal authorities and instruments available.
- Terrorist attacks against America threaten more than the tragic loss of individual lives. Some terrorists hope to provoke a response that undermines our Constitutional system of government. So U.S. leaders must find the appropriate balance by adopting counterterrorism policies which are effective but also respect the democratic traditions which are the bedrock of America's strength.
- Combating terrorism should not be used as a pretext for discrimination against any segment of society. Terrorists often claim to act on behalf of ethnic groups, religions, or even entire nations. These claims are false. Terrorists represent only a minuscule faction of any such group.
- People turn to terrorism for various reasons. Many terrorists act from political, ideological, or religious convictions. Some are simply criminals for hire. Others become terrorists because of perceived oppression or economic deprivation. An astute American foreign policy must take into account the reasons people turn to terror and, where appropriate and feasible, address them. No cause, however, justifies terrorism.

Terrorists attack American targets more often than those of any other country. America's pre-eminent role in the world guarantees that this will continue to be the case, and the threat of attacks creating massive casualties is growing. If the United States is to protect itself, if it is to remain a world leader, this nation must develop and continuously refine sound counterterrorism policies appropriate to the rapidly changing world around us.

Ambassador L. Paul Bremer III
Chairman
Maurice Sonnenberg
Vice Chairman

EXECUTIVE SUMMARY

International terrorism poses an increasingly dangerous and difficult threat to America. This was underscored by the December 1999 arrests in Jordan and at the U.S./Canadian border of foreign nationals who were allegedly planning to attack crowded millennium celebrations. Today's terrorists seek to inflict mass casualties, and they are attempting to do so both overseas and on American soil. They are less dependent on state sponsorship and are, instead, forming loose, transnational affiliations based on religious or ideological affinity and a common hatred of the United States. This makes terrorist attacks more difficult to detect and prevent.

Countering the growing danger of the terrorist threat requires significantly stepping up U.S. efforts. The government must immediately take steps to reinvigorate the collection of intelligence about terrorists' plans, use all available legal avenues to disrupt and prosecute terrorist activities and private sources of support, convince other nations to cease all support for terrorists, and ensure that federal, state, and local officials are prepared for attacks that may result in mass casualties. The Commission has made a number of recommendations to accomplish these objectives:

Priority one is to prevent terrorist attacks. U.S. intelligence and law enforcement communities must use the full scope of their authority to collect intelligence regarding terrorist plans and methods.

- CIA guidelines adopted in 1995 restricting recruitment of unsavory sources should not apply when recruiting counterterrorism sources.
- The Attorney General should ensure that FBI is exercising fully its authority for investigating suspected terrorist groups or individuals, including authority for electronic surveillance.
- Funding for counterterrorism efforts by CIA, NSA, and FBI must be given higher priority to ensure continuation of important operational activity and to close the technology gap that threatens their ability to collect and exploit terrorist communications.

- FBI should establish a cadre of reports officers to distill and disseminate terrorism-related information once it is collected.

U.S. policies must firmly target all states that support terrorists.

- Iran and Syria should be kept on the list of state sponsors until they stop supporting terrorists.
- Afghanistan should be designated a sponsor of terrorism and subjected to all the sanctions applicable to state sponsors.
- The President should impose sanctions on countries that, while not direct sponsors of terrorism, are nevertheless not cooperating fully on counterterrorism. Candidates for consideration include Pakistan and Greece.

Private sources of financial and logistical support for terrorists must be subjected to the full force and sweep of U.S. and international laws.

- All relevant agencies should use every available means, including the full array of criminal, civil, and administrative sanctions to block or disrupt nongovernmental sources of support for international terrorism.
- Congress should promptly ratify and implement the International Convention for the Suppression of the Financing of Terrorism to enhance international cooperative efforts.
- Where criminal prosecution is not possible, the Attorney General should vigorously pursue the expulsion of terrorists from the United States through proceedings which protect both the national security interest in safeguarding classified evidence and the right of the accused to challenge that evidence.

A terrorist attack involving a biological agent, deadly chemicals, or nuclear or radiological material, even if it succeeds only partially, could profoundly affect the entire nation. The government must do more to prepare for such an event.

- The President should direct the preparation of a manual to guide the implementation of existing legal authority in the event of a catastrophic terrorist threat or attack. The President and Congress should determine whether additional legal authority is needed to deal with catastrophic terrorism.
- The Department of Defense must have detailed plans for its role in the event of a catastrophic terrorist attack, including criteria for decisions on transfer of command authority to DoD in extraordinary circumstances.
- Senior officials of all government agencies involved in responding to a catastrophic terrorism threat or crisis should be required to participate in national exercises every year to test capabilities and coordination.

- Congress should make it illegal for anyone not properly certified to possess certain critical pathogens and should enact laws to control the transfer of equipment critical to the development or use of biological agents.
- The President should establish a comprehensive and coordinated long-term research and development program for catastrophic terrorism.
- The Secretary of State should press for an international convention to improve multilateral cooperation on preventing or responding to cyber attacks by terrorists.

The President and Congress should reform the system for reviewing and funding departmental counterterrorism programs to ensure that the activities and programs of various agencies are part of a comprehensive plan.

- The executive branch official responsible for coordinating counterterrorism efforts across the government should be given a stronger hand in the budget process.
- Congress should develop mechanisms for a comprehensive review of the President's counterterrorism policy and budget.

THE INTERNATIONAL TERRORISM THREAT IS CHANGING

... International terrorism once threatened Americans only when they were outside the country. Today international terrorists attack us on our own soil. Just before the millennium, an alert U.S. Customs Service official stopped Ahmad Ressam as he attempted to enter the United States from Canada—apparently to conduct a terrorist attack. This fortuitous arrest should not inspire complacency, however. On an average day, over one million people enter the United States legally and thousands more enter illegally. As the [1993] World Trade Center bombing demonstrated, we cannot rely solely on existing border controls and procedures to keep foreign terrorists out of the United States.

Terrorist attacks are becoming more lethal. Most terrorist organizations active in the 1970s and 1980s had clear political objectives. They tried to calibrate their attacks to produce just enough bloodshed to get attention for their cause, but not so much as to alienate public support. Groups like the Irish Republican Army and the Palestine Liberation Organization often sought specific political concessions.

Now, a growing percentage of terrorist attacks are designed to kill as many people as possible. In the 1990s a terrorist incident was almost 20 percent more likely to result in death or injury than an incident two decades ago. The World Trade Center bombing in New York killed six and wounded about 1,000, but the terrorists' goal was to topple the twin towers, killing tens of thousands of people. The thwarted attacks against New York City's infrastructure in 1993—

which included plans to bomb the Lincoln and Holland tunnels—also were intended to cause mass casualties. In 1995, Philippine authorities uncovered a terrorist plot to bring down 11 U.S. airliners in Asia. The circumstances surrounding the millennium border arrests of foreign nationals suggest that the suspects planned to target a large group assembled for a New Year's celebration. Overseas attacks against the United States in recent years have followed the same trend. The bombs that destroyed the military barracks in Saudi Arabia and two U.S. Embassies in Africa inflicted 6,059 casualties. Those arrested in Jordan in late December had also planned attacks designed to kill large numbers.

The trend toward higher casualties reflects, in part, the changing motivation of today's terrorists. Religiously motivated terrorist groups, such as Usama bin Ladin's group, al-Qaida, which is believed to have bombed the U.S. Embassies in Africa, represent a growing trend toward hatred of the United States. Other terrorist groups are driven by visions of a post-apocalyptic future or by ethnic hatred. Such groups may lack a concrete political goal other than to punish their enemies by killing as many of them as possible, seemingly without concern about alienating sympathizers. Increasingly, attacks are less likely to be followed by claims of responsibility or lists of political demands.

The shift in terrorist motives has contributed to a change in the way some international terrorist groups are structured. Because groups based on ideological or religious motives may lack a specific political or nationalistic agenda, they have less need for a hierarchical structure. Instead, they can rely on loose affiliations with like-minded groups from a variety of countries to support their common cause against the United States.

Al-Qaida is the best-known transnational terrorist organization. In addition to pursuing its own terrorist campaign, it calls on numerous militant groups that share some of its ideological beliefs to support its violent campaign against the United States. But neither al-Qaida's extremist politico-religious beliefs nor its leader, Usama bin Ladin, is unique. If al-Qaida and Usama bin Ladin were to disappear tomorrow, the United States would still face potential terrorist threats from a growing number of groups opposed to perceived American hegemony. Moreover, new terrorist threats can suddenly emerge from isolated conspiracies or obscure cults with no previous history of violence.

These more loosely affiliated, transnational terrorist networks are difficult to predict, track, and penetrate. They rely on a variety of sources for funding and logistical support, including self-financing criminal activities such as kidnapping, narcotics, and petty crimes. Their networks of support include both front organizations and legitimate business and nongovernment organizations. They use the Internet as an effective communications channel.

Guns and conventional explosives have so far remained the weapons of choice for most terrorists. Such weapons can cause many casualties and are relatively easy to acquire and use. But some terrorist groups now show interest in acquiring the capability to use chemical, biological, radiological, or nuclear (CBRN) materials. It is difficult to predict the likelihood of a CBRN attack, but most experts agree that today's terrorists are seeking the ability to use such agents in order to cause mass casualties.

Still, these kinds of weapons and materials confront a non-state sponsored terrorist group with significant technical challenges. While lethal chemicals are easy to come by, getting large quantities and weaponizing them for mass casualties is difficult, and only nation states have succeeded in doing so. Biological agents can be acquired in nature or from medical supply houses, but important aspects of handling and dispersion are daunting. To date, only nation states have demonstrated the capability to build radiological and nuclear weapons.

The 1995 release of a chemical agent in the Tokyo subway by the apocalyptic Aum Shinrikyo group demonstrated the difficulties that terrorists face in attempting to use CBRN weapons to produce mass casualties. The group used scores of highly skilled technicians and spent tens of millions of dollars developing a chemical attack that killed fewer people than conventional explosives could have. The same group failed totally in a separate attempt to launch an anthrax attack in Tokyo.

However, if the terrorists' goal is to challenge significantly Americans' sense of safety and confidence, even a small CBRN attack could be successful.

Moreover, terrorists could acquire more deadly CBRN capabilities from a state. Five of the seven nations the United States identifies as state sponsors of terrorism have programs to develop weapons of mass destruction. A state that knowingly provides agents of mass destruction or technology to a terrorist group should worry about losing control of the terrorists' activities and, if the weapons could be traced back to that state, the near certainty of massive retaliation. However, it is always difficult and sometimes dangerous to attempt to predict the actions of a state. Moreover, a state in chaos, or elements within such a state, might run these risks, especially if the United States were engaged in military conflict with that state or if the United States were distracted by a major conflict in another area of the world.

The Commission was particularly concerned about the persistent lack of adequate security and safeguards for the nuclear material in the former Soviet Union (FSU). A Center for Strategic International Studies panel chaired by former Senator Sam Nunn concluded that, despite a decade of effort, the risk of "loose nukes" is greater than ever. Another ominous warning was given in 1995 when Chechen rebels, many of whom fight side-by-side with Islamic terrorists from bin Ladin's camps sympathetic to the Chechen cause, placed radioactive material in a Moscow park.

Cyber attacks are often considered in the same context with CBRN. Respectable experts have published sobering scenarios about the potential impact of a successful cyber attack on the United States. Already, hackers and criminals have exploited some of our vulnerabilities.

Certainly, terrorists are making extensive use of the new information technologies, and a conventional terrorist attack along with a coordinated cyber attack could exponentially compound the damage. While the Commission considers cyber security a matter of grave importance, it also notes that the measures needed to protect the United States from cyber attack by terrorists are largely identical to those necessary to protect us from such an attack by a hostile foreign country, criminals, or vandals.

Not all terrorists are the same, but the groups most dangerous to the United States share some characteristics not seen 10 or 20 years ago:

- They operate in the United States as well as abroad.
- Their funding and logistical networks cross borders, are less dependent on state sponsors, and are harder to disrupt with economic sanctions.
- They make use of widely available technologies to communicate quickly and securely.
- Their objectives are more deadly.

This changing nature of the terrorist threat raises the stakes in getting American counterterrorist policies and practices right.

GOOD INTELLIGENCE IS THE BEST WEAPON AGAINST INTERNATIONAL TERRORISM

Obtaining information about the identity, goals, plans, and vulnerabilities of terrorists is extremely difficult. Yet, no other single policy effort is more important for preventing, preempting, and responding to attacks.

The Commission has identified significant obstacles to the collection and distribution of reliable information on terrorism to analysts and policymakers. These obstacles must be removed. . . .

Complex bureaucratic procedures now in place send an unmistakable message to Central Intelligence Agency (CIA) officers in the field that recruiting clandestine sources of terrorist information is encouraged in theory but discouraged in practice.

Inside information is the key to preventing attacks by terrorists. The CIA must aggressively recruit informants with unique access to terrorists' plans. That sometimes requires recruiting those who have committed terrorist acts or related crimes, just as domestic law enforcement agencies routinely recruit criminal informants in order to pursue major criminal figures.

CIA has always had a process for assessing a potential informant's reliability, access, and value. However, the CIA issued new guidelines in 1995 in response to concern about alleged serious acts of violence by Agency sources. The guidelines set up complex procedures for seeking approval to recruit informants who may have been involved in human rights violations. In practice, these procedures have deterred and delayed vigorous efforts to recruit potentially useful informants. The CIA has created a climate that is overly risk averse. This has inhibited the recruitment of essential, if sometimes unsavory, terrorist informants and forced the United States to rely too heavily on foreign intelligence services. The adoption of the guidelines contributed to a marked decline in Agency morale unparalleled since the 1970s, and a significant number of case officers retired early or resigned.

Recruiting informants is not tantamount to condoning their prior crimes, nor does it imply support for crimes they may yet commit. The long-standing process in place before 1995 provided managers with adequate guidance to judge the risks of going forward with any particular recruitment.

Recommendations:

- The Director of Central Intelligence should make it clear to the Central Intelligence Agency that the aggressive recruitment of human intelligence sources on terrorism is one of the intelligence community's highest priorities.
- The Director of Central Intelligence should issue a directive that the 1995 guidelines will no longer apply to recruiting terrorist informants. That directive should notify officers in the field that the pre-existing process of assessing such informants will apply.

The Federal Bureau of Investigation (FBI), which is responsible for investigating terrorism in the United States, also suffers from bureaucratic and cultural obstacles to obtaining terrorism information.

The World Trade Center bombers and the foreign nationals arrested before the millennium sought to inflict mass casualties on the American people. These incidents highlight the importance of ensuring that the FBI's investigations of international terrorism are as vigorous as the Constitution allows.

The FBI's terrorism investigations are governed by two sets of Attorney General guidelines. The guidelines for Foreign Intelligence Collection and Foreign Counterintelligence Investigations (FI guidelines), which are classified, cover the FBI's investigations of international terrorism, defined as terrorism occurring outside the United States or transcending national boundaries. Domestic terrorism is governed by the Attorney General guidelines on General Crimes, Racketeering Enterprise and Domestic Security/Terrorism Investigations (domestic guidelines). The domestic guidelines would apply, for example, to an investigation of a foreign terrorist group's activities in the United States if the FBI does not yet have information to make the international connection required for the FI guidelines.

Both guidelines set forth the standards that must be met before the FBI can open a preliminary inquiry or full investigation. The domestic guidelines authorize a preliminary inquiry where there is information or an allegation indicating possible criminal activity. A full investigation may be opened where there is a reasonable indication of a criminal violation, which is described as a standard "substantially lower than probable cause."

The domestic and FI guidelines provide the FBI with sufficient legal authority to conduct its investigations. In many situations, however, agents are unsure as to whether the circumstances of a particular case allow the authority to be invoked. This lack of clarity contributes to a risk-averse culture that causes some agents to refrain from taking prompt action against suspected terrorists.

In 1995, largely in response to the Oklahoma City bombing and indications that confusion was inhibiting investigations, the Department of Justice (DoJ) issued a memorandum to the FBI field offices attempting to clarify the circumstances that would merit opening a preliminary inquiry and full investigation under the domestic guidelines. Nonetheless, there is still considerable confusion among the FBI field agents about the application of the guidelines. Neither the DoJ nor the FBI has attempted to clarify the FI guidelines for international terrorism investigations.

Recommendation:

- The Attorney General and the Director of the Federal Bureau of Investigation should develop guidance to clarify the application of both sets of guidelines. This guidance should specify what facts and circumstances merit the opening of a preliminary inquiry or full investigation and should direct agents in the field to investigate terrorist activity vigorously using the full extent of their authority. . . .

PURSUE A MORE AGGRESSIVE STRATEGY AGAINST TERRORISM

Since the 1980s, the United States has based its counterterrorism policy on four pillars:

- Make no concessions to terrorists and strike no deals;
- Bring terrorists to justice for their crimes;
- Isolate and apply pressure on states that sponsor terrorism to force them to change their behavior; and,

- Bolster the counterterrorism capabilities of countries that work with the United States and require assistance.

The government uses multiple tools to pursue this strategy. Diplomacy is an important instrument, both in gaining the assistance of other nations in particular cases and convincing the international community to condemn and outlaw egregious terrorist practices. Law enforcement is often invaluable in the investigation and apprehension of terrorists. Military force and covert action can often preempt or disrupt terrorist attacks. But meeting the changing terrorist threat requires more aggressive use of these tools and the development of new policies and practices. . . .

The United States should strengthen its efforts to discourage the broad range of assistance that states provide to international terrorists. A key focus of this initiative must be to reduce terrorists' freedom of movement by encouraging countries to stop admitting and tolerating the presence of terrorists within their borders. Nations should bar terrorist groups from activities such as training, recruiting, raising funds, or hiding behind political asylum.

Iran's support for terrorism conducted against American interests remains a serious national security concern. U.S. efforts to signal support for political reform in Iran could be misinterpreted in Iran or by U.S. allies as signaling a weakening resolve on counterterrorism. . . .

There are indications of Iranian involvement in the 1996 Khobar Towers bombing in Saudi Arabia, in which 19 U.S. citizens were killed and more than 500 were injured. In October 1999, President Clinton officially requested cooperation from Iran in the investigation. Thus far, Iran has not responded.

International pressure in the Pan Am 103 case ultimately succeeded in getting some degree of cooperation from Libya. The U.S. Government has not sought similar multilateral action to bring pressure on Iran to cooperate in the Khobar Towers bombing investigation.

Recommendations:

- The President should not make further concessions toward Iran and should keep Iran on the list of state sponsors of terrorism until Tehran demonstrates it has stopped supporting terrorism and cooperates fully in the Khobar Towers investigation.
- The President should actively seek support from U.S. allies to compel Iran to cooperate in the Khobar Towers bombing investigation.

Syria has not ceased its support for terrorists.

The Syrian Government still provides terrorists with safehaven, allows them to operate over a dozen terrorist training camps in the Syrian-controlled Bekaa Valley in Lebanon, and permits the Iranian Government to resupply these camps. Since its designation as a state sponsor of terrorism, Syria has expelled a few terrorist groups from Damascus, such as the Japanese Red Army, but these groups already were of marginal value to Syrian foreign policy. Meanwhile, Damascus continues to support terrorist groups opposed to the peace process. Although Syria recently made a show of "instructing" terrorists based in Damascus not to engage in certain types of attacks, it did not expel the groups or cease supporting them. This suggests Syria's determination to maintain rather than abandon terrorism.

Recommendation:

- The President should make clear to Syria that it will remain on the list of state sponsors of terrorism until it shuts down training camps and other facilities in Syria and the Bekaa Valley and prohibits the resupply of terrorist groups through Syrian-controlled territory.

The U.S. Government has not designated Afghanistan as a state sponsor of terrorism because it does not recognize the Taliban regime as the Government of Afghanistan.

In 1996, the Taliban regime gained control of the capital of Afghanistan and began asserting its control over much of the country. Since then it has provided a safehaven to terrorist groups and terrorist fugitives wanted by U.S. law enforcement, including Usama bin Ladin—who is under indictment for his role in the bombings of U.S. Embassies in Kenya and Tanzania in 1998. The Taliban also supports the training camps of many of these terrorist groups.

Recommendation:

- The Secretary of State should designate Afghanistan as a sponsor of terrorism and impose all the sanctions that apply to state sponsors.

In 1996, Congress enacted a law that authorizes the President to designate as "not cooperating fully" states whose behavior is objectionable but not so egregious as to warrant designation as a "state sponsor of terrorism." This law has not been effectively used.

Some countries use the rhetoric of counterterrorist cooperation but are unwilling to shoulder their responsibilities in practice, such as restricting the travel of terrorists through their territory or ratifying United Nations conventions on terrorism. Other states have relations with terrorists that fall short of the extensive criteria for designation as a state sponsor, but their failure to act against terrorists perpetuates terrorist activities. Newer terrorist groups, many of which are transnational in composition and less influenced by state agendas, can take advantage of such states for safehaven. . . .

Pakistan has cooperated on counterterrorism at times, but not consistently.

In 1995, for example, Pakistan arrested and extradited to the United States Ramzi Ahmed Yousef, who masterminded the World Trade Center bombing in 1993. In December 1999, Pakistan's cooperation was vital in warding off terrorist attacks planned for the millennium. Even so, Pakistan provides safehaven, transit, and moral, political, and diplomatic support to several groups engaged in terrorism including Harakat ul-Mujahidin (HUM), which has been designated by the United States as a Foreign Terrorist Organization (FTO). HUM is responsible for kidnapping and murdering tourists in Indian-controlled Kashmir. Moreover, as part of its support for Usama bin Ladin, HUM has threatened to kill U.S. citizens. . . .

The U.S. Government should vigorously use the "Not Cooperating Fully" category, naming countries—even friends and allies—whose behavior is objectionable but does not justify designation as a state sponsor of terrorism. This designation could be used to warn countries that may be moving toward designation as a state sponsor. . . .

The "Not Cooperating Fully" category could also be used as a "halfway house" for states that have reduced support for terrorism enough to justify removal from the state sponsors list but do not yet deserve to be completely exonerated.

Recommendations:

- The President should make more effective use of authority to designate foreign governments as "Not Cooperating Fully" with U.S. counterterrorism efforts to deter all state support for terrorism. Specifically, the President should direct the Secretary of State to:

  —Consider Greece and Pakistan, among others, as candidates for this designation.

  —Review the current list of state sponsors and recommend that certain states be moved to the "Not Cooperating Fully" designation after they have undertaken specified measures to cease sponsorship of terrorism.

  —Increase publicity of the activities of state sponsors and countries designated as "Not Cooperating Fully" through special reports, making extensive use of the Internet.
- Congress should enact legislation to make countries designated as "Not Cooperating Fully" ineligible for the Visa Waiver Program.

The United States should use all the tools at its disposal to stop or disrupt non-state sources of support for international terrorism.

Today's terrorists rely less on direct state sponsorship and more on private financial and logistical support. Many terrorist groups secretly exploit the resources of international nongovernmental organizations (NGOs), companies, and wealthy individuals. For example, bin Ladin and other extremists have used the Afghanistan-based NGO Maktab al-Khidamat for financial and logistical support. By penetrating an NGO, terrorists gain not only access to funding and international logistics networks, but also the legitimacy of cover employment with a humanitarian organization.

To date, the focus of the U.S. Government's efforts to disrupt private support to terrorists has been on prosecutions under provisions of the Antiterrorism and Effective Death Penalty Act of 1996 (AEDPA). This law requires the Secretary of State to designate groups that threaten U.S. interests and security as Foreign Terrorist Organizations. There are 28 organizations on the most recent list, issued in October of 1999 by the Secretary of State. Current practice is to update the FTO list every two years, although the threat from terrorist groups can change at a faster pace.

The FTO designation makes it a crime for a person in the United States to provide funds or other material support (including equipment, weapons, lodging, training, etc.) to such a group. There is no requirement that the contributor know that the specific resources provided will be used for terrorism. In addition, American financial institutions are required under the law to block funds of FTOs and their agents and report them to the government.

The FTO designation process correctly recognizes that the current threat is increasingly from groups of terrorists rather than state sponsors. In addition to deterring contributions to terrorist organizations, FTO designation serves as a diplomatic tool. It provides the State Department with the ability to use a "carrot and stick" approach to these groups, providing public condemnation and a potential for redemption if the groups renounce terrorism.

There is little doubt that all groups currently on the list belong there. But the exclusion, for example, of the Real Irish Republican Army, which carried out the Omagh car bombing in Northern Ireland in 1998 killing 29 people and injuring more than 200, raises questions about completeness of the list. This diminishes the credibility of the FTO list by giving the impression that political or ethnic considerations can keep a group off the list.

Rather than relying heavily on the FTO process, the U.S. Government should take a broader approach to cutting off the flow of financial support for terrorism from within the United States. Anyone providing funds to terrorist organizations or activities should be investigated with the full vigor of the law and, where possible, prosecuted under relevant statutes, including those covering money laundering, conspiracy, tax or fraud violations. In such cases, assets may also be made subject to civil and criminal forfeiture.

In addition, the Department of the Treasury could use its Office of Foreign Assets Control (OFAC) more effectively. OFAC administers and enforces economic sanctions. For example, any U.S. financial institution holding funds belonging to a terrorist organization or one of its agents must report those assets to OFAC. Under OFAC's regulations, the transfer of such assets can be blocked. OFAC's capabilities and expertise are underutilized in part because of resource constraints.

Other government agencies, such as the Internal Revenue Service and Customs, also possess information and authority that could be used to thwart terrorist fundraising. For instance, the IRS has information on nongovernmental organizations that may be collecting donations to support terrorism, and Customs has data on large currency transactions. But there is no single entity that tracks and analyzes all the data available to the various agencies on terrorist fundraising in the United States.

In addition to domestic efforts, disrupting fundraising for terrorist groups requires international cooperation. A new United Nations convention, the International Convention for the Suppression of the Financing of Terrorism, provides a framework for improved cooperation. Each signing party is to enact domestic legislation to criminalize fundraising for terrorism and provide for the seizure and forfeiture of funds intended to support terrorism. The parties are to cooperate in the criminal investigation and prosecution of terrorism fundraising, and in extraditing suspects.

Recommendations:

- The President should direct the creation of a joint task force consisting of all the agencies in the U.S. Government that possess information or authority relevant to terrorist fundraising. The task force should develop and implement a broad approach toward disrupting the financial activities of terrorists. This approach should use all available criminal, civil, and administrative sanctions, including those for money laundering, tax and fraud violations, or conspiracy charges.
- The Secretary of the Treasury should create a unit within the Office of Foreign Assets Control dedicated to the issue of terrorist fundraising.
- The Congress should promptly ratify the International Convention for the Suppression of the Financing of Terrorism and pass any legislation necessary for full implementation.
- The Secretary of State should ensure the list of FTO designations is credible and frequently updated.
- Congress should review the status of the FTO statute within five years to determine whether changes are appropriate.

Of the large number of foreign students who come to this country to study, there is a risk that a small minority may exploit their student status to support terrorist activity. The United States lacks the nationwide ability to monitor the immigration status of these students. . . .

Beyond the millions who legally come and go, over four million persons reside illegally in the United States. About half of them entered the country without inspection, meaning they crossed U.S. borders between inspection stations or entered by small boat or aircraft. Roughly another two million people entered the United States with a valid visitor's visa, but overstayed their visa and remained here to live. That said, of the millions who come here to live or visit only a minuscule portion of all foreigners in the United States attempt to harm the country in any way.

While the problems of controlling America's borders are far broader than just keeping out terrorists, the Commission found this an area of special concern. For example, thousands of people from countries officially designated as state sponsors of terrorism currently study in the United States. This is not objectionable in itself as a vast majority of these students contribute to America's diversity while here and return home with no adverse impact on U.S. national security. However, experience has shown the importance of monitoring the status of foreign students. Seven years ago, investigators discovered that one of the terrorists involved in bombing the World Trade Center had entered the United States on a student visa, dropped out, and remained illegally. Today, there is still no mechanism for ensuring the same thing won't happen again.

One program holds promise as a means of addressing the issue. The Coordinated Interagency Partnership Regulating International Students (CIPRIS), a regional pilot program mandated by the 1996 Illegal Immigration Reform and Immigrant Responsibility Act (IIR/IRA) collects and makes readily available useful and current information about foreign student visa holders in the United States. For example, CIPRIS would record a foreign student's change in major from English literature to nuclear physics. The CIPRIS pilot program was implemented in 20 southern universities and is being considered for nationwide implementation after an opportunity for notice and comment. The Commission believes that CIPRIS could become a model for a nationwide program monitoring the status of foreign students.

Recommendation:

- The President and Congress should work together to create an effective system for monitoring the status of foreign students nationwide.

Congress provided for the expedited expulsion of terrorists with procedures for the use of secret evidence. The protections contained in these procedures have not been used.

The 1993 World Trade Center bombing brought to light the problem of international terrorists entering and operating in the United States and illustrated the importance of removing suspected terrorists from the United States.

In 1996, Congress established the Alien Terrorist Removal Court (ATRC). The legislation authorized use of classified information in cases involving the expulsion of suspected terrorists, but the law provided several protections for the accused, including the requirement that the alien be provided an unclassified summary of the classified evidence and appellate review by federal courts. For aliens legally admitted for permanent residence, the law allowed the use of special attorneys who hold security clearances (cleared counsel) who are permitted to review secret evidence on behalf of an alien and challenge its veracity.

The ATRC has never been used. Rather, pursuant to other statutes and case law, the Immigration and Naturalization Service (INS) has acted to remove aliens based on classified evidence presented to an immigration judge without disclosure to the alien or defense counsel.

The U.S. Government should not be confronted with the dilemma of unconditionally disclosing classified evidence or allowing a suspected terrorist to remain at liberty in the United States. At the same time, resort to use of secret evidence without disclosure even to cleared counsel should be discontinued, especially when criminal prosecution through an open court proceeding is an option.

Recommendations:

- The Attorney General should direct the Department of Justice to pursue vigorously the criminal prosecution of terrorists in an open court whenever possible.
- The Attorney General should further direct that where national security requires the use of secret evidence in administrative immigration cases, procedures for cleared counsel and unclassified summaries, such as those provided in the ATRC, should be used.

Without international cooperation, the United States cannot protect its national infrastructure from the cyber threat. . . .

Recommendation:

- The Secretary of State, in concert with other departments and agencies, should take the lead in developing an international convention aimed at harmonizing national laws, sharing information, providing early warning, and establishing accepted procedures for conducting international investigations of cyber crime.

The senior official responsible for coordinating all U.S. counterterrorism efforts does not have sufficient authority to ensure that the President's priorities on counterterrorism are reflected in agencies' budgets. . . .

The Commission believes that whoever coordinates the national counterterrorism effort on behalf of the President should also have the authority to ensure that the President's counterterrorism objectives are reflected in agency budgets. That means the coordinator should participate with OMB in the pass-back of counterterrorism budget submissions, as well as in the final phase of the budget process when agencies appeal OMB's decisions.

Recommendation:

- The President should require the Director of the Office of Management and Budget and the national counterterrorism coordinator to agree on all budget guidance to the agencies, including the response to initial budget submissions, and both officials should be involved in presenting agencies' counterterrorism budget appeals to the President.

Congressional responsibility for reviewing the President's counterterrorism budget is divided among several committees and sub-committees, making coordinated review more difficult.

One of the essential tasks for the national counterterrorism coordinator is to prepare a comprehensive counterterrorism plan and budget. Similarly, Congress should develop mechanisms for coordinated review of the President's counterterrorism policy and budget, rather than having each of the many relevant committees moving in different directions without regard to the overall strategy. . . .

Finally, the Commission notes the importance of bipartisanship both in Congress and in the executive branch when considering counterterrorism policy and funding issues.

Recommendations:

- Congress should develop a mechanism for reviewing the President's counterterrorism policy and budget as a whole. The executive branch should commit to full consultation with Congress on counterterrorism issues.
- House and Senate Appropriations Committees should immediately direct full-committee staff to conduct a cross-subcommittee review of counterterrorism budgets.

National Commission on Terrorism Report: Background and Issues for Congress

Raphael F. Perl,
Specialist in International Affairs,
Foreign Affairs, Defense, and Trade Division,
February 6, 2001

SUMMARY

On June 5, 2000, the National Commission on Terrorism (NTC), a congressionally mandated bi-partisan body, issued a report providing a blueprint for U.S. counterterrorism policy with both policy and legislative recommendations. The report could be significant in shaping the direction of U.S. policy and the debate in Congress. It generally argues for a more aggressive U.S. strategy in combating terrorism. Critics, however, argue that NTC conclusions and recommendations ignore competing U.S. goals and interests; i.e. that a proactive strategy might lead to the curbing of individual rights and liberties, damage important commercial interests, and widen disagreements between the U.S. and its allies over using the "stick" as opposed to the "carrot" approach in dealing with states that actively support or countenance terrorism.

The NTC report is likely to stimulate strong congressional interest in counterterrorism policy in the 107th Congress. Likely areas of focus are (1) a more proactive counterterrorism policy; (2) a stronger state sanctions policy; and (3) a more cohesive/better coordinated U.S. federal counterterrorism response. January 23, 2001 press reports indicate that Rep. J.C. Watts (R-Okla) has urged House Speaker Dennis Hastert to create a House Select Committee on Domestic Terrorism. In the 106th Congress, H.R. 4210, which passed the House, would also give added attention to domestic terrorism by establishing a President's Council on Domestic Preparedness in the White House. Moreover, in the 106th Congress, S. 3205, the (Kyl-Feinstein) Counterterrorism Act of 2000, which passed the Senate, incorporated a number of recommendations of the NTC including measures to ensure (1) enhanced policy emphasis on control of biological pathogens and terrorist funding raising; (2) better sharing of FBI intelligence; (3) easier recruitment of CIA counter-terrorism informants; and (4) maintaining Syria and Iran on the list of countries that sponsor terrorism. This report will not be updated.

BACKGROUND

Combating terrorism has emerged as one of the most important U.S. foreign policy and national security priorities. The number of terrorist groups is reportedly growing and the technology to inflict mass casualties is becoming more readily available. The United States and other cooperating nations confront four major tasks, namely, (1) deterring/identifying terrorists and their sponsors/supporters, (2) weakening terrorist financial and other infrastructures, (3) hardening potential targets, and (4) containing damage in the aftermath of terrorist incidents.

The 105th Congress, in response to what is seen as a growing terrorist threat, created the ten-person, bi-partisan National Commission on Terrorism to evaluate U.S. laws, policies, and practices for preventing and punishing terrorism aimed at U.S. citizens (P.L. 105–277). The resulting NTC report, *Countering the Changing Threat of International Terrorism*, was issued on June 5, 2000. It calls on the U.S. government to prepare more actively to prevent and deal with a future mass casualty, catastrophic terrorist attack.

The report advocates: (1) using full, and what can be characterized as proactive, intelligence and law enforcement authority to collect intelligence regarding terrorist plans and methods; (2) targeting firmly—and with sanctions—all states that support terrorists; (3) disrupting non-governmental sources of terrorists' support—especially financial and logistical; (4) enhancing planning and preparation to respond to terrorist attacks involving biological, chemical, radiological or nuclear materials; and (5) creating stronger mechanisms to ensure that funding for individual agency counterterrorism programs reflects priorities integrated into a comprehensive national counterterrorism plan subject to congressional oversight.

The report suggests that the United States is drifting away from a strong policy of combating state support of international terrorism and is generally too passive and not proactive enough in combating a threat that is becoming more deadly, diffuse, and difficult to detect. Implicit in the report is the suggestion that the United States, by drifting away from a strong policy to combat state support of international terrorism, may well be encouraging more terrorism. In citing incidences of such a drift in policy, the report suggests there is a softening of U.S. positions on Iran and Syria and points to a perceived U.S. weakness in not aggressively confronting Pakistan's support for terrorist groups. It also notes U.S. failure to use sanctions, or the threat thereof, in response to Greece's inactivity/reluctance to investigate and prosecute terrorist activity—inaction by Greece which is portrayed as tantamount to complicity. While recognizing the growing danger posed by lone-wolf terrorists and loosely affiliated private transnational groups, the report intimates that U.S. policy may be too heavily focused on Usama Bin Laden.

HIGHLIGHTS OF THE REPORT

Areas addressed in the report's recommendations include the following:

- *Expanding sanctions on state sponsors/uncooperative nations*

Greece and Pakistan

The report notes that "Greece has been disturbingly passive in response to terrorist activities." It comments that since 1975 there have been 146 terrorist attacks against Americans or American interests in Greece with only one case being solved and no meaningful investigation into the others. The report cites examples of past Pakistani anti-terrorism cooperation but stresses that "Pakistan provides safehaven, transit, and moral, political, and diplomatic support to several groups engaged in terrorism" (in Kashmir).

The NTC recommends that the President consider imposing sanctions against Greece and Pakistan under provisions of U.S. law (P.L.104-132) that limit arms sales to countries not "fully cooperating" with the U.S. on anti-terrorism efforts. Enactment of legislation making countries which have been designated as not "fully cooperating" with U.S. counterterrorism efforts ineligible for the U.S. visa waiver program is also called for. In general, the Commission recommends expanding the broad use of sanctions to include, not just state sponsors, but nations not fully cooperating. Currently, U.S. law also requires the withholding of foreign assistance to nations providing lethal military assistance to nations on the U.S. list of state sponsors of terrorism—a little-known provision of P.L.104-132, but one that the Administration has used to help persuade some countries not to provide arms to terrorist list states.

Iran

The report expresses concern that U.S. efforts to signal support for political reform in Iran could be misinterpreted in Iran or by U.S. allies as a weakening of resolve on counterterrorism. The report calls for the President to make no further concessions to Iran and to keep Iran on the terrorism sponsors list until it ceases to support terrorism and cooperates fully in the investigation of the June 1996 Khobar Towers bombing which resulted in the death of U.S. servicemen in Saudi Arabia. It also calls upon the President to actively seek support from US. Allies to compel Iranian cooperation in the Khobar towers investigation.

Syria

The report recommends that the President make it clear that Syria will remain on the state sponsors list until it shuts down terrorist training camps in Syria and the Bekaa valley and prohibits resupply of terrorist groups through Syrian controlled territory.

Afghanistan

The report notes that the United States has not designated Afghanistan as a state sponsor of terrorism because it does not recognize the Taliban regime. Nevertheless, it recommends designating Afghanistan as state sponsor and imposing sanctions against the Kabul regime.

- *Role of the Armed Forces*

Under extraordinary circumstances when a catastrophic event is beyond the capabilities of local, state, and other federal agencies, or is directly related to an armed conflict overseas, the report suggests that the President may want to consider designating the Department of Defense (DoD) as the lead federal agency for the government's response in the event of a catastrophic terrorist attack on U.S. soil. The report calls for detailed contingency plans for the Defense Department's role, which could include transfer of command authority to the Pentagon, in the event of a catastrophic event where the command and control, logistical, communications and specialized ability of the military to respond to chemical/biological/radiological incidents would be required. The Commission believes that advance planning is the best way to prevent curtailment of individual liberties in a weapons of mass destruction scenario.

- *Enhancing foreign student visa data retrieval capability*

Critics of current Immigration and Naturalization Service (INS) student visa status tracking mechanisms often refer to them as being in the "stone age." In a movie which has been characterized as an effort to "substitute computers for shoeboxes," the report recommends expanding an existing computerized pilot program designed to facilitate data retrieval capability to more efficiently monitor the immigration/visa status of students from abroad. This would facilitate access to whereabouts of students from terrorist-list countries and could "flag" a student from such a country who suddenly changes majors from a field such as art to biochemistry or nuclear physics. The report notes that one of the convicted terrorists involved in the World Trade Center bombing entered the U.S. on a student visa, dropped out and remained illegally thereafter.

- *Full use of law enforcement and intelligence authority*

The report recommends that existing CIA guidelines restricting recruitment of unsavory (criminal) sources not apply to recruiting counterterrorism sources. Also recommended is that the FBI guidelines governing criteria for investigating suspected terrorists or groups be clarified to permit full use of legal authorities including the authority to conduct electronic surveillance.

- *Expulsion of suspected terrorists*

Expulsion of suspected terrorists can be a touchy civil liberties issue. In a move designed to minimize what some see as past governmental abuse in expulsion cases handled by INS procedures, the report recommends use of the Alien Terrorist Removal Court (ATRC) (created by Congress in 1996 by section 401 of P.L.104-132, but heretofore unused) to expel terrorists from the United States in instances where criminal prosecution is not possible. This process contains safeguards designed to protect national security and classified evidence (sources and methods), but also accords the accused the right to challenge such evidence.

- *National terrorism response exercises*

The report recommends that senior federal government officials involved in responding to a catastrophe terrorist threat or incident be required to participate in national response exercises every year to test capabilities and coordination.

- *Cyberterrorism/cybercrime*

The report calls on the Secretary of State to take the lead in developing an international convention aimed at harmonizing national laws, sharing information, providing early warning, and establishing accepted procedures for conducting international investigations of cybercrime.

- *Counterterrorism budget process*

The report recommends that the senior National Security Council (NSC) official in charge of coordinating overall U.S. counterterrorism efforts be given a stronger hand in the budget process and that Congress develop a mechanism for comprehensive review of this process and consolidate the process in fewer committees.

ISSUES FOR CONGRESS

Protecting civil liberties, while effectively combating terrorism, remains a strong area of concern in Congress. A number of the Commission's recommendations have drawn sharp criticism from civil libertarian and Arab-American groups. This is especially true of those recommendations which relate to (1) enhancing intelligence gathering; (2) modernizing retrieval capability of databases which monitor the visa status of foreign students; (3) expulsion of suspected terrorists; and (4) contingency planning for an active military role (including a possible lead role) in the event of a catastrophic terrorist attack on U.S. soil. In addition, it is interesting to note that although the Commission's report addresses an impressive array of counterterrorism issues, the list of issues examined is less than exhaustive, leaving a few complex, unresolved, and potentially "prickly" issues unaddressed. These issues would seem to warrant additional congressional attention.

- *Civil liberties concerns*

In democracies such as the United States, the constitutional limits within which policy must operate are sometimes seen to conflict with a desire to more effectively secure the lives of citizens against terrorist activity. Combating terrorism requires government activity designed to gather information on, and restrict the activities of, individual terrorists and groups seeking to engage in direct or indirect terrorist activity. The greater the magnitude of any such acts, the greater the pressure on societal institutions to provide security for their citizens. A challenge facing the policy community is how—in a growing age of globalization, deregulation, democracy and individual freedom—to institute regulatory and monitoring mechanisms which help deter, identify, and track terrorists and generally hinder their operations. Implicit in the reasoning of the Commission's report is that combating terrorism—particularly in the wake of a mass casualty catastrophic incident—may require restrictions on individual liberties. The assumption is that carefully planned and measured restrictions in advance of a catastrophic incident coupled with well thought out contingency planning for a constructive military role in the aftermath of an incident constitute an effective way of *preserving*, and *not* diminishing, individual liberties and democratic freedoms and institutions.

- *Unresolved issues*

The report is noteworthy for what it does not address as well as for what it addresses. Areas not covered in the Commission's report but dealt with by other panels or expert advisory groups include (1) U.S. embassy security (1999 Overseas Advisory Panel Report); (2) security of U.S. military installations overseas (1996 Downing Commission Khobar Towers Report); and (3) weapons of mass destruction (WMD) disaster consequence management (1999 Gilmore Commission Report).

Issues within the purview of the Commission's mandate, but not addressed in its report or in the reports cited above include:

(1) Who should be in charge of U.S. counterterrorism policy, and what are the best organizational mechanisms for policy formulation and implementation;

(2) How does one effectively utilize the gamut of tools available to policy-makers to combat terrorism: i.e., public diplomacy, economic and political sanctions, covert action, military force, and international cooperation and agreements;

(3) How does one prioritize for budget purposes whatever is viewed as an appropriate mix of counterterrorism resources to facilitate assuring that important components are neither short-changed nor overfunded depending on political "clout";

(4) How effective are sanctions and military force as policy tools; how might their use be improved; and how are commercial interests balanced in the equation. For example, how might sanctions be fine tuned or graduated to enhance their effectiveness and make their imposition more likely;

(5) What is an appropriate role for covert operations in a proactive counterterrorism policy (should the U.S. ban on assassinations be reviewed);

(6) How can one insure that the best international talent joins forces to enhance technological research and development efforts to support counterterrorism goals; and

(7) What role, if any, should the media assume in a proactive counterterrorism policy.

Also absent from the report, which largely focuses on the "stick" approach to combating terrorism, are suggestions for use of expanded "carrot" options which may moderate the behavior of rogue states or terrorist groups. Supporters of these types of incentives argue that they facilitate achievement of antiterrorist goals without compromising core values or principles, and without giving in to the demands of terrorists. These approaches include options such as constructive engagement, creative foreign aid or trade packages, or expanded use of rewards for information programs.

For example, if U.S. trade with China is deemed to produce a moderating effect on China's rogue human rights policy, supporters of the "carrot" approach might argue that trade with Libya could have a moderating effect on that nation's rogue terrorism policy. Answers are far from clear, but pursuit of innovative "carrot"-oriented options, coupled with a strong "stick" approach, may, or may not, produce varying degrees of success in dealing with such groups as the IRA and PLO. And many still suggest that use of such options may well produce positive results with countries that seem to be moving in a positive direction such as Iran.

CONCLUSION

The National Commission on Terrorism's report and recommendations on countering the changing threat of international terrorism are likely to spur strong congressional interest in counterterrorism policy during the 107th Congress. The most likely areas of scrutiny include: (1) more productive counterterrorism policies and mindsets; (2) enhanced use of legislative authority to impose sanctions on states that support or actively countenance terrorism, and (3) methods of achieving a more cohesive, better coordinated federal counterterrorism effort through enhanced budget coordination mechanisms.

PART III

Patterns of Global Terrorism

ONCE THE United States began to keep a special eye on terrorist activity over the long term, the question arose of recording data that would chart the phenomenon. At first the Central Intelligence Agency issued occasional public reports. One such analysis in April 1976 was titled *International and Transnational Terrorism: Diagnosis and Prognosis*. Five years later a June 1981 CIA study appeared on *Patterns of International Terrorism: 1980*. That was a public report, but simultaneously at the secret level the intelligence community compiled a national intelligence estimate on terrorism, though its focus was less on terrorist activity than on proving that groups which engaged in this activity were sponsored by other nations. In 1983, George H. W. Bush, then serving as vice president in the Reagan administration, chaired a government-wide panel on terrorism. The Bush panel's public report again relied upon CIA data for its presentation. In the later 1980s the United States decided to regularize the issuance of terrorism data and assigned that task to the State Department, which was already collecting and issuing similar collections of data in such other areas as human rights and arms control.

The task of tracking the terrorist enterprise belonged to the Office for Counter-Terrorism and Emergency Planning. This unit was elevated after 1985 to an ambassador-at-large for counter-terrorism. An annual report appeared in January 1988 titled *Patterns of Global Terrorism: 1986*. By the time the 1989 report appeared (in April 1990), the State Department had again increased the visibility of the issue by creating the Office of the Coordinator for Counter-Terrorism. From 1986 to 1989 the ambassador-at-large for counter-terrorism was L. Paul Bremer, who later chaired the National Commission on Terrorism, whose report appears elsewhere in this collection.

From the beginning, the State Department's annual reports listed government initiatives aimed at countering the political violence that is terrorism. They specified legislation considered necessary for action in this area and recorded laws that had already been passed as well as international actions, agreements, and United Nations activities. The reports presented overviews by continent and country and singled out particular issues for special treatment, such as Libyan connections to terrorist groups, or particular incidents (in 1991), or Osama bin Laden (in 1997, 1998, and 1999). The special sections on bin Laden also appear elsewhere in this volume. In keeping with the theme of state sponsorship of terrorism developed by the Reagan administration, from the beginning the annual reports have contained extended commentaries on this general subject and on the nations considered to be sponsors. The State Department list of state sponsors has acquired greater importance over time as various laws have been enacted to permit sanctions against these countries, prohibit foreign aid to them, or provide the U.S. government with a range of measures that may be applied in specific areas of foreign or economic policy.

The annual reports also provide an extensive chronology of terrorist incidents throughout the world, with statistical data by location, type of incident, numbers of attacks aimed at Americans, casualties, evident targets of the perpetrators, and so on. Another extensive section of each report profiles known groups that engage in terrorism and comments on their origins, affiliations, purposes, and international connections. For a time the reports listed American hostages in terrorist hands, and in recent years they have recorded individual terrorists apprehended abroad by U.S. authorities or arrested in foreign countries and then extradited to the United States. The bulk of the most recent edition of *Patterns of Global Terrorism* appears below. Its discussions of the events in particular countries and profiles of terrorist groups are especially useful. Also appended is an edited version of the Congressional Research Service issue brief "Terrorism, the Future, and U.S. Foreign Policy," which comments on the State Department report and uses it as a point of departure for a set of prescriptions for future action. The latter study is of particular interest in that it has been revised in the wake of the September 11 attacks and now mirrors a number of the actions taken by the U.S. government since then.

The final component of this section is a set of tables which extract the data from the annual reports beginning in 1994. This data shows trends and also illuminates features of terrorist activity. A number of interesting points emerge from examination of the data, some of them perhaps unexpected. Business, not government, the military, or diplomats, has been by far the leading target of terror attacks. Latin America, not the Middle East or South Asia, has been the most common locale for terrorism. Europe surprisingly emerges as a very frequent location for these attacks. Although bombings are the leading type of incident, reflecting terrorist tactics, kidnapping appears to be quite frequent, even though the issue of American hostages abroad has largely disappeared since the 1980s.

While American and international attention has been focused on South Asia and the Middle East, especially since the September 11 attacks, the guerrilla and counter-drug wars in Latin America, where conflict in Colombia spills over into Ecuador and Brazil, account for a great deal of the terrorism in the world today. This is troubling given that the U.S. "war on terrorism" has put Latin American policy on automatic pilot. Persistent troubles in the Balkans lie behind some of the high figures for Europe, though Greece has been a continuing locale for much terrorist activity, and France, with a large expatriate population of Algerian Muslims, has been affected by the ongoing conflict in Algeria between Muslim fundamentalists and a more moderate but authoritarian government. The statistics on terrorism provide much food for thought.

Terrorism Statistics

State Department Annual Reports, 1993–1999

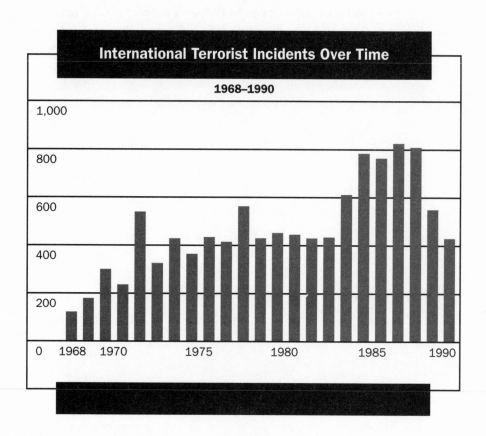

International Terrorist Incidents Over Time

1968–1990

International Terrorist Incidents Over Time, 1976–1995

1976	457	1986	612
1977	419	1987	665
1978	530	1988	605
1979	434	1989	375
1980	499	1990	437
1981	489	1991	565
1982	487	1992	363
1983	497	1993	431
1984	565	1994	322
1985	635	1995	440

In past years, serious violence by Palestinians against other Palestinians in the occupied territories was included in the database of worldwide international terrorist incidents because Palestinians are considered stateless people. This resulted in such incidents being treated differently from intraethnic violence in other parts of the world. In 1989, as a result of further review of the nature of intra-Palestinian violence, such violence stopped being included in the US Government's statistical database on international terrorism. The figures shown above for the years 1984 through 1988 have been revised to exclude intra-Palestinian violence, thus making the database consistent. Investigations into terrorist incidents sometimes yield evidence that necessitates a change in the information previously held true (such as whether the incident fits the definition of international terrorism, which group or state sponsor was responsible, or the number of victims killed or injured). As a result of these adjustments, the statistics given in the report may vary slightly from numbers cited in previous reports.

International Terrorist Incidents, 1990

By Type of Facility	
Business	34.6%
Diplomat	14.4%
Government	7.1%
Military	3.8%
Other	40.1%
By Type of Victim	
Business	10.9%
Military	8.4%
Diplomat	7.9%
Government	7.5%
Other	65.3%
By Type of Event	
Bombing	62.9%
Armed attack	13.8%
Kidnapping	9.9%
Firebombing	5.7%
Arson	4.2%
Sabotage/vandalism	1.5%
Assault	0.9%
Barricade, Hijacking, Other	1.1%

Anti-US Attacks

1990, by Region

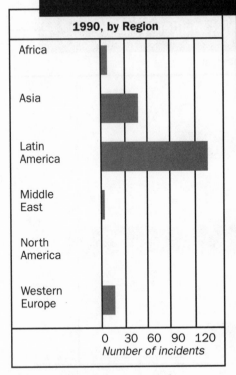

Africa
Asia
Latin America
Middle East
North America
Western Europe

0 30 60 90 120
Number of incidents

1990, by Type of Victim

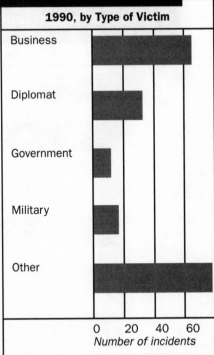

Business
Diplomat
Government
Military
Other

0 20 40 60
Number of incidents

1990, by Type of Event

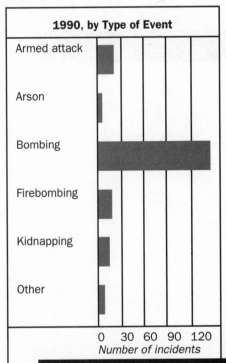

Armed attack
Arson
Bombing
Firebombing
Kidnapping
Other

0 30 60 90 120
Number of incidents

1984–1990, Casualties

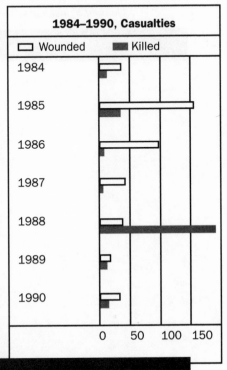

☐ Wounded   ■ Killed

1984
1985
1986
1987
1988
1989
1990

0 50 100 150

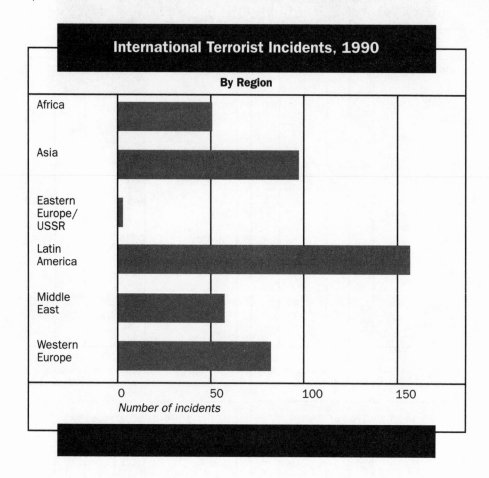

International Terrorist Incidents, 1990

By Region

International Terrorist Incidents, 1992

By Type of Facility

Business	49.5%
Diplomat	14.5%
Government	2.4%
Military	0.8%
Other	32.8%

By Type of Victim

Diplomat	12.5%
Military	11.9%
Government	10.6%
Business	7.5%
Other	57.5%

By Type of Event

Bombing	57.3%
Armed attack	14.7%
Sabotage/vandalism	8.0%
Firebombing	7.5%
Arson	5.3%
Kidnapping	4.7%
Other	2.5%

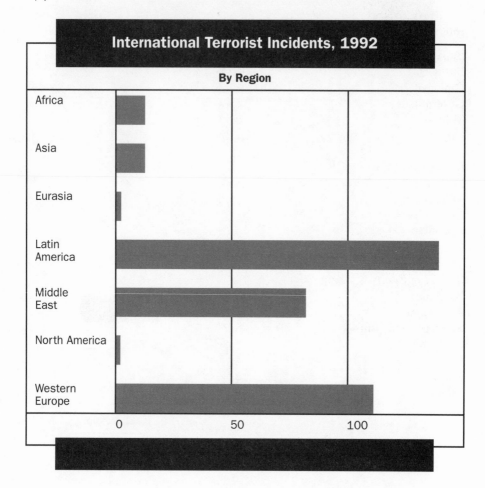

International Terrorist Incidents, 1992

By Region

Anti-US Attacks

1992, by Region

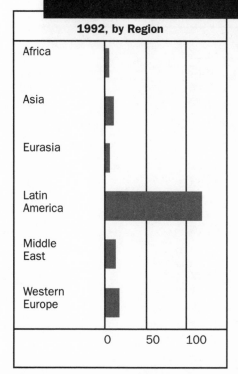

Africa

Asia

Eurasia

Latin America

Middle East

Western Europe

0   50   100

1992, by Type of Victim

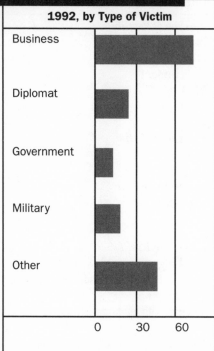

Business

Diplomat

Government

Military

Other

0   30   60

1992, by Type of Event

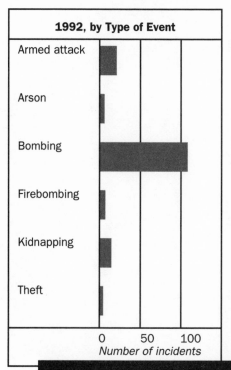

Armed attack

Arson

Bombing

Firebombing

Kidnapping

Theft

0   50   100
Number of incidents

1986–1992, Casualties

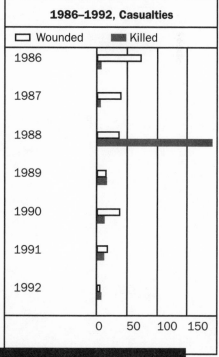

☐ Wounded   ■ Killed

1986

1987

1988

1989

1990

1991

1992

0   50   100   150

International Terrorist Incidents, 1993

By Type of Facility	
Business	61.4%
Diplomat	9.4%
Government	4.5%
Military	2.5%
Other	22.2%
By Type of Victim	
Military	10.5%
Business	10.0%
Government	6.6%
Diplomat	6.1%
Other	66.8%
By Type of Event	
Bombing	32.3%
Armed attack/assault/barricade hostage	21.8%
Firebombing	20.6%
Theft/sabotage/vandalism	16.6%
Kidnapping	8.0%
Hijacking	0.7%

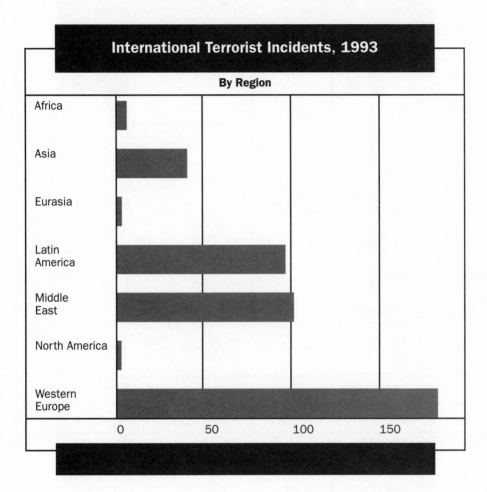

International Terrorist Incidents, 1993

By Region

Anti-US Attacks

1993, by Region

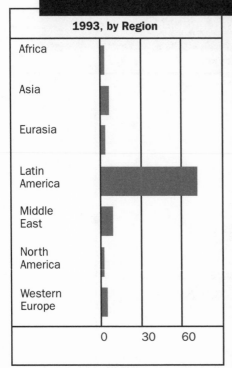

Region	
Africa	
Asia	
Eurasia	
Latin America	
Middle East	
North America	
Western Europe	

0   30   60

1993, by Type of Victim

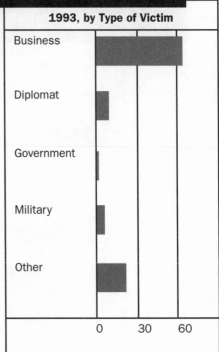

Type	
Business	
Diplomat	
Government	
Military	
Other	

0   30   60

1993, by Type of Event

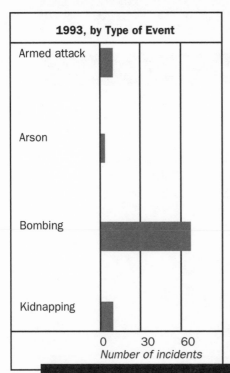

Event	
Armed attack	
Arson	
Bombing	
Kidnapping	

0   30   60
Number of incidents

1987–1993, Casualties

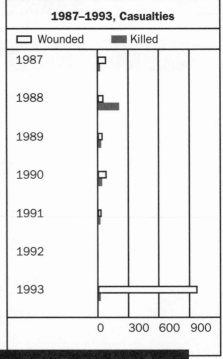

☐ Wounded   ■ Killed

1987	
1988	
1989	
1990	
1991	
1992	
1993	

0   300   600   900

International Terrorist Incidents, 1994

By Region	
Middle East	115
Western Europe	88
Latin America	58
Asia	24
Africa	24
Eurasia	12
By Type of Facility	
Business	126
Government	25
Diplomat	24
Military	5
Other	112
By Type of Targeted Victim	
Business	34
Diplomat	18
Government	11
Military	9
Other	181
By Type of Event	
Bombing	126
Armed attack	101
Kidnapping	42
Firebombing	31
Assault	9
Arson	6
Terrorist skyjacking	2
Vandalism	2
Occupation	1
Barricade hostage	1

International Terrorist Incidents, 1995

By Type of Facility[1]

Business	332
Diplomat	18
Government	17
Military	4
Other	116

By Type of Event

Firebombing	184
Bombing	120
Armed attack/assault	54
Kidnapping	36
Arson	32
Vandalism	13
Chemical attack	1

By Type of Targeted Victim[2]

Business	22
Government	20
Diplomat	7
Military	6
Other	115

Anti-US Attacks, 1995

By Region

Latin America	62
Europe	21
Middle East	6
Asia	6
Africa	3
Eurasia	1

By Type of Event

Bombing	65
Kidnapping	11
Vandalism	9
Armed attack	8
Arson	6

1. Total is greater than 440 because some incidents involved more than one type of target.
2. Includes only those incidents where persons were killed or wounded.

By Type of Targeted Victim

Business	70
Diplomat	6
Military	2
Government	2
Other	22

International Terrorist Incidents, 1996

By Type of Facility[1]

Business	227
Diplomat	25
Government	10
Military	6
Other	79

By Type of Event

Bombing	116
Firebombing	71
Armed attack	39
Arson	31
Kidnapping/hostage	28
Hijacking	2
Other	9

By Type of Targeted Victim[2]

Business	22
Government	11
Diplomat	11
Military	9
Other	72

Anti-US Attacks, 1996

By Region

Latin America	58
Europe	8
Middle East	3
Africa	2
Eurasia	1
Asia	1

1. Total is greater than 296 because some incidents involved more than one type of target.
2. Includes only those incidents where persons were killed or wounded.

By Type of Event

Bombing	55
Arson	7
Kidnapping/hostage	6
Armed attack	3
Assault	1
Firebombing	1

By Type of Targeted Victim[1]

Business	50
Military	4
Diplomat	1
Government	1
Other	19

International Terrorist Incidents, 1997

By Type of Facility[2]

Business	324
Diplomat	26
Government	11
Military	4
Other	74

By Type of Event

Bombing	175
Kidnapping/hostage	54
Armed attack	39
Firebombing	19
Arson	12
Occupation	3
Hijacking/vandalism	2

By Type of Targeted Victim

Business	29
Military	14
Government	13
Diplomat	12
Other	109

1. Includes only those incidents where persons were killed or wounded.
2. Total is greater than 304 because some incidents involved more than one type of target.

Anti-US Attacks, 1997

By Region	
Latin America	97
Europe	7
Asia	6
North America	4
Middle East	4
Eurasia	3
Africa	2
By Type of Event	
Bombing	108
Kidnapping	8
Armed attack	5
Arson	2
By Type of Targeted Victim	
Business	104
Government	4
Diplomat	3
Military	1
Other	14

Total International Attacks, 1998

Total Facilities Struck	
Business	282
Diplomat	35
Government	10
Military	4
Other	68
Type of Event	
Bombing	166
Kidnapping	44
Armed attack	40
Firebombing	11
Arson	8
Hijacking	2
Other	2
Total Casualties	
Diplomat	153
Business	49
Military	23
Government	19
Other	6,449

Total Anti-US Attacks, 1998

Region[1]

Latin America	87
Western Europe	13
Middle East	5
Eurasia	3
Africa	3

Type of Event[2]

Bombing	96
Armed attack	5
Firebombing	5
Kidnapping	4
Arson	1

Total US Casualties

Diplomat	19
Business	1
Other	3

Total International Attacks, 1999

Total Facilities Struck

Business	276
Diplomat	59
Government	27
Military	17
Other	95

Type of Event

Bombing	186
Armed attack	72
Kidnapping	64
Firebombing	22
Arson	16
Occupation	12
Barricade hostage	11
Hijacking	5
Other	4

1. Includes attacks against US facilities and attacks in which US citizens suffered casualties.
2. Includes attacks against US facilities and attacks in which US citizens suffered casualties.

Total Casualties

Military	95
Government	57
Business	57
Diplomat	2
Other	728

Total Anti-US Attacks, 1999

Region[1]

Latin America	96
Western Europe	30
Africa	16
Middle East	11
Eurasia	9
Asia	6
North America	1

Type of Event[2]

Bombing	111
Kidnapping	20
Firebombing	12
Armed attack	11
Arson	6
Hijacking	3
Occupation	2
Barricade hostage	1
Other	3

Total US Casualties

Business	133
Military	9
Diplomat	9
Government	7
Other	26

1. Includes attacks against US facilities and attacks in which US citizens suffered casualties.
2. Includes attacks against US facilities and attacks in which US citizens suffered casualties.

Patterns of Global Terrorism, 2000

Department of State, April 2001

INTRODUCTION

The year 2000 showed that terrorism continues to pose a clear and present danger to the international community. From the millennium-related threats at the beginning of the year to the USS Cole bombing and the rash of hostage takings at the end, the year 2000 highlighted the need for continued vigilance by our government and our allies throughout the world. The tragic death of 19 US citizens at the hands of terrorists is the most sober reminder.

While the threat continues, 2000 saw the international community's commitment to counterterrorism cooperation and ability to mobilize its resources grow stronger than ever. As a result, state-sponsored terrorism has continued to decline, international isolation of terrorist groups and countries has increased, and terrorists are being brought to justice. Indeed, the vigilance of all members of the international community is critical to limiting the mobility and capability of terrorists throughout the world, and both we and the terrorists know it.

We base our cooperation with our international partners on four basic policy tenets:

- First, make no concession to terrorists and strike no deals.
- Second, bring terrorists to justice for their crimes.
- Third, isolate and apply pressure on states that sponsor terrorism to force them to change their behavior.
- Fourth, bolster the counterterrorist capabilities of those countries that work with the United States and require assistance.

These points have been the basis for international cooperation and the foundation for important progress.

UN Security Council Resolution 1333, which levied additional sanctions on the Taliban for harboring Usama Bin Ladin and failing to close down terrorist training camps in Afghanistan, was a major victory for international cooperation against terrorism. This resolution, passed a year after its predecessor resolution 1267, showed the extent to which the international community is prepared to go to isolate those states that refuse to adhere to international norms.

The UN's action also reflected the understanding that Taliban-controlled Afghanistan remains a primary hub for terrorists and a home or transit point for the loosely organized network of "Afghan alumni," a web of informally linked individuals and groups that were trained and fought in the Afghan war. Afghan alumni have been involved in most major terrorist plots or attacks against the United States in the past 15 years and now engage in international militant and terrorist acts throughout the world. The leaders of some of the most dangerous terrorist groups to emerge in the past decade have headquarters or major offices in Afghanistan, and their associates threaten stability in many real and potential trouble spots around the globe—from the Philippines to the Balkans, Central Asia to the Persian Gulf, Western China to Somalia, and Western Europe to South Asia. This is why the Taliban's continued support for these groups is now recognized by the international community as a growing threat to all countries.

International cooperation against agents linked to this network extended far beyond the collaboration on UNSCR 1333. Numerous countries have sent the message to the Taliban and its supporters that the international community—as a whole and as individual member countries—will not stand for such blatant disregard for international law. Good intelligence and law enforcement work—exemplified by the Jordanian Government—enabled partner countries to thwart millennium attacks in early 2000. It has also led to invaluable coordination in the investigation of the October bombing of the USS Cole in Yemen's port of Aden. (It is worth noting that several suspects in the attack on the USS Cole fled back to, not surprisingly, Afghanistan.) We remain fervently committed to ensuring that those who committed and supported the attack on the USS Cole—and killed 17 US service persons—are brought to justice. We will continue to work closely with our allies to ensure that this terrorist incident and others like it do not go unpunished.

The opening in New York of the trial against those accused of perpetrating the bombings of the US embassies in Nairobi and Dar es Salaam in 1998 marked another major victory. Strong international cooperation with our allies—Kenya, Germany, and South Africa, for example—led to the apprehension of several suspects in those crimes. Their trial underlines the importance of cooperative diplomatic, law enforcement, and judicial efforts to combat terrorism. It sends the same strong message that is the cornerstone of US counterterrorism policy: we will be unrelenting in our efforts to bring to justice every individual who chooses terrorism against the United States to advance his or her agenda.

Afghanistan is not the only threat, nor the only rallying point for international cooperation. The conviction of Abdel Basset Ali Mohamed al-Megrahi to life imprisonment for his role in the downing of Pan Am flight 103 over Lockerbie, Scotland, in 1988 also sent a strong message about the international community's determination to bring to justice those responsible for terrorist acts, regardless of how much time has passed. The US Government remains dedicated to maintaining pressure on the Libyan Government until it complies fully with the stipulations required by the UN Security Council to lift sanctions.

Central Asian states have stepped up their fight against terrorist elements in their region, particularly those operating from Afghanistan. At a US Government-hosted conference in June 2000, representatives from five Central Asian states discussed the challenges in their region and committed themselves to developing mechanisms for cooperating to deny sanctuary and financial support to terrorists. We look forward to a follow-up conference and continued constructive engagement with the countries of the region.

While our cooperation with states such as Jordan and Egypt is strong, the terrorism picture in the Middle East remains grim, particularly given the recent escalation of violence in the region. Despite domestic political changes that suggest evolution towards a more moderate policy, Iran remained the primary state sponsor of terrorism, due to its continued support for groups that violently oppose peace between Israel and its Arab neighbors. We expect those states in the region that are committed to peace to distance themselves from all forms of terrorism and to ensure that their countries do not become safehavens or launching points for terrorist acts.

During the past year, increased bilateral and multilateral cooperation with friendly nations has brought unified pressure and action against terrorism. We have expanded our bilateral dialogues with Russia, India, the United Kingdom, Israel, and Canada, and have extended cooperation in intelligence sharing, law enforcement, and antiterrorism training. In addition, we have worked closely with the member states of the G-8, which continued to condemn terrorism emanating from Afghanistan and Iran, and made strides in cutting off terrorist financing.

Like our G-8 counterparts, the United States places a high priority on denying terrorists their sources of financing and blocking their ability to use the funds they already control. In January 2000 we signed the new International Convention for the Suppression of Terrorist Financing. The Convention creates an international legal framework for investigating, apprehending, and prosecuting those involved in terrorist financing and describes preventive measures to identify and choke off sources of income for terrorists and to restrict the movements of such funds across international borders. We look to all members of the international community to join the 35 signatories and to rectify and implement the convention.

In addition, we are strengthening our efforts to fight the spate of hostage taking seen in 2000. Southeast Asia, Central Asia, and South America are just a few of the areas that have been plagued by hostage taking, often linked to terrorist elements. We maintain our policy that we will not concede to terrorist demands or pay ransom. Doing so only rewards the terrorist-criminals and encourages continued criminality. We do remain committed to negotiations with hostage takers for the safety of US citizens and other nationals.

The foundation of our efforts is diplomacy. Our diplomats and representatives maintain relations with countries that are the frontline of defense for US citizens at home and abroad. Our diplomatic efforts build crucial cooperation necessary for joint counterterrorism efforts and raise international political will to fight terrorism. We will continue to reach out to our allies while isolating those who are sympathetic to terrorism. We will continue to use all US tools and cooperation with these allies to disrupt terrorist activity and build a world that is intolerant of terrorists. And we will never rest until we have brought to justice each terrorist that has targeted the United States and its citizens.

Edmund J. Hull
Acting Coordinator for Counterterrorism

NOTE

Adverse mention in this report of individual members of any political, social, ethnic, religious, or national group is not meant to imply that all members of that group are terrorists. Indeed, terrorists represent a small minority of dedicated, often fanatical, individuals in most such groups. It is those small groups—and their actions—that are the subject of this report.

Furthermore, terrorist acts are part of a larger phenomenon of politically inspired violence, and at times the line between the two can become difficult to draw. To relate terrorist events to the larger context, and to give a feel for the conflicts that spawn violence, this report will discuss terrorist acts as well as other violent incidents that are not necessarily international terrorism.

LEGISLATIVE REQUIREMENTS

This report is submitted in compliance with Title 22 of the United States Code, Section 2656f(a), which requires the Department of State to provide Congress a full and complete annual report on terrorism for those countries and groups meeting the criteria of Section (a)(1) and (2) of the Act. As required by legislation, the report includes detailed assessments of foreign countries where significant terrorist acts occurred and countries about which Congress was notified during the preceding five years pursuant to Section 6(j) of the Export Administration Act of 1979 (the so-called terrorist-list countries that have repeatedly provided state support for international terrorism). In addition, the report includes all relevant information about the previous year's activities of individuals, terrorist organizations, or umbrella groups known to be responsible for the kidnapping or death of any US citizen during the preceding five years and groups known to be financed by state sponsors of terrorism.

In 1996, Congress amended the reporting requirements contained in the above-referenced law. The amended law requires the Department of State to report on the extent to which other countries cooperate with the United States in apprehending, convicting, and punishing terrorists responsible for attacking US citizens or interests. The law also requires that this report describe the extent to which foreign governments are cooperating, or have cooperated during the previous five years, in preventing future acts of terrorism. As permitted in the amended legislation, the Department is submitting such information to Congress in a classified annex to this unclassified report.

DEFINITIONS

No one definition of terrorism has gained universal acceptance. For the purposes of this report, however, we have chosen the definition of terrorism contained in Title 22 of the United States Code, Section 2656f(d). That statute contains the following definitions:

- The term "terrorism" means premeditated, politically motivated violence perpetrated against noncombatant* targets by subnational groups or clandestine agents, usually intended to influence an audience.
- The term "international terrorism" means terrorism involving citizens or the territory of more than one country.
- The term "terrorist group" means any group practicing, or that has significant subgroups that practice, international terrorism.

---

*For purposes of this definition, the term "noncombatant" is interpreted to include, in addition to civilians, military personnel who at the time of the incident are unarmed or not on duty. For example, in past reports we have listed as terrorist incidents the murders of the following US military personnel: Col. James Rowe, killed in Manila in April 1989; Capt. William Nordeen, US defense attache killed in Athens in June 1988; the two servicemen killed in the Labelle discotheque bombing in West Berlin in April 1986; and the four off-duty US Embassy Marine guards killed in a cafe in El Salvador in June 1985. We also consider as acts of terrorism attacks on military installations or on armed military personnel when a state of military hostilities does not exist at the site, such as bombings against US bases in Europe, the Philippines, or elsewhere.

The US Government has employed this definition of terrorism for statistical and analytical purposes since 1983.

Domestic terrorism is probably a more widespread phenomenon than international terrorism. Because international terrorism has a direct impact on US interests, it is the primary focus of this report. However, the report also describes, but does not provide statistics on, significant developments in domestic terrorism.

THE YEAR IN REVIEW

There were 423 international terrorist attacks in 2000, an increase of 8 percent from the 392 attacks recorded during 1999. The main reason for the increase was an upsurge in the number of bombings of a multinational oil pipeline in Colombia by two terrorist groups there. The pipeline was bombed 152 times, producing in the Latin American region the largest increase in terrorist attacks from the previous year, from 121 to 193. Western Europe saw the largest decrease—from 85 to 30—owing to fewer attacks in Germany, Greece, and Italy as well as to the absence of any attacks in Turkey.

The number of casualties caused by terrorists also increased in 2000. During the year, 405 persons were killed and 791 were wounded, up from the 1999 totals of 233 dead and 706 wounded.

The number of anti-US attacks rose from 169 in 1999 to 200 in 2000, a result of the increase in bombing attacks against the oil pipeline in Colombia, which is viewed by the terrorists as a US target.

Nineteen US citizens were killed in acts of international terrorism in 2000. Seventeen were sailors who died in the attack against the USS Cole on 12 October in the Yemeni port of Aden. They were:

Kenneth Eugene Clodfeiter
Richard Costelow
Lakeina Monique Francis
Timothy Lee Gauna
Cherone Louis Gunn
James Rodrick McDaniels
Mark Ian Nieto
Ronald Scott Owens
Lakiba Nicole Palmer
Joshua Langdon Parlett
Patrick Howard Roy
Kevin Shawn Rux
Ronchester Mananga Santiago
Timothy Lamont Saunders

Gary Graham Swenchonis
Andrew Triplett
Craig Bryan Wibberley

Two other US citizens were murdered in terrorist attacks during the year:

- Carlos Caceres was one of three aid workers murdered when a militia-led mob in Atambua, West Timor, attacked a United Nations High Commissioner for Refugees aid office on 6 September.
- Kurt Erich Schork was one of two journalists killed when rebels in Sierra Leone shot down a UN helicopter on 25 May.

In December new indictments were issued in connection with the bombings in 1998 at two US embassies in East Africa. A federal grand jury in New York charged five men—Saif Al Adel, Muhsin Musa Matwalli Atwah, Ahmed Mohamed Hamed Ali, Anas Al Liby, and Abdullah Ahmed Adbullah—in connection with the bombing attacks in Nairobi and Dar es Salaam, bringing to 22 the total number of persons charged. At the end of 2000, one suspect had pled guilty to conspiring in the attacks, five were in custody in New York awaiting trial, three were in the United Kingdom pending extradition to the United States, and 13 were fugitives, including Usama Bin Ladin.

A trial began in January 2001 in federal court in the Southern District of New York of four suspects in connection with the bombings at the US embassies in Kenya and Tanzania. Three of the four were extradited to the United States in 1999 to stand trial; the fourth was arrested in this country. The trial is expected to last through 2001.

A trial of two Libyans accused of bombing Pan Am flight 103 in 1988 began in the Netherlands on 3 May 2000. A Scottish court presided over the trial and issued its verdict on 31 January 2001. It found Abdel Basset al-Megrahi guilty of the charge of murdering 259 passengers and crew as well as 11 residents of Lockerbie, Scotland, "while acting in furtherance of the purposes of . . . Libyan Intelligence Services." Concerning the other defendant, Al-Amin Kalifa Fahima, the court concluded it had insufficient evidence to satisfy the high standard of "proof beyond reasonable doubt" that is necessary in criminal cases. The verdict of the court represents a victory for the international effort to hold terrorists accountable for their crimes.

Total International Attacks, 2000

	No. of Attacks	Dead	Wounded
Africa	55	73	29
Asia	98	281	617
Eurasia	31	12	91
Latin America	193	19	1
Middle East	16	19	50
North America	0	0	0
Western Europe	30	1	3

AFRICA OVERVIEW

Africa in 2000 witnessed an increase in the number of terrorist attacks against foreigners or foreign interests—part of a growing trend in which the number of international terrorist incidents on the continent has risen steadily each year since 1995. Most attacks stemmed from internal civil unrest and spillover from regional wars as African rebel movements and opposition groups employed terrorism to further their political, social, or economic objectives. International terrorist organizations, including al-Qaida, Lebanese Hizballah, and Egyptian terrorist groups, continued to operate in Africa during 2000 and to pose a threat to US interests there. . . .

SMART SANCTIONS

United Nations Security Council Resolution 1333, passed in December 2000, targets the Taliban regime in Afghanistan. The Taliban ignored its obligations under UN Security Council Resolution 1267 (passed in November 1999) and has continued to provide shelter to Usama Bin Ladin. In UN Security Council Resolution 1333, the Security Council:

- Demands the Taliban comply with Resolution 1267 and cease providing training and support to international terrorists.
- Insists the Taliban turn over indicted international terrorist Usama Bin Ladin so he can be brought to justice.
- Directs the Taliban to close all terrorist camps in Afghanistan within 30 days.

Until the Taliban fully complies with its obligations under this resolution and Resolution 1267, member states of the United Nations should:

- Freeze the financial assets of Usama Bin Ladin.
- Observe an arms embargo against the Taliban that includes a prohibition against providing military weapons, training, or advice.

Total International Attacks, 2000

Total Facilities Struck	
Business	384
Military	13
Government	17
Diplomat	30
Other	113
Total	557
Type of Event	
Bombing	273
Arson	9
Firebombing	10
Kidnapping	55
Armed attack	68
Other	8
Total	423
Total Casualties	
Diplomat	5
Business	11
Government	51
Military	99
Other	1030
Total	1196

- Close all Taliban offices overseas.
- Reduce the staff at the limited number of Taliban missions abroad.
- Restrict travel of senior Taliban officials except for the purposes of participation in peace negotiations, compliance with the resolution, or for humanitarian reasons, including religious obligations.
- Ban the export to Afghan territory of a precursor chemical, acetic anhydride, which is used to manufacture heroin.
- Close all offices of Ariana Afghan Airlines and ban all nonhumanitarian assistance flights into and out of Afghanistan. Broad exemptions are given to humanitarian flights operated by, or on behalf of, nongovernmental organizations and government relief agencies providing humanitarian assistance to Afghanistan.

The sanctions imposed by these two resolutions are targeted sanctions. They are not economic sanctions.

- These "smart sanctions" provide for broad humanitarian exemptions to avoid harming the Afghan people.

- They permit private-sector trade and commerce, including food, medicine, and consumer products.
- They permit, without impediment, the work of the humanitarian organizations providing assistance to the civilian population of Afghanistan.
- They permit Afghans to travel by air for urgent humanitarian reasons and to fulfill their religious obligations, such as the hajj, including on the banned Ariana Afghan Airline. The UN Sanctions Committee already has approved about 200 flights for 13,000 Afghans in 2001 for this purpose. The Committee never had denied a request for a legitimate humanitarian waiver.
- They permit Taliban officials to travel abroad to participate in a peace process and to discuss fulfilling the demands of the Resolutions.

ASIA OVERVIEW

South Asia

In 2000, South Asia remained a focal point for terrorism directed against the United States, further confirming the trend of terrorism shifting from the Middle East to South Asia. The Taliban continued to provide safehaven for international terrorists, particularly Usama Bin Ladin and his network, in the portions of Afghanistan it controlled.

The Government of Pakistan increased its support to the Taliban and continued its support to militant groups active in Indian-held Kashmir, such as the Harakat ul-Mujahidin (HUM), some of which engaged in terrorism. In Sri Lanka the government continued its 17-year conflict with the Liberation Tigers of Tamil Eelam (LTTE), which engaged in several terrorist acts against government and civilian targets during the year.

Afghanistan

Islamic extremists from around the world—including North America, Europe, Africa, the Middle East, and Central, South, and Southeast Asia—continued to use Afghanistan as a training ground and base of operations for their worldwide terrorist activities in 2000. The Taliban, which controlled most Afghan territory, permitted the operation of training and indoctrination facilities for non-Afghans and provided logistics support to members of various terrorist organizations and *mujahidin*, including those waging *jihads* (holy wars) in Central Asia, Chechnya, and Kashmir.

Throughout 2000 the Taliban continued to host Usama Bin Ladin despite UN sanctions and international pressure to hand him over to stand trial in the United States or a third country. In a serious and ongoing dialogue with the Taliban, the United States repeatedly made clear to the Taliban that it would be held responsible for any terrorist attacks undertaken by Bin Ladin while he is in its territory.

In October, a terrorist bomb attack against the USS Cole in Aden Harbor, Yemen, killed 17 US sailors and injured scores of others. Although no definitive link has been made to Bin Ladin's organization, Yemeni authorities have determined that some suspects in custody and at large are veterans of Afghan training camps.

In August, Bangladeshi authorities uncovered a bomb plot to assassinate Prime Minister Sheikh Hasina at a public rally. Bengladeshi police maintained that Islamic terrorists trained in Afghanistan planted the bomb.

India

Security problems associated with various insurgencies, particularly in Kashmir, persisted through 2000 in India. Massacres of civilians in Kashmir during March and August were attributed to Lashkar-e-Tayyiba (LT) and other militant groups. India also faced continued violence associated with several separatist movements based in the northeast of the country.

The Indian Government continued cooperative efforts with the United States against terrorism. During the year, the US-India Joint Counterterrorism Working Group—founded in November 1999—met twice and agreed to increased cooperation on mutual counterterrorism interests. New Delhi continued to cooperate with US officials to ascertain the fate of four Western hostages—including one US citizen—kidnapped in Indian-held Kashmir in 1995, although the hostages' whereabouts remained unknown.

Pakistan

Pakistan's military government, headed by Gen. Pervez Musharraf, continued previous Pakistani Government support of the Kashmir insurgency, and Kashmiri militant groups continued to operate in Pakistan, raising funds and recruiting new cadre. Several of these groups were responsible for attacks against civilians in Indian-held Kashmir, and the largest of the groups, the Lashkar-e-Tayyiba, claimed responsibility for a suicide car-bomb attack against an Indian garrison in Srinagar in April.

In addition, the Harakat ul-Mujahidin (HUM), a designated Foreign Terrorist Organization, continues to be active in Pakistan without discouragement by the Government of Pakistan. Members of the group were associated with the hijacking in December 1999 of an Air India flight that resulted in the release from an Indian jail of former HUM leader Maulana Masood Azhar. Azhar since has founded his own Kashmiri militant group, Jaish-e-Mohammed, and publicly has threatened the United States.

The United States remains concerned about reports of continued Pakistani support for the Taliban's military operations in Afghanistan. Credible reporting indicates that Pakistan is providing the Taliban with material, fuel, funding, technical assistance, and military advisers. Pakistan has not prevented large numbers of Pakistani nationals from moving into Afghanistan to fight for the Taliban. Islamabad also failed to take effective steps to curb the activities of certain madrassas, or religious schools, that serve as recruiting grounds for terrorism. Pakistan publicly and privately said it intends to comply fully with UNSCR 1333, which imposes an arms embargo on the Taliban.

The attack on the USS Cole in Yemen in October prompted fears of US retaliatory strikes against Bin Ladin's organization and targets in Afghanistan if the investigation pointed in that direction. Pakistani religious party leaders and militant groups threatened US citizens and facilities if such an action were to occur, much as they did after the US attacks on training camps in Afghanistan in August 1998 and following the US diplomatic intervention in the Kargil conflict between Pakistan and India in 1999. The Government of Pakistan generally has cooperated with US requests to enhance security for US facilities and personnel. . . .

East Asia

Japan continued to make progress in its counterrorist efforts. Legal restrictions instituted in 1999 began to take effect on the Aum. Four Aum Shinrikyo members who had personally placed the sarin on the subway in 1995 were sentenced to death. Tokyo also made substantial progress in its efforts to return several Japanese Red Army (JRA) members to Japan. The Government of Japan indicted four JRA members who were forcibly returned after being deported from Lebanon. Tokyo also took two others into custody: Yoshimi Tanaka, a fugitive JRA member involved in hijacking a Japanese airliner in 1970, who was extradited from Thailand, and Fusako Shigenobu, a JRA founder and leader, who had been on the run for 30 years and was arrested in Japan in November.

Several nations in East Asia experienced terrorist violence in 2000. Burmese dissidents took over a provincial hospital in Thailand; authorities stormed the hospital, killed the hostage takers, and freed the hostages unharmed. In Indonesia, there was a sharp increase in international and domestic terrorism, including several bombings, two of which targeted official foreign interests. Pro-Jakarta militia units continued attacks on UN personnel in East Timor. In one incident in September, three aid workers, including one US citizen, were killed.

Small-scale violence in Cambodia, Laos, and Vietnam occurred in 2000, some connected to antigovernment groups, allegedly with support from foreign nationals. Several small-scale bombings occurred in the Laotian capital, some of which targeted tourist destinations and injured foreign nationals. An attack on 24 November in downtown Phnom Penh, Cambodia, resulted in deaths and injuries. The US Government released a statement on 19 December that "deplores and condemns" alleged US national or permanent resident support, encouragement, or participation in violent antigovernment activities in several foreign countries with which the United States is at peace, specifically Vietnam, Cambodia, and Laos. . . .

Malaysia

Malaysia experienced two incidents of international terrorism in 2000, both perpetrated by the Philippine-based Abu Sayyaf Group (ASG). The ASG abducted 21 persons, including 10 foreign tourists, from the Sipadan diving resort in eastern Malaysia on 23 April. A suspected ASG faction also kidnapped three Malaysians from a resort on Pandanan Island in eastern Malaysia on 10 September. The group released most of the hostages from both incidents but continued to hold one Filipino abducted from Sipadan as of the end of the year.

A Malaysian Islamist sect known as Al-Ma'unah targeted domestic security forces for the first time in July. Members of the group raided two military armories in Perak state, about 175 miles north of Kuala Lumpur, and took four locals hostage. Sect members killed two of the hostages—a Malaysian police officer and soldier—before surrendering on 6 July. Malaysian authorities arrested and detained several dozen members following the incident and suspect that 29 of those held also launched attacks against a Hindu temple, a brewery, and an electrical power tower.

Philippines

Islamist separatist groups in the Philippines increased attacks against foreign and domestic targets in 2000. The Abu Sayyaf Group (ASG)—designated one of 29 Foreign Terrorist Organizations by the US Government—conducted operations outside the southern Philippines for the first time when it abducted 21 persons—including 10 foreign tourists—from a Malaysian resort in April. In a series of subsequent, separate incidents, ASG group members abducted several foreign journalists, three Malaysians, and one US citizen in the southern Philippines. Although obtaining ransom money was a primary goal, the hostage takers issued several disparate political demands ranging from releasing international terrorists jailed in the United States to establishing an independent Islamic state. The group released most of the hostages by October allegedly for ransoms totaling several million dollars, while Philippine Government assaults on ASG positions paved the way for some other hostages to escape. The ASG, however, continued to hold the US citizen and a Filipino captive at year's end.

Manila made some legal progress against ASG kidnapping activities in 2000 when a regional trial court sentenced three group members to life in prison for abducting Dr. Nilo Barandino and 10 members of his household in 1992. The Philippine Government also filed charges against ASG members involved in multiple kidnapping cases, although the suspects remained at large.

The Moro Islamic Liberation Front (MILF)—the largest remaining Philippine Islamist separatist group—broke off stalled peace talks with Manila in late April. After the military launched an offensive capturing several MILF strongholds and attacking rebel checkpoints near Camp Abubakar—the MILF headquarters in the southern Philippines—the MILF mounted several terrorist attacks in the southern Philippines against Philippine security and civilian targets. In July, Philippine Armed Forces captured Camp Abubakar, and the MILF responded by declaring a "holy war" against Manila and continuing attacks against civilian and government targets in the southern Philippines. Philippine law enforcement officials also have accused MILF operatives of responsibility for several bombings in Manila, including two at popular shopping malls in May and five at different locations in Manila on 30 December. Police arrested 26 suspected MILF members in connection with the May bombings and still held them at year's end.

Communist rebels also remained active in 2000, occasionally targeting businesses and engaging in sporadic clashes with Philippine security forces. Press reporting indicates that early in the year the Communist Party of the Philippines New People's Army (CPP/NPA) attacked a South Korean construction company and in March issued an order to target foreign businesses "whose operations hurt the country's economy and environment." The Alex Boncayao Brigade (ABB)—a breakaway CPP/NPA faction—strafed Shell Oil offices in the central Philippines in March. The group warned of more attacks against oil companies, including US-owned Caltex, to protest rising oil prices.

Distinguishing between political and criminal motivation for many of the terrorist-related activities in the Philippines continued to be difficult, most notably in the numerous cases of kidnapping for ransom in the southern Philippines. Both Islamist and Communist insurgents sought to extort funds from businesses in their operating areas, occasionally conducting reprisal operations if money was not paid. . . .

EURASIA OVERVIEW

No major terrorist attacks occurred in Eurasia in 2000, but counterterrorist efforts, often in conjunction with counterinsurgency efforts, continued in the states of the former Soviet Union.

Russia, China, and the United States were all involved in regional efforts to combat terrorism. In 2000, members of the Commonwealth of Independent States (CIS) discussed establishing a CIS-wide counterterrorism center in Bishkek, although past efforts have been unsuccessful. The heads of the CIS states security services put forward Gen. Boris Mylnikov, former First Deputy Director of the Russian Federal Security Service (FSB) Department for Protecting the Constitutional Order and Combating Terrorism, to lead the potential CIS Counterterrorism Center, and on 1 December the CIS heads of state agreed on funding for the organization, half of which will be provided by Russia. The center began operations in December 2000 and reportedly has been tasked by the CIS to maintain a database of information on terrorism.

The Shanghai Forum—Kyrgyzstan, Kazakhstan, Tajikistan, Russia, and China—met in July and discussed cooperation among the five states as well as with Uzbekistan against terrorism, insurgency, and Islamic extremism. The Forum supported a proposal to establish a regional counterterrorism center in Bishkek, although no progress had been made in implementing this decision by year's end.

All five Central Asian states participated in the Central Asian Counterterrorism Conference in June sponsored by the US Department of State. Other participants included representatives from Russia, Egypt, and Spain. The United Kingdom, Turkey, China, and the Organization for Security and Cooperation in Europe (OSCE) sent observers.

Several Central Asian states also concluded counterterrorism agreements in 2000. Uzbekistan in early May signed an agreement with India that included an extradition treaty and mutual assistance in criminal investigations with an eye toward counterterrorist operations. In June, Kazakhstan and Kyrgyzstan separately reached bilateral agreements with China to cooperate on counterterrorist matters. In October and November, Uzbekistan also signed agreements on counterterrorism cooperation with Turkey, China, and Italy. . . .

Tajikistan

Several incidents of domestic terrorism occurred in Tajikistan in 2000. A small car bomb, planted on a vehicle belonging to the European Community Humanitarian Organization (ECHO), exploded on 16 July in Dushanbe and injured several children. In addition, in October an unoccupied car belonging to the Chairman of the Democratic Party, Mahmadruzi Iskandarov, was bombed. Bombings and other violence marred Tajikistani Parliamentary elections in February, which concluded the Tajikistani Peace Process ending a five-year civil war. On 1 October and 31 December four churches were bombed. Several deaths and numerous casualties resulted from the bombing in October. There is no evidence that any of the attacks, either on the churches or during the elections, involved international interests. While the Tajikistani Government does not support the Islamic Movement of Uzbekistan (IMU), it has been unable to prevent it from transiting its territory.

Uzbekistan

The Islamic Movement of Uzbekistan (IMU) infiltrated fighters into mountainous areas of Surkhandar'inskaya Oblast southern Uzbekistan during the spring and summer of 2000. Uzbekistani military forces discovered the fighters and drove them back into Tajikistan. Tohir Yuldashev and Juma Khodjiev (a.k.a. Juma Namangani), the leaders of the IMU, were tried in absentia together with 10 other persons accused of terrorism or anticonstitutional activity. All defendants were convicted at a trial that failed to conform to international standards for the protection of the human rights of the defendants. The court sentenced Yuldashev and Khodjiev to death and the remaining defendants to prison terms. On 25 September, the United States designated the IMU a Foreign Terrorist Organization, citing both its armed incursions into Uzbekistan and neighboring Kyrgyzstan and its taking of foreign hostages, including US citizens.

EUROPE OVERVIEW

Western Europe had the largest decline in the number of international terrorist incidents of any region in 2000. Several European states moved to strengthen and codify anti-terrorism legislation, and many signed the International Convention for the Suppression of Terrorist Financing, which was opened for signature on 10 January 2000. There were notable examples of counterterrorism cooperation among several countries, such as the US-UK-Greek collaboration on the British Defense Attache's assassination in Athens, Spanish-French cooperation against the Basque terrorist group Basque Fatherland and Liberty (ETA), and Italy and Spain's agreement to create common judicial space. Greece undertook a series of more stringent counterterrorism measures in the wake of the murder of the UK Defense Attache by the terrorist group 17 November, but Athens still has not made any arrests in connection with any of the group's 21 murders over the past quarter century. France and Turkey both made impressive strides in combating terrorism through aggressively pursuing the perpetrators and their terrorist groups.

In Southeastern Europe, groups of ethnic Albanians have conducted armed attacks against government forces in southern Serbia and in Macedonia since 1999. One group in southern Serbia calls itself the Liberation Army of Presevo, Medvedja, and Bujanovac (PMBLA). One group in Macedonia calls itself the National Liberation Army (NLA). Both groups include members who fought with the Kosovo Liberation Army (KLA) in 1998–99 and have used their wartime connections to obtain funding and weapons from Kosovo and elsewhere. The PMBLA has, on occasion, harassed and detained civilians traveling through areas it controls. Both the PMBLA and the NLA have fired indiscriminately upon civilian centers. (In the same region, ethnic Albanian assailants carried out a terrorist attack against a bus in Kosovo on 16 February 2001, killing at least seven civilians and wounding 43 others.). . .

LATIN AMERICA OVERVIEW

Latin America witnessed an increase in terrorist attacks from the previous year, from 121 to 193. In Colombia, leftist guerilla groups abducted hostages and attacked civil infrastructure, while rightwing paramilitary groups abducted congressional representatives, killed political candidates, and massacred civilians in an attempt to thwart the guerillas. In Ecuador, organized criminal elements with possible links to terrorists and terrorist groups abducted 10 oil workers and also claimed responsibility for oil pipeline bombings that killed seven civilians. Extremist religious groups continued to pose a terrorist concern in the triborder area of Argentina, Brazil, and Paraguay. Terrorist incidents continued a downward trend in Peru despite a deteriorating political situation and the abrupt resignation of hardline President Fujimori. . . .

MIDDLE EAST OVERVIEW

Middle Eastern terrorist groups and their state sponsors continued to plan, train for, and carry out acts of terrorism throughout 2000. The last few months of the year brought a significant increase in the overall level of political violence and terrorism in the region, especially in Israel and the occupied territories. Much of the late-year increase in violence was driven by a breakdown in negotiations and counterterrorism cooperation between Israel and the Palestinian Authority. The breakdown sparked a cycle of violence between Israelis and Palestinians that continued to spiral at the end of the year.

Israeli-Palestinian violence also prompted widespread anger at Israel, as well as the United States, throughout the Middle East, demonstrated in part by numerous, occasionally violent protests against US interests in several Middle Eastern countries. Palestinian terrorist groups, with the assistance of Iran and the Lebanese Hizballah, took advantage of Palestinian and regional anger to escalate their terrorist attacks against Israeli targets.

Other terrorists also keyed on Israeli-Palestinian difficulties to increase their rhetorical and operational activities against Israel and the United States. Usama Bin Ladin's al-Qaida organization, the Egyptian Islamic Jihad, and other terrorist groups that focus on US and Israeli targets escalated their efforts to conduct and promote terrorism in the Middle East. Several disrupted plans to attack US and Israeli targets in the Middle East purportedly were intended to demonstrate anger over Israel's sometimes disproportionate use of force to contain protests and perceptions that the United States "allowed" Israel to act.

Al-Qaida and its affiliates especially used their ability to provide money and training as leverage to establish ties to and build the terrorist capabilities of a variety of small Middle Eastern terrorist groups such as the Lebanese Asbat al-Ansar.

The most significant act of anti-US terrorism in the region in 2000—the bombing of the USS Cole in Yemen on 12 October—was not driven by events in the Levant. Although the joint US-Yemeni investigation into the savage bombing—which killed 17 US sailors and wounded 39 others—continued through the end of 2000, initial indications suggested the attack may have originated in Taliban-controlled Afghanistan, where al-Qaida, the Egyptian Islamic Jihad, and other terrorist groups are based and some of the alleged USS Cole attackers received training. The Yemeni Government, as much a victim of the attack as the United States, was working closely with the US Government to bring to justice those responsible for the act.

Many other Middle Eastern governments also increased their efforts to counter the threat from regional and Afghanistan-based terrorists, including the provision of enhanced security for high-risk US Government targets. The Government of Kuwait, for instance, cooperated with regional counterparts in November to disrupt a suspected international terrorist cell. Kuwait arrested 13 individuals and recovered a large quantity of explosives and weapons. The cell reportedly was planning to attack both Kuwaiti officials and US targets in Kuwait and the region. . . .

Kuwait

In November the Government of Kuwait disrupted a suspected international terrorist cell. Working with regional counterparts, Kuwaiti security services arrested 13 individuals and recovered a large quantity of explosives and weapons. The terrorist cell reportedly was planning to attack both Kuwaiti officials and US targets in Kuwait and the region.

Lebanon

Throughout the year, the Lebanese Government's continued lack of control in portions of the country—including parts of the Bekaa Valley, Beirut's southern suburbs, Palestinian refugee camps, and the southern border area—as well as easy access to arms and explosives, contributed to an environment with a high potential for acts of violence and terrorism.

A variety of terrorist groups—including Hizballah, Usama Bin Ladin's (UBL) al-Qaida network, HAMAS, the PIJ, the PFLP-GC, Asbat al-Ansar, and several local Sunni extremist organizations—continued to operate with varying degrees of impunity, conducting training and other operational activities. Hizballah continued to pose the most potent threat to US interests in Lebanon. Although Hizballah has not attacked US targets in Lebanon since 1991, it continued to pose a significant terrorist threat to US interests globally from its base in Lebanon. Hizballah voiced its support for terrorist actions by Palestinian rejectionist groups in Israel and the occupied territories. While the Lebanese Government expressed support for "resistance" activities along its southern border, it has only limited influence over Hizballah and the Palestinian rejectionists.

UBL's al-Qaida network maintained a presence in Lebanon. Although the Lebanese Government actively monitored and arrested UBL-affiliated operatives, it did not control the Palestinian refugee camps where the operatives conducted terrorist training and anti-US indoctrination.

In the fall, Hizballah kidnapped an Israeli noncombatant whom it may have lured to Lebanon on a false pretense. Hizballah has been using hostages, including captured IDF soldiers, as bargaining chips to win the release of Lebanese prisoners in Israel.

In January, Lebanese security forces clashed in the north with a Sunni extremist movement that had ambushed and killed four Lebanese soldiers. The group had ties to UBL operatives. The same month, Asbat al-Ansar launched a grenade attack against the Russian Embassy. In October, the Sunni extremist group, Takfir wa Hijra, claimed responsibility for a grenade attack against a Christian Member of Parliament's residence, though there are indications others may have been behind this attack.

The Lebanese Government continued to support some international counterterrorist initiatives and moved against UBL-affiliated operatives in 2000. In February, Lebanese authorities arrested members of a UBL cell in Lebanon. In March, the government fulfilled a Japanese Government request and deported four Japanese Red Army (JRA) members after it had refused to do so for years. It allowed one JRA member to remain in Lebanon. It did not act, however, on repeated US requests to turn over Lebanese terrorists involved in the hijacking in 1985 of TWA flight 847 and in the abduction, torture, and—in some cases—murders of US hostages from 1984 to 1991.

Saudi Arabia

Several threats against US military and civilian personnel and facilities in Saudi Arabia were reported in 2000, but there were no confirmed terrorist incidents.

At year's end Saudi authorities were investigating a shooting by a lone gunman who opened fire on British and US nationals near the town of Khamis Mushayt in early August 2000. The gunman fired more than 100 rounds on a Royal Saudi Air Force checkpoint, killing one Saudi and wounding two other Saudi guards. The gunman was wounded in the exchange of fire.

Terrorist Usama Bin Ladin, whose Saudi citizenship was revoked in 1994, continued to publicly threaten US interests in Saudi Arabia during the year. In a videotaped statement released in September, Bin Ladin once again publicly threatened US interests.

The Government of Saudi Arabia continued to investigate the bombing in June 1996 of the Khubar Towers housing facility near Dhahran that killed 19 US military personnel and wounded some 500 US and Saudi personnel. The Government of Saudi Arabia publicly stated that it still was looking for three Saudi suspects whom it wanted for questioning in connection with the bombing and whom authorities believed to be currently outside Saudi Arabia. The Saudis continued to hold in detention a number of Saudi citizens linked to the attack, including Hani al-Sayegh, whom the United States expelled to Saudi Arabia in 1999.

The Government of Saudi Arabia reaffirmed its commitment to combating terrorism. It required nongovernmental organizations and private voluntary agencies to obtain government authorization before soliciting contributions for domestic or international causes. It was not clear that these regulations were enforced consistently; however, allegations continued to surface that some international terrorist organization representatives solicited and collected funds from private citizens in Saudi Arabia.

Yemen

On 12 October a boat carrying explosives was detonated next to the USS Cole, killing 17 US Navy members and injuring another 39. The US destroyer, en route to the Persian Gulf, was making a prearranged fuel stop in the Yemeni port of Aden when the attack occurred. At least three groups reportedly claimed responsibility for the attack, including the Islamic Army of Aden, Muhammad's Army, and a previously unknown group called the Islamic Deterrence Force.

The Yemeni Government strongly condemned the attack on the USS Cole and actively engaged in investigative efforts to find the perpetrators. On 29 November, Yemen and the United States signed a memorandum of agreement delineating guidelines for joint investigation to further facilitate cooperation between the two governments. The Yemeni Government's ability to conduct international terrorism investigations was enhanced by joint investigative efforts undertaken pursuant to these guidelines.

Several terrorist organizations maintained a presence in Yemen. HAMAS and the Palestinian Islamic Jihad continued to be recognized as legal organizations and maintained offices in Yemen but did not engage in terrorist activities there. Other international terrorist groups that have an illegal presence in Yemen included the Egyptian Islamic Jihad, al-Gama'a al-Islamiyya, Libyan opposition groups, the Algerian Armed Islamic Group, and al-Qaida. Press reports indicated indigenous groups such as the Islamic Army of Aden remained active in Yemen.

The Government of Yemen did not provide direct or indirect support to terrorists, but its inability to control fully its borders, territory, or its own travel documents did little to discourage the terrorist presence in Yemen. Improved cooperation with Saudi Arabia as a result of the Yemeni-Saudi border treaty, concluded in June, promised to reduce illegal border crossings and trafficking in weapons and explosives, although border clashes continued after the agreement's ratification. The government attempted to resolve some of its passport problems in 2000 by requiring proof of nationality when submitting an application, although terrorists continued to have access to forged Yemeni identity documents.

OVERVIEW OF STATE-SPONSORED TERRORISM

The designation of state sponsors of terrorism by the United States—and the imposition of sanctions—is a mechanism for isolating nations that use terrorism as a means of political expression. US policy seeks to pressure and isolate state sponsors so they will renounce the use of terrorism, end support to terrorists, and bring terrorists to justice for past crimes. The United States is committed to holding terrorists and those who harbor them accountable for past attacks, regardless of when the acts occurred. The US Government has a long memory and will not simply expunge a terrorist's record because time has passed. The states that choose to harbor terrorists are like accomplices who provide shelter for criminals. They will be held accountable for their "guests'" actions. International terrorists should know, before they contemplate a crime, that they cannot hunker down in safehaven for a period of time and be absolved of their crimes.

The United States is firmly committed to removing countries from the list once they have taken necessary steps to end their link to terrorism. In fact, the Department of State is engaged in ongoing discussions with North Korea and Sudan with the object of getting those governments completely out of the terrorism business and off the terrorism list.

Iran, Iraq, Syria, Libya, Cuba, North Korea, and Sudan continue to be the seven governments that the US Secretary of State has designated as state sponsors of international terrorism. Iran remained the most active state sponsor of terrorism in 2000. It provided increasing support to numerous terrorist groups, including the Lebanese Hizballah, HAMAS, and the Palestine Islamic Jihad (PIJ), which seek to undermine the Middle East peace negotiations through the use of terrorism. Iraq continued to provide safehaven and support to a variety of Palestinian rejectionist groups, as well as bases, weapons, and protection to the Mujahedin-e-Khalq (MEK), an Iranian terrorist group that opposes the current Iranian regime. Syria continued to provide safehaven and support to several terrorist groups, some of which oppose the Middle East peace negotiations. Libya at the end of 2000 was attempting to mend its international image following its surrender in 1999 of two Libyan suspects for trial in the Pan Am 103 bombing. (In early 2001, one of the suspects was convicted of murder. The judges in the case found that he acted "in furtherance of the purposes of . . . Libyan Intelligence Services.") Cuba continued to provide safehaven to several terrorists and US fugitives and maintained ties to state sponsors and Latin American insurgents. North Korea harbored several hijackers of a Japanese Airlines flight to North Korea in the 1970s and maintained links to other terrorist groups. Finally, Sudan continued to serve as a safehaven for members of al-Qaida, the Lebanese Hizballah, al-Gama'a al-Islamiyya, Egyptian Islamic Jihad, the PIJ, and HAMAS, but it has been engaged in a counterterrorism dialogue with the United States since mid-2000.

State sponsorship has decreased over the past several decades. As it decreases, it becomes increasingly important for all countries to adopt a "zero tolerance" for terrorist activity within their borders. Terrorists will seek safehaven in those areas where they are able to avoid the rule of law and to travel, prepare, raise funds, and operate. The United States continued actively researching and gathering intelligence on other states that will be considered for designation as state sponsors. If the United States deems a country to "repeatedly provide support for acts of international terrorism," the US Government is required by law to add it to the list. In South Asia, the United States has been increasingly concerned about reports of Pakistani support to terrorist groups and elements active in Kashmir, as well as Pakistani support, especially military support, to the Taliban, which continues to harbor terrorist groups, including al-Qaida, the Egyptian Islamic Jihad, al-Gama'a al-Islamiyya, and the Islamic Movement of Uzbekistan. In the Middle East, the United States was concerned that a variety of terrorist groups operated and trained inside Lebanon, although Lebanon has acted against some of those groups. Lebanon also has been unresponsive to US requests to bring to justice terrorists who conducted attacks against US citizens and property in Lebanon in previous years. . . .

Iraq

Iraq planned and sponsored international terrorism in 2000. Although Baghdad focused on antidissident activity overseas, the regime continued to support various terrorist groups. The regime has not attempted an anti-Western terrorist attack since its failed plot to assassinate former President Bush in 1993 in Kuwait.

Czech police continued to provide protection to the Prague office of the US Government-funded Radio Free Europe/Radio Liberty (RFE/RL), which produces Radio Free Iraq programs and employs expatriate journalists. The police presence was augmented in 1999, following reports that the Iraqi Intelligence Service (IIS) might retaliate against RFE/RL for broadcasts critical of the Iraqi regime.

To intimidate or silence Iraqi opponents of the regime living overseas, the IIS reportedly opened several new stations in foreign capitals during 2000. Various opposition groups joined in warning Iraqi dissidents abroad against newly established "expatriates' associations," which, they asserted, are IIS front organizations. Opposition leaders in London contended that the IIS had dispatched women agents to infiltrate their ranks and was targeting dissidents for assassination. In Germany, an Iraqi opposition figure denounced the IIS for murdering his son, who had recently left Iraq to join him abroad. Dr. Ayad 'Allawi, Secretary General of the Iraqi National Accord, an opposition group, stated that relatives of dissidents living abroad are often arrested and jailed to intimidate activists overseas.

In northern Iraq, Iraqi agents reportedly killed a locally well-known religious personality who declined to echo the regime line. The regional security director in As Sulaymaniyah stated that Iraqi operatives were responsible for the car-bomb explosion that injured a score of passersby. Officials of the Iraqi Communist Party asserted that an attack on a provincial party headquarters had been thwarted when party security officers shot and wounded a terrorist employed by the IIS.

Baghdad continued to denounce and delegitimize UN personnel working in Iraq, particularly UN de-mining teams, in the wake of the killing in 1999 of an expatriate UN de-mining worker in northern Iraq under circumstances suggesting regime involvement. An Iraqi who opened fire at the UN Food and Agriculture Organization (FAO) office in Baghdad, killing two persons and wounding six, was permitted to hold a heavily publicized press conference at which he contended that his action had been motivated by the harshness of UN sanctions, which the regime regularly excoriates.

The Iraqi regime rebuffed a request from Riyadh for the extradition of two Saudis who had hijacked a Saudi Arabian Airlines flight to Baghdad, but did return promptly the passengers and the aircraft. Disregarding its obligations under international law, the regime granted political asylum to the hijackers and gave them ample opportunity to ventilate in the Iraqi Government–controlled and international media their criticisms of alleged abuses by the Saudi Arabian Government, echoing an Iraqi propaganda theme.

While the origins of the FAO attack and the hijacking were unclear, the Iraqi regime readily exploited these terrorist acts to further its policy objectives.

Several expatriate terrorist groups continued to maintain offices in Baghdad, including the Arab Liberation Front, the inactive 15 May Organization, the Palestine Liberation Front (PLF), and the Abu Nidal organization (ANO). PLF leader Abu 'Abbas appeared on state-controlled television in the fall to praise Iraq's leadership in rallying Arab opposition to Israeli violence against Palestinians. The ANO threatened to attack Austrian interests unless several million dollars in a frozen ANO account in a Vienna bank were turned over to the group.

The Iraq-supported Iranian terrorist group, Mujahedin-e Khalq (MEK), regularly claimed responsibility for armed incursions into Iran that targeted police and military outposts, as well as for mortar and bomb attacks on security organization headquarters in various Iranian cities. MEK publicists reported that in March group members killed an Iranian colonel having intelligence responsibilities. An MEK claim to have wounded a general was denied by the Iranian Government. The Iraqi regime deployed MEK forces against its domestic opponents.

Libya

In 2000, Libya continued efforts to mend its international image in the wake of its surrender in 1999 of two Libyans accused of the bombing of Pan Am flight 103 over Lockerbie, Scotland, in 1988. Trial proceedings for the two defendants began in the Netherlands in May and were ongoing at year's end. (The court issued its verdict on 31 January 2001. It found Abdel Basset al-Megrahi guilty of murder, concluding that he caused an explosive device to detonate on board the airplane resulting in the murder of the flight's 259 passengers and crew as well as 11 residents of Lockerbie, Scotland. The judges found that he acted "in furtherance of the purposes of . . . Libyan Intelligence Services." Concerning the other defendant, Al-Amin Kalifa Fahima, the court concluded that the Crown failed to present sufficient evidence to satisfy the high standard of "proof beyond reasonable doubt" that is necessary in criminal cases.)

In 1999, Libya paid compensation for the death of a British policewoman,*

---

*In April 1984, a British policewoman was killed and 11 demonstrators were wounded when gunmen in the Libyan People's Bureau in London fired on a peaceful anti-Qadhafi demonstration outside their building.

a move that preceded the reopening of the British Embassy. Libya also paid damages to the families of victims in the bombing of UTA flight 772. Six Libyans were convicted in absentia in that case, and the French judicial system is considering further indictments against other Libyan officials, including Libyan leader Muammar Qadhafi.

Libya played a high-profile role in negotiating the release of a group of foreign hostages seized in the Philippines by the Abu Sayyaf Group, reportedly in exchange for a ransom payment. The hostages included citizens of France, Germany, Malaysia, South Africa, Finland, the Philippines, and Lebanon. The payment of ransom to kidnappers only encourages additional hostage taking, and the Abu Sayyaf Group, emboldened by its success, did seize additional hostages—including a US citizen—later in the year. Libya's behavior and that of other parties involved in the alleged ransom arrangement served only to encourage further terrorism and to make that region far more dangerous for residents and travelers.

At year's end, Libya had yet to comply fully with the remaining UN Security Council requirements related to Pan Am 103: accepting responsibility, paying appropriate compensation, disclosing all it knows, and renouncing terrorism. The United States remains dedicated to maintaining pressure on the Libyan Government until it does so. Qadhafi stated publicly that his government had adopted an antiterrorism stance, but it remains unclear whether his claims of distancing Libya from its terrorist past signify a true change in policy.

Libya also remained the primary suspect in several other past terrorist operations, including the Labelle discotheque bombing in Berlin in 1986 that killed two US servicemen and one Turkish civilian and wounded more than 200 persons. The trial in Germany of five suspects in the bombing, which began in November 1997, continued in 2000. Although Libya expelled the Abu Nidal organization and distanced itself from the Palestinian rejectionists in 1999, it continued to have contact with groups that use violence to oppose the Middle East Peace Process, including the Palestine Islamic Jihad and the Popular Front for the Liberation of Palestine-General Command. . . .

Sudan

The United States and Sudan in mid-2000 entered into a dialogue to discuss US counterterrorism concerns. The talks, which were ongoing at the end of the year, were constructive and obtained some positive results. By the end of the year Sudan had signed all 12 international conventions for combating terrorism and had taken several other positive counterterrorism steps, including closing down the Popular Arab and Islamic Conference, which served as a forum for terrorists.

Sudan, however, continued to be used as a safehaven by members of various groups, including associates of Usama Bin Ladin's al-Qaida organization, Egyptian al-Gama'a al-Islamiyya, Egyptian Islamic Jihad, the Palestine Islamic Jihad, and HAMAS. Most groups used Sudan primarily as a secure base for assisting compatriots elsewhere.

Khartoum also still had not complied fully with UN Security Council Resolutions 1044, 1054, and 1070, passed in 1996—which demand that Sudan end all support to terrorists. They also require Khartoum to hand over three Egyptian Gama'a fugitives linked to the assassination attempt in 1995 against Egyptian President Hosni Mubarak in Ethiopia. Sudanese officials continued to deny that they had a role in the attack. . . .

WEAPONS-OF-MASS-DESTRUCTION (WMD) TERRORISM

At the dawn of a new millennium, the possibility of a terrorist attack involving weapons of mass destruction (WMD)—chemical, biological, radiological, nuclear (CBRN), or large explosive weapons—remained real. As of the end of 2000, however, the most notorious attack involving chemical weapons against a civilian target remained Aum Shinrikyo's sarin nerve agent attack against the Tokyo subway in March 1995.

Most terrorists continued to rely on conventional tactics, such as bombing, shooting, and kidnapping, but some terrorists—such as Usama Bin Ladin and his associates—continued to seek CBRN capabilities.

- Popular literature and the public dialog focused on the vulnerability of civilian targets to CBRN attacks. Such attacks could cause lasting disruption and generate significant psychological impact on a population and its infrastructure.
- A few groups, notably those driven by distorted religious and cultural ideologies, showed signs they were willing to cause large numbers of casualties. Other potentially dangerous but less predictable groups had emerged, and those groups may not abide by traditional targeting constraints that would prohibit using indiscriminate violence or CBRN weapons.
- Some CBRN materials, technology, and especially information continued to be widely available, particularly from commercial sources and the Internet.

TERRORIST USE OF INFORMATION TECHNOLOGY

Terrorists have seized upon the worldwide practice of using information technology (IT) in daily life. They embrace IT for several reasons: it improves communication and aids organization, allows members to coordinate quickly with large numbers of followers, and provides a platform for propaganda. The Internet also allows terrorists to reach a wide audience of potential donors and recruits who may be located over a large geographic area.

In addition, terrorists are taking note of the proliferation of hacking and the use of the computer as a weapon. Extremists routinely post messages to widely accessible Web sites that call for defacing Western Internet sites and disrupting online service, for example. The widespread availability of hacking software and its anonymous and increasingly automated design make it likely that terrorists will more frequently incorporate these tools into their online activity. The appeal of such tools may increase as news media continue to sensationalize hacking. . . .

TERRORIST GROUPS

The following descriptive list of terrorist groups is presented in two sections. The first section lists the 28 groups that currently are designated by the Secretary of State as Foreign Terrorist Organizations (FTOs), pursuant to section 219 of the Immigration and Nationality Act, as amended by the Antiterrorism and Effective Death Penalty Act of 1996. The designations carry legal consequences:

- It is unlawful to provide funds or other material support to a designated FTO.
- Representatives and certain members of a designated FTO can be denied visas or excluded from the United States.
- US financial institutions must block funds of designated FTOs and their agents and must report the blockage to the US Department of the Treasury.

The second section includes other terrorist groups that were active during 2000. Terrorist groups whose activities were limited in scope in 2000 are not included.

I. Designated Foreign Terrorist Organizations

Abu Nidal organization (ANO) *a.k.a. Fatah Revolutionary Council, Arab Revolutionary Brigades, Black September, and Revolutionary Organization of Socialist Muslims*

Description. International terrorist organization led by Sabri al-Banna. Split from PLO in 1974. Made up of various functional committees, including political, military, and financial.

Activities. Has carried out terrorist attacks in 20 countries, killing or injuring almost 900 persons. Targets include the United States, the United Kingdom, France, Israel, moderate Palestinians, the PLO, and various Arab countries. Major attacks included the Rome and Vienna airports in December 1985, the Neve Shalom synagogue in Istanbul and the Pan Am flight 73 hijacking in Karachi in September 1986, and the City of Poros day-excursion ship attack in Greece in July 1988. Suspected of assassinating PLO deputy chief Abu Iyad and PLO security chief Abu Hul in Tunis in January 1991. ANO assassinated a Jordanian diplomat in Lebanon in January 1994 and has been linked to the killing of the PLO representative there. Has not attacked Western targets since the late 1980s.

Strength. A few hundred plus limited overseas support structure.

Location/Area of Operation. Al-Banna relocated to Iraq in December 1998, where the group maintains a presence. Has an operational presence in Lebanon, including in several Palestinian refugee camps. Financial problems and internal disorganization have reduced the group's activities and capabilities. Authorities shut down the ANO's operations in Libya and Egypt in 1999. Has demonstrated ability to operate over wide area, including the Middle East, Asia, and Europe.

External Aid. Has received considerable support, including safehaven, training, logistic assistance, and financial aid from Iraq, Libya, and Syria (until 1987), in addition to close support for selected operations.

Abu Sayyaf Group (ASG)

Description. The ASG is the smallest and most radical of the Islamic separatist groups operating in the southern Philippines. Some ASG members have studied or worked in the Middle East and developed ties to *mujahidin* while fighting and training in Afghanistan. The group split from the Moro National Liberation Front in 1991 under the leadership of Abdurajik Abubakar Janjalani, who was killed in a clash with Philippine police on 18 December 1998. Press reports place his younger brother, Khadafi Janjalani, as the nominal leader of the group, which is composed of several factions.

Activities. Engages in bombings, assassinations, kidnappings, and extortion to promote an independent Islamic state in western Mindanao and the Sulu Archipelago, areas in the southern Philippines heavily populated by Muslims. Raided the town of Ipil in Mindanao in April 1995—the group's first large-scale action—and kidnapped more than 30 foreigners, including a US citizen, in 2000.

Strength. Believed to have about 200 core fighters, but more than 2,000 individuals motivated by the prospect of receiving ransom payments for foreign hostages allegedly joined the group in August.

Location/Area of Operation. The ASG primarily operates in the southern Philippines with members occasionally traveling to Manila, but the group expanded its operations to Malaysia this year when it abducted foreigners from two different resorts.

External Aid. Probably receives support from Islamic extremists in the Middle East and South Asia.

Armed Islamic Group (GIA)

Description. An Islamic extremist group, the GIA aims to overthrow the secular Algerian regime and replace it with an Islamic state. The GIA began its violent activities in 1992 after Algiers voided the victory of the Islamic Salvation Front (FIS)—the largest Islamic opposition party—in the first round of legislative elections in December 1991.

Activities. Frequent attacks against civilians and government workers. Between 1992 and 1998 the GIA conducted a terrorist campaign of civilian massacres, sometimes wiping out entire villages in its area of operation. Since announcing its campaign against foreigners living in Algeria in 1993, the GIA has killed more than 100 expatriate men and women—mostly Europeans—in the country. The group uses assassinations and bombings, including car bombs, and it is known to favor kidnapping victims and slitting their throats. The GIA hijacked an Air France flight to Algiers in December 1994. In late 1999 several GIA members were convicted by a French court for conducting a series of bombings in France in 1995.

The Salafi Group for Call and Combat (GSPC) splinter faction appears to have eclipsed the GIA since approximately 1998 and is currently assessed to be the most effective remaining armed group inside Algeria. Both the GIA and GSPC leadership continue to proclaim their rejection of President Bouteflika's amnesty, but in contrast to the GIA, the GSPC has stated that it limits attacks on civilians. The GSPC's planned attack against the Paris-Dakar Road Rally in January 2000 demonstrates, however, that the group has not entirely renounced attacks against high-profile civilian targets.

Strength. Unknown; probably several hundred to several thousand.

Location/Area of Operation. Algeria.

External Aid. Algerian expatriates and GSPC members abroad, many of whom reside in Western Europe, provide financial and logistic support. In addition, the Algerian Government has accused Iran and Sudan of supporting Algerian extremists.

Aum Supreme Truth (Aum) a.k.a. Aum Shinrikyo, Aleph

Description. A cult established in 1987 by Shoko Asahara, the Aum aimed to take over Japan, then the world. Approved as a religious entity in 1989 under Japanese law, the group ran candidates in a Japanese parliamentary election in 1990. Over time the cult began to emphasize the imminence of the end of the world and stated that the United States would initiate Armageddon by starting World War III with Japan. The Japanese Government revoked its recognition of the Aum as a religious organization in October 1995, but in 1997 a government panel decided not to invoke the Anti-Subversive Law against the group, which would have outlawed the cult. In 2000, Fumihiro Joyu took control of the Aum following his three-year jail sentence for perjury. Joyu was previously the group's spokesman and Russia Branch leader. Under Joyu's leadership the Aum changed its name to Aleph and claims to have rejected the violent and apocalyptic teachings of its founder.

Activities. On 20 March 1995, Aum members simultaneously released the chemical nerve agent sarin on several Tokyo subway trains, killing 12 persons and injuring up to 6,000. (Recent studies put the number of persons who suffered actual physical injuries closer to 1,300, with the rest suffering from some form of psychological trauma.) The group was responsible for other mysterious chemical accidents in Japan in 1994. Its efforts to conduct attacks using biological agents have been unsuccessful. Japanese police arrested Asahara in May 1995, and he remained on trial, facing 17 counts of murder at the end of 2000. Since 1997 the cult continued to recruit new members, engage in commercial enterprise, and acquire property, although the cult scaled back these activities significantly in 2000 in response to public outcry. The cult maintains an Internet homepage.

Strength. The Aum's current membership is estimated at 1,500 to 2,000 persons. At the time of the Tokyo subway attack, the group claimed to have 9,000 members in Japan and up to 40,000 worldwide.

Location/Area of Operation. The Aum's principal membership is located only in Japan, but a residual branch comprising an unknown number of followers has surfaced in Russia.

External Aid. None.

Basque Fatherland and Liberty (ETA) a.k.a. Euzkadi Ta Askatasuna

Description. Founded in 1959 with the aim of establishing an independent homeland based on Marxist principles in the northern Spanish provinces of Vizcaya, Guipuzcoa, Alava, and Navarra and the southwestern French departments of Labourd, Basse-Navarra, and Soule.

Activities. Primarily bombings and assassinations of Spanish Government officials, especially security and military forces, politicians, and judicial figures. ETA finances its activities through kidnappings, robberies, and extortion. The group has killed more than 800 persons since it began lethal attacks in the early 1960s. In November 1999, ETA broke its "unilateral and indefinite" cease-fire and began an assassination and bombing campaign that killed 23 individuals and wounded scores more by the end of 2000.

Strength. Unknown; may have hundreds of members, plus supporters.

Location/Area of Operation. Operates primarily in the Basque autonomous regions of northern Spain and southwestern France, but also has bombed Spanish and French interests elsewhere.

External Aid. Has received training at various times in the past in Libya, Lebanon, and Nicaragua. Some ETA members allegedly have received sanctuary in Cuba while others reside in South America. Also appears to have ties to the Irish Republican Army through the two groups' legal political wings.

Al-Gama'a al-Islamiyya (Islamic Group, IG)

Description. Egypt's largest militant group, active since the late 1970s; appears to be loosely organized. Has an external wing with a worldwide presence. The group issued a cease-fire in March 1999, but its spiritual leader, Shaykh Umar Adb al-Rahman, incarcerated in the United States, rescinded his support for the cease-fire in June 2000. The Gama'a has not conducted an attack inside Egypt since August 1998. Rifa'i Taha Musa—a hardline former senior member of the group—signed Usama Bin Ladin's February 1998 *fatwa* calling for attacks against US civilians. The IG since has publicly denied that it supports Bin Ladin and frequently differs with public statements made by Taha Musa. Taha Musa has in the last year sought to push the group toward a return to armed operations, but the group, which still is led by Mustafa Hamza, has yet to break the unilaterally declared cease-fire. In late 2000, Taha Musa appeared in an undated video with Bin Ladin and Ayman al-Zawahiri threatening retaliation against the United States for Abd al-Rahman's continued incarceration. The IG's primary goal is to overthrow the Egyptian Government and replace it with an Islamic state, but Taha Musa also may be interested in attacking US and Israeli interests.

Activities. Group specialized in armed attacks against Egyptian security and other government officials, Coptic Christians, and Egyptian opponents of Islamic extremism before the cease-fire. From 1993 until the cease-fire, al-Gama'a launched attacks on tourists in Egypt, most notably the attack in November 1997 at Luxor that killed 58 foreign tourists. Also claimed responsibility for the attempt in June 1995 to assassinate Egyptian President Hosni Mubarak in Addis Ababa, Ethiopia. The Gama'a has never specifically attacked a US citizen or facility but has threatened US interests.

Strength. Unknown. At its peak the IG probably commanded several thousand hard-core members and a like number of sympathizers. The 1998 cease-fire and security crackdowns following the attack in Luxor in 1997 probably have resulted in a substantial decrease in the group's numbers.

Location/Area of Operation. Operates mainly in the Al-Minya, Asyu't, Qina, and Sohaj Governorates of southern Egypt. Also appears to have support in Cairo, Alexandria, and other urban locations, particularly among unemployed graduates and students. Has a worldwide presence, including Sudan, the United Kingdom, Afghanistan, Austria, and Yemen.

External Aid. Unknown. The Egyptian Government believes that Iran, Bin Ladin, and Afghan militant groups support the organization. Also may obtain some funding through various Islamic nongovernmental organizations.

HAMAS (Islamic Resistance Movement)

Description. Formed in late 1987 as an outgrowth of the Palestinian branch of the Muslim Brotherhood. Various HAMAS elements have used both political and violent means, including terrorism, to pursue the goal of establishing an Islamic Palestinian state in place of Israel. Loosely structured, with some elements working clandestinely and others working openly through mosques and social service institutions to recruit members, raise money, organize activities, and distribute propaganda. HAMAS's strength is concentrated in the Gaza Strip and a few areas of the West Bank. Also has engaged in peaceful political activity, such as running candidates in West Bank Chamber of Commerce elections.

Activities. HAMAS activists, especially those in the Izz el-Din al-Qassam Brigades, have conducted many attacks—including large-scale suicide bombings—against Israeli civilian and military targets. In the early 1990s, they also targeted suspected Palestinian collaborators and Fatah rivals. Claimed several attacks during the unrest in late 2000.

Strength. Unknown number of hard-core members; tens of thousands of supporters and sympathizers.

Location/Area of Operation. Primarily the occupied territories, Israel. In August 1999, Jordanian authorities closed the group's Political Bureau offices in Amman, arrested its leaders, and prohibited the group from operating on Jordanian territory.

External Aid. Receives funding from Palestinian expatriates, Iran, and private benefactors in Saudi Arabia and other moderate Arab states. Some fundraising and propaganda activities take place in Western Europe and North America.

Harakat ul-Mujahidin (HUM)

Description. Formerly known as the Harakat al-Ansar, the HUM is an Islamic militant group based in Pakistan that operates primarily in Kashmir. Long-time leader of the group, Fazlur Rehman Khalil, in mid-February stepped down as HUM emir, turning the reins over to the popular Kashmiri commander and his second-in-command, Farooq Kashmiri. Khalil, who has been linked to Bin Ladin and signed his *fatwa* in February 1998 calling for attacks on US and Western interests, assumed the position of HUM Secretary General. Continued to operate terrorist training camps in eastern Afghanistan.

Activities. Has conducted a number of operations against Indian troops and civilian targets in Kashmir. Linked to the Kashmiri militant group al-Faran that kidnapped five Western tourists in Kashmir in July 1995; one was killed in August 1995 and the other four reportedly were killed in December of the same year. The new millennium brought significant developments for Pakistani militant groups, particularly the HUM. Most of these sprang from the hijacking of an Indian airliner on 24 December by militants believed to be associated with the HUM. The hijackers negotiated the release of Masood Azhar, an important leader in the former Harakat ul-Ansar imprisoned by the Indians in 1994. Azhar did not, however, return to the HUM, choosing instead to form the Jaish-e-Mohammed (JEM), a rival militant group expressing a more radical line than the HUM.

Strength. Has several thousand armed supporters located in Azad Kashmir, Pakistan, and India's southern Kashmir and Doda regions. Supporters are mostly Pakistanis and Kashmiris and also include Afghans and Arab veterans of the Afghan war. Uses light and heavy machineguns, assault rifles, mortars, explosives, and rockets. HUM lost some of its membership in defections to the JEM.

Location/Area of Operation. Based in Muzaffarabad, Rawalpindi, and several other towns in Pakistan and Afghanistan, but members conduct insurgent and terrorist activities primarily in Kashmir. The HUM trains its militants in Afghanistan and Pakistan.

External Aid. Collects donations from Saudi Arabia and other Gulf and Islamic states and from Pakistanis and Kashmiris. The sources and amount of HUM's military funding are unknown.

Hizballah (Party of God) a.k.a. Islamic Jihad, Revolutionary Justice Organization, Organization of the Oppressed on Earth, and Islamic Jihad for the Liberation of Palestine

Description. Radical Shia group formed in Lebanon; dedicated to increasing its political power in Lebanon and opposing Israel and the Middle East peace negotiations. Strongly anti-West and anti-Israel. Closely allied with, and often directed by, Iran but may have conducted operations that were not approved by Tehran.

Activities. Known or suspected to have been involved in numerous anti-US terrorist attacks, including the suicide truck bombing of the US Embassy and US Marine barracks in Beirut in October 1983 and the US Embassy annex in Beirut in September 1984. Elements of the group were responsible for the kidnapping and detention of US and other Western hostages in Lebanon. The group also attacked the Israeli Embassy in Argentina in 1992 and is a suspect in the 1994 bombing of the Israeli cultural center in Buenos Aires. In fall 2000, it captured three Israeli soldiers in the Shabaa Farms and kidnapped an Israeli noncombatant whom it may have lured to Lebanon under false pretenses.

Strength. Several thousand supporters and a few hundred terrorist operatives.

Location/Area of Operation. Operates in the Bekaa Valley, the southern suburbs of Beirut, and southern Lebanon. Has established cells in Europe, Africa, South America, North America, and Asia.

External Aid. Receives substantial amounts of financial, training, weapons, explosives, political, diplomatic, and organizational aid from Iran and Syria.

Islamic Movement of Uzbekistan (IMU)

Description. Coalition of Islamic militants from Uzbekistan and other Central Asian states opposed to Uzbekistan President Islom Karimov's secular regime. Goal is the establishment of an Islamic state in Uzbekistan. The group's propaganda also includes anti-Western and anti-Israeli rhetoric.

Activities. Believed to be responsible for five car bombs in Tashkent in February 1999. Took hostages on several occasions in 1999 and 2000, including four US citizens who were mountain climbing in August 2000, and four Japanese geologists and eight Kyrgyzstani soldiers in August 1999.

Strength. Militants probably number in the thousands.

Location/Area of Operation. Militants are based in Afghanistan and Tajikistan. Area of operations includes Uzbekistan, Tajikistan, Kyrgyzstan, and Afghanistan.

External Aid. Support from other Islamic extremist groups in Central and South Asia. IMU leadership broadcasts statements over Iranian radio.

Japanese Red Army (JRA) a.k.a. Anti-Imperialist International Brigade (AIIB)

Description. An international terrorist group formed around 1970 after breaking away from Japanese Communist League-Red Army Faction. The JRA was led by Fusako Shigenobu until her arrest in Japan in November 2000. The JRA's historical goal has been to overthrow the Japanese Government and monarchy and to help foment world revolution. After her arrest Shigenobu announced she intended to pursue her goals using a legitimate political party rather than revolutionary violence. May control or at least have ties to Anti-Imperialist International Brigade (AIIB); also may have links to Antiwar Democratic Front—an overt leftist political organization—inside Japan. Details released following Shigenobu's arrest indicate that the JRA was organizing cells in Asian cities, such as Manila and Singapore. Has history of close relations with Palestinian terrorist groups—based and operating outside Japan—since its inception, primarily through Shigenobu. The current status of these connections is unknown.

Activities. During the 1970s, the JRA carried out a series of attacks around the world, including the massacre in 1972 at Lod Airport in Israel, two Japanese airliner hijackings, and an attempted takeover of the US Embassy in Kuala Lumpur. In April 1988, JRA operative Yu Kikumura was arrested with explosives on the New Jersey Turnpike, apparently planning an attack to coincide with the bombing of a USO club in Naples, a suspected JRA operation that killed five, including a US servicewoman. He was convicted of the charges and is serving a lengthy prison sentence in the United States. Tsutomu Shirosaki, captured in 1996, is also jailed in the United States. In 2000, Lebanon deported to Japan four members it arrested in 1997, but granted a fifth operative, Kozo Okamoto, political asylum. Longtime leader Shigenobu was arrested in November 2000 and faces charges of terrorism and passport fraud.

Strength. About six hard-core members; undetermined number of sympathizers.

Location/Area of Operations. Location unknown, but possibly traveling in Asia or Syrian-controlled areas of Lebanon.

External Aid. Unknown.

Al-Jihad a.k.a. Egyptian Islamic Jihad, Jihad Group, Islamic Jihad

Description. Egyptian Islamic extremist group active since the late 1970s. Close partner of Bin Ladin's al-Qaida organization. Suffered setbacks as a result of numerous arrests of operatives worldwide, most recently in Lebanon and Yemen. Primary goals are to overthrow the Egyptian Government and replace it with an Islamic state and attack US and Israeli interests in Egypt and abroad.

Activities. Specializes in armed attacks against high-level Egyptian Government personnel, including cabinet ministers, and car-bombings against official US and Egyptian facilities. The original Jihad was responsible for the assassination in 1981 of Egyptian President Anwar Sadat. Claimed responsibility for the attempted assassinations of Interior Minister Hassan al-Alfi in August 1993 and Prime Minister Atef Sedky in November 1993. Has not conducted an attack inside Egypt since 1993 and has never targeted foreign tourists there. Responsible for Egyptian Embassy bombing in Islamabad in 1995; in 1998, planned attack against US Embassy in Albania was thwarted.

Strength. Not known but probably has several hundred hard-core members.

Location/Area of Operation. Operates in the Cairo area. Has a network outside Egypt, including Yemen, Afghanistan, Pakistan, Sudan, Lebanon, and the United Kingdom.

External Aid. Not known. The Egyptian Government claims that both Iran and Bin Ladin support the Jihad. Also may obtain some funding through various Islamic nongovernmental organizations, cover businesses, and criminal acts.

Kach and Kahane Chai

Description. Stated goal is to restore the biblical state of Israel. Kach (founded by radical Israeli-American rabbi Meir Kahane) and its offshoot Kahane Chai, which means "Kahane Lives" (founded by Meir Kahane's son Binyamin following his father's assassination in the United States), were declared to be terrorist organizations in March 1994 by the Israeli Cabinet under the 1948 Terrorism Law. This followed the groups' statements in support of Dr. Baruch Goldstein's attack in February 1994 on the al-Ibrahimi Mosque—Goldstein was affiliated with Kach—and their verbal attacks on the Israeli Government. Palestinian gunmen killed Binyamin Kahane and his wife in a drive-by shooting on 31 December in the West Bank.

Activities. Organize protests against the Israeli Government. Harass and threaten Palestinians in Hebron and the West Bank. Have threatened to attack Arabs, Palestinians, and Israeli Government officials. Have vowed revenge for the death of Binyamin Kahane and his wife.

Strength. Unknown.

Location/Area of Operation. Israel and West Bank settlements, particularly Qiryat Arba' in Hebron.

External Aid. Receives support from sympathizers in the United States and Europe.

Kurdistan Workers' Party (PKK)

Description. Founded in 1974 as a Marxist-Leninist insurgent group primarily composed of Turkish Kurds. The group's goal has been to establish an independent Kurdish state in southeastern Turkey, where the population is predominantly Kurdish. In the early 1990s, the PKK moved beyond rural-based insurgent activities to include urban terrorism. Turkish authorities captured Chairman Abdullah Ocalan in Kenya in early 1999; the Turkish State Security Court subsequently sentenced him to death. In August 1999, Ocalan announced a "peace initiative," ordering members to refrain from violence and withdraw from Turkey and requesting dialogue with Ankara on Kurdish issues. At a PKK Congress in January 2000, members supported Ocalan's initiative and claimed the group now would use only political means to achieve its new goal, improved rights for Kurds in Turkey.

Activities. Primary targets have been Turkish Government security forces in Turkey. Conducted attacks on Turkish diplomatic and commercial facilities in dozens of West European cities in 1993 and again in spring 1995. In an attempt to damage Turkey's tourist industry, the PKK bombed tourist sites and hotels and kidnapped foreign tourists in the early-to-mid-1990s.

Strength. Approximately 4,000 to 5,000, most of whom currently are located in northern Iraq. Has thousands of sympathizers in Turkey and Europe.

Location/Area of Operation. Operates in Turkey, Europe, and the Middle East.

External Aid. Has received safehaven and modest aid from Syria, Iraq, and Iran. The Syrian Government expelled PKK leader Ocalan and known elements of the group from its territory in October 1998.

Liberation Tigers of Tamil Eelam (LTTE) *Other known front organizations: World Tamil Association (WTA), World Tamil Movement (WTM), the Federation of Associations of Canadian Tamils (FACT), the Ellalan Force, the Sangilian Force*

Description. Founded in 1976, the LTTE is the most powerful Tamil group in Sri Lanka and uses overt and illegal methods to raise funds, acquire weapons, and publicize its cause of establishing an independent Tamil state. The LTTE began its armed conflict with the Sri Lankan Government in 1983 and relies on a guerrilla strategy that includes the use of terrorist tactics.

Activities. The Tigers have integrated a battlefield insurgent strategy with a terrorist program that targets not only key personnel in the countryside but also senior Sri Lankan political and military leaders in Colombo and other urban centers. The Tigers are most notorious for their cadre of suicide bombers, the Black Tigers. Political assassinations and bombings are commonplace. The LTTE has refrained from targeting foreign diplomatic and commercial establishments.

Strength. Exact strength is unknown, but the LTTE is estimated to have 8,000 to 10,000 armed combatants in Sri Lanka, with a core of trained fighters of approximately 3,000 to 6,000. The LTTE also has a significant overseas support structure for fundraising, weapons procurement, and propaganda activities.

Location/Area of Operations. The Tigers control most of the northern and eastern coastal areas of Sri Lanka but have conducted operations throughout the island. Headquartered in northern Sri Lanka, LTTE leader Velupillai Prabhakaran has established an extensive network of checkpoints and informants to keep track of any outsiders who enter the group's area of control.

External Aid. The LTTE's overt organizations support Tamil separatism by lobbying foreign governments and the United Nations. The LTTE also uses its international contacts to procure weapons, communications, and any other equipment and supplies it needs. The LTTE exploits large Tamil communities in North America, Europe, and Asia to obtain funds and supplies for its fighters in Sri Lanka. Information obtained since the mid-1980s indicates that some Tamil communities in Europe are also involved in narcotics smuggling. Tamils historically have served as drug couriers moving narcotics into Europe.

Mujahedin-e Khalq Organization (MEK or MKO) a.k.a. The National Liberation Army of Iran (NLA, the militant wing of the MEK), the People's Mujahidin of Iran (PMOI), National Council of Resistance (NCR), Muslim Iranian Student's Society (front organization used to garner financial support)

Description. Formed in the 1960s by the college-educated children of Iranian merchants, the MEK sought to counter what it perceived as excessive Western influence in the Shah's regime. Following a philosophy that mixes Marxism and Islam, has developed into the largest and most active armed Iranian dissident group. Its history is studded with anti-Western activity, and, most recently, attacks on the interests of the clerical regime in Iran and abroad.

Activities. Worldwide campaign against the Iranian Government stresses propaganda and occasionally uses terrorist violence. During the 1970s the MEK staged terrorist attacks inside Iran and killed several US military personnel and civilians working on defense projects in Tehran. Supported the takeover in 1979 of the US Embassy in Tehran. In April 1992 conducted attacks on Iranian embassies in 13 different countries, demonstrating the group's ability to mount large-scale operations overseas. The normal pace of anti-Iranian operations increased during the "Operation Great Bahman" in February 2000, when the group claimed it launched a dozen attacks against Iran. During the remainder of the year, the MEK regularly claimed that its members were involved in mortar attacks and hit-and-run raids on Iranian military, law enforcement units, and government buildings near the Iran-Iraq border. The MEK also claimed six mortar attacks on civilian government and military buildings in Tehran.

Strength. Several thousand fighters based in Iraq with an extensive overseas support structure. Most of the fighters are organized in the MEK's National Liberation Army (NLA).

Location/Area of Operation. In the 1980s the MEK's leaders were forced by Iranian security forces to flee to France. Most resettled in Iraq by 1987. In the mid-1980s the group did not mount terrorist operations in Iran at a level similar to its activities in the 1970s. In the 1990s, however, the MEK claimed credit for an increasing number of operations in Iran.

External Aid. Beyond support from Iraq, the MEK uses front organizations to solicit contributions from expatriate Iranian communities.

National Liberation Army (ELN)—Colombia

Description. Marxist insurgent group formed in 1965 by urban intellectuals inspired by Fidel Castro and Che Guevara. Began a dialogue with Colombian officials in 1999 following a campaign of mass kidnappings—each involving at least one US citizen—to demonstrate its strength and continuing viability and to force the Pastrana administration to negotiate. Bogota and the ELN spent most of 2000 discussing where to establish an ELN safehaven in which to hold peace talks. A proposed location in north central Colombia faces stiff local and paramilitary opposition.

Activities. Kidnapping, hijacking, bombing, extortion, and guerrilla war. Modest conventional military capability. Annually conducts hundreds of kidnappings for ransom, often targeting foreign employees of large corporations, especially in the petroleum industry. Frequently assaults energy infrastructure and has inflicted major damage on pipelines and the electric distribution network.

Strength. Approximately 3,000 to 6,000 armed combatants and an unknown number of active supporters.

Location/Area of Operation. Mostly in rural and mountainous areas of north, northeast, and southwest Colombia and Venezuela border regions.

External Aid. Cuba provides some medical care and political consultation.

The Palestine Islamic Jihad (PIJ)

Description. Originated among militant Palestinians in the Gaza Strip during the 1970s. Committed to the creation of an Islamic Palestinian state and the destruction of Israel through holy war. Because of its strong support for Israel, the United States has been identified as an enemy of the PIJ, but the group has not specifically conducted attacks against US interests in the past. In July 2000, however, publicly threatened to attack US interests if the US Embassy is moved from Tel Aviv to Jerusalem. Also opposes moderate Arab governments that it believes have been tainted by Western secularism.

Activities. Conducted at least three attacks against Israeli interests in late 2000, including one to commemorate the anniversary of former PIJ leader Fathi Shaqaqi's murder in Malta on 26 October 1995. Conducted suicide bombings against Israeli targets in the West Bank, Gaza Strip, and Israel.

Strength. Unknown.

Location/Area of Operation. Primarily Israel and the occupied territories and other parts of the Middle East, including Jordan and Lebanon. Headquartered in Syria.

External Aid. Receives financial assistance from Iran and limited logistic assistance from Syria.

Palestine Liberation Front (PLF)

Description. Broke away from the PFLP-GC in mid-1970s. Later split again into pro-PLO, pro-Syrian, and pro-Libyan factions. Pro-PLO faction led by Muhammad Abbas (Abu Abbas), who became member of PLO Executive Committee in 1984 but left it in 1991.

Activities. The Abu Abbas–led faction is known for aerial attacks against Israel. Abbas's group also was responsible for the attack in 1985 on the cruise ship Achille Lauro and the murder of US citizen Leon Klinghoffer. A warrant for Abu Abbas's arrest is outstanding in Italy.

Strength. Unknown.

Location/Area of Operation. PLO faction based in Tunisia until Achille Lauro attack. Now based in Iraq.

External Aid. Receives support mainly from Iraq. Has received support from Libya in the past.

Popular Front for the Liberation of Palestine (PFLP)

Description. Marxist-Leninist group founded in 1967 by George Habash as a member of the PLO. Joined the Alliance of Palestinian Forces (APF) to oppose the Declaration of Principles signed in 1993 and suspended participation in the PLO. Broke away from the APF, along with the DFLP, in 1996 over ideological differences. Took part in meetings with Arafat's Fatah party and PLO representatives in 1999 to discuss national unity and the reinvigoration of the PLO but continues to oppose current negotiations with Israel.

Activities. Committed numerous international terrorist attacks during the 1970s. Since 1978 has conducted attacks against Israeli or moderate Arab targets, including killing a settler and her son in December 1996.

Strength. Some 800.

Location/Area of Operation. Syria, Lebanon, Israel, and the occupied territories.

External Aid. Receives safehaven and some logistic assistance from Syria.

Popular Front for the Liberation of Palestine — General Command (PFLP-GC)

Description. Split from the PFLP in 1968, claiming it wanted to focus more on fighting and less on politics. Violently opposed to Arafat's PLO. Led by Ahmad Jabril, a former captain in the Syrian Army. Closely tied to both Syria and Iran.

Activities. Carried out dozens of attacks in Europe and the Middle East during 1970s–80s. Known for cross-border terrorist attacks into Israel using unusual means, such as hot-air balloons and motorized hang gliders. Primary focus now on guerrilla operations in southern Lebanon, small-scale attacks in Israel, West Bank, and Gaza Strip.

Strength. Several hundred.

Location/Area of Operation. Headquartered in Damascus with bases in Lebanon.

External Aid. Receives logistic and military support from Syria and financial support from Iran.

al-Qaida

Description. Established by Usama Bin Ladin in the late 1980s to bring together Arabs who fought in Afghanistan against the Soviet invasion. Helped finance, recruit, transport, and train Sunni Islamic extremists for the Afghan resistance. Current goal is to establish a pan-Islamic Caliphate throughout the world by working with allied Islamic extremist groups to overthrow regimes it deems "non-Islamic" and expelling Westerners and non-Muslims from Muslim countries. Issued statement under banner of "the World Islamic Front for Jihad Against the Jews and Crusaders" in February 1998, saying it was the duty of all Muslims to kill US citizens—civilian or military—and their allies everywhere.

Activities. Plotted to carry out terrorist operations against US and Israeli tourists visiting Jordan for millennial celebrations. (Jordanian authorities thwarted the planned attacks and put 28 suspects on trial.) Conducted the bombings in August 1998 of the US Embassies in Nairobi, Kenya, and Dar es Salaam, Tanzania, that killed at least 301 persons and injured more than 5,000 others. Claims to have shot down US helicopters and killed US servicemen in Somalia in 1993 and to have conducted three bombings that targeted US troops in Aden, Yemen, in December 1992. Linked to the following plans that were not carried out: to assassinate Pope John Paul II during his visit to Manila in late 1994, simultaneous bombings of the US and Israeli Embassies in Manila and other Asian capitals in late 1994, the midair bombing of a dozen US trans-Pacific flights in 1995, and to kill President Clinton during a visit to the Philippines in early 1995. Continues to train, finance, and provide logistic support to terrorist groups in support of these goals.

Strength. May have several hundred to several thousand members. Also serves as a focal point or umbrella organization for a worldwide network that includes many Sunni Islamic extremist groups such as Egyptian Islamic Jihad, some members of al-Gama'at al-Islamiyya, the Islamic Movement of Uzbekistan, and the Harakat ul-Mujahidin.

Location/Area of Operation. Al-Qaida has a worldwide reach, has cells in a number of countries, and is reinforced by its ties to Sunni extremist networks. Bin Ladin and his key lieutenants reside in Afghanistan, and the group maintains terrorist training camps there.

External Aid. Bin Ladin, son of a billionaire Saudi family, is said to have inherited approximately $300 million that he uses to finance the group. Al-Qaida also maintains moneymaking front organizations, solicits donations from likeminded supporters, and illicitly siphons funds from donations to Muslim charitable organizations.

Revolutionary Armed Forces of Colombia (FARC)

Description. Established in 1964 as the military wing of the Colombian Communist Party, the FARC is Colombia's oldest, largest, most capable, and best-equipped Marxist insurgency. The FARC is governed by a secretariat, led by septuagenarian Manuel Marulanda, a.k.a. "Tirofijo," and six others, including senior military commander Jorge Briceno, a.k.a. "Mono Jojoy." Organized along military lines and includes several urban fronts. In 2000, the group continued a slow-moving peace negotiation process with the Pastrana Administration, which has gained the group several concessions, including a demilitarized zone used as a venue for negotiations.

Activities. Bombings, murder, kidnapping, extortion, hijacking, as well as guerrilla and conventional military action against Colombian political, military, and economic targets. In March 1999 the FARC executed three US Indian rights activists on Venezuelan territory after it kidnapped them in Colombia. Foreign citizens often are targets of FARC kidnapping for ransom. Has well-documented ties to narcotics traffickers, principally through the provision of armed protection.

Strength. Approximately 9,000 to 12,000 armed combatants and an unknown number of supporters, mostly in rural areas.

Location/Area of Operation. Colombia with some activities—extortion, kidnapping, logistics, and R&R—in Venezuela, Panama, and Ecuador.

External Aid. Cuba provides some medical care and political consultation.

Revolutionary Organization 17 November (17 November)

Description. Radical leftist group established in 1975 and named for the student uprising in Greece in November 1973 that protested the military regime. Anti-Greek establishment, anti-US, anti-Turkey, anti-NATO, and committed to the ouster of US bases, removal of Turkish military presence from Cyprus, and severing of Greece's ties to NATO and the European Union (EU).

Activities. Initial attacks were assassinations of senior US officials and Greek public figures. Added bombings in 1980s. Since 1990 has expanded targets to include EU facilities and foreign firms investing in Greece and has added improvised rocket attacks to its methods. Most recent attack claimed was the murder in June 2000 of British Defense Attache Stephen Saunders.

Strength. Unknown, but presumed to be small.

Location/Area of Operation. Athens, Greece.

Revolutionary People's Liberation Party/Front (DHKP/C)
a.k.a. Devrimci Sol (Revolutionary Left), Dev Sol

Description. Originally formed in 1978 as Devrimsi Sol, or Dev Sol, a splinter faction of the Turkish People's Liberation Party/Front. Renamed in 1994 after factional infighting, it espouses a Marxist ideology and is virulently anti-US and anti-NATO. Finances its activities chiefly through armed robberies and extortion.

Activities. Since the late 1980s has concentrated attacks against current and retired Turkish security and military officials. Began a new campaign against foreign interests in 1990. Assassinated two US military contractors and wounded a US Air Force officer to protest the Gulf war. Launched rockets at US Consulate in Istanbul in 1992. Assassinated prominent Turkish businessman and two others in early 1996, its first significant terrorist act as DHKP/C. Turkish authorities thwarted DHKP/C attempt in June 1999 to fire light antitank weapon at US Consulate in Istanbul. Series of safehouse raids, arrests by Turkish police over last two years has weakened group significantly. Turkish security forces stormed prison wards controlled by the DHKP/C in December 2000, transforming militants to cell-type penitentiaries and further undermining DHKP/C cohesion.

Strength. Unknown.

Location/Area of Operation. Conducts attacks in Turkey, primarily in Istanbul, Ankara, Izmir, and Adana. Raises funds in Western Europe.

External Aid. Unknown.

Revolutionary People's Struggle (ELA)

Description. Extreme leftist group that developed from opposition to the military junta that ruled Greece from 1967 to 1974. Formed in 1971, ELA is a self-described revolutionary, anti-capitalist, and anti-imperialist group that has declared its opposition to "imperialist domination, exploitation, and oppression." Strongly anti-US and seeks the removal of US military forces from Greece.

Activities. Since 1974 has conducted bombings against Greek Government and economic targets as well as US military and business facilities. In 1986 stepped up attacks on Greek Government and commercial interests. Raid on a safehouse in 1990 revealed a weapons cache and direct contacts with other Greek terrorist groups, including 1 May and Revolutionary Solidarity. In 1991, ELA and 1 May claimed joint responsibility for more than 20 bombings. Greek police believe they have established links between ELA and Revolutionary Organization 17 November. Although ELA has not claimed an attack since January 1995, other groups have emerged with similar modus operandi. Of these, Revolutionary Nuclei (a.k.a. Revolutionary Cells) appears most likely to be the successor group to ELA.

Strength. Unknown.

Location/Area of Operation. Greece.

External Aid. Received weapons and other assistance from international terrorist Carlos during 1980s. Currently no known foreign sponsors.

Sendero Luminoso (Shining Path, or SL)

Description. Former university professor Abimael Guzman formed Sendero Luminoso in the late 1960s, and his teachings created the foundation of SL's militant Maoist doctrine. In the 1980s, SL became one of the most ruthless terrorist groups in the Western Hemisphere—approximately 30,000 persons have died since Shining Path took up arms in 1980. Its stated goal is to destroy existing Peruvian institutions and replace them with a communist peasant revolutionary regime. It also opposes any influence by foreign governments, as well as by other Latin American guerrilla groups, especially the Tupac Amaru Revolutionary Movement (MRTA).

In 2000, government authorities continued to arrest and prosecute active SL members, including, in April, commander Jose Arcela Chiroque, a.k.a. Ormeno. Counterterrorist operations targeted pockets of terrorist activity in the Upper Huallaga River Valley and the Apurimac/Ene River Valley, where SL columns continued to conduct periodic attacks.

Activities. Conducted indiscriminate bombing campaigns and selective assassinations. Detonated explosives at diplomatic missions of several countries in Peru in 1990, including an attempt to car-bomb the US Embassy in December. SL continued in 2000 to clash with Peruvian authorities and military units in the countryside and conducted periodic raids on villages. Despite numerous threats, the remaining active SL guerrillas were unable to cause any significant disruption to the Peruvian national elections held on 9 April.

Strength. Membership is unknown but estimated to be 100 to 200 armed militants. SL's strength has been vastly diminished by arrests and desertions.

Location/Area of Operation. Peru, with most activity in rural areas.

External Aid. None.

Tupac Amaru Revolutionary Movement (MRTA)

Description. Traditional Marxist-Leninist revolutionary movement formed in 1983 from remnants of the Movement of the Revolutionary Left, a Peruvian insurgent group active in the 1960s. Aims to establish a Marxist regime and to rid Peru of all imperialist elements (primarily US and Japanese influence). Peru's counterterrorist program has diminished the group's ability to carry out terrorist attacks, and the MRTA has suffered from infighting, the imprisonment or deaths of senior leaders, and loss of leftist support. Several MRTA members also remain imprisoned in Bolivia.

Activities. Previously conducted bombings, kidnappings, ambushes, and assassinations, but recent activity has fallen drastically. In December 1996, 14 MRTA members occupied the Japanese Ambassador's residence in Lima and held 72 hostages for more than four months. Peruvian forces stormed the residence in April 1997, rescuing all but one of the remaining hostages and killing all 14 group members, including the remaining leaders. The group has not conducted a significant terrorist operation since and appears more focused on obtaining the release of imprisoned MRTA members.

Strength. Believed to be no more than 100 members, consisting largely of young fighters who lack leadership skills and experience.

Location/Area of Operation. Peru with supporters throughout Latin America and Western Europe. Controls no territory.

External Aid. None.

II. Other Terrorist Groups

Alex Boncayao Brigade (ABB)

Description. The ABB, the breakaway urban hit squad of the Communist Party of the Philippines New People's Army, was formed in the mid-1980s.

Activities. Responsible for more than 100 murders and believed to have been involved in the murder in 1989 of US Army Col. James Rowe in the Philippines. In March 1997 the group announced it had formed an alliance with another armed group, the Revolutionary Proletarian Army. In March 2000, the group claimed credit for a rifle grenade attack against the Department of Energy building in Manila and strafed Shell Oil offices in the central Philippines to protest rising oil prices.

Strength. Approximately 500.

Location/Area of Operation. Operates in Manila and central Philippines.

External Aid. Unknown.

Army for the Liberation of Rwanda (ALIR)
a.k.a. Interahamwe, Former Armed Forces (ex-FAR)

Description. The FAR was the army of the Rwandan Hutu regime that carried out the genocide of 500,000 or more Tutsis and regime opponents in 1994. The Interahamwe was the civilian militia force that carried out much of the killing. The groups merged after they were forced from Rwanda into the Democratic Republic of the Congo (then-Zaire) in 1994. They are now often known as the Army for the Liberation of Rwanda (ALIR), which is the armed branch of the PALIR or Party for the Liberation of Rwanda.

Activities. The group seeks to topple Rwanda's Tutsi-dominated government, reinstitute Hutu control, and, possibly, complete the genocide. In 1996, a message—allegedly from the ALIR—threatened to kill the US Ambassador to

Rwanda and other US citizens. In 1999, ALIR guerrillas critical of alleged US-UK support for the Rwandan regime kidnapped and killed eight foreign tourists, including two US citizens, in a game park on the Congo-Uganda border. In the current Congolese war, the ALIR is allied with Kinshasa against the Rwandan invaders.

Strength. Several thousand ALIR regular forces operate alongside the Congolese Army on the front lines of the Congo civil war, while a like number of ALIR guerrillas operate behind Rwanda lines in eastern Congo closer to the Rwandan border and sometimes within Rwanda.

Location/Area of Operation. Mostly Democratic Republic of the Congo and Rwanda, but a few may operate in Burundi.

External Support. From the Rwandan invasion of 1998 until his death in early 2001, the Laurent Kabila regime in the Democratic Republic of the Congo provided the ALIR with training, arms, and supplies.

Continuity Irish Republican Army (CIRA) a.k.a. Continuity Army Council

Description. Radical terrorist splinter group formed in 1994 as the clandestine armed wing of Republican Sinn Fein (RSF), a political organization dedicated to the reunification of Ireland and to forcing British troops from Northern Ireland. RSF formed after the Irish Republican Army announced a cease-fire in September 1994.

Activities. Bombings, assassinations, extortion, and robberies. Targets include British military and Northern Ireland security targets and Northern Ireland Loyalist paramilitary groups. Also has launched bomb attacks against civilian targets in Northern Ireland. Does not have an established presence or capability to launch attacks on the UK mainland.

Strength. Fewer than 50 hard-core activists.

Location/Area of Operation. Northern Ireland, Irish Republic.

External Aid. Suspected of receiving funds and arms from sympathizers in the United States. May have acquired arms and material from the Balkans in cooperation with the Real IRA.

First of October Antifascist Resistance Group (GRAPO)
Grupo de Resistencia Anti-Fascista Premero de Octubre

Description. Formed in 1975 as the armed wing of the illegal Communist Party of Spain of the Franco era. Advocating the overthrow of the Spanish Government and replacement with a Marxist-Lenin regime, GRAPO is vehemently anti-US, calls for the removal of all US military forces from Spanish territory, and has conducted and attempted several attacks against US targets since 1977.

Activities. GRAPO has killed more than 80 persons and injured more than 200. The group's operations customarily have been designed to cause material damage and gain publicity rather than inflict casualties, but the terrorists have conducted lethal bombings and close-range assassinations. In November 2000, GRAPO operatives shot to death a Spanish policeman in reprisal for the arrest that month in France of several group leaders, while in May, GRAPO operatives murdered two guards during a botched robbery against an armored security van.

Strength. Unknown but likely fewer than a dozen hard-core activists. Numerous GRAPO members also currently are in Spanish prisons.

Location/Area of Operation. Spain.

External Aid. None.

Irish Republican Army (IRA) a.k.a. Provisional Irish Republican Army (PIRA), the Provos

Description. Terrorist group formed in 1969 as clandestine armed wing of Sinn Fein, a legal political movement dedicated to removing British forces from Northern Ireland and unifying Ireland. Has a Marxist orientation. Organized into small, tightly knit cells under the leadership of the Army Council.

Activities. Bombings, assassinations, kidnappings, punishment beatings, extortion, smuggling, and robberies. Targets have included senior British Government officials, British military and police in Northern Ireland, and Northern Ireland Loyalist paramilitary groups. Bombing campaigns have been conducted against train and subway stations and shopping areas on mainland Britain, as well as against British and Royal Ulster Constabulary targets in Northern Ireland, and a British military facility on the European Continent. The IRA has been observing a cease-fire since July 1997 and previously observed a cease-fire from 1 September 1994 to February 1996.

Strength. Largely unchanged—several hundred members, plus several thousand sympathizers—despite the defection of some members to the dissident splinter groups.

Location/Area of Operation. Northern Ireland, Irish Republic, Great Britain, Europe.

External Aid. Has in the past received aid from a variety of groups and countries and considerable training and arms from Libya and the PLO. Is suspected of receiving funds, arms, and other terrorist-related material from sympathizers in the United States. Similarities in operations suggest links to the ETA.

Jaish-e-Mohammed (JEM) (Army of Mohammed)

Description. The Jaish-e-Mohammed (JEM) is an Islamist group based in Pakistan that has rapidly expanded in size and capability since Maulana Masood Azhar, a former ultrafundamentalist Harakat ul-Ansar (HUA) leader, announced its formation in February. The group's aim is to unite Kashmir with Pakistan. It is politically aligned with the radical, pro-Taliban, political party, Jamiat-i Ulema-i Islam (JUI-F).

Activities. The JEM's leader, Masood Azhar, was released from Indian imprisonment in December 1999 in exchange for 155 hijacked Indian Airlines hostages in Afghanistan. The 1994 HUA kidnappings of US and British nationals in New Delhi and the July 1995 HUA/AI Faran kidnappings of Westerners in Kashmir were two of several previous HUA efforts to free Azhar. Azhar organized large rallies and recruitment drives across Pakistan throughout 2000. In July, a JEM rocket-grenade attack failed to injure the Chief Minister at his office in Srinagar, India, but wounded four other persons. In December, JEM militants launched grenade attacks at a bus stop in Kupwara, India, injuring 24 persons, and at a marketplace in Chadoura, India, injuring 16 persons. JEM militants also planted two bombs that killed 21 persons in Qamarwari and Srinagar.

Strength. Has several hundred armed supporters located in Azad Kashmir, Pakistan, and in India's southern Kashmir and Doda regions. Following Maulana Masood Azhar's release from detention in India, a reported three quarters of Harakat ul-Mujahedin (HUM) members defected to the new organization, which has managed to attract a large number of urban Kashmiri youth. Supporters are mostly Pakistanis and Kashmiris and also include Afghans and Arab veterans of the Afghan war. Uses light and heavy machineguns, assault rifles, mortars, improvised explosive devices, and rocket grenades.

Location/Area of Operation. Based in Peshawar and Muzaffarabad, but members conduct terrorist activities primarily in Kashmir. The JEM maintains training camps in Afghanistan.

External Aid. Most of the JEM's cadre and material resources have been drawn from the militant groups Harakat ul-Jihad al-Islami (HUJI) and the Harakat ul-Mujahedin (HUM). The JEM has close ties to Afghan Arabs and the Taliban. Usama Bin Ladin is suspected of giving funding to the JEM.

Lashkar-e-Tayyiba (LT) (Army of the Righteous)

Description. The LT is the armed wing of the Pakistan-based religious organization, Markaz-ud-Dawa-wal-Irshad (MDI)—a Sunni anti-US missionary organization formed in 1989. One of the three largest and best-trained groups fighting in Kashmir against India, it is not connected to a political party. The LT leader is MDI chief, Professor Hafiz Mohammed Saeed.

Activities. Has conducted a number of operations against Indian troops and civilian targets in Kashmir since 1993. The LT is suspected of eight separate attacks in August that killed nearly 100, mostly Hindu Indians. LT militants are suspected of kidnapping six persons in Akhala, India, in November 2000 and killing five of them. The group also operates a chain of religious schools in the Punjab.

Strength. Has several hundred members in Azad Kashmir, Pakistan, and in India's southern Kashmir and Doda regions. Almost all LT cadres are foreigners—mostly Pakistanis from seminaries across the country and Afghan veterans of the Afghan wars. Uses assault rifles, light and heavy machineguns, mortars, explosives, and rocket propelled grenades.

Location/Area of Operation. Based in Muridke (near Lahore) and Muzaffarabad. The LT trains its militants in mobile training camps across Pakistan-administered Kashmir and Afghanistan.

External Aid. Collects donations from the Pakistani community in the Persian Gulf and United Kingdom, Islamic NGOs, and Pakistani and Kashmiri businessmen. The amount of LT funding is unknown. The LT maintains ties to religious/military groups around the world, ranging from the Philippines to the Middle East and Chechnya through the MDI fraternal network.

Loyalist Volunteer Force (LVF)

Description. Terrorist group formed in 1996 as a faction of the mainstream loyalist Ulster Volunteer Force (UVF) but did not emerge publicly until February 1997. Composed largely of UVF hardliners who have sought to prevent a political settlement with Irish nationalists in Northern Ireland by attacking Catholic politicians, civilians, and Protestant politicians who endorse the Northern Ireland peace process. Has been observing a cease-fire since 15 May 1998. The LVF decommissioned a small but significant amount of weapons in December 1998, but it has not repeated this gesture and in fact threatened in 2000 to resume killing Catholics.

Activities. Bombings, kidnappings, and close-quarter shooting attacks. LVF bombs often have contained Powergel commercial explosives, typical of many loyalist groups. LVF attacks have been particularly vicious: the group has murdered numerous Catholic civilians with no political or terrorist affiliations, including an 18-year-old Catholic girl in July 1997 because she had a Protestant boyfriend. The terrorists also have conducted successful attacks against Irish targets in Irish border towns. In 2000, the LVF also engaged in a brief but violent feud with other loyalists in which several individuals were killed.

Strength. Approximately 150 activists.

Location/Area of Operation. Northern Ireland, Ireland.

External Aid. None.

New People's Army (NPA)

Description. The military wing of the Communist Party of the Philippines (CPP), the NPA is a Maoist group formed in March 1969 with the aim of overthrowing the government through protracted guerrilla warfare. Although primarily a rural-based guerrilla group, the NPA has an active urban infrastructure to conduct terrorism and uses city-based assassination squads called sparrow units. Derives most of its funding from contributions of supporters and so-called revolutionary taxes extorted from local businesses.

Activities. The NPA primarily targets Philippine security forces, corrupt politicians, and drug traffickers. Opposes any US military presence in the Philippines and attacked US military interests before the US base closures in 1992. Press reports in 1999 indicated that the NPA would target US troops participating in joint military exercises under the Visiting Forces Agreement and US Embassy personnel.

Strength. Estimated between 6,000 and 8,000.

Location/Area of Operations. Operates in rural Luzon, Visayas, and parts of Mindanao. Has cells in Manila and other metropolitan centers.

External Aid. Unknown.

Orange Volunteers (OV)

Description. Terrorist group comprised largely of disgruntled loyalist hardliners who split from groups observing the cease-fire. OV seeks to prevent a political settlement with Irish nationalists by attacking Catholic civilian interests in Northern Ireland.

Activities. The OV declared a cease-fire in September 2000, but the group maintains ability to conduct bombings, arson, beatings, and possibly robberies.

Strength. Up to 20 hard-core members, some of whom are experienced in terrorist tactics and bombmaking.

Location/Area of Operations. Northern Ireland.

External Aid. None.

People Against Gangsterism and Drugs (PAGAD)

Description. PAGAD was formed in 1996 as a community anticrime group fighting drugs and violence in the Cape Flats section of Cape Town but by early 1998 had also become antigovernment and anti-Western. PAGAD and its Islamic ally Qibla view the South African Government as a threat to Islamic values and consequently promote greater political voice for South African Muslims. The group is led by Abdus Salaam Ebrahim. PAGAD's G-Force (Gun Force) operates in small cells and is believed responsible for carrying out acts of terrorism. PAGAD uses several front names, including Muslims Against Global Oppression (MAGO) and Muslims Against Illegitimate Leaders (MAIL), when launching anti-Western protests and campaigns.

Activities. PAGAD is suspected of conducting recurring bouts of urban terrorism—particularly bomb sprees—in Cape Town since 1998, including nine bombings in 2000. Bombing targets have included South African authorities, moderate Muslims, synagogues, gay nightclubs, tourist attractions, and Western-associated restaurants. PAGAD is believed to have masterminded the bombing on 25 August 1998 of the Cape Town Planet Hollywood.

Strength. Estimated at several hundred members. PAGAD's G-Force probably contains fewer than 50 members.

Location/Area of Operation. Operates mainly in the Cape Town area, South Africa's foremost tourist venue.

External Aid. Probably has ties to Islamic extremists in the Middle East.

Real IRA (RIRA) a.k.a. True IRA

Description. Formed in February–March 1998 as clandestine armed wing of the 32-County Sovereignty Movement, a "political pressure group" dedicated to removing British forces from Northern Ireland and unifying Ireland. The 32-County Sovereignty Movement opposed Sinn Fein's adoption in September 1997 of the Mitchell principles of democracy and nonviolence and opposed the December 1999 amendment of Articles 2 and 3 of the Irish Constitution, which lay claim to Northern Ireland. Former IRA "quartermaster general" Mickey McKevitt leads the group; Bernadette Sands-McKevitt, his common-law wife, is the vice-chair of the 32-County Sovereignty Movement.

Activities. Bombings, assassinations, smuggling, extortion, and robberies. Many Real IRA members are former IRA who opposed the IRA's cease-fire and bring to RIRA a wealth of experience in terrorist tactics and bombmaking. Targets include British military and police in Northern Ireland and Northern Ireland civilian targets. Has attempted several unsuccessful bomb attacks on the UK mainland. Claimed responsibility for the car bomb attack in Omagh, Northern

Ireland, on 15 August 1998 that killed 29 and injured 220 persons. The group declared a cease-fire following Omagh but in early 2000 resumed attacks in Northern Ireland and on the UK mainland. These include a bombing of Hammersmith Bridge and a rocket attack against MI-6 Headquarters in London.

Strength. 150 to 200 activists plus possible limited support from IRA hardliners dissatisfied with the IRA cease-fire and other republican sympathizers.

Location/Area of Operation. Northern Ireland, Irish Republic, Great Britain.

External Aid. Suspected of receiving funds from sympathizers in the United States. RIRA also is thought to have purchased sophisticated weapons from the Balkans, according to press reports.

Red Hand Defenders (RHD)

Description. Extremist terrorist group composed largely of Protestant hardliners from loyalist groups observing a cease-fire. RHD seeks to prevent a political settlement with Irish nationalists by attacking Catholic civilian interests in Northern Ireland.

Activities. RHD was quiet in 2000, following a damaging security crackdown in late 1999. In recent years, however, the group has carried out numerous pipe bombings and arson attacks against "soft" civilian targets, such as homes, churches, and private businesses, to cause outrage in the republican community and to provoke IRA retaliation. RHD claimed responsibility for the car-bombing murder on 15 March 1999 of Rosemary Nelson, a prominent Catholic nationalist lawyer and human rights campaigner in Northern Ireland.

Strength. Up to 20 members, some of whom have considerable experience in terrorist tactics and bomb-making.

Location/Area of Operation. Northern Ireland.

External Aid. None.

Revolutionary United Front (RUF)

Description. The RUF is a loosely organized group—but an effective guerrilla force because of its flexibility and brutal discipline—seeking to topple the current government of Sierra Leone and to retain control of the lucrative diamond-producing regions of the country. The group funds itself largely through the extraction and sale of diamonds obtained in areas of Sierra Leone that it controls.

Activities. The RUF uses guerrilla, criminal, and terror tactics, such as murder, torture, and mutilation, to fight the government, intimidate civilians, and keep UN peacekeeping units in check. In 2000 they held hundreds of UN peacekeepers hostage until their release was negotiated, in part, by the RUF's chief sponsor Liberian President Charles Taylor. The group also has been accused of attacks in Guinea at the behest of President Taylor.

Strength. Estimated at several thousand fighters and possibly a similar number of supporters and sympathizers.

Location/Area of Operation. Sierra Leone, Liberia, Guinea.

External Aid. A UN experts panel report on Sierra Leone said President Charles Taylor of Liberia provides support and leadership to the RUF. The UN has identified Libya, Gambia, and Burkina Faso as conduits for weapons and other material for the RUF.

United Self-Defense Forces/Group of Colombia
(AUC-Autodefensas Unidas de Colombia)

Description. The AUC—commonly referred to as autodefensas or paramilitaries—is an umbrella organization formed in April 1997 to consolidate most local and regional paramilitary groups each with the mission to protect economic interests and combat insurgents locally. The AUC—supported by economic elites, drug traffickers, and local communities lacking effective government security—claims its primary objective is to protect its sponsors from insurgents. The AUC now asserts itself as a regional and national counterinsurgent force. It is adequately equipped and armed and reportedly pays its members a monthly salary. AUC leader Carlos Castaño in 2000 claimed 70 percent of the AUC's operational costs were financed with drug-related earnings, the rest from "donations" from its sponsors.

Activities. AUC operations vary from assassinating suspected insurgent supporters to engaging guerrilla combat units. Colombian National Police reported the AUC conducted 804 assassinations, 203 kidnappings, and 75 massacres with 507 victims during the first 10 months of 2000. The AUC claims the victims were guerrillas or sympathizers. Combat tactics consist of conventional and guerrilla operations against main force insurgent units. AUC clashes with military and police units are increasing, although the group has traditionally avoided government security forces. The paramilitaries have not taken action against US personnel.

Strength. In early 2001, the government estimated there were 8,000 paramilitary fighters, including former military and insurgent personnel.

Location/Areas of Operation. AUC forces are strongest in the north and northwest: Antioquia, Cordoba, Sucre, Bolivar, Atlantico, and Magdalena Departments. Since 1999, the group demonstrated a growing presence in other northeastern and southwestern departments and a limited presence in the Amazon plains. Clashes between the AUC and the FARC insurgents in Putumayo in 2000 demonstrated the range of the AUC to contest insurgents throughout Colombia.

External Aid. None.

Total International Terrorist Attacks, 1981–2000

1981	489	1991	565
1982	487	1992	363
1983	498	1993	431
1984	565	1994	322
1985	635	1995	440
1986	612	1996	296
1987	666	1997	304
1988	605	1998	274
1989	375	1999	392
1990	437	2000	423

In past years, serious violence by Palestinians against other Palestinians in the occupied territories was included in the database of worldwide international terrorist incidents because Palestinians are considered stateless people. This resulted in such incidents being treated differently from intraethnic violence in other parts of the world. In 1989, as a result of further review of the nature of intra-Palestinian violence, such violence stopped being included in the US Government's statistical database on international terrorism. The figures shown above for the years 1984 through 1988 have been revised to exclude intra-Palestinian violence, thus making the database consistent.

Investigations into terrorist incidents sometimes yield evidence that necessitates a change in the information previously held true (such as whether the incident fits the definition of international terrorism, which group or state sponsor was responsible, or the number of victims killed or injured). As a result of these adjustments, the statistics given in this report may vary slightly from numbers cited in previous reports.

International Attacks and Casualties by Region, 1995–2000

	1995	1996	1997	1998	1999	2000
Africa						
Attacks	10	11	11	21	52	55
Casualties	8	80	28	5379	185	102
Asia						
Attacks	16	11	21	49	72	98
Casualties	5639	1507	344	635	690	898
Eurasia						
Attacks	5	24	42	14	35	31
Casualties	29	20	27	12	8	103
Latin America						
Attacks	92	84	128	111	121	193
Casualties	46	18	11	195	9	20
Middle East						
Attacks	45	45	37	31	25	16
Casualties	445	1097	480	68	31	69
North America						
Attacks	0	0	13	0	2	0
Casualties	0	0	7	0	0	0
Western Europe						
Attacks	272	121	52	48	85	30
Casualties	287	503	17	405	16	4

Facilities Struck by International Attacks, 1995–2000

	1995	1996	1997	1998	1999	2000
Business	338	235	327	282	276	384
Diplomat	22	24	30	35	59	30
Government	20	12	11	10	27	17
Military	4	6	4	4	17	13
Other	126	90	80	67	95	113

Total U.S. Citizen Casualties Caused by International Attacks, 1995–2000

	1995	1996	1997	1998	1999	2000
Dead	10	25	6	12	5	19
Wounded	60	510	21	11	6	43

Total Anti-U.S. Attacks, 2000
(Includes attacks against U.S. facilities and attacks
in which U.S. citizens suffered casualties)

Latin America	172
Middle East	2
Eurasia	4
Africa	6
Western Europe	7
Asia	9
Total	21
Firebombing	1
Arson	2
Armed attack	4
Kidnapping	11
Other	3
Total	21
Government	2
Diplomat	3
Military	6
Business	178
Other	17
Total	206

Signatories to the International Convention for the Suppression of Terrorist Financing

North America
  Canada
  United States

Latin America
  Costa Rica
  Ecuador
  Mexico
  Peru

Africa and the Middle East
  Algeria
  Botswana
  Comoros
  Egypt
  Gabon
  Israel
  Lesotho
  Nigeria
  Sudan

Europe and Eurasia
  Czech Republic
  Estonia
  Finland
  France
  Georgia
  Germany
  Greece
  Italy
  Macedonia
  Malta
  Netherlands
  Portugal
  Romania
  Russia
  San Marino
  Ukraine
  United Kingdom

Asia/Oceania
  India
  New Zealand
  Sri Lanka

Terrorism, the Future, and U.S. Foreign Policy

Raphael F. Perl,
Foreign Affairs, Defense, and Trade Division,
September 13, 2001

SUMMARY

International terrorism has long been recognized as a foreign and domestic security threat. The tragic events of September 11th in New York, Washington, and Pennsylvania have dramatically re-energized the nation's focus and resolve on terrorism. This issue brief examines international terrorist actions and threats and the U.S. policy response. Available policy options range from diplomacy, international cooperation and constructive engagement to economic sanctions, covert action, physical security enhancement and military force.

The recent terrorist incidents in the United States, as well the U.S.S. Cole, Oklahoma City, 1993 World Trade Center, the U.S. embassy bombings in Kenya and Tanzania, and the Tokyo subway gas attack, have brought the issue of terrorism to the forefront of American public interest. Questions relate to whether U.S policy and organizational mechanisms are adequate to deal with both state sponsored or abetted terrorism and that undertaken by independent groups.

Formal definitions of terrorism do not include terrorist activity for financial profit or terrorists motivated by religious goals. Non-traditional harm such as computer "violence" may not be included as well. Such activity may well be on the rise.

Terrorist activities supported by sophisticated planning and logistic as well as possible access to chemical, biological, or nuclear weaponry raise a host of new issues. Faced with such prospects, governments are increasingly likely to consider utilizing covert operations to protect their citizenry.

What in the recent past has been some analysts' belief that a comprehensive review of U.S. terrorism policy, organizational structure, and preparedness to respond to major terrorist incidents in the United States is needed, has by necessity become a mainstream view.

Another issue is whether PDD 62, which established a terrorism coordinator at the National Security Council (NSC), takes too much of the terrorism decisionmaking process out of the realm of congressional oversight as NSC members do not generally testify before Congress.

Radical Islamic fundamentalist groups pose a major terrorist threat to U.S. interests and friendly regimes. Nations facing difficult challenges include Algeria, Bahrain, Egypt, Israel, Jordan, Pakistan, and to a lesser degree, Russia and Saudi Arabia. One of the seven states on the State Department's terrorism list, Iran, is seen as the most active state sponsor. Iran has been aggressively seeking nuclear weapons technology. Sanctions have not deterred such activity to any meaningful degree. Some see utility in creation of an informal "watch-list" of nations not currently qualifying for inclusion on the terrorism list.

MOST RECENT DEVELOPMENTS

On September 11, 2001, in an apparent well financed/coordinated attack, hijackers rammed jetliners into each of the New York's World Trade Center's Towers and ultimately collapsed them, causing loss of life believed to be in the many thousands. A third hijacked airliner ploughed into the Pentagon causing extensive damage and loss of life, and a fourth hijacked airliner crashed near Pittsburgh raising speculation that a related mission . . . had failed. . . . Rescue operations are continuing, law enforcement authorities are investigating leads, and response options are being considered. Radical individuals/groups affiliated with Saudi exile Usama bin Laden are high on the list of suspected perpetrators.

President Bush, in addressing the nation, stressed that the United States, in responding to the attacks, will make no distinction between the terrorists who committed these acts and those who harbor them.

The United Nations Security Council has condemned the attacks in a unanimous declaration and NATO Secretary General George Robertson has characterized the attacks, in terms of article V (mutual defense provision) of the NATO Treaty, as an attack on all members of the NATO alliance. Leaders around the world have expressed their condolences and support for the United States in these times of tragedy. . . .

BACKGROUND AND ANALYSIS

. . . Both timing and target selection by terrorist groups can have significant political and economic impact on many activities ranging from U.S. commercial activities to the Middle East peace process. Some analysts have expressed concern that radical Islamic groups may seek to exploit economic and political instabilities in Saudi Arabia. Other potential target nations of such groups include Algeria, Bahrain, Egypt, India, Jordan, Turkey, and Pakistan. Inherent in *Patterns 2000* is concern that a decline in state sponsorship of terrorism has moved terrorism eastward from Libya, Syria, and Lebanon to South Asia. The result: more U.S. policy focus on Usama bin Laden and the alliance of groups operating out of Afghanistan with the acquiescence of the Taliban. A heavy area of focus remains the ability of terrorists to raise funds through non-state sources, often through charitable contributions, kidnaping, and drug trafficking. . . .

The destruction of the World Trade and the severe damage to the Pentagon, together with other incidents such as the bombings of the U.S. Embassies in East Africa, of the World Trade Center in 1993, and of the Jewish cultural center in Buenos Aires may indicate a desire to inflict higher casualties on what are generally less protected civilian targets. It may be that state-sponsored terrorism is decreasing significantly as, in a post-Cold War era, groups find it harder to obtain sponsors and rogue states are less willing to risk exposure to broad based and severe international sanctions. In this environment, access to private sources of funding for terrorist enterprises becomes critical. . . .

DEFINITIONS

There is no universally accepted definition of international terrorism. One definition widely used in U.S. government circles, and incorporated into law, defines "international terrorism" as terrorism involving the citizens or property of more than one country. Terrorism is broadly defined as politically motivated violence perpetrated against noncombatant targets by subnational groups or clandestine agents. A "terrorist group" is defined as a group which practices or which has significant subgroups which practice terrorism (22 U.S.C. 2656f). One potential shortfall of this traditional definition is its focus on groups and group members and exclusion of individual (non-group organized) terrorist activity which has recently risen in frequency and visibility. Another possible weakness of these standard definitions is the criterion of violence in a traditional form. Analysts pointing to computer "virus" sabotage incidents warn that terrorists acts could include more sophisticated forms of destruction and extortion such as disabling a national infrastructure by penetrating vital computer software. . . .

Current definitions of terrorism all share one common element: politically motivated behavior. Such definitions do not include violence for financial profit or religious motivation. Additionally, the rapid growth of transnational criminal organizations and the growing range and scale of such operations could well result in their use of violence to achieve objectives with financial profit as the driving motivation. Thus, although the basic assumption today is that all terrorist acts are politically motivated, some are driven by other factors, and this number may grow in light of expanding international criminal activity and an increasing number of extremist acts carried out in the name of religious and cultural causes. A new approach might focus more on defining terrorist acts, giving less emphasis to the motivation behind the acts.

U.S. POLICY RESPONSE

Framework

Past Administrations have employed a range of options to combat international terrorism, from diplomacy and international cooperation and constructive engagement to economic sanctions, covert action, protective security measures and military force. The application of sanctions is one of the most frequently used anti-terrorist tools of U.S. policymakers. . . .

In the wake of the September 2001 World Trade Center and Pentagon attacks, President Bush, in addressing the nation, stressed that the United States in responding to the attacks, will make no distinction between the terrorists who committed these acts and those who harbor them. The President characterized the incidents as "acts of war." Secretary of State Colin Powell called for a "full scale assault against terrorism" and announced plans to launch a world wide coalition against terrorism. A military response option, once perpetrators and/or supporters have been identified, is a strong probability.

Most experts agree that the most effective way to fight terrorism is to gather as much intelligence as possible; disrupt terrorist plans and organizations before they act; and organize multinational cooperation against terrorists and countries that support them. The U.S.'s role in mandating sanctions against Libya for its responsibility in the 1988 Pan Am 103 bombing was significant as the first instance when the world community imposed sanctions against a country in response to its complicity in an act of terrorism. Several factors made the action possible. First, terrorism has touched many more countries in recent years, forcing governments to put aside parochial interests. (Citizens from over 30 countries have reportedly died in Libyan-sponsored bombings.) Second, the end of the Cold War has contributed to increased international cooperation against terrorism. And third, U.S. determination to punish terrorist countries, by military force in some instances, once their complicity was established, was a major factor spurring other countries to join U.S.-sponsored action.

In the past, governments have often preferred to handle terrorism as a national problem without outside interference. Some governments were also wary of getting involved in others' battles and possibly attracting additional terrorism in the form of reprisals. Others were reluctant to join in sanctions if their own trade interests might be damaged or they sympathized with the perpetrators' cause. Finally, there is the persistent problem of extraditing terrorists without abandoning the long-held principle of asylum for persons fleeing persecution for legitimate political or other activity.

Dilemmas

In their desire to combat terrorism in a modern political context, nations often face conflicting goals and courses of action: (1) providing security from terrorist acts, i.e. limiting the freedom of individual terrorists, terrorist groups, and support networks to operate unimpeded in a relatively unregulated environment versus (2) maximizing individual freedoms, democracy, and human rights. Efforts to combat terrorism are complicated by a global trend towards deregulation, open borders, and expanded commerce. Particularly in democracies such as the United States, the constitutional limits within which policy must operate are often seen by some to conflict directly with a desire to secure the lives of citizens against terrorist activity more effectively. This issue will likely come to the fore as the United States develops its response to the September 2001 incidents.

Another dilemma for policymakers is the need to identify the perpetrators of particular terrorist acts and those who train, fund, or otherwise support or sponsor them. Moreover, as the international community increasingly demonstrates its ability to unite and apply sanctions against rogue states, states will become less likely to overtly support terrorist groups or engage in state sponsored terrorism.

Today a non-standard brand of terrorist may be emerging: individuals who do not work for any established terrorist organization and who are apparently not agents of any state sponsor. The worldwide threat of such individual or "boutique" terrorism, or that of "spontaneous" terrorist activity such as the bombing of bookstores in the United States after Ayatollah Khomeini's death edict against British author Salman Rushdie, appears to be on the increase. Thus, one likely profile for the terrorist of the 21st century may well be a private individual not affiliated with any established group. Another profile might be a group-affiliated individual acting independent of the group, but drawing on other similarly minded individuals for support. Because U.S. international counter-terrorism policy framework has been sanctions-oriented, and has traditionally sought to pin responsibility on state-sponsors, it appears that changes in policy will be considered.

Another problem surfacing in the wake of the number of incidents associated with Islamic fundamentalist groups is how to condemn and combat such terrorist activity, and the extreme and violent ideology of specific radical groups, without appearing to be anti-Islamic in general. A desire to punish a state for supporting international terrorism may also be subject to conflicting foreign policy objectives.

Policy Tools

... Diplomacy/Constructive Engagement. Most responses to international terrorism involve use of diplomacy in some form as governments seek cooperation to apply pressure on terrorists. One such initiative was the active U.S. role taken in the March 1996 Sharm al-Sheikh peacemaker/anti-terrorism summit. Another is the ongoing U.S. effort to get Japan and major European nations to join in U.S. trade and economic sanctions against Iran. Some argue that diplomacy holds little hope of success against determined terrorists or the countries that support them. However, in most cases, diplomatic measures are considered least likely to widen the conflict and therefore are usually tried first.

In incidents of international terrorism by subnational groups, implementing a policy response of constructive engagement is complicated by the lack of existing channels and mutually accepted rules of conduct between governmental entities and the group in question. In some instances, as was the case with the PLO, legislation may specifically prohibit official contact with a terrorist organization or its members. Increasingly, however, governments appear to be pursuing policies which involve verbal contact with terrorist groups or their representatives. . . .

Economic Sanctions. In the past, use of economic sanctions was usually predicated upon identification of a nation as an active supporter or sponsor of international terrorism. . . .

Economic sanctions fall into six categories: restrictions on trading, technology transfer, foreign assistance, export credits and guarantees, foreign exchange and capital transactions, and economic access. Sanctions may include a total or partial trade embargo, embargo on financial transactions, suspension of foreign aid, restrictions on aircraft or ship traffic, or abrogation of a friendship, commerce, and navigation treaty. Sanctions usually require the cooperation of other countries to make them effective, and such cooperation is not always forthcoming.

The President has a variety of laws at his disposal, but the broadest in its potential scope is the International Emergency Economic Powers Act. The Act permits imposition of restrictions on economic relations once the President has declared a national emergency because of a threat to the U.S. national security, foreign policy, or economy. While the sanctions authorized must deal directly with the threat responsible for the emergency, the President can regulate imports, exports, and all types of financial transactions, such as the transfer of funds, foreign exchange, credit, and securities, between the United States and the country in question. . . . Other major laws that can be used against countries supporting terrorism are the Export Administration Act, the Arms Export Control Act, and specific items or provisions of foreign assistance legislation.

P.L. 104-132 prohibits the sale of arms to any country the President certifies is not cooperating fully with U.S. anti-terrorism efforts. The seven terrorist list countries and Afghanistan are currently on this list. The law also requires that aid be withheld to any nation providing lethal military aid a country on the terrorism list.

Covert Action. Intelligence gathering, infiltration of terrorist groups and military operations involve a variety of clandestine or so called "covert" activities. Much of this activity is of a passive monitoring nature. A more active form of covert activity occurs during events such as a hostage crisis or hijacking when a foreign country may quietly request advice, equipment or technical support during the conduct of operations, with no public credit to be given the providing country.

Some nations have periodically gone beyond monitoring or covert support activities and resorted to unconventional methods beyond their territory for the express purpose of neutralizing individual terrorists and/or thwarting pre-planned attacks. Examples of activities might run the gamut from intercepting or sabotaging delivery of funding or weapons to a terrorist group to seizing and transporting a wanted terrorist to stand trial for assassination or murder. Arguably, such activity might be justified as preemptive self defense under Article 51 of the U.N. charter. On the other hand, it could be argued that such actions violate customary international law and can delegate such authority to the Attorney General level, should the national interest so require.

Assassination is specifically prohibited by U.S. Executive Order (most recently, E.O. 12333), but bringing of wanted criminals to the United States for trial is not. There exists an established U.S. legal doctrine that allows an individual's trial to proceed regardless of whether he is forcefully abducted from another country, or from international waters or airspace. For example, Fawaz Yunis, a Lebanese who participated in the 1985 hijacking of a Jordanian airliner with two Americans among its 70 passengers, was lured aboard a yacht in international waters off the coast of Cyprus in 1987 by federal agents, flown to the United States for trial, and convicted.

Experts warn that bringing persons residing abroad to U.S. justice by means other than extradition or mutual agreement with the host country, i.e., by abduction and their surreptitious transportation, can vastly complicate U.S. foreign relations, sometimes jeopardizing interests far more important than "justice," deterrence, and the prosecution of a single individual. For example, the abduction of a Mexican national in 1990 to stand trial in Los Angeles on charges relating to torture and death of a DEA agent led to vehement protests from the government of Mexico, a government subsequently plagued with evidence of high level drug related corruption. Subsequently, in November 1994, the two countries signed a Treaty to Prohibit Transborder Abductions. Notwithstanding the unpopularity of such abductions in nations that fail to apprehend and prosecute those accused, the "rendering" of such wanted criminals to U.S. courts is permitted under limited circumstances by a January 1993 Presidential Decision Directive issued under the first Bush Administration, and reaffirmed by former President Clinton. Such conduct, however, raises prospects of other nations using similar tactics against U.S. citizens.

Although conventional explosives—specifically car bombs—appear to be the terrorism weapon of choice, the world is increasingly moving into an era in which terrorists may gain access to nuclear, chemical or biological weaponry. Faced with the potential of more frequent incidents and higher conventional casualty levels, or a nuclear or biological attack, nations may be more prone to consider covert operations designed to neutralize such threats.

Rewards for Information Program. Money is a powerful motivator. Rewards for information have been instrumental in Italy in destroying the Red Brigades and in Colombia in apprehending drug cartel leaders. A State Department program is in place, supplemented by the aviation industry, offering rewards of up to $5 million to anyone providing information that would prevent or resolve an act of international terrorism against U.S. citizens or U.S. property, or that leads to the arrest or conviction of terrorist criminals involved in such acts. This program was at least partly responsible for the arrest of Ramzi Ahmed Yousef, the man accused of masterminding the World Trade Center bombing, and of the CIA personnel shooter, Mir Amal Kansi. The program was established by the 1984 Act to Combat International Terrorism (P.L. 98-533), and is administered by State's Diplomatic Security Service. Rewards over $250,000 must be approved by the Secretary of State. . . . Expanded participation by the private sector in funding and publicizing such reward programs has been suggested by some observers.

Extradition/Law Enforcement Cooperation. International cooperation in such areas as law enforcement, customs control, and intelligence activities is an important tool in combating international terrorism. One critical law enforcement tool in combating international terrorism is extradition of terrorists. International extradition traditionally has been subject to several limitations, including the refusal to extradite for political or extraterrestrial offenses and the refusal of some countries to extradite their nationals. The United States has been encouraging the negotiation of treaties with fewer limitations, in part as a means of facilitating the transfer of wanted terrorists. Because much terrorism involves politically motivated violence, the State Department has sought to curtail the availability of the political offense exception, found in many extradition treaties, to avoid extradition. Increasingly, rendition is being employed by the U.S. as a vehicle for gaining physical custody over terrorist suspects.

Military Force. Although not without difficulties, military force, particularly when wielded by a superpower such as the United States, can carry substantial clout. Proponents of selective use of military force usually emphasize the military's unique skills and specialized equipment. The April 1986 decision to bomb Libya for its alleged role in the bombing of a German discotheque exemplifies use of military force. Other examples are: (1) the 1993 bombing of Iraq's military intelligence headquarters by U.S. forces in response to Iraqi efforts to assassinate former President George Bush during a visit to Kuwait and (2) the August 1998 missile attacks against bases in Afghanistan and an alleged chemical production facility in Sudan.

Concerns about the terrorist threat prompted an extensive buildup of the military's counter-terrorist organization. A special unit known as "Delta Force" at Fort Bragg, NC, has been organized to perform anti-terrorist operations when needed. Details about the unit are secret, but estimates are that it has about 800 assigned personnel.

Use of military force presupposes the ability to identify a terrorist group or sponsor and its location, knowledge often unavailable to law enforcement officials. Risks of military force include (1) military casualties or captives, (2) foreign civilian casualties, (3) retaliation and escalation by terrorist groups, (4) holding the wrong parties responsible, (5) sympathy for the "bullied" victim, and (6) perception that the U.S. ignores rules of international law.

P.L. 104-264 includes a sense of the Senate statement that if evidence suggests "beyond a clear and reasonable doubt" that an act of hostility against any U.S. citizen was a terrorist act sponsored, organized, condoned or directed by any nation, then a state of war should be considered to exist between the United States and that nation.

International Conventions. To date, the United States has joined with the world community in developing all of the major anti-terrorism conventions. These conventions impose on their signatories an obligation either to prosecute offenders or extradite them to permit prosecution for a host of terrorism-related crimes including hijacking vessels and aircraft, taking hostages, and harming diplomats. An important convention is the Convention for the Marking of Plastic Explosives. Implementing legislation is in P.L. 104-132. On September 8, 1999 the U.S. signed the U.N. Convention on the Suppression of Terrorist Bombings; and on January 12, 2000, the U.N. Anti-Terrorism Financing Convention was signed as well. Both these conventions were submitted to the Senate for advice and consent during the 106th Congress and currently remain there.

Potential Tools

An International Court for Terrorism. Each year bills are introduced urging that an international court be established, perhaps under the U.N., to sit in permanent session to adjudicate cases against persons accused of international terrorist crimes. The court would have broad powers to sentence and punish anyone convicted of such crimes. Critics point out many administrative and procedural problems associated with establishing such a court and making it work, including jurisdictional and enforcement issues. An International Court of Justice in the Hague exists, but it deals with disputes between states and lacks compulsory jurisdiction and enforcement powers.

Media Self-Restraint. For some, the term "media self-restraint" is an oxymoron; the sensational scoop is the golden fleece and dull copy is to be avoided. The media are occasionally manipulated into the role of mediator and often that of publicist of terrorist goals. . . . Notably, there have been attempts by the media to impose its own rules when covering terrorist incidents. . . . Such standards are far from uniformly accepted. In an intensely competitive profession consisting of a multinational worldwide press corps, someone is likely to break the story. . . .

U.S. ORGANIZATION AND PROGRAM RESPONSE

The chain of command on anti-terrorism planning runs from the President through the National Security Council's (NSC's) Principals Committee, through the NSC's Deputies Committee, a representative of which chairs a senior interagency Counterterrorism & National Preparedness Policy Coordinating Committee (PCC). The PCC oversees four working groups charged with overseeing policy in four generic areas: (1) continuity of federal operations; (2) preventing and responding to foreign terrorism; (3) preventing and responding to weapons of mass destruction (WMD) attacks; and (4) preventing and responding to cyberthreats. The State Department's Federal Bureau of Investigation (FBI) is the lead agency for domestic terrorism; and the Federal Aviation Administration is the lead for hijackings when a plane's doors are closed. These roles were reaffirmed by Presidential Decision Directive (PDD) No. 39 in June 1995. PDD 62 (Protection Against Unconventional Threats) and PDD 63 (Critical Infrastructure Protection) of May 22, 1998: (1) established within the NSC a National Coordinator for Security, Infrastructure Protection, and Counterterrorism who also provides "advice" regarding the counterterrorism budget; (2) established within the NSC two Senior Directors who report to the National Coordinator—one for infrastructure protection and one for counterterrorism; (3) established a new inter-agency working group primarily focused on domestic preparedness for WMD incidents; and (4) laid out the architecture for critical infrastructure protection.

On February 14, 2001, President Bush signed National Security Presidential Directive Number 1, which fine-tuned the existing NSC structure and replaced what were formerly referred to as interagency working groups with four groups designed as Policy Coordination Committees.

Under the current structure, intelligence information among the various agencies is coordinated by an Intelligence Committee, chaired by a representative of the CIA. An important policy question is whether current organizational structure brings excessive focus on state-sponsored actions at the expense of attention on so-called "gray area" terrorist activity (i.e. terrorist activity not clearly linked to any perpetrator, group, or supporting/sponsoring nation). In light of the recent terrorist attacks, it is likely that a comprehensive review of counterterrorism policy, organizational structure, and preparedness to respond to major terrorist incidents in the United States will be undertaken. Whether PDD 62, by establishing a national terrorism coordinator at the NSC, takes too much terrorism decisionmaking out of the realm of congressional oversight is another issue as NSC members generally do not testify before Congress. . . .

Counter-Terrorism Research and Development Program

The State Department's Counter-Terrorism Research and Development Program, which is jointly funded by the Departments of State and Defense, constitutes a response to combat the threat posed by increasingly sophisticated equipment and explosives available to terrorist groups. Recent projects include detectors for nuclear materials, decontaminants for chemical and biological weapons, law enforcement and intelligence database software and surveillance technology. . . .

Diplomatic Security Program

The Diplomatic Security Program of the State Department is designated to protect U.S. personnel, information and facilities domestically and abroad. Constructing secure facilities abroad, providing security guards, and supporting counter intelligence are some important elements of the program. Detection and investigation of passport and visa fraud is another important component. The Diplomatic Security Program is contained in three budget accounts: the Diplomatic and Consular Programs account (which covers salaries and operating expenses such as guards and armored vehicles), the Embassy Security, Construction, and Maintenance account (which covers our overseas offices and residences), and the Protection of Foreign Missions and Officials account (which provides extraordinary protection for these purposes in the United States). . . .

Options for Program Enhancement

Some notable areas cited for improvement of programs to combat terrorism include contingency planning; explosives detection; joint or multinational research, operational and training programs/exercises; nuclear materials safeguarding; chemical/biological weapon detection equipment development and disaster/crisis consequence management including training of first responders. Some have suggested that U.S. public diplomacy/media programs could be broadened to support anti-terrorism policy objectives. Cyber security remains an important area for program enhancement. Another option includes enhancing investigative, law enforcement, and prosecution capabilities in other countries to include the area of terrorism fundraising. An enhanced role for the National Academies and the National Laboratories in facilitating more concerted and better coordinated involvement of the U.S. scientific community in assessing threats, developing countermeasures, and in designing responses to terrorism is another option which has been recommended by a number of bipartisan congressional commissions.

STATE-SUPPORTED TERRORISM

The Secretary of State maintains a list of countries that have "repeatedly provided support for acts of international terrorism." Data supporting this list is drawn from the intelligence community. Listed countries are subject to severe U.S. export controls, particularly of dual use technology, and selling them military equipment is prohibited. Providing foreign aid under the Foreign Assistance Act is also prohibited. Section 6(j) of the 1979 Export Administration Act stipulates that a validated license shall be required for export of controlled items and technology to any country on the list, and that the Secretaries of Commerce and State must notify the House Committee on Foreign Affairs, and both the Senate Committees on Banking, Housing, and Urban Affairs, and Foreign Relations, at least 30 days before issuing any validated license required by this Act. In addition, Section 509(a) of the 1986 omnibus anti-terrorism act (P.L. 99-399) bars export of munitions list items to countries on the terrorism list. Indirect state sponsorship or sponsorship by proxy is addressed in a second State Department terrorist category (required by P.L. 104-132)—which is distinct from the list of state sponsors that is generally referred to as the "list"—prohibits the sale of arms to nations not fully cooperating with U.S. anti-terrorism efforts. Strong language critical of Lebanon in *Patterns 2000* prompts some to question whether Lebanon should be included in the latter category of nations. The category designation of countries "not fully cooperating" includes the seven state supporters of terrorism plus Afghanistan. P.L 104-132 also requires the withholding of foreign assistance to nations providing lethal military aid to countries on the list of state sponsors.

Adding and Removing Countries on the List

In late January each year, . . . the Secretary of Commerce in consultation with the Secretary of State provides Congress with a list of countries supporting terrorism. Compilation of the list is the result of an ongoing process. Throughout the year the Department of State gathers data on terrorist activity worldwide, and then beginning about November, the list is formally reviewed. . . .

When a government comes to power (i.e., a government different from that in power at the time of the last determination), the President's report, submitted before the proposed rescission would take effect, must certify that (1) there has been a fundamental change in the leadership and policies of the government of the country concerned (this means an actual change of government as a result of an election, coup, or some other means); (2) the new government is not supporting acts of international terrorism; and (3) the new government has provided assurances that it will not support acts of international terrorism in the future. When the same government is in power, the President's report—submitted at least 45 days before the proposed rescission would take effect—must justify the rescission and certify that, (1) the government concerned has not provided support for international terrorism during the preceding 6-month period; and (2) the government concerned had provided assurances that it will not support acts of international terrorism in the future. Congress can let the President's action take effect, or pass legislation to block it, the latter most likely over the President's veto. To date Congress has passed no such legislation or resolution, although Syria would be the likely target of such endeavors, should the Administration act soon to seek its removal from the terrorism list. *Patterns 2000* notes that "the United States is firmly committed to removing countries from the list once they have taken necessary steps to end their link of terrorism."

Countries on the List

Currently seven countries are on the "terrorism list": Cuba, Iran, Iraq, Libya, North Korea, Sudan and Syria. (For further information on states sponsoring international terrorism, see *Patterns of Global Terrorism (Patterns 2000)*, Department of State, April 2001.) Of the seven, five are Middle Eastern nations with predominantly Muslim populations. . . . Of these, Iran and Iraq could currently be characterized on one extreme as active supporters of terrorism: nations that use terrorism as an instrument of policy or warfare beyond their borders. Iran, Iraq, and Libya are major oil producers, producing, in 1999, about 11% of the world's oil consumption, 35% of Europe's (OECD) oil imports, and 10.8% of Japan's imports. Such dependence on oil complicates universal support for sanctions against these nations.

On the other extreme one might place countries such as Cuba or North Korea, which at the height of the Cold War were more active, but in recent years have seemed to settle for a more passive role in granting ongoing safe haven to previously admitted individual terrorists. Sudan, which *Patterns* 2000 notes continues to serve as a safe haven for members of terrorist groups, has by-and-large shut down their training camps and is engaged with the Department of State in ongoing dialogue on anti-terrorism issues. Closer to the middle of an active/passive spectrum is Libya, which grants safe haven to wanted terrorists. Syria, though not formally detected in an active role since 1986, reportedly serves as the primary transit point for terrorist operatives in Lebanon and for the resupply of weapons to groups in Syria and Lebanon to project power into Israel. Syria allows groups to train in territory under its control, placing it somewhere in the middle to active end of the spectrum.

A complex challenge facing those charged with compiling and maintaining the list is the degree to which diminution of hard evidence of a government's active involvement indicates a real change in behavior, particularly when a past history of active support or use of terrorism as an instrument of foreign policy has been well established. Removing a country from the list is likely to result in some level of confrontation with Congress, so the bureaucratically easier solution is to maintain the status quo, or add to the list, but not to delete from it.

Iran. In a change from *Patterns* 1998, *Patterns* 1999, as well as *Patterns* 2000 names Iran as the most active—and increasingly active—state sponsor of terrorism. Iran continues to be deeply involved in the planning and execution of terrorist acts by its own agents and surrogate groups. It provides "increasing support"—ongoing direction, safe haven, funding, training, weapons and other support—to a variety of radical Islamic terrorist groups including Hizballah in Lebanon, as well as Hammas and Palestinian Islamic Jihad (PIJ) to undermine the Middle East peace process. There are press reports that Iran is building a terrorist infrastructure in the region by providing political indoctrination, military training, and financial help to dissident Shia groups in neighboring countries, including Kuwait, Bahrain, and Saudi Arabia. According to *Patterns* 2000, Iran provides "funding, training, and logistics assistance to extremist groups in the Gulf, Africa, Turkey, and Central Asia." Iran was placed on the terrorism list in January of 1984. President Clinton has halted U.S. trade with Iran and barred U.S. companies from any involvement in the Iranian oil sector. The threat per-

ceived from Iran as a leading supporter of terrorism is substantially raised by reports that Iran is seeking to acquire nuclear technology and seeking nuclear
weapons technology.

Iraq. On September 13, 1990, Iraq was placed once again on the terrorism
list, after having been removed in 1982. Iraq's ability to instigate terror has been
curbed by U.S. and U.N. sanctions which were imposed after the Kuwait invasion. Nevertheless, *Patterns 2000* indicates that Saddam Hussein's regime continues to murder dissidents and provide a safe haven for a variety of Palestinian
rejectionist groups. There are numerous claims that Iraqi intelligence is behind
killings of dissidents on foreign soil during 2000. Iraq also provides active assistance to the MEK, a terrorist group opposed to the Teheran regime. In the past,
Iraq has temporarily expelled terrorists, only to invite them back later.

Libya. Libya has a long history of involvement in international terrorism.
Libya was placed on the terrorism list when it was started in December 1979
and approximately $1 billion in bank deposits belonging to Libya are frozen by
the United States. Libyan terrorism has been sharply reduced after imposition
of U.N. sanctions in the wake of Libyan involvement in the bombings of Pan
Am flight 103 and in the 1989 bombings of French UTA flight 772. The response of the international community and U.S. Congress (P.L. 104-172) seems
to have been relatively effective in restraining the level of Libya's outlaw behavior and may provide one model for future international action. There is no evidence of Libyan involvement in recent acts of international terrorism. In April
2000, Libya took what *Patterns 1999* noted as "an important step by surrendering . . . two Libyans accused of bombing Pan Am flight 103 . . . in 1988" to a
court in the Hague.

Syria. Syria was placed on the first terrorism list in December 1979. It is
generally believed within the western community that Syria has a long history
of using terrorists to advance its own interests. The United States has said that it
has no evidence of Syrian government direct involvement in terrorism since
1986. Informed sources suggest, however, that the Syrian government remains
active, hiding behind the sophisticated operational level of their intelligence
services and their ability to mask such involvement. According to *Patterns 2000*,
many major terrorist groups are known to maintain an active presence (including training camps and operational headquarters) in Syria or in Syrian-
controlled Lebanon and Syria has allowed Iran to supply Hizballah with
weaponry via Damascus. Providing such support, free movement, and safe
haven has caused prominent Members of Congress to contend that Syria
should remain on the terrorism list. Terrorism aside, some observers also argue
that Syria should continue to be subject to U.S. sanctions because of involvement in drug trafficking by some of its ruling elites and their alleged involvement in counterfeiting of U.S. currency.

Sudan. Sudan was added to the terrorism list in August 1993. Sudan continues to harbor members of some of the world's most violent organizations and according to *Patterns 2000* continues to serve as a safe haven for a number of terrorist organizations including Palestine Islamic Jihad, Hamas, and bin Laden's al-Qaida organization. Egypt and Ethiopia have charged the Sudanese government with involvement in a failed assassination attempt against President Hosni Mubarak while in Ethiopia in June 1995. Sudan, however, in mid-2000, entered into a counterterrorism dialogue with the U.S.; it has signed all 12 international anti-terrorism conventions, and has reportedly "by-and-large" shut down terrorist training camps on its territory, steps some observers suggest pave the way for its removal from the terrorism list.

Cuba. Fidel Castro's government has a long history of providing arms and training to terrorist organizations. A cold war carryover, Cuba was added to the 1982 U.S. list of countries supporting international terrorism based on its support for the M-19 guerrilla organization in Colombia. *Patterns 2000* does not cite evidence that Cuban officials were directly involved in sponsoring an act of terrorism in 2000, but notes that Havana remains a safe haven to several international terrorists and U.S. fugitives as well. Implicit in *Patterns 2000* is language from *Patterns 1999* that Cuba no longer actively supports armed struggles in Latin America or elsewhere. Nevertheless, Havana continues to maintain close ties to other state sponsors of terrorism. The Castro regime also reportedly maintains close ties with leftist insurgent groups in Latin America.

North Korea. North Korea was added to the "official" list of countries supporting terrorism because of its implication in the bombing of a South Korean airliner on November 29, 1987, which killed 115 persons. According to the State Department, North Korea is not conclusively linked to any terrorist acts since 1987. A North Korean spokesman in 1993 condemned all forms of terrorism, and said his country resolutely opposed the encouragement and support of terrorism. A similar statement was made in November 1995. Nevertheless, North Korea continues to provide political sanctuary to members of a group that hijacked a Japan Airlines flight in 1970 and is still believed to be linked to the murder of a South Korean diplomat in Vladivostoc in 1996. *Patterns 2000* notes that North Korea has engaged in terrorism talks with the U.S.; has reiterated its opposition to terrorism; and has "agreed to support international actions against such activity."

An Informal Watchlist?

Some suggest that there is utility in drawing to Congress' attention countries that do not currently qualify for inclusion in the terrorism list but where added scrutiny may be warranted. Such a list would be similar to the Attorney General's National Security Threat List that includes sponsors of international terrorism, the activities of which warrant monitoring by the FBI within the United States. Although informal, it would be controversial and speculative. But it would reflect legitimate concerns of those in the intelligence and policy community and might serve as an informal warning mechanism to countries that their activities are being scrutinized. For example, the State Department warned Pakistan in January 1993 that it was under "active continuing review" to determine whether it should be placed on the terrorism list. When the list came out in April 1993, Pakistan was not on it. A similar warning was issued to Pakistan in January 2000. . . . Sudan was also warned that it was being subjected to special review prior to its being placed on the terrorism list in August 1993.

Currently, some informally discussed candidates for such a list include (1) Afghanistan, which *Patterns 2000* characterizes as "a training ground and base of operations" for worldwide terrorist activities. Concerns are that Islamic fundamentalist terrorists linked to numerous international plots continue to train and operate out of the country and/or enter or exit with impunity, and more specifically that the Taliban continues to offer sanctuary to Usama bin Laden and his associated terror networks; (2) Pakistan—*Patterns 2000* notes that Pakistan has tolerated terrorists living and moving freely within its territory; supported groups that engage in violence in Kashmir; and is "providing the Taliban with material, fuel, funding, technical assistance, and military advisers"; (3) Lebanon—ongoing concern exists over terrorist groups operating with impunity from there, often under Syrian protection, in areas ostensibly controlled by the Government of Lebanon; and (4) Yemen—despite growing military cooperation and assistance in the U.S.S. Cole bombing investigation, Yemen, a nation where a thriving kidnapping industry flourishes in remote areas, remains a safe haven for international terrorist groups with the Government of Yemen, according to *Patterns 2000*, apparently unable "to discourage the terrorist presence in Yemen." Not specifically stated in *Patterns 2000* is a growing concern in U.S. policy circles that Chechnya may increasingly become a magnet for Islamic radicals. *Patterns 1999*, however, noted that concern exists that "increased radicalization of Islamist populations connected to the Chechnya conflict would encourage violence and spread instability elsewhere in Russia and beyond." Concerns also remain that militant Iranian elements and militants linked to Usama bin Laden remaining in the territory of Nations of the Former Yugoslavia may resort to terrorist violence.

PART IV

Osama bin Laden

THIS SECTION contains an assortment of biographical profiles of Osama bin Laden which were released at various times in the late 1990s. The most detailed is a Central Intelligence Agency briefing note completed in early 1996. Following it are inset articles on bin Laden which appeared in the State Department publication *Patterns of Global Terrorism* in 1997, when bin Laden was first singled out for special attention, and in the following two years. The pieces have been edited to show assertions about bin Laden in the first instance in which they appear and to eliminate duplication. These materials show the initial U.S. official statement on bin Laden and how that commentary has evolved in subsequent years. Note that by this measure, U.S. agencies began to focus on the Saudi activist only at a relatively late date. The section ends with the text of the *fatwa* or religious decree issued by bin Laden on February 23, 1998, on the occasion of his alliance with other Islamic political and religious leaders in a "World Islamic Front."

What is striking about the set of biographical profiles is how little they reveal about the man and the origins of his political movement. Osama bin Laden was born in Riyadh, Saudi Arabia, on March 10, 1957 (his birthdate has also been reported as July 30). "Osama" is the Arabic for "Young Lion." He was the seventeenth of 25 sons (and many daughters) of Mohammed bin Oud bin Laden, a bricklayer who became friends with the Saudi crown prince, started a construction company, and became rich on Saudi government and international contracts. Today the company, now known as the Saudi Binladen Group

(SGB), is a multinational corporation that employs 35,000 persons and has assets of more than $5 billion. The company remains personally held and is controlled by one of Osama's half-brothers, with others sitting on a board of directors.

Socially conservative as it is, Saudi society permits multiple marriages, and Mohammed bin Laden fully availed himself of this practice. Osama's mother was exceptional among the wives, a Syrian woman, the sole foreigner in the Saudi family. Mohammed had met her while on a construction project in Syria. In older age she returned to that country and continues to live there. The woman bore a son and two daughters. Osama was focused, dutiful, and a good student. With Syria even more a closed world than Saudi Arabia, and only periodic sojourns in Saudi Arabia for family visits or study, Osama grew up admiring his father but not especially close to his numerous siblings. Mohammed died in 1968 when his private jet crashed in the mountainous region of Saudi Arabia along the Yemeni border.

Unlike the Saudi side of the family, many of whom attended private academies abroad, especially in England, Osama went to local schools. For college he remained in the Middle East, in Saudi Arabia, where he studied at the King Abdel Azziz University, named for the royal ruler who had befriended his father, in Jidda. Bin Laden had been involved with SBG in minor capacities as a boy, and for college he chose engineering as a field of study. At Jidda too, bin Laden came under the influence of Dr. Abdullah Azzam, a proponent of the fundamentalist Wahhabi strain of Islam. Osama was graduated in 1979, a deeply religious engineer.

The combination of practical work in service of religious conviction seems to have characterized Osama bin Laden's career from the beginning. In the early 1980s, for example, when Islam was undergoing a revival in Spain (the number of Muslims in Spain would grow from about thirty thousand at that time to as many as half a million by the turn of the century), Osama with his brother Tarek showed up in Granada on the lookout for construction projects in which they could participate. But the family business soon lost its luster for the young zealot.

Bin Laden completed his education at a moment when the Middle East and South Asia were in ferment. The Iranian revolution had just toppled the shah and brought to power a Shiite Muslim theocracy. Egypt was in the throes of intense struggle between a moderate government and the more fundamentalist Muslim Brotherhood, which would lead in a matter of months to the assassination of President Anwar Sadat. Afghanistan was in revolt against a Communist dictatorship, and before the end of the year a Russian army would intervene in force in that country to prop up the regime. When that happened the call came throughout the Muslim world to travel to Afghanistan and join with the Resistance to fight the Russians. Political action seemed necessary. Saudi Arabia itself was intervening alongside the U.S. Central Intelligence Agency to support the Afghan Resistance. Then bin Laden's spiritual guide, Abdullah Azzam, formed an organization in Pakistan, the rear base of the Resistance, called the Office of Support. Bin Laden went to assist in the struggle. In *Holy War, Inc.*, journalist Peter L. Bergen quotes bin Laden as saying, "My father was very keen that one of his sons should fight against the enemies of Islam. So I am the one who is acting according to the wishes of his father."

By some accounts bin Laden took earth movers and heavy construction equipment to Pakistan with him. By most accounts his money was a key aspect of his participation, but that inheritance was much less than the $325 million figure that has appeared in many press accounts. More recent estimates of $30 to $60 million are in line with the number of $27 million used by Saudi Prince Bandar bin Sultan, currently ambassador to the United States, in an October 2001 interview. In any case, use of that lesser fortune on massive construction efforts is unlikely; if equipment was involved, the more likely provenance was Saudi Arabia's intelligence service, headed since 1976 by Prince Turki al-Faisal Saud. There are reports that Turki and bin Laden cooperated, which are entirely plausible given the closeness of the families and the intensity with which Turki pursued the Afghan war, matching CIA funding every step of the way.

Osama bin Laden used his own money on more modest endeavors that gradually took wing. Abdullah Azzam set up a guest house at Peshawar, Pakistan, for Arab fighters on their way to join the Resistance. Bin Laden worked on that project, then, in 1984, set up his own guest house called "Beit al-Ansar," the House of the Supporters. In 1986 he created a separate military and religious course with his own training camp called "Al Masadah," or The Lion's Den. Later he funded a second facility open only to more trusted Arab fighters. Reports that the CIA funded bin Laden or gave him his start are almost certainly false. Agency officers who worked on the Afghan war did not know bin Laden or were only vaguely aware of his efforts. Milton Bearden, the officer who headed the CIA base at Peshawar from 1986 to 1989, recalls that he had no dealings with bin Laden. A French intelligence chief of that era, Admiral Pierre Lacoste, has since asserted that he warned the CIA against becoming involved with Islamic extremists like bin Laden.

On Osama bin Laden's side, a record of cooperation with the CIA is equally improbable. Bin Laden was already looking askance at America. As early as 1982, associates recall him saying that good Muslims should boycott American products. Bin Laden himself told an interviewer in 1999 that by the mid-1980s he had been giving talks in Saudi Arabia that urged both a boycott of American products and actual attacks on U.S. forces. In 1988 he founded a group of his own called "Al Qaeda," or The Base. Meanwhile the Masadah camp had been specializing in training for strikes in the Persian Gulf area, a locale where targets would have had to be related more to the United States than to any aspect of the Afghan war. Bin Laden's outlook could not have been improved by the 1989 assassination of the Office of Support leader Abdullah Azzam with two of his sons, by a car bomb as they entered a mosque for services. As the Office of Support splintered, its more extreme faction joined Al Qaeda.

The Afghan war also ended in 1989. Osama bin Laden returned to Saudi Arabia, for a time a hero. The tall (6 foot, 5 inch), distinguished leader had earned respect. Having first married in 1974, along the way he had acquired two more wives (though elsewhere the man is reported to have four wives in all) and sired fifteen children. But domestic concerns did not remain long on his mind. In 1990, Iraq invaded Kuwait, and Iraqi armies threatened Saudi Arabia. Bin Laden wanted to organize a legion of Arab fighters to halt the Iraqi aggression. Saudi authorities rejected the proposal, instead relying upon a major deployment of U.S. and coalition military forces to protect the kingdom. The United States and an international coalition ejected Iraq from Kuwait in the Gulf War campaign of 1991, but afterward U.S. forces remained in Saudi Arabia to help enforce the United Nations resolutions and the American declaration of a "no-fly zone" over parts of Iraq that had marked the end of the war. This presence of U.S. military forces in Saudi Arabia enraged bin Laden and led him to begin his anti-American terrorist efforts. Those activities were unacceptable to the Saudi government, and bin Laden was forced to leave the country of which he was now a citizen.

With the help of Muslim fundamentalist leaders and officials of the Office of Support, bin Laden was able to set up shop in the Sudan. There he established a construction company, Al-Hijrah for Construction and Development Ltd., which built a 185-mile highway from Khartoum to Port Sudan; bought a tannery; formed the Taba Investment Company Ltd., which invested in commodities, cornering the Sudanese export market in gum, sunflower, and sesame products; and created an import-export firm, Wadi al-Aqiq Company Ltd. The executive who headed the construction company has since recalled that bin Laden paid special attention to this operation, participating in the decisions on exactly what heavy equipment to procure, and that he showed he knew how to work every piece of this machinery. Bin Laden reportedly also invested $50 million in a new venture, the Al Shamal Islamic Bank, established in Khartoum. (Officials of the bank have denied the connection and insist that their total initial capitalization and value are less than the alleged bin Laden investment.)

Bin Laden paid travel expenses for as many as 480 Muslim fighters to come to Sudan, which waived all its immigration and registration rules for the jihadists. Al Qaeda opened training camps for the fighters. The Islamic insurgent offered his fighters to the Muslim government of that time for service in the civil war that still rages in the Sudan, but he was turned down. Al Qaeda also looked for opportunities to strike at Americans. At the end of 1992, when the United States began a humanitarian intervention in the nearby East African nation of Somalia, bin Laden sent his military chief and co-founder of Al Qaeda, Muhammed Atef (killed in November 2001 in the U.S. air campaign in Afghanistan), to scout the Somali situation. As a result, Al Qaeda specialists Saif al-Adel and Muhsin Musa Matwalli Atwah were sent to Somalia to train the troops of warlords, such as Mohammed Aideed, who were fighting the Americans. The battle in Mogadishu on October 3, 1993, in which eighteen American soldiers were killed, involved Qaeda-trained troops. U.S. intelligence did not learn of this for several years afterward. By January 1994, Al Qaeda had several training camps in Sudan.

Foreigners in the Sudan have been routinely subjected to some degree of surveillance by the Sudanese intelligence service, the Mukhabarat, and bin Laden and his Al Qaeda were not exceptions. The Sudanese recorded the names and vital details of Qaeda members, photographed them, and followed their activities. As early as 1992, security officers noted that bin Laden hosted an extended visit by Egyptian Islamic activist Ayman al-Zawahiri, later to become a bin Laden ally.

Osama bin Laden himself rented a house in one of Khartoum's best districts, and a downtown office on Mak Nimer street. He dressed in the traditional Sudanese manner, played soccer with children from his neighborhood, and went swimming in the Nile. He bought horses and raced them on Fridays at Khartoum's track. He displayed few signs of the fundamentalism that remained at his core (covering his ears when he heard music, which he deplored, was one of them). Some acquaintances saw Osama as putting down roots in this African country, but the genteel veneer overlaid his more disquieting political activities.

The Sudanese, who helped French authorities in 1994 to arrest the notorious terrorist Carlos (Illyich Ramirez Sanchez), attempted to share their bin Laden files with the United States or deal directly with the FBI in 1997 and 1998, without success. When the United States made demands in 1996 that Sudan expel the Al Qaeda leader, the Sudanese offered to turn him over to the United States, but American officials rejected that option. The United States at that time lacked the concrete evidence necessary to bring bin Laden to trial as a terrorist. Sudan expelled him in May 1996, though security officials there believed that to be a mistake—constant monitoring of bin Laden was being traded for a situation in which there would be no surveillance at all. Estimated to number several hundred, the Sudanese intelligence files were eventually accepted by the United States, but only after the September 11 attacks on New York and Washington.

Earlier, in 1993, Muslim terrorists in the United States had made a first attempt at destroying New York's World Trade Center. Subsequent investigation revealed that a key facility for the cell involved in that attack, and in other planned but abortive terrorist attacks on important New York targets (including United Nations headquarters, tunnels leading to the city, and the Statue of Liberty), had been an Islamic center, Al Khifa, in Brooklyn. That center had been founded by the Office of Support. A Muslim cleric implicated in the plots, Omar Abdul Rahman, had also been instrumental in helping bin Laden gain entry into the Sudan, had been a colleague of Abdullah Azzam, and had also run one of the Peshawar guest houses during the anti-Soviet war in Afghanistan. Again these connections were not known at the time, though there remains no evidence directly linking Al Qaeda with the 1993 Trade Center bombing. (In fact, some observers suspect that Iraq was behind that attack.)

The Trade Center bombing and other incidents energized the Clinton administration's efforts to counter terrorism, and Osama bin Laden became a focus of these activities. With his impending expulsion from the Sudan in 1996, he looked for a new base. That could not be Saudi Arabia, against which Al Qaeda had been conducting a propaganda campaign since about 1992. At that time the Saudis had uncovered evidence that bin Laden had been involved in smuggling weapons to dissidents within the monarchy. In 1994 Saudi Arabia had stripped him of his Saudi citizenship. From 1995 to 1998 he funded an organization in London, the Advisory and Reform Committee headed by Khalid al-Fawwaz, which created and circulated propaganda rejecting the Saudi monarchy. Fawwaz was arrested and the office broken up after the 1998 embassy bombings in Africa. In addition, Al Qaeda had expressed its approval for a terrorist attack in late 1995 against Americans stationed in Saudi Arabia. The next year bin Laden's group repeated its expressions of approval after the Khobar Barracks bombing. But the Saudi government found no direct connection between Al Qaeda and these incidents.

Afghanistan became bin Laden's new center of operations. The Taliban fundamentalist sect that had taken over the Afghan capital in 1995 were willing to offer him shelter. In turn, he used his money to cement relations with the Taliban government. In April 1997 bin Laden made his center of operations Kandahar, the city where the Taliban itself had originated and was headquartered.

By 1998 bin Laden had a network of training camps for agent recruits and several houses in Afghanistan. He formed an alliance with Egyptian, Pakistani, and other fundamentalist groups in the so-called World Islamic Front, whose statement appears in this section. It is notable that bin Laden, who was in no sense a religious leader (though he is known to be an intensely religious man), saw no problem in characterizing this and subsequent pronouncements as *fat-*

was, which in Muslim practice are supposed to be edicts issued by learned religious leaders. The *fatwa* and its successors called for attacks on Americans. The bombings of American embassies in Africa, which are covered by documents in the next section of this collection, followed within months of the *fatwa*.

The United States retaliated after the embassy attacks. On August 20, 1998, cruise missiles hit bin Laden training camps in Afghanistan and mistakenly struck a factory in the Sudan thought to be a bin Laden entity. American authorities confirmed that the missiles had targeted bin Laden. Reportedly the Afghan attacks were intended to strike a meeting of senior Al Qaeda leaders that included bin Laden, but the group broke up hours before the missiles hit, and bin Laden escaped. In February 1999 there were reports that by intercepting Al Qaeda electronic communications, the CIA had managed to foil at least seven planned Al Qaeda attacks against U.S. facilities in Saudi Arabia, Albania, Azerbaijan, Tadjikistan, Uganda, Uruguay, and the Ivory Coast. President Clinton had signed an intelligence finding in the summer of 1998 permitting the CIA to go after bin Laden, and several additional attempts were made, including an ambush by CIA-trained paramilitary units of a road convoy carrying the Al Qaeda leader. At one point the Taliban announced falsely that bin Laden had left Afghanistan, and another time that it had closed his training camps in the country. The U.S. government presented the Taliban with evidence to substantiate charges against bin Laden on at least two occasions in an effort to induce the Taliban to hand him over to U.S. authorities. The Taliban publicly expressed itself willing to take such action if evidence were convincing, but they consistently rejected the evidence presented. Saudi intelligence chief Prince Turki also made at least two attempts along the same lines, in June and September 1998, without success. Meanwhile bin Laden escalated his own terrorist efforts in tandem with the attempts to neutralize him. On June 7, 1999, he was placed on the FBI's Ten Most Wanted list, and a $5 million reward for his capture was posted. By early 2000, Al Qaeda had about a dozen training camps in Afghanistan and was reported to have trained at least five thousand fighters.

In the wake of the September 2001 attacks, bin Laden publicly denied any connection with the tragedies at the same time he threatened America and the West. But strong evidence links Al Qaeda to the events of September 11. Most recently a privately made Afghan videotape, captured during the Afghan military operation, shows bin Laden commenting in the immediate aftermath of the bombings in a way that demonstrates foreknowledge of the plans.

At this writing American forces in Afghanistan and local tribal allies have overthrown Taliban power in that country and have attacked a series of cave systems and Al Qaeda base camps in the high mountains and also the plains along the Pakistani border and in eastern Afghanistan, places where Al Qaeda figures were believed to have hid, or where fighters apparently gathered following the collapse of organized resistance. Osama bin Laden was believed to have holed up in the mountain caves called Tora Bora, but when that base fell in mid-December he was nowhere to be found. Perhaps bin Laden died in the heavy bombardment of Tora Bora, but the terrorist chieftain may have escaped across the Pakistani border. The reward for the capture of bin Laden and his top Al Qaeda confederates was increased to $25 million in November.

Usama Bin Ladin: Islamic Extremist Financier

Central Intelligence Agency, February 1996

Usama bin Muhammad bin Awad Bin Ladin is one of the most significant financial sponsors of Islamic extremist activities in the world today. One of some 20 sons of wealthy Saudi construction magnate Muhammed Bin Ladin—founder of the Kingdom's Bin Ladin Group business empire—Usama joined the Afghan resistance movement following the 26 December 1979 Soviet invasion of Afghanistan. "I was enraged and went there at once," he claimed in a 1993 interview, "I arrived within days, before the end of 1979."

Bin Ladin gained prominence during the Afghan war for his role in financing the recruitment, transportation, and training of Arab nationals who volunteered to fight alongside the Afghan mujahadin. By 1985, Bin Ladin had drawn on his family's wealth, plus donations received from sympathetic merchant families in the Gulf region, to organize the Islamic Salvation Foundation, or al-Qaida, for this purpose.

- A network of al-Qaida recruitment centers and guesthouses in Egypt, Saudi Arabia, and Pakistan has enlisted and sheltered thousands of Arab recruits. This network remains active.
- Working in conjunction with extremist groups like the Egyptian al-Gama'at al-Islamiyyah, also known as the Islamic Group, al-Qaida organized and funded camps in Afghanistan and Pakistan that provided new recruits paramilitary training in preparation for the fighting in Afghanistan.
- Under al-Qaida auspices, Bin Ladin imported bulldozers and other heavy equipment to cut roads, tunnels, hospitals, and storage depots through Afghanistan's mountainous terrain to move and shelter fighters and supporters.

After the Soviets withdrew from Afghanistan in 1989, Bin Ladin returned to work in the family's Jeddah-based construction business. However, he continued to support militant Islamic groups that had begun targeting moderate Islamic governments in the region. Saudi officials held Bin Ladin's passport during 1989–1991 in a bid to prevent him from solidifying contacts with extremists whom he had befriended during the Afghan war.

Bin Ladin relocated to Sudan in 1991, where he was welcomed by National Islamic Front (NIF) leader Hassan al-Turabi. In a 1994 interview, Bin Ladin claimed to have surveyed business and agricultural investment opportunities in Sudan as early as 1983. He embarked on several business ventures in Sudan in 1990, which began to thrive following his move to Khartoum. Bin Ladin also formed symbiotic business relationships with wealthy NIF members by undertaking civil infrastructure development projects on the regime's behalf.

- Bin Ladin's company Al-Hijrah for Construction and Development, Ltd. built the rahaddi (challenge) road linking Khartoum with Port Sudan, as well as a modern international airport near Port Sudan.
- Bin Ladin's import-export firm Wadi al-Aqiq Company, Ltd., in conjunction with his Taba Investment Company, Ltd., acquired a near monopoly over Sudan's major agricultural exports of gum, corn, sunflower, and sesame products in cooperation with prominent NIF members. At the same time, Bin Ladin's Al-Themar al-Mubarakah Agriculture Company, Ltd., grew to encompass large tracts of land near Khartoum and in eastern Sudan.
- Bin Ladin and wealthy NIF members capitalized Al-Shamal Islamic Bank in Khartoum. Bin Ladin invested $50 million in the bank.

Bin Ladin's work force grew to include militant Afghan war veterans seeking to avoid a return to their own countries, where many stood accused of subversive and terrorist activities. In May 1993, for example, Bin Ladin financed the travel of 300 to 480 Afghan war veterans to Sudan after Islamabad launched a trackdown against extremists lingering in Pakistan. In addition to safehaven in Sudan, Bin Ladin has provided financial support to militants actively opposed to moderate Islamic governments and the West:

- Islamic extremists who perpetrated the December 1992 attempted bombings against some 100 U.S. servicemen in Aden—billeted there to support the U.N. relief operations in Somalia—claimed that Bin Ladin financed their group.
- A joint Egyptian-Saudi investigation revealed in May 1993 that Bin Ladin business interests helped funnel money to Egyptian extremists, who used the cash to buy unspecified equipment, printing presses, and weapons.

- By January 1994, Bin Ladin had begun financing at least three terrorist training camps in southern Sudan—camp residents included Egyptian, Algerian, Tunisian, and Palestinian extremists—in cooperation with the NIF. Bin Ladin's Al-Hijrah for Construction and Development works directly with Sudanese military officials to transport and provision terrorists training in such camps.
- Pakistani investigators have said that Ramzi Ahmed Yousef, the alleged mastermind of the February 1993 World Trade Center bombing, resided at the Bin Ladin-funded Bayt Ashuhada (house of martyrs) guesthouse in Peshawar during most of the three years before his apprehension in February 1995.
- A leading member of the Egyptian extremist group al-Jihad claimed in a July 1995 interview that Bin Ladin helped fund the group and was at times aware of specific terrorist operations mounted by the group against Egyptian interests.
- Bin Ladin remains the key financier behind the "Kunar" camp in Afghanistan, which provides terrorist training to al-Jihad and al-Gama'at al-Islamiyyah members, according to suspect terrorists captured recently by Egyptian authorities.

Bin Ladin's support for extremist causes continues despite criticisms from regional governments and his family. Algeria, Egypt, and Yemen have accused Bin Ladin of financing militant Islamic groups on their soil (Yemen reportedly sought INTERPOL's assistance to apprehend Bin Ladin during 1994). In February 1994, Riyadh revoked Bin Ladin's Saudi citizenship for behavior that "contradicts the Kingdom's interests and risks harming its relations with fraternal countries." The move prompted Bin Ladin to form the Advisory and Reformation Committee, a London-based dissident organization that by July 1995 had issued over 350 pamphlets critical of the Saudi Government. Bin Ladin has not responded to condemnation leveled against him in March 1994 by his eldest brother, Hakr Bin Ladin, who expressed through the Saudi media his family's "regret, denunciation, and condemnation" of Bin Ladin's extremist activities.

Usama Bin Ladin

Profiles, Department of State, 1997, 1998, 1999

Usama bin Muhammad bin Awad Bin Ladin is one of the most significant sponsors of Sunni Islamic terrorist groups. The youngest son of Saudi construction magnate Muhammad Bin Ladin, Usama joined the Afghan resistance almost immediately after the Soviet invasion in December 1979. He played a significant role in financing, recruiting, transporting, and training Arab nationals who volunteered to fight in Afghanistan. During the war, Bin Ladin founded al-Qaida—the Base—to serve as an operational hub, predominantly for like-minded Sunni Islamic extremists. The Saudi Government revoked his citizenship in 1994 and his family officially disowned him. He had moved to Sudan in 1991, but international pressure on that government forced him to move to Afghanistan in 1996.

In August 1996, Bin Ladin issued a statement outlining his organization's goals: drive US forces from the Arabian Peninsula, overthrow the Government of Saudi Arabia, "liberate" Muslim holy sites in "Palestine," and support Islamic revolutionary groups around the world. To these ends, his organization has sent trainers throughout Afghanistan as well as to Tajikistan, Bosnia, Chechnya, Somalia, Sudan, and Yemen and has trained fighters from numerous other countries including the Philippines, Egypt, Libya, and Eritrea. Bin Ladin also has close associations with the leaders of several Islamic terrorist groups and probably has aided in creating new groups since the mid-1980s. He has trained their troops, provided safehaven and financial support, and probably helps them with other organizational matters.

Since August 1996, Bin Ladin has been very vocal in expressing his approval of and intent to use terrorism. He claimed responsibility for trying to bomb US soldiers in Yemen in late 1992 and for attacks on them in Somalia in 1993, and reports suggest his organization aided the Egyptian al-Gama'at al-Islamiyya in its assassination attempt on Egyptian President Mubarak in Ethoipia in 1995. In

November 1996 he called the 1995 and 1996 bombings against US military personnel in Saudi Arabia "praiseworthy acts of terrorism" but denied having any personal participation in those bombings. At the same time, he called for further attacks against US military personnel, saying: "If someone can kill an American soldier, it is better than wasting time on other matters." . . .

(1997)

The bombings of the US Embassies in Nairobi, Kenya, and Dar es Salaam, Tanzania on 7 August 1998 underscored the global reach of Usama Bin Ladin—a long-time sponsor and financier of Sunni Islamic extremist causes—and his network. A series of public threats to drive the United States and its allies out of Muslim countries foreshadowed the attacks. The foremost threat was presented as a Muslim religious decree and published on 23 February 1998 by Bin Ladin and allied groups under the name "World Islamic Front for Jihad Against the Jews and Crusaders." The statement asserted that it was a religious duty for all Muslims to wage war on US citizens, military and civilian, anywhere in the world.

The 17th son of Saudi construction magnate Muhammad Bin Ladin, Usama joined the Afghan resistance almost immediately after the Soviet invasion in December 1979. He played a significant role in financing, recruiting, transporting, and training Arab nationals who volunteered to fight in Afghanistan. During the war, Bin Ladin founded al-Qaida—the "Base"—to serve as an operational hub for like-minded Sunni Islamic extremists. In 1994 the Saudi Government revoked his citizenship and his family officially disowned him. He moved to Sudan in 1991 but international pressure on Khartoum forced him to move to Afghanistan in 1996.

Bin Ladin leads a broad-based, versatile organization. Suspects named in the wake of the Embassy bombings—four Egyptians, one Comoran, one Jordanian, three Saudis, one US citizen, one or possibly two Kenyan citizens, and one Tanzanian—reflect the range of al-Qaida operatives. The diverse groups under his umbrella afford Bin Ladin resources beyond those of the people directly loyal to him. With his own inherited wealth, business interests, contributions from sympathizers in various countries, and support from close allies like the Egyptian and South Asian groups that signed his so-called *fatwa*, he funds, trains, and offers logistic help to extremists not directly affiliated with his organization.

Bin Ladin seeks to aid those who support his primary goal—driving US forces from the Arabian Peninsula, removing the Saudi ruling family from power, and "liberating Palestine"—or his secondary goals of removing Western military forces and overthrowing what he calls corrupt, Western-oriented governments in predominantly Muslim countries. To these ends, his organization has sent trainers throughout Afghanistan as well as to Tajikistan, Bosnia and Herzegovina, Chechnya, Somalia, Sudan, and Yemen, and has trained fighters from numerous other countries, including the Philippines, Egypt, Libya, Pakistan, and Eritrea.

Using the ties al-Qaida has developed, Bin Ladin believes he can call upon individuals and groups virtually worldwide to conduct terrorist attacks. His Egyptian and South Asian allies, for example, publicly threatened US interests in the latter half of 1998. Bin Ladin's own public remarks underscore his expanding interests, including a desire to obtain a capability to deploy weapons of mass destruction.

On 4 November indictments were returned in the US District Court for the Southern District of New York in connection with the two US Embassy bombings in Africa. Charged in the indictment were: Usama Bin Ladin, his military commander Muhammad Atef, and Wadih El Hage, Fazul Abdullah Mohammed, Mohammed Sadeek Odeh, and Mohamed Rashed Daoud al-Owhali, all members of al-Qaida. Two of these suspects, Odeh and al-Owhali, were turned over to US authorities in Kenya and brought to the United States to stand trial. Another suspect, Mamdouh Mahmud Salim, was arrested in Germany and extradited to the United States in December. On 16 December five others were indicted for their role in the Dar es Salaam Embassy bombing: Mustafa Mohammed Fadhil, Khalfan Khamis Mohamed, Ahmed Khalfan Ghailani, Fahid Mohammed Ally Msalam, and Sheikh Ahmed Salim Swedan.

(1998)

The bombings of the US Embassies in Nairobi, Kenya, and in Dar es Salaam, Tanzania, on 7 August 1998 underscored the global reach of Usama Bin Ladin—a longtime sponsor and financier of extremist causes—and brought to full public awareness his transition from sponsor to terrorist. A series of public threats to drive the United States and its allies out of Muslim countries foreshadowed the attacks, including what was presented as a *fatwa* (Muslim legal opinion) published on 23 February 1998 by Bin Ladin and allied groups under the name "World Islamic Front for Jihad Against the Jews and Crusaders." The statement asserted it was a religious duty for all Muslims to wage war on US citizens, military and civilian, anywhere in the world.

The 17th son of Saudi construction magnate Muhammad Bin Ladin, Usama joined the Afghan resistance almost immediately after the Soviet invasion in December 1979. He played a significant role in financing, recruiting, transporting, and training Arab nationals who volunteered to fight in Afghanistan. During the war, Bin Ladin founded al-Qaida (the Base) to serve as an operational hub for like-minded extremists. The Saudi Government revoked his citizenship in 1994, and his family officially disowned him. He moved to Sudan in 1991, but international pressure on Khartoum forced him to move to Afghanistan in 1996.

Bin Ladin has stated publicly that terrorism is a tool to achieve the group's goal of bringing Islamic rule to Muslim lands and "cleanse" them of Western influence and corruption. To this end, Bin Ladin in 1999 led a broadbased, versatile organization. Suspects named in the wake of the Embassy bombings — Egyptians, one Comoran, one Palestinian, one Saudi, and US citizens — reflect the range of al-Qaida operatives. The diverse groups under his umbrella afford Bin Ladin resources beyond those of the people directly loyal to him. With his own inherited wealth, business interests, contributions from sympathizers in various countries; and support from close allies like the Egyptian and South Asian groups that signed his *fatwa*, he funds, trains, and offers logistic help to extremists not directly affiliated with his organization. He seeks to aid those who support his primary goals — driving US forces from the Arabian Peninsula, removing the Saudi ruling family from power, and "liberating Palestine" — or his secondary goals of removing Western military forces and overthrowing what he calls corrupt, Western-oriented governments in predominantly Muslim countries. His organization has sent trainers throughout Afghanistan as well as to Tajikistan, Bosnia, Chechnya, Somalia, Sudan, and Yemen and has trained fighters from numerous other countries, including the Philippines, Egypt, Libya, Pakistan, and Eritrea.

Using the ties al-Qaida has developed, Bin Ladin believes he can call upon individuals and groups virtually worldwide to conduct terrorist attacks. In December 1998, Bin Ladin gave a series of interviews in which he denied involvement in the East Africa bombings but said he "instigated" them and called for attacks on US citizens worldwide in retaliation for the strikes against Iraq. Bin Ladin's public statements then ceased under increased pressure from his Taliban hosts. Nonetheless, in 1999, Bin Ladin continued to influence like-minded extremists to his cause, and his organization continued to engage in terrorist planning. His Egyptian and South Asian allies, for example, continued publicly to threaten US interests. Bin Ladin's public remarks also underscored his expanding interests, including a desire to obtain a capability to deploy weapons of mass destruction.

(1999)

Jihad Against Jews and Crusaders

Statement of World Islamic Front, February 23, 1998

Shaykh Usamah Bin-Muhammad Bin-Ladin
Ayman al-Zawahiri, amir of the Jihad Group in Egypt
Abu-Yasir Rifa'i Ahmad Taha, Egyptian Islamic Group
Shaykh Mir Hamzah, secretary of the Jamiat-ul-Ulema-e-Pakistan
Fazlur Rahman, amir of the Jihad Movement in Bangladesh

Praise be to God, who revealed the Book, controls the clouds, defeats factionalism, and says in His Book: "But when the forbidden months are past, then fight and slay the pagans wherever ye find them, seize them, beleaguer them, and lie in wait for them in every stratagem (of war)"; and peace be upon our Prophet, Muhammad Bin-'Abdallah, who said: I have been sent with the sword between my hands to ensure that no one but God is worshipped, God who put my livelihood under the shadow of my spear and who inflicts humiliation and scorn on those who disobey my orders.

The Arabian Peninsula has never—since God made it flat, created its desert, and encircled it with seas—been stormed by any forces like the crusader armies spreading in it like locusts, eating its riches and wiping out its plantations. All this is happening at a time in which nations are attacking Muslims like people fighting over a plate of food. In the light of the grave situation and the lack of support, we and you are obliged to discuss current events, and we should all agree on how to settle the matter.

No one argues today about three facts that are known to everyone; we will list them, in order to remind everyone:

First, for over seven years the United States has been occupying the lands of Islam in the holiest of places, the Arabian Peninsula, plundering its riches, dictating to its rulers, humiliating its people, terrorizing its neighbors, and turning its bases in the Peninsula into a spearhead through which to fight the neighboring Muslim peoples.

If some people have in the past argued about the fact of the occupation, all the people of the Peninsula have now acknowledged it. The best proof of this is the Americans' continuing aggression against the Iraqi people using the Peninsula as a staging post, even though all its rulers are against their territories being used to that end, but they are helpless.

Second, despite the great devastation inflicted on the Iraqi people by the crusader-Zionist alliance, and despite the huge number of those killed, which has exceeded 1 million . . . despite all this, the Americans are once again trying to repeat the horrific massacres, as though they are not content with the protracted blockade imposed after the ferocious war or the fragmentation and devastation.

So here they come to annihilate what is left of this people and to humiliate their Muslim neighbors.

Third, if the Americans' aims behind these wars are religious and economic, the aim is also to serve the Jews' petty state and divert attention from its occupation of Jerusalem and murder of Muslims there. The best proof of this is their eagerness to destroy Iraq, the strongest neighboring Arab state, and their endeavor to fragment all the states of the region such as Iraq, Saudi Arabia, Egypt, and Sudan into paper statelets and through their disunion and weakness to guarantee Israel's survival and the continuation of the brutal crusade occupation of the Peninsula.

All these crimes and sins committed by the Americans are a clear declaration of war on God, his messenger, and Muslims. And ulema have throughout Islamic history unanimously agreed that the jihad is an individual duty if the enemy destroys the Muslim countries. This was revealed by Imam Bin-Qadamah in "Al-Mughni," Imam al-Kisa'i in "Al-Bada'i," al-Qurtubi in his interpretation, and the shaykh of al-Islam in his books, where he said: "As for the fighting to repulse [an enemy], it is aimed at defending sanctity and religion, and it is a duty as agreed [by the ulema]. Nothing is more sacred than belief except repulsing an enemy who is attacking religion and life."

On that basis, and in compliance with God's order, we issue the following fatwa to all Muslims:

The ruling to kill the Americans and their allies—civilians and military—is an individual duty for every Muslim who can do it in any country in which it is possible to do it, in order to liberate the al-Aqsa Mosque and the holy mosque [Mecca] from their grip, and in order for their armies to move out of all the lands of Islam, defeated and unable to threaten any Muslim. This is in accordance with the words of Almighty God, "and fight the pagans all together as they fight you all together," and "fight them until there is no more tumult or oppression, and there prevail justice and faith in God."

This is in addition to the words of Almighty God: "And why should ye not fight in the cause of God and of those who, being weak, are ill-treated (and oppressed)?—women and children, whose cry is: 'Our Lord, rescue us from this town, whose people are oppressors; and raise for us from thee one who will help!"

We—with God's help—call on every Muslim who believes in God and wishes to be rewarded to comply with God's order to kill the Americans and plunder their money wherever and whenever they find it. We also call on Muslim ulema, leaders, youths, and soldiers to launch the raid on Satan's U.S. troops and the devil's supporters allying with them, and to displace those who are behind them so that they may learn a lesson.

Almighty God said: "Oh ye who believe, give your response to God and His Apostle, when He calleth you to that which will give you life. And know that God cometh between a man and his heart, and that it is He to whom ye shall all be gathered."

Almighty God also says: "O ye who believe, what is the matter with you, that when ye are asked to go forth in the cause of God, ye cling so heavily to the earth! Do ye prefer the life of this world to the hereafter? But little is the comfort of this life, as compared with the hereafter. Unless ye go forth, He will punish you with a grievous penalty, and put others in your place; but Him ye would not harm in the least. For God hath power over all things."

Almighty God also says: "So lose no heart, nor fall into despair. For ye must gain mastery if ye are true in faith."

PART V

Terrorist Groups and Methods

THE VARIETY of terrorist groups is as broad as the array of issues, ethnicities, and religions that motivate people. Annual surveys like the State Department's, which appears earlier, provide capsule commentaries on the most important movements. The paper on Near Eastern Groups and State Sponsors which leads this section uses that material along with other research to provide more detailed commentaries. They concentrate primarily on movements in the Middle East, the main theater of activity in the present war on terrorism. Although there is a certain amount of overlap between the treatments here and in the State Department's *Patterns of Global Terrorism*, both have been included in order to take advantage of the depth of the present study and the scope of the State Department's effort. The paper also contains a useful discussion of strategies to counter terrorism and some of the actions taken against these organizations in recent years. The acronym FTO that appears in the paper refers to Foreign Terrorist Organization. An SDT is a Specially Designated Terrorist.

In most of the huge outpouring of commentary that has appeared recently on the subjects of new terrorist targets or methods—such as whether groups like the Al Qaeda will attack with chemical or biological weapons, or will hack into computer networks to disrupt security or financial systems or other key services—little attention has been paid to some of the practical difficulties involved. The assumption seems to be that technology, techniques, and tactics are perfectly fungible and can be changed without effort or cost. The second reading in this section provides a much more nuanced view of the steps actually required to assimilate new technology. The author, a RAND Corporation analyst and academic expert on the subject, discusses the general question of innovation as it relates to terrorist groups and uses the analogy of a large corporation or other organization to define the dimensions of the problem.

Although these materials speak to overall aspects of the present situation regarding terrorism, they are less revealing of the specifics of terrorist operations. These details come into better focus in the third reading of this section, a terrorist manual. Several earlier documents of this kind exist. One was entered into evidence at the trial of suspects who were convicted for the 1993 bombing of the World Trade Center. It had been in the possession of one of the defendants, Ahmad M. Ajaj, who had spent four months in Pakistan the previous year. Mistranslated at the time, the manual covered necessary subjects in making and detonating bombs and had been published by Al Qaeda in Afghanistan in 1989. The second document was a CD-ROM recovered by Belgian police in 1995 from a member of an Algerian terrorist cell in Brussels. It contained several versions of a manual known to have circulated among terrorist cells in Western Europe in the early 1990s. It covered a broad range of subjects, from CIA recruitment methods to Israeli intelligence organization to the place of psychological warfare in Islam. A third document of this type is a multi-volume study called the "Encyclopedia of the Afghan Jihad," seized by Jordanian authorities during their investigations into failed terrorist disruption of the millennium celebrations in 2000.

A different manual is included here. This one is more of a nuts-and-bolts approach to field operations. It includes such subjects as maintaining the secrecy of meetings, houses, bases, and members; the use of communications; codes and ciphers; the proper use of pistols, rifles, and explosives in assassinations; and other related items. Unlike some of the other documents in this volume, the manual draws almost all its examples from Arab or Islamic experience, such as allusions to historical events in the Muslim past, operations against Israeli targets, or the attempted assassinations of government ministers in some countries and of Egyptian President Hosni Mubarak while visiting Ethiopia in 1995. Titled "Military Studies in the Jihad Against the Tyrants," the manual consists of eighteen "lessons," each on one of its discreet subjects. The editing here has excluded much of the more esoteric material, such as lessons on codes or weapons, in order to use available space for material that shows tactical procedures. Written in Arabic and clearly from the pen or pens of devout fundamentalists, the manual nevertheless goes out of its way in several places to warn users to avoid Arab dress, shave beards, and take other measures to blend in with Western societies.

This manual was in the possession of Anas al-Liby, a thirty-seven-year-old member of a Libyan group opposed to the government of Muammar Qaddhafi. He worked with Ali A. Mohamed, a participant in the Islamic circle in Brooklyn that hatched plots against targets in New York in 1993 (Mohamed later became an informant for U.S. authorities). Liby also had connections with Al Qaeda and in some accounts is identified as its leading computer specialist until a 1995 split over money. He is alleged to have participated in Al Qaeda's scouting of the U.S. embassy in Nairobi in 1993 and 1995, taking photographs for planning purposes. In any case, Liby lived in Manchester, England, until discovering he was under suspicion, when he disappeared. Scotland Yard raided his apartment in May 2000 to find that Liby had flown the coop, but detectives seized a trove of computer materials and documents, including the "Military Studies" manual. Liby was indicted in the United States in December 2000 for conspiracy to bomb the Nairobi embassy, and in October 2001 he was included in the FBI's list of most-wanted terrorists.

Although there is no evidence that the perpetrators of the September 11 attacks used or had access to the "Military Studies" manual, there are plentiful indications that the assailants took the same or similar security measures. For example, the manual advises against putting all "operational funds" in one place, it favors leaving money with nonmembers of the cell and spending it as needed. Investigation of the activities of participants prior to September 11 has established that money *was* parceled out and distributed in increments, many by a certain individual in Bahrain with links to Al Qaeda, and others from bank accounts in Western Europe thought to be controlled by Osama bin Laden. Similarly the manual warns that communication should be carried out from public places, and indeed the September 11 hijackers kept in touch by e-mails sent from computers in public libraries.

Al Qaeda has also typically used go-betweens to shield leaders from direct involvement in plots. In the 1998 embassy bombings at Nairobi and Dar es Salaam, a senior supervisor was in and out of Kenya days in advance of the attacks, evidently finalizing details of the plot. The same individual, in fact, was in Yemen in January 2000, shortly before the failure of a plot to attack a U.S. warship in the port of Aden, and again before the successful October 2000 attack in Aden against the *USS Cole*. This individual was spotted on film from a surveillance camera in Malaysia early in 2001, meeting with one of the team leaders of the attacks of September 11, 2001. The security measures taken in all these activities were of a high order, comparable to those of intelligence agents and their case officers.

Terrorist groups also make considerable use of the globe as, in effect, an international locale for dispersing their personnel and activities. The mastermind of the 1993 attack against the World Trade Center, Ramsi Ahmad Youssef, shuttled between the United States and Pakistan before the attacks, is linked in some accounts to Iraq, and fled to the Philippines, from where he again went to Pakistan. In the Philippines, Youssef associated with others, including another participant in the World Trade Center operation, and plotted to murder the pope, destroy airliners, and fly one into the headquarters building outside Washington of the Central Intelligence Agency. The Al Qaeda apparently forged links in the early 1990s with the Filipino Muslim group Abu Sayyaf through personal connections between Osama bin Laden and Filipino terrorist leaders, and these may have helped Youssef when he sought shelter. Similarly bin Laden had been an early associate of the founder of the Armed Islamic Front in Algeria, and in the plot to disrupt millennium celebrations in 2000 the Al Qaeda operative sent to bomb Los Angeles International Airport turned out to be an Algerian. A Jordanian fundamentalist group with ties to Al Qaeda received help in the early 1990s for a string of bombings of movie theaters and other cultural targets it deemed corrupt, then made its own contribution to the millennium plot. Also late in 2000, Kuwaiti police arrested a suspect with Al Qaeda links who revealed a cache of three hundred pounds of explosives and fourteen hundred detonators and reported that attacks against Kuwaiti and local American targets had been planned. The modus operandi seems to be that terrorist groups in different cities or countries develop plans which they propose to Al Qaeda senior representatives; the plots are then accepted or rejected for Al Qaeda support. These patterns are not clear in the terrorist manual below, but they are representative of the same kind of approach that is reflected in the manual's strictures.

Terrorism: Near Eastern Groups and State Sponsors, 2001

Kenneth Katzman,
Foreign Affairs, Defense, and Trade Division,
September 10, 2001

SUMMARY

Signs continue to point to a decline in state sponsorship of terrorism, as well as a rise in the scope of threat posed by the independent network of exiled Saudi dissident Usama bin Ladin. During the 1980s and the early 1990s, Iran and terrorist groups it sponsors were responsible for the most politically significant acts of Middle Eastern terrorism. Although Iran continues to actively sponsor terrorist groups, since 1997 some major factions within Iran have sought to change Iran's image to that of a more constructive force in the region. Pressured by international sanctions and isolation, Sudan and Libya appear to have sharply reduced their support for international terrorist groups, and Sudan has told the United States it wants to work to achieve removal from the "terrorism list."

Usama bin Ladin's network, which is independently financed and enjoys safe haven in Afghanistan, poses an increasingly significant threat to U.S. interests in the Near East and perhaps elsewhere. The primary goals of bin Ladin and his cohort are to oust pro-U.S. regimes in the Middle East and gain removal of U.S. troops from the region. Based on U.S. allegations of past plotting by the bin Ladin network, suggest that the network wants to strike within the United States itself.

The Arab-Israeli peace process is a longstanding major U.S. foreign policy interest, and the Administration and Congress are concerned about any terrorist groups or state sponsors that oppose the Arab-Israel peace process. Possibly because of a breakdown in the Palestinian-Israeli peace process in September 2000, Palestinian Islamic organizations such as Hamas have stepped up operations against Israelis, after a few years of diminished terrorist activity. Some observers blame Palestinian Authority President Yasir Arafat, accusing his regime of ending efforts to constrain these and other groups. Others assert that Israel's actions against the Palestinians have been provocative and have contributed to increased Palestinian support for violence against Israel.

There is no consensus on the strategies for countering terrorism in the Near East. The United States, in many cases, differs with its allies on how to deal with state sponsors of terrorism; most allied governments believe that engaging these countries diplomatically might sometimes be more effective than trying to isolate or punish them. The United States is more inclined than its European allies to employ sanctions, military action, and legal pressure to compel state sponsors and groups to abandon terrorism. In a few cases since 1998, the United States has pursued an engagement strategy by easing sanctions or conducting dialogue with those state sponsors willing to distance themselves from international terrorism. The United States also believes that greater counterterrorism cooperation with allies and other countries, including Russia, is yielding benefits in reducing the threat from terrorism.

INTRODUCTION

Please Note: This report was completed immediately prior to the terrorist attacks on the World Trade Center and the Pentagon on September 11, 2001. It is offered as essential background for policymakers.

This report is an annual analysis of Near Eastern terrorist groups and countries on the U.S. "terrorism list," a list of countries that the Secretary of Commerce and Secretary of State have determined provide repeated support for international terrorism. Five out of the seven states currently on the terrorism list are located in the Near East region—Iran, Iraq, Syria, Libya, and Sudan. (The other two are Cuba and North Korea, which will not be covered in this report). The composition of the list has not changed since Sudan was added in 1993. The groups analyzed in this report include, but are not limited to, those designated as "Foreign Terrorist Organizations" (FTO's), pursuant to the Anti-Terrorism and Effective Death Penalty Act of 1996 (P.L. 104-132). The last section of the report discusses significant themes in U.S. unilateral and multilateral efforts to combat terrorism in or from the region. The State Department's annual report on international terrorism, entitled *Patterns of Global Terrorism: 2000* is a significant source for this report; other sources include press reports and conversations with U.S. counter-terrorism officials, experts, investigative journalists, and foreign diplomats.

Near Eastern terrorist groups and their state sponsors have been the focus of U.S. counter-terrorism policies for several decades. Since the 1970s, many of the most high-profile acts of terrorism against American citizens and targets have been conducted by these groups, sometimes with the encouragement or at the instigation of their state sponsors. Few recent terrorist attacks — either in or outside the Near East region — compare in scale to the August 7, 1998 bombings of the U.S. embassies in Kenya and Tanzania, which killed 224 persons, including 12 Americans. The October 12, 2000 bombing of the U.S. destroyer Cole in the harbor of Aden, Yemen, killed 17 U.S. Navy personnel, nearly sank the ship, and caused at least a temporary halt in growing U.S. military relations with Yemen. . . .

The terrorist groups analyzed often differ in their motivations, objectives, ideologies, and levels of activity. The Islamist groups remain generally the most active, stating as their main objective the overthrow of secular, pro-Western governments, the derailment of the Arab-Israeli peace process, the expulsion of U.S. forces from the region, or the end of what they consider unjust occupation of Muslim lands. Some groups, such as the Kurdistan Workers' Party (PKK), fight for cultural and political rights or the formation of separate ethnically-based states. Table 1 below shows the 19 Near Eastern groups currently designated by the State Department as FTO's. The designations were mostly made when the FTO list was inaugurated in October 1997 and revised in October 1999. A revised list is due out in October 2001. A group can be added to the list at any time; Al-Qaida (the bin Ladin network) was added on August 21, 1998 and the Islamic Movement of Uzbekistan was designated on September 25, 2000.

Under the Anti-Terrorism and Effective Death Penalty Act, the designation of a group as an FTO blocks its assets in the United States and makes it a criminal offense for U.S. persons to provide it with material support or resources, such as financial contributions. Executive order 12947 of January 23, 1995, also bars U.S. dealings (contributions to or financial transactions) with any individuals named as "Specially Designated Terrorists (SDTs)." An SDT, according to the Executive order, is a person found to pose a significant risk of disrupting the Middle East peace process, or to have materially supported acts of violence toward that end.

In contrast to Patterns 2000, this report analyzes the following:

- The Palestine Liberation Organization (PLO), which has not been the subject of a separate section in Patterns since Patterns 1995, is analyzed in this report because of the debate over whether or not PLO leader Yasir Arafat is taking sufficient steps to prevent terrorism by other groups in areas under the control of the Palestinian Authority. Since late 2000, there has been discussion about the degree to which certain PLO factions are involved in violence against Israel and whether or not they should be named as FTO's.

- When the FTO list was reviewed and re-issued in October 1999, the Democratic Front for the Liberation of Palestine (DFLP) was dropped, largely because it has reconciled with Arafat. The group's past involvement in terrorism, and the recent revival of its operations against Israel, are discussed in this report.

- This report, in contrast to last year's, contains a section on the Abu Sayyaf Group operating in the Philippines, as well as analysis of several Pakistani Islamist groups that are fighting Indian control of part of Kashmir Province. These groups are discussed in this report, even though they operate outside the Near East region, because of their alleged connections to the bin Ladin network and the Taliban of Afghanistan.

Table 1. Near Eastern Foreign Terrorist Organizations (FTOs)

Group	Description	Terrorist Activity Level
Abu Nidal Organization	Palestinian, nationalist	Very Low
Abu Sayyaf Group	Filipino, Islamist	Moderate
Armed Islamic Group	Algerian, Islamist	Moderate
Hamas	Palestinian, Islamist	Very High
Harakat ul-Mujahidin	Kashmir, Islamist	High
Hizballah	Lebanese, Shiite Islamist	High
Islamic Group	Egyptian, Islamist	Moderate
Islamic Movement of Uzbekistan	Uzbek, Islamist	Moderate
Al-Jihad	Egyptian, Islamist	Moderate
Kach	Jewish extremist	Low
Kahane Chai	Jewish extremist	Low
Kurdistan Workers' Party	Kurdish, anti-Turkey	Low
Palestinian Islamic Jihad	Palestinian, Islamist	Very High
Palestine Liberation Front	Palestinian, nationalist	Very Low
Popular Front for the Liberation of Palestine	Palestinian, Marxist	Low
Popular Front for the Liberation of Palestine— General Command	Palestinian, nationalist	Moderate

Group	Description	Terrorist Activity Level
People's Mojahedin Organization of Iran	Iranian, leftwing anti-regime	Moderate
Al-Qaida (Bin Ladin Network)	Multinational Islamist, Afghanistan-based	Extremely High
Revolutionary People's Liberation Party/Front	Turkish, leftwing anti-government	Low

RADICAL ISLAMIC GROUPS

Since the 1979 Islamic revolution in Iran, and particularly since the seizure of the U.S. Embassy in Tehran in November of that year, radical Islam has attracted widespread press attention as the driving ideology of the most active Middle Eastern terrorist groups and state sponsors. Of the 19 FTOs listed above, ten are Islamic organizations.

Hizballah (Party of God)

Lebanon-based Hizballah appears to be groping for direction following Israel's May 2000 withdrawal from Lebanon. Having accomplished its main goal of ousting Israel from southern Lebanon, some in the organization want it to change from a guerrilla and terrorist organization into a mainstream political movement, focusing mainly on its work in parliament (it holds 8 out of 128 total seats) and its charity and reconstruction works with Lebanon's Shiite community. Hardliners in Hizballah want it to battle Israeli forces over the border and in the disputed Shib'a farms area. Other hardliners in the organization believe that the Israeli withdrawal validated its guerrilla strategy and are helping Palestinian groups apply similar tactics against Israeli forces in the West Bank and Gaza Strip.

Although initially encouraged by Hizballah's relative restraint following the Israeli withdrawal, Israel and the United States remain wary of Hizballah. Hizballah's 15 year military campaign against Israeli and Israeli surrogate forces in southern Lebanon—activity that is not technically considered terrorism by the U.S. State Department—often included rocket attacks on Israeli civilians. Even though the United Nations has certified that Israel's withdrawal is complete, Hizballah has asserted that Israel still occupies some Lebanese territory (the Shib'a farms) and, on that basis, has conducted a few military attacks on Israel since the withdrawal. In October 2000, Hizballah captured three Israeli soldiers in the Shib'a farms area and kidnapped an Israeli noncombatant whom it had lured to Lebanon. Hizballah has indicated a willingness to return these captives in exchange for several Lebanese prisoners captured or kidnapped by Israel since the late 1980s.

Founded in 1982 by Lebanese Shiite clerics inspired by the Islamic revolutionary ideology of Iran's Ayatollah Khomeini, Hizballah's original goal was to establish an Islamic republic in Lebanon. During the 1980s, Hizballah was a principal sponsor of anti-Western, and particularly anti-U.S., terrorism. It is known or suspected to have been involved in suicide truck bombings of the U.S. Embassy (April 1983), the U.S. Marine barracks (October 1983, killing 220 Marine, 18 Navy and 3 Army personnel), and the U.S. Embassy annex (September 1984), all in Beirut. It also hijacked TWA Flight 847 in 1985, killing a Navy diver, Robert Stethem, who was on board, and its factions were responsible for the detention of most, if not all, U.S. and Western hostages held in Lebanon during the 1980s and early 1990s. Eighteen Americans were held hostage in Lebanon during that period, three of whom were killed.

In the early 1990s, Hizballah also demonstrated an ability to conduct terrorism far from the Middle East. In May 1999, Argentina's Supreme Court, after an official investigation, formally blamed Hizballah for the March 17, 1992 bombing of Israel's embassy in Buenos Aires and issued an arrest warrant for Hizballah terrorist leader Imad Mughniyah. Hizballah did not claim responsibility for the attack outright, but it released a surveillance tape of the embassy, implying responsibility. In May 1998, FBI Director Louis Freeh told Argentina the FBI believes that Hizballah, working with Iranian diplomats, was also responsible for the July 18, 1994 bombing of the Argentine-Jewish Mutual Association (AMIA) building in Buenos Aires that left 86 dead. In July 1999, Argentine investigators brought charges against 20 suspected Argentine collaborators in the AMIA bombings, and the trial is set to begin in September 2001.

Hizballah has continued to conduct surveillance of the U.S. Embassy in Lebanon and its personnel, according to recent Patterns reports, but no major terrorist attacks have been attributed to it since 1994. However, according to numerous press reports and Hizballah leaders' own statements, the organization is helping Palestinian groups fight against Israel in the latest Palestinian uprising, which began in September 2000. In late August 2001, Jordanian officials discovered a cache of rockets at a Hizballah-owned location in Jordan, igniting fears that Hizballah might fire rockets on Israel from there or might provide the weapons to Palestinian militants there or in the West Bank.

Hizballah's Persian Gulf Connections. Hizballah maintains connections with similar groups in the Persian Gulf. Saudi and Bahraini investigations of anti-regime unrest have revealed the existence of local chapters of Hizballah composed of Shiite Muslims, many of whom have studied in Iran's theological seminaries and received terrorist training there and in Lebanon. Saudi and U.S. officials believe that Saudi Shiite Muslims with connections to Lebanese

Hizballah were responsible for the June 25, 1996 bombing of the Khobar Towers housing complex for U.S. military personnel, near Dhahran, Saudi Arabia. This allegation was reaffirmed in the June 2001 U.S. indictments of 14 Khobar suspects. According to Patterns 1998, in November 1998 Bahraini authorities uncovered an alleged bomb plot that they blamed on persons linked to Bahraini and Lebanese Hizballah.

Patterns 1999 reiterates that Hizballah receives "substantial" amounts of financial assistance, weapons, and political and organizational support from both Syria and Iran, although it does not mention specific figures. Then Secretary of State Christopher said on May 21, 1996 that Iran gave Hizballah about $100 million per year, a figure that U.S. officials have not since deviated from. About 150 of Iran's Revolutionary Guards remain in Lebanon to coordinate Iran's aid to Hizballah. Syria permits Iran to supply weapons to Hizballah through the international airport in Damascus, although a recent Turkish shutdown of the air corridor connecting Iran and Syria has made Iranian deliveries more difficult. . . .

Blocked Assets. According to the Treasury Department's "Terrorist Assets Report" for 2000, the Bureau of alcohol, Tobacco and Firearms has seized $283,000 in assets belonging to 18 persons arrested in North Carolina in July 2000 on suspicion of smuggling goods to generate funds for Hizballah.

Hamas and Palestinian Islamic Jihad (PIJ)

Prior to the September 2000 outbreak of the Palestinian uprising, it appeared that the bulk of the leadership of the Sunni Muslim Palestinian group Hamas (Islamic Resistance Movement) was accommodating Yasir Arafat's leadership of the Palestinian Authority (PA). Hamas leaders also appeared resigned to an eventual final peace agreement between Israel and the PA, although they continued to criticize Arafat as too eager to compromise with Israel. Since the uprising began, Hamas and its smaller ally, Palestinian Islamic Jihad (PIJ), have escalated terrorist attacks against Israelis. Hamas claimed responsibility for the June 1, 2001 suicide bombing of the "Dolphinarium" discotheque in Tel Aviv, which killed 21, and for an August 9, 2001 suicide bombing at a pizza restaurant in Jerusalem that killed 18, including one American. PIJ has conducted several recent suicide bombings, many of which killed only the bomber(s). Many experts believe that the renewed terrorist activity is at least partly attributable to a breakdown in security cooperation between Israel and the Palestinian Authority—cooperation that was widely credited with keeping terrorist attacks to a minimum in the preceding few years. The renewed terrorist threat has led Israel to adopt a policy—criticized by the United States and many other countries—of assassinating Hamas and PIJ activists to preempt their suspected attacks.

Hamas was formed by Muslim Brotherhood activists during the early stages of the earlier Palestinian uprising (intifada) in 1987. Its spiritual leader, Shaykh Ahmad Yassin, who is paralyzed, was released from prison by Israel in October 1997. He seems to serve as a bridge between Hamas' two main components— the extremists who orchestrate terrorist attacks (primarily through a clandestine wing, the Izz ad-Din al-Qassam Brigades), and the more moderate elements affiliated with Hamas' social services, charity, and educational institutions. PIJ was, in part, inspired by the Iranian revolution of 1979 even though PIJ is a Sunni Muslim, not a Shiite Muslim organization. PIJ remains almost purely a guerrilla organization, with no overt component. It is led by Ramadan Abdullah Shallah, a Gaza-born, 43 year old academic who previously was an adjunct professor at the University of South Florida. He was chosen leader in 1995 after his predecessor, Fathi al-Shiqaqi was assassinated, allegedly by Israeli agents. Recent Patterns reports characterizes Hamas' strength as "an unknown number of hardcore members [and] tens of thousands of supporters and sympathizers," and PIJ's strength as "unknown."

Hamas receives funding from Iran, from wealthy private benefactors in the Persian Gulf monarchies, and Palestinian expatriates, according to Patterns 2000, which adds that the group conducts fundraising and propaganda activities in Western Europe and North America. Many individual donors appear to believe their contributions go to charitable activities for poor Palestinians served by Hamas' social services network, and are not being used for terrorism. PIJ is politically closer to Iran than is Hamas, and apparently derives most of its funding from state sponsors, especially Iran. PIJ receives some logistical support from Syria, according to Patterns 2000.

Hamas and PIJ have not targeted the United States or Americans directly, although Americans have died in attacks by these groups, along with Israelis and often the bombers themselves. Five out of the 65 killed in a series of four Hamas/PIJ bombings in Israel during February—March 1996 were American citizens. These bombings had the apparent effect of shifting public opinion toward Benjamin Netanyahu in Israeli national elections on May 29, 1996, possibly proving decisive in his election victory as Prime Minister over then Labor Party leader Shimon Peres. Neither group conducted major attacks in the run-up to the May 1999 Israeli elections, although they did carry out attacks in an attempt to derail the negotiation and implementation of the October 23, 1998 Israeli-Palestinian Wye River Memorandum. In total, the two groups have conducted about 80 suicide bombings or attempted suicide bombings, killing more than 450 Israelis, since the signing of the Israeli-PLO Declaration of Principles in 1993.

Blocked Assets. The United States has blocked the assets of some alleged Hamas/PIJ leaders, using the authority of President Clinton's January 23, 1995 Executive order on Middle East terrorism. As of the end of 2000, a total of about $17,000 in PIJ assets in the United States were blocked, consisting of a bank account belonging to PIJ leader Shallah.

SDTs. Several Hamas and PIJ activists have been named as SDTs. They include: (1) Hamas founder Shaykh Ahmad Yassin; (2) PIJ leader Ramadan Abdullah Shallah; (3) PIJ ideologist Abd al-Aziz Awda; (4) Hamas political leader Musa Abu Marzuq, who was barred from returning to Jordan when that country shut Hamas's offices in Amman in August 1999; and (5) alleged U.S. fundraiser for Hamas, Mohammad Salah.

The Islamic Group and Al-Jihad

Egyptian security authorities continue to gain the upper hand in their battle against the opposition Islamic Group and its ally, Al-Jihad, groups that, over the past several decades, periodically have gone underground and then resurfaced. There have been no large scale terrorist attacks by these groups since the Islamic Group's November 17, 1997 attack on tourists near Luxor, and no attacks inside Egypt at all since August 1998. The gunmen in the Luxor attack killed 58 tourists and wounded 26 others, and then committed suicide or were killed by Egyptian security forces. Sensing that they are on the defensive and that terrorism has made them unpopular, in late 1997 leaders of both groups, including their common spiritual leader, the 63 year old blind cleric Shaykh Umar Abd al-Rahman, declared a ceasefire with the Egyptian government. Muhammad Hamza, who is in operational control of the Islamic Group in Egypt while Abd al-Rahman remains incarcerated in the United States, has abided by the truce.

Despite the decline of the groups' activities within Egypt, factions of the groups that are in exile have gravitated to the network of Usama bin Ladin. Several SDTs from the Islamic Group and Al-Jihad now serve in bin Ladin's inner circle as his top lieutenants, including Ayman al-Zawahiri, Rifai Taha Musa, and Abu Hafs Masri (Mohammad Atef). These leaders forswear any truce with the Egyptian government and also seek, in concert with bin Ladin, to attack U.S. interests directly.

Abd al-Rahman was not convicted specifically for the February 1993 bombing of the World Trade Center in New York, but he was convicted for related unsuccessful plots in the New York area, and those convicted in the Trade Center bombing were allegedly associated with him. There has been much speculation about the relationship, if any, between Abd al-Rahman and bin Ladin. Both recruited fighters for the Afghan conflict against the Soviet Union through centers in the United States and elsewhere, but it is not clear that the two men had any direct contact with each other in Afghanistan. The two also had close connections to the Islamic government of Sudan, although Abd al-Rahman left Sudan in 1990, before bin Ladin relocated there. Abd al-Rahman's two sons reportedly have been in or around Afghanistan since the war ended in 1989. Before the February 1993 World Trade Center bombing, some of Abd al-Rahman's aides reportedly had personal contact with bin Ladin associates in the United States. Although their recruiting presence has raised questions as to whether or not the United States gave bin Ladin or Abd al-Rahman assistance during the Afghan war, the Central Intelligence Agency has told CRS that it found no evidence that the Agency provided any direct assistance to either of them. The U.S. assistance program for the anti-Soviet groups in Afghanistan focused primarily on indigenous Afghan mujahedin and not Arab volunteers such as those sponsored by bin Ladin or Abd al-Rahman.

The Islamic Group and Al-Jihad formed in the early 1970s as offshoots of the Muslim Brotherhood, which opted to work within the political system after being crushed by former President Gamal Abd al-Nasser. Both seek to replace Egypt's pro-Western, secular government with an Islamic state. Al-Jihad was responsible for the assassination of President Anwar Sadat in October 1981. The Islamic Group has been responsible for several attacks on high-ranking Egyptian officials, including the killing of the People's Assembly Speaker in October 1990 and the wounding of the Minister of Information in April 1993. The Islamic Group also has a nonviolent arm which recruits and builds support openly in poor neighborhoods in Cairo, Alexandria and throughout southern Egypt, and runs social service programs. Al-Jihad has operated only clandestinely, focusing almost exclusively on assassinations.

SDTs. The following Egyptian Islamist figures have been named as SDTs: (1) Shaykh Umar Abd al-Rahman, who was acquitted in 1984 of inciting Egyptian President Anwar Sadat's assassination, is in a medical detention facility in Missouri following his October 1995 conviction for planning terrorist conspiracies in the New York area; (2) Ayman al-Zawahiri, about 50, who is a top lieutenant of bin Ladin (see below) and was convicted in Egypt for the Sadat assassination; (3) Rifa'i Taha Musa, about 47, another top aide to bin Ladin; (4) Abbud al-Zumar, leader of the remnants of the original Jihad who is serving a 40 year sentence in Egypt; (5) Talat Qasim, about 44, a propaganda leader of the Islamic Group; and (6) Muhammad Shawqi Islambouli, about 46, the brother of the lead gunman in the Sadat assassination. Islambouli, a military leader of the Islamic Group, also is believed to be associated with bin Ladin in Afghanistan.

Al-Qaida (Usama bin Ladin Network)

Over the past six years, Al-Qaida (Arabic for "the base"), the network of Usama bin Ladin, has evolved from a regional threat to U.S. troops in the Persian Gulf to a global threat to U.S. citizens and national security interests. In building this network, bin Ladin has assembled a coalition of disparate radical Islamic groups of varying nationalities to work toward common goals—the expulsion of non-

Muslim control or influence from Muslim-inhabited lands. The network's ideology, laid out in several pronouncements signed by bin Ladin and his allies, has led bin Ladin to support Islamic fighters or terrorists against Serb forces in Bosnia; against Soviet forces in Afghanistan and now Russian forces in Chechnya; against Indian control over part of Kashmir; against secular or pro-Western governments in Egypt, Algeria, Saudi Arabia, and Uzbekistan; and against U.S. troops and citizens in the Persian Gulf, Somalia, Yemen, Jordan, and against the U.S. mainland itself.

The backbone of the Saudi dissident's network is the ideological and personal bond among the Arab volunteers who were recruited by bin Ladin for the fight against the Soviet occupation of Afghanistan (1979–1989). Financially, it draws on the personal fortune of bin Ladin, estimated at about $300 million, but also reportedly including funding from many other sources. Al-Qaida now encompasses members and factions of several major Islamic militant organizations, including Egypt's Islamic Group and Al-Jihad, Algeria's Armed Islamic Group, Pakistan's Harakat ul-Mujahidin, the Islamic Movement of Uzbekistan, and opposition groups in Saudi Arabia. The network reportedly also has links to the Abu Sayyaf Islamic separatist group in the Philippines. Although there are few evident links to Hamas, bin Ladin was a follower of Dr. Abdullah al-Azzam, a Palestinian of Jordanian origin who was influential in the founding of both Hamas and al-Qaida. Reflecting its low level of early activity, al-Qaida was not discussed in U.S. government reports until Patterns 1993. That report, which did not mention a formal group name, said that several thousand non-Afghan Muslims fought in the war against the Soviets and the Afghan Communist government during 1979 to 1992. Although the Taliban movement of Afghanistan, which controls about 90% of that country, gives bin Ladin and his subordinates safehaven, bin Ladin does not appear to be acting on behalf of the Taliban, or vice versa.

Bin Ladin's network has been connected to a number of acts of terrorism. Bin Ladin himself has been indicted by a U.S. court for involvement in several of them. They include the following:

- Bin Ladin has claimed responsibility for the December 1992 attempted bombings against 100 servicemen in Yemen—there to support U.N. relief operations in Somalia (Operation Restore Hope). No one was killed.
- In press interviews, bin Ladin has openly boasted that he provided weapons to anti-U.S. militias in Somalia during Operation Restore Hope and that his loyalists fought against U.S. forces there. His involvement with the Somali militias appeared to have strengthened his view that terrorism and low-technology combat can succeed in causing the United States to withdraw from military involvement abroad.

- The four Saudi nationals who confessed to the November 13, 1995 bombing of a U.S. military training facility in Riyadh, Saudi Arabia, admitted on Saudi television to being inspired by bin Ladin and other Islamic radicals. Three of the confessors were veterans of conflicts in Afghanistan, Bosnia, and Chechnya.
- According to Patterns 1997, members of bin Ladin's organization might have aided the Islamic Group assassination attempt against Egyptian President Mubarak in Ethiopia in June 1995.
- There is no direct evidence that bin Ladin was involved in the February 1993 bombing of the World Trade Center. However, Patterns 1999 says that bin Ladin's network was responsible for plots in Asia believed orchestrated by Ramzi Ahmad Yusuf, who was captured in Pakistan, brought to the United States, and convicted in November 1997 of masterminding the Trade Center bombing. The plots in Asia, all of which failed, were: to assassinate the Pope during his late 1994 visit to the Philippines and President Clinton during his visit there in early 1995; to bomb the U.S. and Israeli embassies in Manila in late 1994; and to bomb U.S. trans-Pacific flights.
- The August 7, 1998 U.S. embassy bombings in Kenya and Tanzania, which killed 224 persons, including 12 American citizens, occurred just after a six month period in which bin Ladin had issued repeated and open threats, including a February 1998 pronouncement calling for the killing of U.S. civilians and servicemen worldwide. On August 20, 1998, the United States launched cruise missiles on bin Ladin's training camps in eastern Afghanistan, based on U.S. evidence of his network's involvement in the bombings. The United States also struck a pharmaceutical plant in Sudan that the Administration alleged was linked to bin Ladin and was producing chemical weapons agents. U.S. officials add that the bombings were intended to disrupt planning for a new attack. For their alleged role in the bombings, 17 alleged members of al-Qaida have been indicted by a U.S. court, including bin Ladin. Four of the six in U.S. custody have been tried and convicted; three are in custody in Britain.
- In December 1999, U.S. and Jordanian law enforcement authorities uncovered and thwarted two alleged plots—one in the United States and one in Jordan—to attack U.S. citizens celebrating the new millennium. The United States plot, allegedly to bomb Los Angeles international airport, was orchestrated by a pro-bin Ladin cell of Algerian Armed Islamic Group members coming from Canada. In June 2000, Jordan tried 28 who allegedly were planning to attack tourists during millennium festivities in that country, but 15 of those charged are still at large. Also in June 2000, Lebanon placed 29 alleged followers of bin Ladin on trial for planning

terrorist attacks in Jordan. The presence of bin Ladin cells in Jordan and Lebanon—coupled with Israeli arrests of alleged bin Ladin operatives in the West Bank and Gaza Strip—suggests that Al-Qaida might plan acts of terrorism in connection with the Palestinian uprising.

- Patterns 2000 says that "supporters" of bin Ladin are suspected in the October 12, 2000 bombing of the destroyer U.S.S. Cole in the harbor of the port of Aden, Yemen. The blast, which severely damaged the ship, killed 17 and injured 39 Navy personnel.

Since the August 1998 U.S. retaliatory strikes on the Afghan camps and the Sudan pharmaceutical plant, the Taliban leadership has tried to dissociate itself from bin Ladin by asserting that he is no longer its guest. However, Taliban officials have rebuffed repeated U.S. requests to extradite him, claiming that the United States has not provided the Taliban with convincing evidence that bin Ladin might have been involved in anti-U.S. terrorism. Adding to the U.S. concerns, several hundred U.S. shoulder-held anti-aircraft weapons ("Stingers") are still at large in Afghanistan, and, because of bin Ladin's financial resources, it is highly likely he has acquired some of them. U.S. officials say bin Ladin's fighters have experimented with chemical weapons and might be trying to purchase nuclear or other weapons of mass destruction materials. From those comments, it is reasonable to assume that bin Ladin's organization has at least a rudimentary chemical weapons capability.

SDTs/August 20, 1998 Executive Order. President Clinton's August 20, 1998 Executive Order 13099 amended an earlier January 23, 1995 Executive order (12947) by naming al-Qaida and its aliases (the World Islamic Front for Jihad Against Jews and Crusaders, the Islamic Army for the Liberation of the Holy Places, the Islamic Salvation Foundation, and the Group for the Preservation of the Holy Sites), as an FTO. The effect of the order was to ban U.S. financial transactions with bin Ladin's organization and to allow U.S. law enforcement to freeze any bin Ladin assets in the United States that can be identified. The order also named bin Ladin as an SDT, along with Rifai Taha Musa, of the Egyptian Islamic Group (see that section above) and another associate, Abu Hafs al-Masri (Mohammad Atef). Atef and Al-Jihad guerrilla leader Ayman al-Zawahiri (see above) were indicted along with bin Ladin on November 4, 1998 for the Kenya/Tanzania bombings; both are viewed as potential successors to bin Ladin. A $5 million reward is offered for the capture of Atef, who, according to the U.S. indictment against him, was sent by bin Ladin to Somalia in 1992 to determine how to combat U.S. troops sent there for Operation Restore Hope. Zawahiri, a medical doctor, met bin Ladin in the late 1980s in Afghanistan and is considered his closest adviser on policy and strategy.

Blocked Assets. No assets have been firmly linked to bin Ladin, in the

United States or elsewhere, and hence none are frozen at this time, according to the Treasury Department's report on terrorist assets for 2000. U.S. officials say they are encouraging other governments to help dismantle bin Ladin's financial empire and they have persuaded Saudi Arabia and the United Arab Emirates to end the handling of some of bin Ladin's money by a few of their banks. About $254 million in assets of the Taliban movement are blocked under Executive order 13129, issued in July 1999 on the grounds that the Taliban continued to harbor bin Ladin.

The Armed Islamic Group (GIA)

The Armed Islamic Group (GIA, after its initials in French) is experiencing pressure in Algeria similar to that faced by Egyptian Islamist groups in Egypt. According to Patterns 2000, a GIA splinter group, the Salafi Group for Call and Combat, is now the more active armed group inside Algeria, although it is considered somewhat less violent in its tactics than is the GIA. Led by Antar Zouabri, the GIA is highly fragmented, in part because it does not have an authoritative religious figure who can hold its various factions together and arbitrate disputes. Some GIA members in exile appear to have gravitated to bin Ladin's network, according to information coming out of the thwarted December 1999 plot to detonate a bomb in the United States. As noted above, it now appears that the target of the plot was Los Angeles international airport.

Founded by Algerian Islamists who fought in Afghanistan, the GIA formed as a breakaway faction of the then legal Islamic Salvation Front (FIS) political party in 1992, after the regime canceled the second round of parliamentary elections on fears of an FIS victory. According to Patterns 2000, the GIA has killed over 100 expatriates in Algeria (mostly Europeans) since 1992, but, in a possible indication of regime counterterrorism success, no foreigners have been killed in Algeria since 1997. Over the past six years, the GIA has conducted a campaign of civilian massacres, sometimes wiping out entire villages in their areas of operations, in an effort to intimidate rival groups and to demonstrate that the government lacks control over the country. The GIA conducted its most lethal terrorist attack on December 31, 1997, when it killed 400 Algerian civilians in a town 150 miles southwest of Algiers, according to Patterns 1997. It should be noted that there are allegations that elements of the regime's security forces and other opposition groups have also conducted civilian massacres. Among its acts outside Algeria, the GIA hijacked an Air France flight to Algiers in December 1994, and the group is suspected of bombing the Paris subway system on December 3, 1996, killing four. Patterns 2000 repeats previous descriptions of the GIA's strength as probably between several hundred to several thousand. The organization receives financial and logistical aid from Algerian expatriates, many of whom reside in Western Europe and in Canada.

Harakat ul-Mujahidin/Islamist Groups in Pakistan

The Harakat ul-Mujahidin (HUM) is a Pakistan-based Islamic militant group that seeks to end Indian control of Muslim-inhabited parts of the divided region of Kashmir. It is composed of militant Islamist Pakistanis and Kashmiris, as well as Arab veterans of the Afghan war against the Soviet Union who view the Kashmir struggle as a "jihad" (Islamic crusade). The HUM was included in the original October 1997 FTO designations when its name was Harakat al-Ansar. It subsequently changed its name to Harakat ul-Mujahidin, possibly in an attempt to avoid the U.S. sanctions that accompanied its designation as an FTO. Under its new name, the group was redesignated as an FTO in October 1999. An offshoot of the HUM kidnapped and reportedly later killed five Western tourists in Kashmir in 1995. The HUM is believed responsible for the December 1999 hijacking of an Indian airliner because the hijackers demanded the release of an HUM leader, Masood Azhar, in exchange for the release of the jet and its passengers (one of whom was killed by the hijackers).

The group appears to be allied with or part of bin Ladin's militant Islamic network, although its goal is the expulsion of Indian troops that occupy parts of Kashmir—it does not appear to be part of bin Ladin's more far-reaching struggle against the United States. A senior leader of the HUM, Fazlur Rehman Khalil, signed bin Ladin's February 1998 pronouncement calling for terrorist attacks on American troops and civilians and, according to Patterns 1999, some HUM fighters were killed in the August 20, 1998 U.S. retaliatory strikes on bin Ladin's training camps in Afghanistan. Khalil stepped down in February 2000 as leader of the HUM in favor of his second-in-command, Faruq Kashmiri. Kashmiri is not viewed as closely linked to bin Ladin as is Khalil, and the move could suggest that the HUM wants to distance itself from bin Ladin. Khalil remains as Secretary General of the organization.

Other Islamist Groups in Pakistan. The HUM fights alongside other Pakistani Islamist groups that have not been named as FTOs. They include the following:

- Jaish-e-Mohammed (JEM, Army of Mohammed). This is a more radical splinter group of the HUM formed by Masood Azhar (see above) in February 2000. The group is analyzed in a section of Patterns 2000 but it is not named as an FTO. The group, which attracted a large percentage (up to 75%) of HUM fighters who defected to it when it was formed, is politically aligned with bin Ladin, the Taliban, and the pro-Taliban Islamic Scholars Society (Jamiat-i Ulema-i Islam) party of Pakistan. It probably receives some funds from bin Ladin, according to Patterns 2000.
- Lashkar-e-Tayyiba (Army of the Righteous) is analyzed separately in Patterns 2000 as "one of the three largest and best trained groups fighting in

Kashmir against India." Led by Professor Hafiz Mohammed Saeed and operating through a missionary organization known as the MDI (Center for Islamic Call and Guidance), its fighters are Pakistanis from religious schools throughout Pakistan, as well as Arab volunteers for the Kashmir "jihad."

• A few other Kashmir-related groups are mentioned in press reports or in Patterns 2000, but they are not analyzed separately in the report or discussed in depth. One is the Harakat-ul Jihad Islami (Islamic Jihad Movement), many of whose fighters defected to the Jaish-e-Mohammed when it was formed. Another group, Lashkar-e-Jhangvi, has called for attacks on the United States and declared itself an ally of bin Ladin. The Hizb-ul Mujahedin (Mujahedin Party) is an older, more established, and somewhat more moderate group with few apparent links to bin Ladin or to Arab volunteers for the Kashmir struggle.

Islamic Movement of Uzbekistan (IMU)

The Islamic Movement of Uzbekistan (IMU) was named as an FTO on September 25, 2000 after kidnapping four U.S. citizens who were mountain climbing in Kyrgyzstan in August 2000. The IMU's primary objective is to replace the secular, authoritarian government of Uzbekistan's President Islam Karimov with an Islamic regime, and it is believed responsible for setting off five bombs in Tashkent, Uzbekistan on February 16, 1999. One of the bombs exploded in a government building just minutes before Karimov was to attend a meeting there. The government of Uzbekistan blamed the plot on two IMU leaders, Tahir Yuldashev and Juma Namangani, both of whom are reported to enjoy safehaven in Taliban-controlled Afghanistan.

Among its insurgency operations, in August 1999, Namangani led about 800 IMU guerrillas in an unsuccessful attempt to establish a base in Kyrgyzstan from which to launch cross-border attacks into Uzbekistan. In the course of their operations, the IMU guerrillas kidnapped four Japanese geologists and eight Kyrgyz soldiers. In early August 2000, about 100 guerrillas presumably linked to the IMU seized several villages just inside Uzbekistan, on the Uzbekistan-Tajikistan border. At the same time, a related group of guerrillas battled security forces in neighboring Kyrgyzstan. Some press reports indicate that bin Ladin contributes funds to the IMU, although Patterns 2000 says only that the IMU receives "support from other Islamic extremist movements in Central Asia."

Abu Sayyaf Group

The Abu Sayyaf Group, which is a designated FTO, is an Islamic separatist organization operating in the southern Philippines. Although it is not known to operate in the Near East region, Abu Sayyaf is discussed in this report because of its alleged ties to Islamic extremists based in Afghanistan, possibly including bin Ladin. The group, led by Khadafi Janjalani, raises funds for operations and recruitment by kidnapping foreign hostages. As of late August 2001, it was holding about 20 hostages, including two American citizens, in the southern Philippines. It has also expanded its kidnappings into Malaysia and is suspected of shipping weapons to Muslim extremists in Indonesia.

Islamic Army of Aden

The Islamic Army of Aden, also called the Aden-Abyan Islamic Army, is a Yemen-based radical Islamic organization. It has not been designated by the State Department as an FTO and it is not analyzed separately in Patterns 2000, although it is mentioned in that report's discussion of terrorism in Yemen. Little is known about the group, but it advocates the imposition of Islamic law in Yemen and the lifting of international sanctions against Iraq, and opposes the use of Yemeni ports and bases by U.S. or other Western countries. Some of the group's members are suspected of having links to bin Ladin, and the group was one of three to claim responsibility for the bombing of the U.S.S. Cole on October 12, 2000. However, some experts, note that the Islamic Army of Aden is not, as a whole, closely linked to bin Ladin and is therefore not the likely perpetrator of that attack.

The group first achieved notoriety in December 1998, when it kidnaped sixteen tourists, including two Americans. Three British and one Australian tourist were killed in the course of a rescue attempt by Yemeni security forces; the rest were saved. The group's leader at the time, Zein al-Abidine al-Midhar (Abu Hassan), admitted to the kidnapping and was executed by the Yemeni government in October 1999. No new leader has been publicly identified.

Yemen's President Ali Abdullah al-Salih has publicly vowed to eradicate terrorism from Yemen and there is no evidence that the government, as a matter of policy, supports radical Islamist groups or alleged bin Ladin sympathizers living in Yemen. However, there are areas of Yemen under tenuous government control and experts believe that the Yemeni government has, to some extent, tolerated the presence of Islamic extremists in Yemen. Some government workers are believed to have personal ties to individual Islamists there. Yemen has interrogated many people and made a number of arrests in the Cole attack, but some U.S. law enforcement officials are unsatisfied with its cooperation in that investigation. The former South Yemen (People's Democratic Republic of Yemen, PDRY) was on the U.S. terrorism list during 1979–1990 for supporting leftwing Arab terrorist groups, but was removed from the list when South Yemen merged with more conservative North Yemen in 1990 to form the Republic of Yemen.

RADICAL JEWISH GROUPS: KACH AND KAHANE CHAI

Some radical Jewish groups are as opposed to the Arab-Israeli peace process as are radical Islamic groups. The Jewish groups, which derive their support primarily from Jewish settlers in the occupied territories, have been willing to engage in terrorism to try to derail the process. The incidents involving these Jewish groups have declined in recent years, although settlers possibly linked to Kach and Kahane Chai have attacked Palestinians throughout the latest Palestinian uprising that began in September 2000.

Kach was founded by Rabbi Meir Kahane, who was assassinated in the United States in 1990. Kahane Chai (Kahane Lives) was founded by Kahane's son, Binyamin, following his father's assassination. Binyamin Kahane and his wife were killed on December 31, 2000 by a Palestinian group calling itself the "Martyr's of Al-Aqsa." The two Jewish movements seek to expel all Arabs from Israel and expand Israel's boundaries to include the occupied territories and parts of Jordan. They also want strict implementation of Jewish law in Israel. To try to accomplish these goals, the two groups have organized protests against the Israeli government, and threatened Palestinians in Hebron and elsewhere in the West Bank.

On March 13, 1994, the Israeli Cabinet declared both to be terrorist organizations under a 1948 Terrorism Law. The declaration came after the groups publicly stated their support for a February 25, 1994 attack on a Hebron mosque by a radical Jewish settler, Baruch Goldstein, who was a Kach affiliate and an immigrant from the United States. The attack killed 29 worshipers and wounded about 150. Patterns 2000 says that the numerical strength of Kach and Kahane Chai is unknown and repeats previous assertions that both receive support from sympathizers in the United States and Europe. Prime Minister Yitzhak Rabin was killed by Israeli extremist Yigal Amir in November 1995, shortly after signing the Oslo II interim agreement with the Palestinians. Neither Amir nor his two accomplices were known to be formal members of Kach or Kahane Chai, although Amir appears to espouse ideologies similar to those of the two groups.

Blocked Assets. According to the Terrorist Assets Report for 2000, about $200 belonging to Kahane Chai has been blocked since 1995.

LEFTWING AND NATIONALIST GROUPS

Some Middle Eastern terrorist groups are guided by Arab nationalism or left-wing ideologies rather than Islamic fundamentalism. With the collapse of the Soviet Union and the loss of much of their backing from state sponsors, the left-wing and nationalist groups became progressively less active since the late 1980s and were largely eclipsed by militant Islamic groups. However, some of the left-wing nationalist groups have reactivated their terrorist and commando operations during the Palestinian uprising.

Palestine Liberation Organization (PLO)

The PLO formally renounced the use of terrorism in 1988, and it reaffirmed that commitment as part of its September 1993 mutual recognition agreement with Israel. The PLO has not been named an FTO by the State Department and Patterns 1995 was the last Patterns report to contain a formal section analyzing the PLO. . . .

Patterns 2000 generally credits the PA with working with Israel to disrupt Hamas and PIJ attacks against Israel in the first half of 2000, but the report notes Israel's dissatisfaction with PA anti-terrorism cooperation after the uprising began. Patterns 2000, and an Administration report to Congress on PLO compliance with its commitments (covering June–December 2000) cite Israeli allegations that factions of the PLO encouraged or participated in violence against Israel. The factions mentioned include the Fatah movement, a wing of Fatah called the "Tanzim" (Organization) and a PLO security apparatus called Force 17. The PLO compliance report added that Israeli officials are divided on the degree to which senior PLO and PA officials were willing or able to halt violence by these factions. Neither report clearly states whether or not the U.S. government concurs with the Israeli allegations, although U.S. officials acknowledge that the inclusion of the Israeli views in these reports suggests a degree of U.S. concurrence. . . .

Popular Front for the Liberation of Palestine — General Command (PFLP-GC)

Ahmad Jibril, a former captain in the Syrian army, formed the PFLP–GC in October 1968 as a breakaway faction of the Popular Front for the Liberation of Palestine (PFLP, see below), which he considered too willing to compromise with Israel. He also believed that a conventional military arm was needed to complement terrorist operations, and the group operates a small tank force at its bases in Lebanon, according to observers. During Israel's occupation of a strip of southern Lebanon, which ended in May 2000, Jibril's several hundred guerrillas fought against Israeli forces alongside Hizballah. Recent Patterns reports have not attributed any significant terrorist attacks to the PFLP-GC in the past few years. In May 2001, Jibril claimed responsibility for shipping a boatload of weapons to the Palestinians in the occupied territories, although the shipment was intercepted by Israel's navy.

Probably because of Jibril's service in the Syrian military, Syria has always been the chief backer of the PFLP-GC, giving it logistical and military support.

In the late 1980s, the PFLP-GC also built a close relationship with Iran, and it receives Iranian financial assistance. There have been persistent reports that Iran approached the PFLP-GC to bomb a U.S. passenger jet in retaliation for the July 3, 1988 U.S. Navy's downing of an Iranian passenger airplane (Iran Air flight 655). The PFLP-GC allegedly pursued such an operation and abandoned it or, according to other speculation, handed off the operation to Libya in what became a successful effort to bomb Pan Am flight 103 in December 1988. Patterns 2000 drops assertions in previous Patterns reports that Libya, formerly a major financier of the group, retains ties to the PFLP-GC. . . .

Popular Front for the Liberation of Palestine (PFLP)

The PFLP's opposition to Arafat and to eventual peace with Israel appears to be weakening. The PFLP opposed the Palestinians' decision to join the Madrid peace process and suspended its participation in the PLO after the September 1993 Israel-PLO Declaration of Principles. In August 1999, in apparent recognition of Arafat's growing control over Palestinian territory, the PFLP held reconciliation talks with him. Arafat reportedly invited the PFLP to send a delegate to the U.S.-brokered summit talks with Israel at Camp David in July 2000, but the PFLP refused. Its terrorist wing had been almost completely inactive in the four years prior to the latest Palestinian uprising, but since then has conducted five car bombings and a few other attacks on Israelis, according to Israeli officials. Patterns 2000 repeats previous estimates of the PFLP's strength as about 800, and says that the group receives logistical assistance and safehaven from Syria. The PFLP is headquartered in Damascus and it reportedly has training facilities in Syrian-controlled areas of Lebanon.

The PFLP was founded in December 1967, following the Arab defeat in the Six Day War with Israel in June of that year, by Marxist-Leninist ideologue and medical doctor George Habash, a Christian. The PFLP was active in international terrorism during the late 1960s and the 1970s; on September 6, 1970, PFLP guerrillas simultaneously hijacked three airliners and, after evacuating the passengers, blew up the aircraft. . . .

Democratic Front for the Liberation of Palestine (DFLP)

The DFLP, still led by its 67-year-old founder Nayif Hawatmeh, abandoned its call for the destruction of Israel in the 1980s. However, it sought stringent conditions for Palestinian participation in the October 1991 Madrid peace conference and opposed the September 1993 Israel-PLO mutual recognition accords. Although it still opposes the interim agreements reached between Israel and the Palestinians since 1993, the DFLP began reconciling with Arafat in August 1999 and stated that it might recognize Israel if there was a permanent Israeli-Palestinian peace. In response to the DFLP's apparent moderation, the State

Department removed the group from the list of FTOs when that list was revised in October 1999. Also that month, Israel permitted Hawatmeh to relocate to the Palestinian-controlled areas, although he apparently has not moved there permanently.* Patterns 1999 is the first Patterns report to exclude the group from its analysis of terrorist organizations. In July 2000, the DFLP was part of the Palestinian delegation to the U.S.-brokered Israeli-Palestinian final status summit negotiations at Camp David. However, since the Palestinian uprising began in September 2000, the group has claimed responsibility for a few attacks on Israeli military patrols and settlers in the occupied territories, and has openly encouraged the Palestinian uprising. Two commandos from the group attacked a heavily fortified Israeli military position in the Gaza Strip on August 25, 2001, and killed three Israeli soldiers; the two guerrillas were killed in the exchange of fire. . . .

Abu Nidal Organization (ANO)

The international terrorist threat posed by the Abu Nidal Organization has receded because of Abu Nidal's reported health problems (leukemia and a heart condition), internal splits, friction with state sponsors, and clashes with Arafat loyalists. It still has a few hundred members and a presence in Palestinian refugee camps in Lebanon, but it has not attacked Western targets since the late 1980s. During the 1970s and 1980s, the ANO carried out over 90 terrorist attacks in 20 countries, killing about 300 people. One of its most well-known operations was a December 27, 1985 attack at airports in Rome and Vienna, in which 18 died and 111 were injured. One month earlier, ANO members hijacked Egypt Air 648, resulting in the deaths of 60 people. On September 6, 1986, ANO gunmen killed 22 at a synagogue (Neve Shalom) in Istanbul. The group is suspected of assassinating top Arafat aides in Tunis in 1991 and a Jordanian diplomat in Lebanon in January 1994.

Also known as the Fatah Revolutionary Council, the ANO was created in 1974 when Abu Nidal (real name, Sabri al-Banna), then Arafat's representative in Iraq, broke with the PLO over Arafat's willingness to compromise with Israel. U.S. engagement with Iraq in the early stages of the 1980-88 Iran-Iraq war contributed to Iraq's expulsion of Abu Nidal to Syria in November 1983, but Syria expelled the group four years later to reduce scrutiny on the country as a sponsor of terrorism. Abu Nidal left his next home, Libya, in April 1998, after a schism between pro and anti-Arafat members of Abu Nidal's group. He relocated to Cairo, where he stayed until December 1998, when more infighting caused his presence in Egypt to become public, and therefore a foreign policy

---

*Hawatmeh was killed by Israeli security forces in the summer of 2001.

problem for Egypt. He has been in Iraq since, but there is no hard evidence that Abu Nidal is reviving his international terrorist network on his own or on Baghdad's behalf.

SDTs. Abu Nidal, who was born in 1937 in Jaffa (part of what is now Israel), is the only ANO member named an SDT. He faces no legal charges in the United States, according to an ABC News report of August 25, 1998, but he is wanted in Britain and Italy. His aide, Nimer Halima, was arrested in Austria in January 2000. . . .

Libya

The Pan Am 103 bombing issue has been at the center of U.S. policy toward Libya for more than a decade, and will likely prevent any major rapprochement as long as Muammar Qadhafi remains in power. The Pan Am attack, on December 21, 1988, killed 259 people aboard plus 11 on the ground, and the families of the victims are vocal advocates of a hardline U.S. stance on Libya. Three U.N. Security Council resolutions—731 (January 21, 1992); 748 (March 31, 1992); and 883 (November 11, 1993)—called on Libya to turn over the two Libyan intelligence agents (Abd al-Basit Ali al-Megrahi and Al Amin Khalifah Fhimah) suspected in the bombing, and to help resolve the related case of the 1989 bombing of French airline UTA's Flight 772. The U.N. resolutions prohibited air travel to or from Libya and all arms transfers to that country (Resolution 748); and froze Libyan assets and prohibited the sale to Libya of petroleum-related equipment (Resolution 883). In accordance with U.N. Security Council Resolution 1192 (August 27, 1998), the sanctions were suspended, but not terminated, immediately upon the April 5, 1999 handover of the two to the Netherlands. There, their trial under Scottish law began on May 3, 2000 and ended on January 31, 2001 with the conviction of al-Megrahi and the acquittal of Fhimah.

The handover of the Pan Am suspects, along with Libya's growing distance from radical Palestinian groups, reportedly prompted the Clinton Administration to review whether to remove Libya from the terrorism list. In 1998, prior to the handover, Libya had expelled Abu Nidal, it was reducing its contacts with other radical Palestinian organizations, and it expressed support for Yasir Arafat. In an effort to reward Libya's positive steps, in 1999 a U.S. official met with a Libyan diplomat for the first time since 1981, and the U.S. trade ban was modified to permit exports of food and medicine. In March 2000, a group of U.S. security officials visited Libya briefly to assess whether or not to lift the U.S. restriction on the use of U.S. passports for travel to Libya. No decision was announced.

The January 31, 2001 conviction of al-Megrahi brought some closure to the Pan Am case but also reinforced the perception among the Pan Am victims' families and others that Libyan leader Muammar Qadhafi knew about, if not orchestrated, the bombing. Immediately upon the conviction, President Bush stated that the United States would maintain unilateral sanctions on Libya and opposes permanently lifting U.N. sanctions until Libya: (1) accepts responsibility for the act; (2) compensates the families of the victims; (3) renounces support for terrorism; and (4) discloses all it knows about the plot. Since the conviction, no U.S. official has suggested that Libya would receive consideration for removal from the terrorism list in the near future. Patterns 2000 was more critical of Libya than was Patterns 1999, stating that it is unclear whether or not Libya's distancing itself from its "terrorist past" signifies a true change in policy.

Libya has tried to appear cooperative in resolving other past acts of terrorism. In March 1999, a French court convicted six Libyans, in absentia, for the 1989 bombing of a French airliner, UTA Flight 772, over Niger. One of them is Libyan leader Muammar Qadhafi's brother-in-law, intelligence agent Muhammad Sanusi. Although it never acknowledged responsibility or turned over the indicted suspects, in July 1999 Libya compensated the families of the 171 victims of the bombing, who included seven U.S. citizens. In July 1999, Britain restored diplomatic relations with Libya after it agreed to cooperate with the investigation of the 1984 fatal shooting of a British policewoman, Yvonne Fletcher, outside Libya's embassy in London. It is alleged that a Libyan diplomat shot her while firing on Libyan dissidents demonstrating outside the embassy.

In what some construe as part of the effort to improve its international image, Libya also has tried to mediate an end to conflicts between Eritrea and Ethiopia, and within Sudan and the Democratic Republic of the Congo. However, some believe Libya is trying to extend its influence in Africa rather than broker peace, and some in Congress and the Administration assert that Libya continues to arm rebel groups in Africa, such as the Revolutionary United Front in Sierra Leone.

Sudan

Sudan appears closest of any of the Near Eastern countries on the terrorism list to being removed, despite congressional and outside criticism over its prosecution of the war against Christian and other rebels in its south. The State Department says it is engaged in discussions with Sudan with the objective of getting Sudan "completely out of the terrorism business and off the terrorism list." Since shortly after being placed on the terrorism list, Sudan has signaled a willingness to assuage international concerns about its support for terrorism. In August 1994, Sudan turned over the terrorist Carlos (Ilyich Ramirez Sanchez) to France. In December 1999, Sudan's President Umar Hassan al-Bashir, a military leader, politically sidelined Sudan's leading Islamist figure, Hassan al-Turabi. In February 2001, Turabi was arrested, and has remained under house arrest since May 2001. Turabi was the primary proponent of Sudan's ties to region-wide Islamic movements, including Al Qaida, the Abu Nidal Organization, Hamas, PIJ, Egypt's Islamic Group and Al Jihad, Hizballah, and Islamist rebel movements in East Africa. According to Patterns 2000, by the end of 2000 Sudan had signed all 12 international conventions on combating terrorism.

The key outstanding terrorism issue is Sudan's compliance with three Security Council resolutions adopted in 1996: (1044 of January 31; 1054, of April 26; and 1070 of August 16). The resolutions demanded that Sudan extradite the three Islamic Group suspects in the June 1995 assassination attempt against President Mubarak in Ethiopia, restricted the number of Sudanese diplomats abroad, and authorized a suspension of international flights of Sudanese aircraft, although the last measure was never put into effect. According to the *Washington Post* of August 21, 2001, the Bush Administration has concluded that Sudan has ended its support for the terrorists involved in the bomb plot. Some Administration officials want the United States to agree to a lifting of the U.N. sanctions if and when Sudan seeks such a move, possibly as early as late September 2001. Others believe that the U.N. sanctions should remain as a signal, in part, of U.S. displeasure with Sudan's overall poor human rights record and its war against southern Sudanese rebels.

The United States has tried to promote further progress on terrorism by slowly increasing engagement with Sudan. The United States closed its embassy in Khartoum in February 1996, although diplomatic relations were not broken. U.S. diplomats posted to Sudan have since worked out of the U.S. Embassy in Kenya, but have made consular visits to the embassy in Khartoum. Several times since mid-2000, U.S. counterterrorism experts have visited Sudan to discuss U.S. terrorism concerns and monitor Sudan's behavior on the issue.

There is lingering resentment among some Sudanese against the United States because of the August 20, 1998 cruise missile strike on the al-Shifa pharmaceutical plant in Khartoum, conducted in conjunction with the strike on bin Ladin's bases in Afghanistan. The United States destroyed the plant on the grounds that it was allegedly contributing to chemical weapons manufacture for bin Ladin. Although the Clinton Administration asserted that the al-Shifa strike was justified, several outside critics maintained that the plant was a genuine pharmaceutical factory with no connection to bin Ladin or to the production of chemical weapons. The plant owner's $24 million in U.S.-based assets were unfrozen by the Administration in 1999, a move widely interpreted as a tacit U.S. admission that the strike was in error.

Iraq

U.S.-Iraq differences over Iraq's regional ambitions and its record of compliance with post-Gulf war ceasefire requirements will probably keep Iraq on the terrorism list as long as Saddam Husayn remains in power. Observers are virtually unanimous in assessing Iraq's record of compliance with its postwar obligations as poor, and its human rights record as abysmal. However, international pressure on Iraq on these broader issues appears to have constrained Iraq's ability to use terrorism. Patterns 2000, as have the past few Patterns reports, notes that Iraq continues to plan and sponsor international terrorism, although Iraq's activities are directed mostly against anti-regime opposition, symbols of Iraq's past defeats, or bodies that represent or implement international sanctions against Iraq. In October 1998, Iraqi agents allegedly planned to attack the Prague-based Radio Free Iraq service of Radio Free Europe/Radio Liberty, although no attack occurred. Iraq organized a failed assassination plot against former President Bush during his April 1993 visit to Kuwait, which triggered a U.S. retaliatory missile strike on Iraqi intelligence headquarters. Since 1991, it has sporadically attacked international relief workers in Kurdish-controlled northern Iraq.

Iraq, which historically has had close ties to Yasir Arafat, has given some support to anti-peace process Palestinian groups, and hosts the Abu Nidal Organization, Abu Abbas' Palestine Liberation Front, and other minor groups. As a lever in its relations with Iran, Iraq continues to host and provide some older surplus weaponry to the PMOI's army, the National Liberation Army (NLA), which has bases near the border with Iran. However, Iraq apparently has reduced support for the group as Iraq's relations with Tehran have improved over the past two years.

Table 2. Blocked Assets of Middle East Terrorism List States (As of End 2000)

Country	Assets in U.S.
IRAN (added to terrorism list January 19, 1984)	$23.2 million, consisting of blocked diplomatic property and related accounts. (A reported additional $400 million in assets remain in a Defense Dept. account pending resolution of U.S.-Iran military sales cases)
IRAQ (on list at inception, December 29, 1979. Removed March 1982, restored to list September 13, 1990)	$2.356 billion, primarily blocked bank deposits. Includes $596 million blocked in U.S. banks' foreign branches, and $173 million in Iraqi assets loaned to a U.N. escrow account.
SYRIA (on list since inception)	No blocked assets.

SUDAN	$33.3 million in blocked bank deposits.
(added August 12, 1993)	
LIBYA	$1.073 billion, primarily blocked bank
(on list since inception)	deposits.

Principal Source: 2000 Annual Report to Congress on Assets in the United States Belonging to Terrorist Countries or International Terrorist Organizations. Office of Foreign Assets Control, Department of the Treasury. January 2001.

COUNTERING NEAR EASTERN TERRORISM

There is no universally agreed strategy for countering the terrorism threats discussed above, partly because the challenge is so complex and the potential anti-terrorism methods so diverse. However, a central tenet of U.S. policy is not to capitulate to the demands of terrorists. Observers also tend to agree that the success of almost any strategy depends on bilateral, multilateral, or international cooperation with U.S. efforts. Not all options focus on pressuring states or groups; some believe that engagement with state sponsors and U.S. efforts to address terrorists' grievances are more effective over the long term. The United States has claimed some successes for its policy of pressuring state sponsors, but there are signs that the United States is now incorporating a greater degree of engagement into its policy framework. At the same time, the United States has not dropped the longstanding stated U.S. policy of refusing to make concessions to terrorists or of pursuing terrorism cases, politically or legally, as long as is needed to obtain a resolution.

An exhaustive discussion of U.S. efforts to counter terrorism emanating from the region is beyond the scope of this paper, but the following sections highlight key themes in U.S. efforts to reduce this threat.

Military Force

The United States has used military force against terrorism in selected cases. U.S. allies in Europe have sometimes been the victims of Near Eastern terrorism, but they generally view military retaliation as a last resort, believing that it could inspire a cycle of attack and reaction that might be difficult to control. On some occasions, however, allies have provided logistic and diplomatic support for unilateral U.S. retaliatory attacks. U.S. military actions against terrorists have almost always received strong congressional support.

Major U.S. attacks have been conducted in retaliation for terrorist acts sponsored by Libya and Iraq, as well as those allegedly sponsored by the bin Ladin network. On April 15, 1986, the United States sent about 100 U.S. aircraft to bomb military installations in Libya. The attack was in retaliation for the

April 2, 1986 bombing of a Berlin nightclub in which 2 U.S. military personnel were killed, and in which Libya was implicated. On June 26, 1993, the United States fired cruise missiles at the headquarters in Baghdad of the Iraqi Intelligence Service, which allegedly sponsored a failed assassination plot against former President George Bush during his April 14-16, 1993 visit to Kuwait. (Other U.S. retaliation against Iraq since 1991 has been triggered by Iraqi violations of ceasefire terms not related to terrorism.) The August 20, 1998 cruise missile strikes against the bin Ladin network in Afghanistan represented a U.S. strike against a group, not a state sponsor. The related strike on a pharmaceutical plant in Sudan could have been intended as a signal to Sudan to sever any remaining ties to bin Ladin.

The effectiveness of U.S. military action against terrorist groups or state sponsors is difficult to judge. Libya did not immediately try to retaliate after the 1986 U.S. strike, but many believe that it did eventually strike back by orchestrating the Pan Am 103 bombing. Since the 1993 U.S. strike, Iraq has avoided terrorist attacks against high profile U.S. targets, but it has continued to challenge the United States on numerous issues related to its August 1990 invasion of Kuwait. The 1998 airstrikes against bin Ladin did not prompt the Taliban leadership to extradite or expel him from Afghanistan, nor did the strikes deter bin Ladin's network from engaging in further terrorist activities.

Unilateral Economic Sanctions

The United States has been willing to apply economic sanctions unilaterally. Under a number of different laws, the placement of a country on the terrorism list triggers a wide range of U.S. economic sanctions, including:

- a ban on direct U.S. foreign aid, including Export-Import Bank guarantees.
- a ban on sales of items on the U.S. Munitions Control List.
- a requirement that the United States vote against lending to that country by international institutions.
- strict licensing requirements for sales to that country, which generally prohibit exports of items that can have military applications, such as advanced sensing, computation, or transportation equipment.

A U.S. trade ban has been imposed on every Middle Eastern terrorism list state, except Syria, under separate Executive orders. Placement on the terrorism list *does not* automatically trigger a total ban on U.S. trade with or investment by the United States. In addition, foreign aid appropriations bills since the late 1980s have barred direct and indirect assistance to terrorism list and other selected countries, and mandated cuts in U.S. contributions to international programs that work in those countries. As shown in Table 2 above, the United

States also tries to maintain some leverage over terrorism list states and groups by blocking some of their assets in the United States.

Some sanctions are aimed at countries that help or arm terrorism list countries. Sections 325 and 326 of the Anti-Terrorism and Effective Death Penalty Act (P.L. 104-132) amended the Foreign Assistance Act by requiring the President to withhold U.S. foreign assistance to any government that provides assistance or lethal military aid to any terrorism list country. In April 1999, three Russian entities were sanctioned under this provision for providing anti-tank weaponry to Syria; sanctions on the Russian government were waived.

The 1996 Anti-Terrorism act also gave the Administration another option besides placing a country on the terrorism list. Section 303 of that Act created a new list of states that are deemed "not cooperating with U.S. anti-terrorism efforts," and provided that states on that list be barred from sales of U.S. Munitions List items. Under that provision, and every year since 1997, Afghanistan— along with the seven terrorism list countries—has been designated as not cooperating. No U.S. allies have been designated as "not cooperating," although the provision was enacted following an April 1995 incident in which Saudi Arabia did not attempt to detain Hizballah terrorist Imad Mughniyah when a plane, on which he was believed to be a passenger, was scheduled to land in Saudi Arabia. Possibly in an attempt to avoid similar incidents, on June 21, 1995, President Clinton signed Presidential Decision Directive 39 (PDD-39), enabling U.S. law enforcement authorities to capture suspected terrorists by force from foreign countries that refuse to cooperate in their extradition.

The Clinton Administration rejected several outside recommendations— most recently those issued in June 2000 by the congressionally-mandated National Commission on Terrorism—to place Afghanistan on the terrorism list. The Clinton Administration said that placing Afghanistan on the list would imply that the United States recognizes the Taliban movement as the legitimate government of Afghanistan. However, President Clinton, on July 4, 1999, issued Executive order 13129 imposing sanctions on the Taliban that are similar to those imposed on terrorism list countries and on foreign terrorist organizations. The order imposed a ban on U.S. trade with areas of Afghanistan under Taliban control, froze Taliban assets in the United States, and prohibited contributions to Taliban by U.S. persons. The President justified the move by citing the Taliban's continued harboring of bin Ladin.

Also in its June 2000 report, the National Commission on Terrorism recommended naming Greece and Pakistan as not fully cooperating with U.S. anti-terrorism efforts. The Clinton Administration rejected those recommendations as well. In Patterns 2000, the State Department implied that Pakistan and Lebanon were potential candidates for the terrorism list, or possibly the "not cooperating" list, for supporting or tolerating operations by terrorist groups. On the other hand, Patterns 2000 did credit both Pakistan and Lebanon with anti-terrorism cooperation in selected cases. Most experts believe the United States does not want to alienate those countries by placing them on the terrorism list, although designating them as "not cooperating" might have less of an effect on U.S. relations with them.

Analysts doubt that unilateral U.S. economic sanctions, by themselves, can force major changes in the behavior of state sponsors of terrorism. Major U.S. allies did not join the U.S. trade ban imposed on Iran in May 1995 and the move did not, in itself, measurably alter Iran's support for terrorist groups. On the other hand, virtually all Middle Eastern terrorism list states have publicly protested their inclusion on the list and other U.S. sanctions, suggesting that these sanctions are having an effect politically and/or economically. U.S. officials assert that U.S. sanctions, even if unilateral, have made some terrorism state sponsors "think twice" about promoting terrorism.

To demonstrate that improvements in behavior can be rewarded, in April 1999 the Clinton Administration announced that it would permit, on a case-by-case basis, commercial sales of U.S. food and medical products to Libya, Sudan, and Iran. The move relaxed the bans on U.S. trade with the three countries. As noted previously, all three have recently shown some signs of wanting to improve their international images.

Multilateral Sanctions

In concert with U.S. unilateral actions, the United States has sought to apply multilateral sanctions against Middle Eastern terrorism. As noted above, the United States led efforts to impose international sanctions on Libya and Sudan for their support of terrorism, and both those states have sought to improve their international standings since international sanctions were imposed. The United States and Russia jointly worked successfully to persuade the United Nations Security Council to adopt sanctions on the Taliban because of its refusal to extradite bin Ladin. U.N. Security Council Resolution 1267, adopted October 15, 1999, banned flights outside Afghanistan by its national airline, Ariana, and directed U.N. member states to freeze Taliban assets. The United States and Russia teamed up again to push another resolution (U.N. Security Council Resolution 1333, adopted December 19, 2000) that, among other measures, imposed an international arms embargo on the Taliban only, not on opposition factions. These measures are beginning to be implemented and have not, to date, caused the Taliban to waiver in its refusal to hand over bin Ladin. Pakistan has said it will comply with the resolutions, possibly resulting in Pakistan's reducing its patronage of the Taliban movement.

Counterterrorism Cooperation

Successive administrations have identified counterterrorism cooperation with friendly countries as a key element of U.S. policy. In one important regional example, the United States has sought to contain Hizballah by providing military and law enforcement assistance to the government of Lebanon. In the past few years, the United States has sold Lebanon non-lethal defense articles such as armored personnel carriers. In 1994, on a one-time basis, the United States provided non-lethal aid, including excess trucks and equipment, to Palestinian Authority security forces in an effort to strengthen them against Hamas and PIJ, although some in Israel now fear that the PA or PLO factions might use some of this equipment against Israel. Several Middle Eastern countries, including Egypt, Israel, Jordan, Kuwait, Saudi Arabia, Tunisia, and Turkey, receive anti-terrorism assistance through the Anti-Terrorism Assistance Program run by the State Department Bureau of Diplomatic Security, in which the United States provides training in airport security, explosives detection, and crisis management.

In cooperating against the bin Ladin network, the United States has expanded and formalized a counterterrorism dialogue with Russia and begun bilateral dialogues on the issue with the Central Asian states. Every year since 1999, the State Department has hosted a multilateral conference of senior counterterrorism officials from the Middle East, Central Asia, and Asia, focusing on combating the terrorism threat from Afghanistan. These conferences and meetings have often resulted in agreements to exchange information, to conduct joint efforts to counter terrorist fundraising, and to develop improved export controls on explosives and conventions against nuclear terrorism. The United States has provided some detection equipment to the Central Asian states to help them prevent the smuggling of nuclear and other material to terrorist groups such as the bin Ladin network or terrorism list countries. The measure yielded some results in April 2000, when Uzbek border authorities used this equipment to detect and seize ten containers with radioactive material bound for Pakistan. During a trip to the region a few weeks after this incident, then Secretary of State Albright pledged $3 million each to Uzbekistan, Kyrgyzstan, and Kazakhstan to help their border police combat drug smuggling and terrorism. In June 2001, the U.S. National Academy of Sciences began a program of cooperation with the Russian Academy of Sciences to combat the use of high technology for terrorism.

The United States has worked with the European Union (EU) to exert influence on Iran to end its sponsorship of terrorism. In exchange for relaxing enforcement of U.S. sanctions under the Iran-Libya Sanctions Act (P.L. 104-172), which would have sanctioned EU firms that invest in Iran's energy industry, in mid 1998 the United States extracted a pledge from the EU to increase cooperation with the United States against Iranian terrorism. In May 1998, the EU countries agreed on a "code of conduct" to curb arms sales to states, such as Iran, that might use the arms to support terrorism. However, the code is not legally binding on the EU member governments. In January 2000, the United States signed a new International Convention for the Suppression of Terrorist Financing, which creates an international legal framework to investigate those involved in terrorist financing.

Selective Engagement

As noted in the discussions of terrorism list countries, the Administration has shown increasing willingness to engage state sponsors, once these countries have demonstrated some willingness to curb support for terrorism. U.S. officials justify engagement with the argument that doing so creates incentives for terrorism list countries to continue to reduce their support for international terrorism. On the other hand, critics believe that terrorism list countries are likely to view a U.S. policy of engagement as a sign that supporting terrorism will not adversely affect relations with the United States.

Of the Middle Eastern terrorism list countries, the United States engages in bilateral dialogue with all except Iran and Iraq. The United States has called for a dialogue with Iran, but Iran has thus far refused on the grounds that the United States has not dismantled what Iran calls "hostile" policies toward that country—a formulation widely interpreted to refer to U.S. sanctions. Iraq has asked for direct talks with the United States, but the United States has rejected the suggestion on the grounds that Iraq is too far from compliance with Gulf war-related requirements to make official talks useful.

Legal Action

Legal action against terrorist groups and state sponsors is becoming an increasingly large component of U.S. counterterrorism strategy. In the case of the bombing of Pan Am 103, the Bush Administration chose international legal action—a trial of the two Libyan suspects—over military retaliation. A similar choice has apparently been made in the Khobar Towers bombing case, although that legal effort consists of U.S. indictments of suspects and not a U.N.-centered legal effort.

Congress has attempted to give victims of international terrorism a legal option against state sponsors. The Anti-Terrorism and Effective Death Penalty Act of 1996 (Section 221) created an exception to the Foreign Sovereign Immunity for Certain Cases (28 U.S.C., Section 1605), allowing victims of terrorism to sue terrorism list countries for acts of terrorism by them or groups they support. Since this provision was enacted, a number of cases have been brought in U.S.

courts, and several multimillion dollar awards have been made to former hostages and the families of victims of groups proven in court to have been sponsored by Iran. In 2000, the Clinton Administration accepted compromise legislation to use general revenues to pay compensatory damage awards to these successful claimants, with the stipulation that the President try to recoup expended funds from Iran as part of an overall reconciliation in relations and settlement of assets disputes. The provision, called the "Justice for Victims of Terrorism Act," was incorporated into the Victims of Trafficking and Violence Protection Act of 2000 (P.L. 106-386). The Clinton Administration had opposed directly tapping frozen Iranian assets in the United States—such as selling Iran's former embassy in Washington—on the grounds that doing so could violate diplomatic sovereignty or provoke attacks on U.S. property or citizens.

The Domestic Front

The February 1993 World Trade Center bombing exposed the vulnerability of the United States homeland to Middle Eastern-inspired terrorism as did no other previous event. The bombing sparked stepped up law enforcement investigation into the activities of Islamic networks in the United States and alleged fundraising in the United States for Middle East terrorism. In January 1995, President Clinton targeted terrorism fundraising in his Executive order 12947 (see above). Congress included many of the measures in that Executive order in the Anti-Terrorism and Effective Death Penalty Act of 1996. The additional law enforcement powers and efforts in recent years might have accounted for the foiling of the alleged plot by bin Ladin supporters to detonate a bomb at Los Angeles airport on the eve of the millennium.

Some observers allege that Middle Eastern groups have extensive fundraising and political networks in the United States, working from seemingly innocent religious and research institutions and investment companies. PIJ leader Shallah, before being tapped to lead PIJ, taught at the University of South Florida in the early 1990s and ran an affiliated Islamic studies institute called the World and Islam Studies Enterprise (WISE). In May 2000, the parents of an Israeli-American teenager killed in a 1996 Hamas attack in Israel filed suit against several Islamic charity groups in the United States alleging that they raised money for Hamas. Groups named in the suit included the Quranic Literary Institute, the Holy Land Foundation for Relief and Development, the Islamic Association for Palestine, and the United Association for Studies and Research. Representatives of these groups have consistently denied any involvement with fundraising for terrorism or involvement in Hamas/PIJ activities.

Others have challenged this view, saying that most American Muslims who support such groups oppose the use of violence, and donate money to organizations that they believe use the funds solely for humanitarian purposes. Some

U.S. domestic counterterrorism efforts, particularly those dealing with immigration and investigative powers, have drawn substantial criticism from U.S. civil liberties groups, which have expressed concern about excessive intrusions by law enforcement authorities. These groups also have said that the prohibition on donations to groups allegedly involved in terrorism infringes free speech. Some Arab-American and American Muslim organizations have complained that U.S. residents and citizens of Arab descent are being unfairly branded as suspected terrorists, and point to erroneous initial accusations by some terrorism experts that Islamic extremists perpetrated the Oklahoma City bombing in April 1995.

Technology Acquisition by Terrorist Groups

Brian A. Jackson

Terrorism, the systematic and premeditated use or threatened use of violence for politically motivated purposes, has been called the "weapon of the weak." By staging attacks that are unexpected and that intimidate a larger audience than their immediate victims, a small group of terrorists can influence public opinion and, through this, gain a measure of control over the policies of much larger and militarily stronger nations. Although there was a period in history when hidden daggers and public murder were sufficient to generate such fear, today, terrorist campaigns are far larger in scope and innovative in their methods. Like all modern warfare, advances in military technology have greatly broadened the operational possibilities of today's terrorist groups and have made possible significant increases in their scale. It is the technology applied by the terrorist—the explosive device that destroys a target, the automatic weapon that intimidates and, potentially, the chemical or biological weapon that inflicts mass casualties—that make today's "high impact" terrorist strikes possible and makes the threat of future violence credible to a mass audience.

In addition to the role of military technology in terrorism, it is also important to appreciate the broader effect of technology on the potential activities of terrorists. For every advance that improves the quality of life there is a corresponding new vulnerability: airliners can be blown up, a poisoned consumer product can be efficiently distributed to many potential targets, electrical substations can be destroyed, plunging cities into darkness, and sites on the Inter-

This article was originally published as "Technology Acquisition by Terrorist Groups: Threat Assessment Informed by Lessons from Private Sector Technology Acquisition," *Studies in Conflict and Terrorism*, 24:183–213, 2001, and is revised and reprinted here by permission.

net are vulnerable to tampering or direct cyber-assault. The events of September 11th, 2001, underscore that some technology advances can produce very significant vulnerabilities which are recognized only after they are brutally and disastrously exploited by terrorists.

Although technology is key to the credibility and effectiveness of a terrorist threat, it is also the main driver behind improvements in counter-terrorism. In response to the threat of hidden weaponry, detection devices such as metal detectors and x-ray machines have been deployed at vulnerable and attractive targets. Given the potential for use of chemical and biological weapons, one goal of current counter-terrorism research is developing methods to detect and defeat these new categories of threats. Beyond detection technologies, the abilities of modern computer systems to collect information, process data to identify patterns, and allow investigations by law enforcement in disparate countries to benefit from each others' work have also been of utmost importance in fighting terrorist groups. This relationship between the technology of terrorism and the technology of those fighting it can be viewed as one of the more important modern arms races, not between superpowers in missile construction but between small groups and states vying for the ability either to perpetrate or to prevent low-intensity conflict.

The centrality of technology to all terrorist and counter-terrorist operations represents an important incentive for individual groups to seek out and master new techniques and weapons. Although the desire for new technology by terrorist groups is not new—Karl Heinzen discussed the necessity of new technology for terrorist groups as early as 1849—it has been reinforced as society-as-a-whole has become more advanced. The opportunities presented by the technological dependence of society will also be inaccessible unless terrorist groups master the techniques necessary to capitalize on them. Although the Internet can make it possible to attack enemies, gain intelligence, accumulate financial resources, and publicize the agenda of a group, in the absence of computer skills many of these options are inaccessible.

For groups seeking legitimacy and "respect" in today's technologically advanced world, the sophistication of a group's attacks can be of utmost importance. Such a distinction is important both for public reactions—where a more technological attack may result in greater impact—and in the ability of terrorists to gain the attention of the world press necessary to transmit their propaganda to a broad audience. This pressure to gain media attention and prominence has been suggested as one of the reasons why terrorist acts in recent years have gradually escalated in their scale and lethality (Hoffman 1998, 177—see the references at the end of this article). New technologies and weapons are absolutely necessary in the escalation and, as a result, the ability of a group to absorb and deploy them is a critical factor in determining the success of this escalation process. If, for example, a group familiar with simple hand-thrown explosives were unable to master sophisticated timing and detonator technology, delayed-action and remotely detonated devices would be inaccessible and the group's effectiveness and ability to escalate its operations would be constrained.

Work in the broader field of technology studies has shown that the process of technology acquisition by *any* organization is often a very complex process which is both promoted and inhibited by many different pressures and variables. Such studies have sought to explain, for example, why different companies with access to the same technologies might use them at varying levels of effectiveness, why the possession of a "recipe" for an industrial process is often not sufficient to successfully replicate it, and why even conscientious attempts to transfer knowledge or technology between different organizations can and do fail. In light of this deeper understanding, it is relevant to re-examine the topic of technology and terrorism from a dynamic perspective by examining not what happens when terrorists gain a new technology but the steps and missteps that are taken as part of the acquisition process. Understanding this dynamic is of particular relevance for contemporary problems in technology and terrorism—including terrorist use of weapons of mass destruction and the Internet as a terrorist tool or venue for attack—and could suggest novel routes to discourage or inhibit the adoption and deployment of new technologies by such groups.

Since terrorist organizations do not generally open themselves to direct study, an understanding of their technology acquisition processes must be approached indirectly. In this attempt, it is profitable to draw on what is known about how technology is acquired and applied by *commercial* organizations. The terrorist organization is simply a "business" which, rather than producing financial profits, seeks to produce fear and media coverage that are used to pressure governments or the public to further the group's political goals. Given that terrorist groups and companies face analogous pressures—including dealing with external "competition," managing internal group dynamics, and preserving a level of "trade secrecy" necessary for their operations—and similar organizational constraints, such an approach provides a new way to gain insight into extremist groups' activities.

LESSONS FROM COMMERCIAL TECHNOLOGY ACQUISITION

Given its clear impact on spheres as disparate as public health, economic development, individual communication, and national security, researchers in many fields have long been interested in technology and how it affects society. For many years this interest focused on the effects of technological advance—for example, how an industry adapted when a new process or product was introduced to compete against those dominating a market. In recent years researchers have increasingly found that the discovery of new knowledge and its spread from organization to organization are very complex processes. Furthermore, the efficiency of these processes can differ markedly for different organizations.

There are two general mechanisms through which an organization can acquire new technology. One mechanism is to develop the new technology within the firm; this *internal innovation* provides the opportunity for a temporary monopoly on the new knowledge which the organization may use to gain an advantage over its competitors. To one extent or another, all firms have some internal innovation processes as they develop and apply the basic ideas they need to make and sell their products. Alternatively, companies can utilize technology produced *externally* by other researchers in the public or private sectors. In many studies of technology in both the commercial and military spheres, this distinction between internally "developed" knowledge and eternally "purchased" knowledge was assumed to illuminate fully the process of technology application as well as acquisition. In the strongest version of this view, while development of knowledge internally might involve a long process of research, purchased knowledge could be easily transferred into a firm and quickly put to use. Recent studies of technological innovation, however, have shown that the adoption of new knowledge is not so simple. Although a purchased technology may not entail the specific costs involved in developing new knowledge, often even well-understood technologies do not readily transfer into a firm and are not easily applied.

Scholars of technology have drawn a distinction between different types of knowledge. The first is *explicit knowledge*, information like the recipe for a food product, a scientific protocol, or the blueprints for an automobile which can be readily codified and written down or embodied in a physical object. Because it is easy to "capture" explicit knowledge, it is also readily transferred between one firm and another. In contrast, *tacit knowledge* is much more difficult to transfer among individuals or firms. Examples of tacit knowledge include the general "know-how" of engineers used in product design, the understanding of a machine's operation gained by its user through long experience, and a plant manager's intuition about the most critical factors in a production process. Since tacit knowledge is hard to identify, much less codify, transfer is far more difficult. Although a great deal of the knowledge that underlies an organization is explicit, it is now broadly appreciated that the body of tacit knowledge that exists in an organization is critical for its operation. *It could be argued that this tacit knowledge makes it possible to apply and use explicit knowledge effectively.* This "tacit component" of an organization's knowledge base, which can be quite large, is also very important from the perspective of a company's competitiveness. Because it is difficult to describe, tacit knowledge represents a set of practices and understanding which tend to "stick" to an organization and its personnel—they are hard to appropriate or steal—and therefore are easier to keep secret.

Although the "stickiness" of tacit knowledge can be positive for preserving trade secrets, when organizations want to transfer technology it can be a significant stumbling block. Even if the company selling a machine or other technology makes every effort to communicate its knowledge about usage, much of the tacit knowledge associated with the machine's operation will not be effectively transferred. As a result, a purchaser will *always* have to go through a subsequent internal learning process where necessary tacit knowledge is "discovered" and the technology is adapted to the user's specific needs. The extent of this learning will be related to both the nature of the technology and the characteristics of the firms and individuals involved.

TECHNOLOGY ADOPTION IN LEGAL AND ILLEGAL ORGANIZATIONS

The tendency of many terrorist groups to limit themselves to a small range of tactics, predominantly hijackings, kidnappings, bombings, and assassinations, and their overwhelming preference for operations using only firearms and explosives, has led some researchers to discount the desire for innovation among most terrorist organizations. Although there are certain areas of terrorist operations where this characterization may apply, such a broad statement does not consider the critical role that technological advance and tactical improvement have played in many groups' operations and the differences in technological aspirations that exist among different groups. There are many examples in the literature of terrorist groups, even those who have restricted themselves to certain weapons, being violently and effectively innovative. Two particularly good case studies are the advances made in bomb-making by the Provisional Irish Republican Army (PIRA) and the numerous operational improvements made by the Red Army Faction (RAF) over the course of its organizational lifetime. In the case of the PIRA, Hoffman has described how the group improved its detonator technology to incorporate first crude timers, then radio control, and finally triggers using radar detectors or remote photographic flash units (Hoffman 1998, 180–182). In the case of the RAF, the group devoted significant effort to defeating law enforcement's attempts to capture members of its organization. From studies of police tactics and trial transcripts, the group researched ways to thwart the police, including developing a special ointment which, when applied to the fingers, eliminated fingerprints. As a result of such innovations, one former member of the group declared that before its cease fire in 1992, the RAF had reached "maximum efficiency" (Hoffman 1999(2), 25–26). From the perspective of threat assessment, the most important question is what made these organizations different from the many other groups that sustained extended "careers" without marked improvements in the tools of their trade.

The process of technology adoption by any organization can be broken down into two interrelated stages. The first entails the individual or group decision-making process in choosing to adopt a new weapon or new tactical options. During this stage the hard limits of a group's technology trajectory are defined: if it is unwilling to seek out a new innovation, it is an obvious and inescapable result that the group will never have that new technology to use and apply. Like any decision-making processes, understanding such technology choices requires delineating the many internal and external factors that may influence a group's preferences and perceived constraints. If analysis stops here, however, a significant portion of the technology acquisition process and many factors that can affect the technological trajectory of a terrorist group will be overlooked. In addition to being *unwilling* to adopt a technology, a group may be *unable* to successfully absorb it and gain the knowledge required to deploy it effectively. As a result, understanding the forces that may influence a group's ability to apply technologies is equally critical for accurate threat assessment. Even if a terrorist organization decides and devotes itself to the acquisition and deployment of a particular weapon, if organizational or resource constraints doom the endeavor to failure, the group's choice to pursue the new technology may result in it posing a reduced rather than an increased threat.

Factors Influencing the Decision to Innovate

Characterization of an organization's desire to innovate, whether in the commercial or military realm, begins with a few simple questions. Does the organization seek out new ideas, or is it "satisfied" with its current options? Does it strive to improve upon currently used technologies? When presented with a new technological opportunity, does the organization choose to adopt it? If so, how rapidly does it attempt to absorb the new knowledge? The answers to these questions approach the broader idea of whether a given organization is innovative or conservative towards technology. Understanding this first level of the technology adoption process—controlled by the organization's "desire for innovation"—is critical for assessing the likely technology trajectory of a group and is therefore a relevant starting point for an assessment of the threat of technology-based terrorism.

Organizations, whether they are legitimate or underground, do not innovate for the sake of innovating. Rather, a company or terrorist group will choose to pursue a new piece of technology because it believes there is something to be gained by doing so. Innovation and new technology are not ends in themselves but only means to accomplish other organizational objectives.

Depending on the nature and mission of the terrorist organization, in some cases a new technology's impact is clearly positive or negative, and an informed adoption decision can be made. These cases are based on the relationship between the terrorist organization and the constituency or audience for its activities. For a group that is highly dependent on a constituency and therefore concerned with causing the "minimum necessary" level of damage during attacks, adopting and using a highly destructive chemical weapon or biological agent would be catastrophic to the group's "bottom line." Groups like this would therefore have a strong incentive not to adopt such technologies. On the other hand, a group seeking maximum destruction for the benefit of a divine audience would likely conclude that such destructive weapons would be appropriate to its goals. An interesting example of this calculus can be found in the behavior of the LTTE in Sri Lanka. Although it used chlorine gas against a military camp in 1990, it has not used it again; one reason cited to explain this change in behavior is a new concern on the part of the organization to appeal to an international audience (Hoffman 1999(1), 46–47). A similar distinction in weapons choice can also sometimes be drawn based on the geographic area in which a terrorist group operates. If a nationalist terrorist group carries out its operations within its home country—and therefore within the communities from which it draws its support—the organization will likely be more restrained in its attacks for fear of alienating its supporters. If that same nationalist group carried out attacks abroad, where its core constituency would no longer be directly exposed to their effects, such "restraints" might no longer apply since the perceived costs and benefits would change.

Unlike the relatively simple cases above, it is often difficult to predict the costs and benefits of a new technology, which makes adoption decisions more difficult. In the absence of any solid analytical method to guide technology adoption, most of these decisions are made based on organizational culture and intuition. The technology strategy of a given firm, for example, might be characterized as "offensive" if it always strives to be the first adopter of new techniques to gain an advantage over competing firms. In contrast, a firm might choose a "defensive" technology strategy by allowing other firms to exploit new technology first. Such behavior could be advantageous if the technology is further perfected or more broadly accepted before adoption by the defensive firm. At the other end of the spectrum, a firm might chose to ignore most new technologies if it doesn't believe that modification of its product will be accepted by the market. This is termed a "traditional" technology strategy. At the risk of ascribing too many human traits to organizations, these strategies can be viewed as a group's "self-image" with respect to technology—groups that see themselves as "advanced" or "cutting edge" will logically move to adopt new technology more rapidly than those who do not.

Just as commercial firms base their technology strategies on incomplete information and intuition, technology acquisition decisions by extremist organizations will also be inexact and non-quantitative beyond the simplest cases where the impact is clear. It is reasonable to assume, for example, that the specific and attributable benefits of adopting surface-to-air missiles will be no easier for a terrorist group to predict *a priori* than it is for a company to foresee the exact profit impact of a given manufacturing technology. Due to the many convoluting factors affecting the political influence of extremist groups, in many cases it may not even be possible to deduce the effect of specific technological changes on the "success" of groups even with the benefit of hindsight. As a result, terrorist groups, like the companies discussed in the previous paragraph, will also likely adopt broader "technology strategies" to guide their technology acquisition activities. The construction of such a strategy, as one would expect, is a non-quantitative process which can be influenced by many psychological and organizational factors. Successfully deducing these factors from the nature of the terrorist organization is one way to characterize the technology strategy of the group and predict what technologies the group is likely to pursue. Four of the factors that have been singled out are the organization's technological awareness, how open it is to new ideas, its attitude toward risk, and the nature of the environment in which it operates.

Technological Awareness

Although seemingly trivial when reduced to a single statement, the fact that no terrorist group can adopt a technology of which it is unaware is a constraint that is potentially very important for some organizations. To learn about the existence of new technologies, groups must be in contact with the "outside world." As a result, any barriers raised between the group and the larger world—including physical isolation, intellectual distance, or lack of contact out of a desire to avoid scrutiny or law enforcement attention—might serve as an impediment to technology adoption. These types of barriers would be expected to impact significantly religious groups and cults that isolate themselves from the world for philosophical (or paranoid) reasons and groups forced deeply underground. If such a terrorist group sequesters itself and prevents all mixing between its members and outsiders, it will likely remain locked at the level of technological advancement it had when its isolation began. In contrast, groups may isolate themselves from outside society in certain ways but still remain in open technical communication in others. A salient example of this behavior is the millennial cult Aum Shinrikyo which, while setting itself apart from the world, continually sought sources of new technology. Group parameters that impact the level of this "external" communication include the level of recruiting of knowledgeable individuals into the group, the number of group members per-

mitted actively to seek information outside the organization, and group participation in activities specific to the gathering and integration of new knowledge
and technology.

One example of prominent public concern about the technological awareness of terrorist organizations is the recent controversy over information being
placed on the Internet. Because of its universal accessibility and emblematic
representation of modern technology, the Internet stands out as a source of
worry in the proliferation of knowledge about explosives and more dangerous
weapons technologies. As a result, it is thought that access to the 'net provides a
way for groups to increase their technology at low risk. This role in providing
technology information could be particularly important for the types of
"closed" organizations alluded to in the preceding paragraph; the international
scope of the Internet could allow these organizations access to broad sources of
information even from the privacy of their own fortified compounds. The ready
accessibility of bomb-making manuals like *The Anarchist's Cookbook* or *The Big
Book of Mischief*, for example, has generated enough fear at the national level
that, independent of free speech implications, U.S. lawmakers have attempted
to ban their dissemination.

Openness to New Ideas

Even if a group becomes aware of a new innovation in weaponry or tactics, if it
is hostile to novel ideas or resistant to change there will be no incentive to
adopt it. Although the level of such "open mindedness" can be affected by
many things, the philosophical perspective of the group and its leaders and the
internal group dynamics of the organization are likely to be dominant factors.
Many authors have broadly characterized terrorist groups as "operationally conservative" and generally hesitant to adopt new tactics and methods. This con-
servatism has previously been interpreted as their desire to succeed at their
operations with a minimum of risk (discussed in more detail below) combined
with a reticence to make large changes in their modes of operation. Such an
"organizational inertia" that works against new ideas is not unlike a corporation
which, over the years, has developed standard ways of operating. Such a reticence was singled out—and labeled the "not invented here" syndrome—as a
primary cause for difficulties in the competitive performance of U.S. companies in the 1980s.

In an analogous manner, the longer a terrorist organization exists and the
better established it becomes, the more likely it is that expertise in its "current"
technologies will be a strong disincentive to replacing them. In addition to the
psychological price an organization might pay by displacing a mastered technology with a new one, significant financial costs may also be involved if materials and systems will be made obsolete by the change. For example, the fact

that Czechoslovakia reportedly shipped thousands of tons of Semtex plastic explosive to Libya, Syria, North Korea, Iran, and Iraq during the 1980s (Hoffman 1999(2), 14) means that groups sponsored by those nations will have a financial and material disincentive to give up explosives as a weapon. Although the level of impact that such an investment will have on states that likely have sufficient resources to ignore the expenditures, the accessibility and costs (both direct and perceived) of procuring and using alternate weapons could affect that judgment. In addition to affecting the decision to adopt new weapons, if a significant percentage of the group is "tied" to an older technology, it is much less likely that those individuals will actively strive to master a new technique even if it is pursued.

Invariably the response of any organization to external stimuli, while not fully determined by its leadership, is strongly affected by the characteristics of its leaders and how information is transmitted from the leadership to the remainder of the group. At the simplest level, groups led by individuals who are open to new technology will be much more likely to seek and adopt innovations than those led by individuals hostile to it. For example, groups whose leaders have technical backgrounds would be expected to have a greater organizational "desire" to innovate than a group led by a conservative Islamic cleric who has spoken publicly against modern science. As a result, to the extent that the background and views of individual terrorist leaders can be assessed, those characteristics can be used to help predict the desire to pursue a given course of action.

In addition to these organizational and investment pressures, the philosophical and ideological views of a group—including both the espoused "philosophy" of the organization and the "actual" philosophy revealed by the group's actions—are also critical in determining whether it will seek out new technology. Given that a great deal of analysis has been devoted to how groups' philosophical frameworks affect their operations, one example is sufficient to suggest their effect on technology and innovation. At one extreme there is Aum Shinrikyo whose philosophy and metaphysics specifically included "diagnostic" tests and "scientific" examination as part of cult indoctrination and initiation. Such a viewpoint would clearly predispose the group to inputs of a scientific or technological nature. The writings of Abd Al-Salam Faraj, leader of *Al-Jihad*, have a markedly different view of novelty and new ideas: "The most reliable speech is the Book of God and the best guidance is the guidance of Mohammed. . . . The worst of all things are novelties and every innovation is deviation and all deviation is in Hell" (Faraj, J.J. quoted in Rapoport, 103–130). As a result, it is unsurprising that it was the former of these two groups that sought out and attempted to deploy chemical, biological, and nuclear weapons.

Attitudes Toward Risk

A central consideration for the terrorist group seeking new weapons or tactics is the level of risk inherent in any attempt at technological adoption. In the legitimate business world, these risks are financial—the costs of purchasing and adopting a new technique may not be recouped, and the company may go out of business. The risks to a terrorist group, because of the lethality and illegitimacy of its "business," can be significantly higher. The choice to integrate a new technology into a group's repertoire and use it in operations instead of currently "proven" methods entails both the risk inherent in learning a new military technology and the operational risks of failure associated with deploying it. At the most basic level, mastering a new military technique can be physically dangerous. Failures during the process of deploying bomb-making technology, more than just leading to financial costs, are likely to result in the death or dismemberment of members of the group. It has been estimated that PIRA, for example, in the period from 1970 to 1996, lost approximately 120 members due to accidental shooting incidents or premature explosions. These explosions were most common in the seventies when the group was less experienced and became less frequent as members gained a greater mastery of the technology and learned how to integrate safety features into the devices. Similar incidents have occurred in Middle East terrorist organizations, including explosions killing Kamal Ismail Hafez Kahil, a leader of the *Izzedine al-Qassam* brigade, in April 1995, and in April 1999 killing Muhi a-din Sharif, called "The Engineer's Apprentice" for his relationship with the noted *Hamas* bomb-maker. It should be noted that when groups have members who are willing to commit suicide to advance their cause, the impact of these types of risks changes dramatically.

Beyond the obvious "costs" to the individuals involved, these technological failures can also have a significant impact on the terrorist group as a whole. Depending on the value of the members who are lost in the accidents, such individual casualties may be crippling to a group. If an organization loses, for example, its most experienced bomb-maker, the technological capabilities of the group may be decimated by a single "research" accident. In addition, these types of events may also exert a significant strategic and intelligence cost on an underground organization. An unexpected explosion will almost certainly result in the loss of a safe-house or facility that was part of the organization's physical infrastructure. The investigations that follow the accidents may also provide law enforcement officials with information about the group's activities and plans. An accidental fire resulting from bomb-making activities led to the capture of Ramzi Yousef and his laptop computer, which contained his plans to destroy multiple U.S. aircraft and assassinate Pope John Paul II. It should be noted that the level of these risks an organization is willing to bear is related to the size and resources it has available. Just as a $2 million investment is a very different risk to a ten-person company than it is to a multibillion dollar multinational firm, the perceived risk level associated with the same action will almost certainly differ among terrorist organizations.

Beyond the risk of the physical and human costs of using new technologies, operational failures or "research accidents" also place the perceived effectiveness of the terrorist organization at risk. For groups whose success depends on credible threats of future violence, public failure can severely diminish the impact of terrorist actions. If a group believes it needs a "100 percent" success rate to ensure it will gain world attention for its views or agenda, the risk of failure may be a significant stumbling block to the adoption of new weapons technology. Although clear data on the number of terrorist "failures" that have occurred and their effect on the groups involved are not readily available, examples of groups attempting to shift responsibility for mistakes presumably to avoid these perceived consequences do exist. For example, in the aforementioned 1995 accident that resulted in the death of Kamal Kahil, *Hamas* attempted to blame Israel and the PLO for the bombing presumably to avoid this "loss of face."

Nature of the Environment

Beyond group characteristics, the nature of the environment surrounding an organization may also have a significant effect on how it chooses to pursue new knowledge. From the commercial perspective, the most critical influences exerted by the external environment are the level of demand in the market for the products associated with a new technology and the actions of the organization's competitors. In the case of terrorism, this market "demand" is construed to be the requirement that groups' attacks are dramatic enough to warrant media attention and notoriety. One way this has manifested itself is the perceived pressure for terrorist groups to escalate the lethality of their attacks. Timothy McVeigh, discussing the bombing of the Murrah Building in Oklahoma City, was quoted as saying that a "body count" was needed to make a political point (Hoffman 1998, 177). Such an escalation essentially requires adoption of newer, more destructive technologies.

In addition to market pull, the actions of a firm's competitors can also exert a powerful effect on technology acquisition. In a very competitive market, for example, the fear that competitors will gain an advantage using a new technology can overwhelm the uncertainty associated with the costs of innovation and "force" a firm to adopt. From the perspective of terrorist groups, this "competitive advantage" is the shock value associated with the first uses of a new weapon. For example, Aum Shinrikyo gained a level of notoriety by using chemical weapons, which will set it apart from other extremist groups for many years to come. In balance, it should also be noted that the group's failure to use these weapons to their full potential demonstrates the risks associated with being an early adopter of a new technology.

Besides such "customer-driven" influences, terrorist groups also are subject to a category of pressures that legitimate organizations are not. The impact of law enforcement and counter-terrorist forces, in addition to affecting operations that are under way, may have a significant effect on a group's technology adoption process. Like the small business owner who lacks the time to investigate new techniques or the leisure to reflect on how new technology might change his or her business plan, a terrorist group under pressure of pursuit will also have a serious disincentive to seek out or attempt to adopt new technologies. The efforts of counter-terrorist forces could push groups toward new technology as well. If law enforcement groups use technology extensively in their attempts to defeat the terrorist organization, this pressure could move the organization to adopt new tactics and weapons in response. Furthermore, if the efforts of law enforcement cut a group off from accessible sources of weapons, it may be forced to innovate and devise new ones to continue operations. In the case of LTTE, this process operated in reverse. Earlier in its history it lacked access to basic weapons and so pursued tactics such as chemical warfare (see above); when standardized military technology became available, it had much less of an incentive to innovate (Hoffman 1999(1), 47).

FACTORS INFLUENCING SUCCESSFUL TECHNOLOGY ADOPTION

Although the intent to acquire a new technology is the initiator of the adoption process, making the decision is the easier part of the procedure. Once it is so committed, the organization must move past the point of planning to the second stage of the process and actually adopt the technology. This transition requires that the group devote the resources necessary to purchase or develop the technology and, having made that investment, assume the risk associated with the endeavor. At this point the question is no longer whether the group is "innovative" or "non-innovative" but whether it will be successful in completing its desired course of action. As a result, *successful* technology adoption becomes a question of effectiveness of implementation in addition to sustained organizational desire. The examination of technology adoption, beyond simply characterizing an activity as a success or failure, can also consider whether a given terrorist organization has the abilities to use a technology up to its full potential. A bomb planted in a building by one terrorist group, for example, might cause few casualties and some property damage while the same device planted by a more experienced group would lead to a far more lethal attack. The second group, because of a greater knowledge of explosives and tacit understanding of where to place them for maximum effect, has arguably adopted the technology more completely. As a result, all other variables being equal, the second group poses a far greater threat and is more worthy of counter-terrorist attention.

It should be noted from the outset that there is great variation among terrorist groups in these organizational characteristics and therefore in their abilities to deploy technology well. As a result, rather than providing general "rules" about technology and all terrorist groups, this framework is more appropriately a method to examine individual organizations. To the extent that these characteristics can be identified *via* intelligence or analysis for specific groups, more informed projections can be made about particular organizations' potential to innovate upon current weapons choices or to seek out and deploy new ones.

The Nature of the Technology

Beginning from the most basic characteristics of different technologies, variations in "inherent complexity" affect the ability of groups to successfully adopt techniques or devices. At one end of the spectrum, the use of simple firearms and explosives requires very little tacit or explicit knowledge and can therefore be mastered by almost any terrorist. These two routes are arguably the terrorists' "lowest technology" and "lowest training" tactical options, and it is unsurprising that they have remained popular through the entire history of modern terrorism. Conversely, the construction of a working nuclear weapon, even assuming all the physical ingredients were readily available, would require a broader range and greater degree of scientific knowledge and experience and, as a result, much more effort by a terrorist group.

Although the ability of terrorist groups to produce complex weapons systems internally is restricted by constraints of technological adoption, much of the literature focusing on technology and terrorism considers the "easier" case where terrorists procure such technologies from external sources. If a group can obtain a weapon in such a form that much of the required knowledge is already embodied in the hardware—purchasing a timer-controlled, fully operational nuclear device as opposed to assembling one, for example—the chance of the group successfully using a technology that is otherwise "beyond its ability" is greatly increased. Although such weapons systems are readily available to the terrorist organization and do pose a significant threat, the assumption is often made that there are *no* knowledge constraints to their successful use. In reality, even "off-the-shelf" weapons, like a new machine purchased by a commercial firm, require the accumulation of tacit and experiential knowledge regarding their use. Terrorist use of free-flight, armor-piercing missiles to attack vehicles and buildings is one such example. Although a seemingly "simple" weapon, terrorist groups "have generally failed to achieve the clean hit at the right angle in the right place on which hollow-charge missiles depend for their effect" (Clutterbuck, 45). For example, in September 1981 in Germany, an armored limousine carrying U.S. Army General Kroesen was stopped at a traffic light. An attack using an armor-piercing missile was attempted at short range, but the missile bounced off the trunk and inflicted only superficial injuries (Clutterbuck, 45). Even more dramatically, in 1975, Black September Organization terrorists attempted to destroy an El Al airliner at the Orly Airport in Paris using a Soviet 40mm RPG-7 grenade launcher; as a result of their improper use of the weapon, they missed and hit a Yugoslav Airlines plane instead (Wardlaw, 27). Such examples demonstrate that simply assuming that the purchase of a technology implies its successful adoption may overestimate the actual threat posed by terrorist possession of some weapons.

Beyond its usefulness as a rudimentary predictor of the ease of technology adoption, this basic distinction between "simple" and "complex" technologies is also useful in predicting whether terrorist organizations will be able to modify and customize a weapon for their unique use. The ability to adapt a technology for "local" requirements demands a much deeper understanding than that required simply to use the technique or product. If someone wanted to disassemble their video cassette recorder and alter its operation to better suit his or her needs, the level of knowledge required to do so is more extensive than that needed to use it to record television programs. All other variables being equal, it will be more likely that a terrorist organization will acquire this level of mastery of simple technologies rather than more complex ones. In light of this distinction, the extensive amount of innovation that has been shown by terrorist groups in the use of explosives, a very simple technology, is not surprising. The basic grenade, an application of plastic explosives mixed with nails or metal fragments and controlled by a short time fuse, is a common weapon that has been made successfully by almost all terrorist groups. Organizations with a greater mastery of the technology have gone beyond basic construction, however. The PIRA attempted to improve on the design with the construction of the drogue grenade—a hollow charge grenade designed to penetrate armored personnel carriers and tanks. The innovation in design is the addition of a kite-like tail to the explosive which is intended to guide the flight of the grenade and force it to strike the target at the right orientation for its hollow charge to penetrate the armor (Clutterbuck, 49–50). More advanced adaptations also include innovations in remote detonation (discussed previously) and the cruelly innovative bomb designs used by groups targeting civilian airliners. Assessment of the level of innovation in bomb design was, for example, a key part of the investigation of the attack on Pan Am flight 103. Other modifications of basic explosives technology by terrorists have included construction of booby traps, letter bombs, car bombs, and mines for targeting vehicles or personnel (Mullins, 298–322).

In the case of complex "off-the-shelf" systems—such as precision-guided munitions or anti-aircraft missiles—this argument can be extrapolated to predict that terrorist organizations will be unable to customize these technologies. This inability serves as a "bound" on the ways these systems might be applied by terrorist groups. As a result, the operational parameters of a missile used by that same organization can be predicted to conform to the original capabilities imparted by the weapon's manufacturer. Although the quality and effectiveness of modern weapons systems makes this foreknowledge insufficient to provide clear ways of defeating attacks using these weapons, it can serve as a guide to countermeasure design which is unavailable for weapons that are more easily modified by the terrorist.

External Communications Links and the Characteristics of Technology Sources

Just as the extent to which a group communicates with the outside world has a significant impact on its choice of technology, its communication characteristics will also affect the success of a technology adoption effort. The presence of information conduits into a terrorist organization will significantly impact its ability to secure the necessary additional information needed to successfully deploy technology. In obtaining this auxiliary (often tacit) knowledge, the characteristics of the group's sources of information are critical. Because it has been singled out as a potential source of terrorist know-how, it is worthwhile to explore these parameters with respect to information on the Internet. At the most basic level, the quality of the information that is available from a source is of utmost importance. Although the Internet does represent an important source of knowledge about terrorist technology, much of the available information is of questionable quality. Even though the "free-wheeling" nature of the Internet makes bomb-making manuals readily available, those same characteristics mean that the knowledge delivered has likely not been "validated" and could simply be wrong.

In addition to the quality of the information, the types of knowledge transmitted by a source may significantly affect the chances of successful technology deployment. Although bomb-making manuals may be easy to download, is important to recognize that the information transmitted in these manuals is *explicit* alone, and the tacit and experiential understanding needed to apply the technology effectively is not included. Beyond the factual information contained in these sources, the additional tacit knowledge that is required will have to be gained through experimentation by the aspiring terrorist, a process which can be more dangerous to the participant (and likely to lead to arrest and prosecution) than to his or her potential targets. One of the authors of an Internet terrorist handbook blew off both his hands while making one of the formulas contained in his own publication. Whether this was due to inaccuracy in the information or a lack of tacit understanding on the part of the author is impossible to tell, but it underscores the risks of such technology sources (Mullins, 300). Further emphasizing the personal danger in acquiring this tacit knowledge, it has been estimated that approximately 30 percent of the deaths caused by homemade explosives are the bomb-makers themselves (Mullins, 307). In this light, worries about information on bomb-making and instructions for chemical and biological weaponry available on the Internet sound very similar to the arguments made over the last twenty years that nuclear bombs could be assembled by "two graduate students from information in the open literature" and would therefore soon be in the hands of terrorists. One reason that assembly of such a weapon by a terrorist group is now considered a low probability event are the significant obstacles that exist in the construction of technology from explicit knowledge alone.

From a threat assessment perspective, far more worrisome sources of technology are those where terrorists can either obtain technologies as readily usable, "point-and-click" devices, or those which transfer tacit knowledge and training to the group alongside new technology. Sources that meet these criteria to differing degrees are state sponsors, other better-equipped terrorist groups, sympathetic scientists, and members of the international arms market. Because of their desire to sell weapons, arms dealers may have a financial incentive to ensure that their customers are "satisfied" with the operational performance of their products. This could lead to training in their use and a higher probability of terrorists using the weapons to their full potential; like training by the group on its own, however, such activities will be subject to the pressures of international counter-terrorist activities and, if performed in an "unfriendly" country, may call unwanted attention to the group's location and intentions. In the case of the September 11th hijackers, the individuals involved sought pilot training to learn the tacit knowledge needed to carry out the attack. It is unlikely they would have been as tactically successful if they had gained all their piloting information from books. This case represents an important example where the terrorists' technology acquisition strategy provided an opportunity to gain early information into their tactical plans.

Examples also exist of sympathetic scientists or engineers providing technical information to terrorist organizations. State sponsorship of terrorist groups has long been appreciated as a source of advanced weapons technology. Beyond simply providing weapons, states also provide a location for the groups to train and access to potential "experts" who are experienced in the use of the technologies. Once inside a friendly nation, the insulation of the group from threat also provides the opportunity to evaluate a new technology fully and integrate it into the organization's operational repertoire. Reflecting these influences, terrorist acts by state-sponsored groups have been shown, on average, to be eight times more lethal than those by groups without sponsors (Hoffman 1992, 9); although this difference has been ascribed to the access to armaments and technologies made available by the state sponsors, it is also relevant to consider the effects that state sponsorship can have on the groups' adoption of the technologies.

The potential for international cooperation among terrorist groups for operational or ideological reasons has long been a focus of interest. More relevant from the perspective of the current subject, however, is international cooperation that can lead to technology transfer among extremist groups. Examples of such cooperation among terrorist groups include Middle Eastern groups training and supplying weapons to European organizations in the 1970s and the PIRA passing on its "special knowledge on the design of booby-traps and radio-controlled bombs to other terrorist groups in exchange for services rendered, while at the same time learning new techniques from foreign terrorists" (Wilkinson, 40).

The Environment of the Terrorist Group

Just as environmental factors strongly influence the technology choices of a terrorist group, they can also exert a significant effect on the chances of success of their adoption efforts. In the same way that pressure from law enforcement can restrict an organization's choices by preventing it from exploring new technologies, these pressures can also deprive it of the time necessary to adopt them. Successful use of new techniques requires training and, if the risk of coming "above ground" and taking the time to train is too great, the techniques will never be mastered. Increasing pressure from authorities has also been theorized to have sped up the timetable for Aum Shinrikyo's nerve-gas attack on the Tokyo subway which resulted in far fewer deaths than could have occurred had the attack been better orchestrated (Hoffman 1998, 126).

Characteristics of Group Leadership and Structure

In addition to affecting technology choice by an organization, the personal characteristics of a group's leadership also influence the chances of adoption activities being successful. If a leader only values "action," for example, the time spent by a group member practicing or "researching" a newly acquired technology will not be positively reinforced. As a result, when that technology is applied to "action," it will likely be done so prematurely before the group has had the chance to master its full potential. In addition to these effects, the internal group dynamics imposed by the leadership can also affect technological innovation and should be considered. In the adoption of a new technology, inevitably there will be problems during early use or difficulties in adapting the technology to better suit the needs of the organization. Such a "debugging" process—the development of the tacit knowledge needed to use the technology well—is highly dependent on the nature of the relationships between group members and between the group and its leader. For example, a leadership style that does not tolerate internal questioning may inhibit the communication necessary for troubleshooting a new weapon or tactical choice; if discussion of problems and solutions is viewed as dissent or criticism of the leader for choosing the technology, no such questioning will occur, and the group will lose the chance to optimize its use of the techniques.

Beyond the personal characteristics of group leaders and the dynamics within a group, the actual structure of a terrorist organization may also significantly impact how efficiently new technology is adopted. The observation that good technology transfer in commercial organizations requires extensive face-to-face interaction and hands-on training, for example, has significant consequences for underground groups. If a movement chooses to organize itself using a "cell" or "leaderless resistance" model—where small independent groups operate in varying degrees of ignorance about the plans and intentions other group members—technology adoption by the entire movement will be essentially impossible. Large corporations, even those whose members gather at the same meetings and share social time with one another, find that transfer of information from one company division to another is far from easy and often takes a great deal of effort. In a sense, the cell structure of a terrorist organization is specifically designed to minimize such "intergroup" transfer. In this case the advantages of security and being able to minimize "damage" if a section of the group is compromised prevent the communication of tacit or experiential knowledge among members necessary for efficient technological adoption. Although electronic communication over the Internet may partially offset this disadvantage by allowing some interaction among isolated cells, such written communication is limited to explicit knowledge and cannot transmit tacit knowledge effectively.

Availability of Financial and Human Resources

New technology, especially military technology, is expensive. Organizations must raise funds to purchase the materials or weapons necessary for their innovative activities and gain access to the knowledge required to put those materials to work. As a result, terrorist groups that are well funded or supported by states have a distinct advantage. For other groups, alternate sources must be pursued. When explaining a series of bank robberies performed by their organization, the RAF stated they were gathering resources because "only the 'solution of logistics problems' could secure the continuity of the revolutionary organization"; the statement goes further to say that "the technical means could be acquired only in a collective process of working and learning together" (Horchem, 201), thereby explicitly linking the need for resources with the technical capabilities and training needs of the group. Similar statements, including both the focus on group learning and the revolutionary tone, echo modern "cutting-edge" companies' statements as they appeal for investor funding.

Beyond financial assets, a terrorist organization seeking new technology must either possess or gain access to the needed human resources; the absence of such assets can serve as an insurmountable barrier to successful adoption. Beyond a group's current stock of human capital, it is also important to consider its ability to recruit new members with appropriate technical knowledge. Aum Shinrikyo, for example, made extensive efforts to gather members in the scientific and technical disciplines so it would have the resources necessary to produce chemical and biological agents. Consideration of this "recruiting dimension" emphasizes the risk posed by technical personnel who were employed in the former Soviet Union; if a terrorist group has the necessary resources to tap into such an international reservoir of talent, many more technology adoption options will become available and chances of success will markedly increase. It should also be noted, however, that the human resource challenges for terrorist organizations can be significantly more serious than those for commercial firms. Because of the illicit nature of their activities, extremist groups cannot take advantage of the labor mobility that exists among commercial firms; if a group is in need of an expert bomb-maker, for example, it cannot simply "hire one away" from a competing organization.

In addition to constraints on the knowledge stock of a group's members, limits on their activities may also greatly affect the success of technology adoption efforts. In light of the tacit knowledge and locally specific knowledge required to apply new technology, a firm must also have workers who are able to perform the "research" required to gain experience with the techniques or devices and adapt them to the organization's needs. Such experimentation will necessarily consume those members' efforts, and the organization must be able to afford the "costs" associated with part of its staff not participating in current operations. It should be noted that although this "learning by doing" is an important component in the successful adoption of new technology, the converse is also true. If an organization does not use a technology regularly, even one that was successfully adopted earlier, the group may lose its ability to effectively use it.

Because the nature and quality of human resources are so important to technological adoption and successful deployment, the size of terrorist organizations also becomes an important variable to consider in such a personnel analysis. Throughout history, terrorist groups have varied considerably in size. On the upper end, Aum Shinrikyo was estimated to have as many as 50,000 members worldwide (Hoffman 1998, 122), and the Osama bin Laden organization was recently estimated to consist of an extended network of 4,000 to 5,000 individuals. In contrast, the Abu Nidal organization was thought to consist of approximately 500 people, the PIRA and ETA between 200 and 400, and groups like the Japanese Red Army or the Red Army Faction between 20 and 30 individuals (Hoffman 1999(2), 10). In the absence of confounding factors, the larger an organization, the more likely its members are to possess the appropriate explicit and tacit knowledge base to efficiently absorb new technology, and the more likely it is that the organization can "afford" to devote some of its members to technology acquisition activities. In addition, for small groups, the effect of other barriers, such as lack of knowledge, resources, and time, are likely to be magnified.

Group Longevity

Just as having a large number of members to experiment with and perfect the use of a new weapons technology is an advantage, groups that use a technology over an extended period of time will gradually master it and adopt it more fully. The many improvements in detonator technology made by the PIRA (discussed in the opening of this section) would not have occurred if that group had not had thirty years to work on its designs. The life expectancy of many terrorist groups is very short; it has been estimated that 90 percent do not last a year, and 50 percent of those that survive their first year do not last for a decade (Rapoport quoted in Hoffman 1998, 170). The short life of most terrorist groups could serve as a partial explanation of why most operations are relatively "non-innovative." Beyond simply the chronological time that a group exists, the frequency with which the group carries out terrorist operations is also an important consideration. Although significant advances may be made through research alone, it is often only through the actual use of technology that tacit knowledge is acquired and effectiveness is improved. As a result, groups that stage attacks frequently will be more likely to improve their mastery of technology than those that use it only rarely. In recent years, the rise of "free-agent terrorism"—groups that contract their services to others independent of the issue or mission—is particularly troubling with respect to this impediment to innovation. Beyond the reductions in ideological constraints on technology choice that these groups may have, compared to more traditional terrorist groups, their international scope and flexibility may afford them longer lifetimes and higher operational frequencies to perfect and adopt damaging technologies.

ASSESSING TERRORIST TECHNOLOGY ACQUISITION

The term "innovation" applied to terrorist groups may carry a number of meanings across a spectrum of technology acquisition activities. It may refer to an organization pursuing external innovation by obtaining explicit knowledge as written information or as the technology embodied in weapons and, potentially, the tacit knowledge needed to use them both effectively. It may also denote internal learning processes, including both routine "learning by doing" which moves a group toward more complete mastery of a given tactic or weapon, and the development of new knowledge to improve on an existing technology or develop a novel one through experimentation and development. Because of the potential of all these learning processes to increase the lethality and operational spectrum of these organizations, the approaches of terrorist groups to innovation are critically important to accurate threat assessment.

The characteristics highlighted in this analysis, to the extent they can be determined for a given terrorist group, provide a way to predict more accurately both the technology strategies of the organization and its chances to implement those strategies successfully. At the technology strategy stage, such an assessment can allow a more reasoned deployment of both intelligence and counterterrorist resources. A group that is philosophically and operationally closed to new ideas and options will, at most, improve the technologies they already possess through iterative learning and therefore pose a more "bounded" threat than another, more innovative group. At the technology deployment stage, collecting data about the forces that influence group adoption efforts provides the analyst with a window into what otherwise is an entirely restricted space—the actual group activities as it learns to use a new tactic or weapon. Although tabulating the attitudes of a leader toward risk and failure, the network of possible technology sources available to a group, and the educational backgrounds of the people involved does not provide a foolproof method of predicting whether a given adoption effort will be successful, estimates informed by such an analysis are far superior to those based on fear and worst-case scenarios alone.

In light of this analysis, one might reasonably ask, What are the characteristics of a terrorist group that make it most likely to pursue and successfully deploy new technologies? The answer to this question is found most readily in the commercial realm in the form of the small high-technology firm. Any group that is tapped into new technology options, open and hungry for new ideas, willing to take risks, not afraid to fail, and driven by its environment to pursue novelty will clearly have the most positive and acquisitive approach toward technology. If that aggressive strategy is complemented by the necessary human resources, collaborations with sources of technology that transmit both tacit and explicit knowledge, appropriate leadership and structural support, and an environment that provides both enough pressure to force the firm to try many technology experiments and enough leisure to learn from their results, its technology adoption efforts are likely to be very successful. From the perspective of terrorist threat analysis, it is a fortunate observation that no terrorist groups have truly possessed *all* of these technology-reinforcing characteristics. While some organizations have brought together some of them (examples of which are cited throughout this paper), the nature of terrorist activities and the individuals who are attracted to them make it unlikely that an organization will arise with the innovative power of a high-tech start-up firm.

APPLICATIONS AND IMPLICATIONS OF THE FRAMEWORK

By examining not only the technological aspirations of terrorist organizations but also the inherent obstacles that exist in the process of technological adoption and deployment, the framework described here represents an improved method of performing technology-based threat assessment of terrorist organizations. Such an understanding of the obstacles and diverse pressures groups face when deploying new technology also provides a better way to examine current topics of concern in terrorism—many of which hinge on technology adoption—and design ways to address them.

Chemical and Biological Weapons: A Technology Adoption Problem. Over the past few decades, one area which seems to have suffered from such "incomplete" technology-based threat assessment is the use of weapons of mass destruction (WMD) by terrorist organizations. After many years in which the broad-based assumption was made that WMD were incompatible with the desired goals of terrorist groups, the use of chemical agents by Aum Shinrikyo fundamentally altered the framework of discussion on the issue. Analysts spoke of a "taboo" being broken for terrorists; now that such agents had been used once, a barrier to being the first to do so was gone. Discussions of the topic turned to the seeming certainty that extremist groups would quickly gain such agents from sympathetic states, poorly guarded stockpiles, or by manufacturing them independently, and use them for terrorism (see Hoffman, 1999 (1)). Throughout much of the literature, most authors have assumed that few technical hurdles stand between the desirous terrorist organization and WMD. Fortunately, however, there have been few serious imitators since Aum Shinrikyo's attack, and to date rogue states have been seemingly unwilling to place finished weapons in the hands of terrorists. Grave predictions of the widespread use of WMD by terrorists have not come to pass.

Examining chemical and biological weapons from the perspective of this framework produces some insight into the possible reasons why their use has not spread broadly among terrorist groups. Contrary to assumptions in much of the literature, chemical and biological weapons are not simple technologies. Recent assessments of the technological requirements associated with making effective chemical or biological weapons (see Stern, 48–68) highlight the significant technical obstacles to producing and using WMD. That the subway attack by Aum Shinrikyo, an endeavor supported by an extensive scientific staff and nearly a billion dollars in assets, produced only a small fraction of the potential number of fatalities, suggests that there are significant technological hurdles to using these weapons at their full potential. It is not surprising that the specific delivery requirements and instabilities of chemical and biological weapons would require that groups accumulate a level of experience and a considerable stock of tacit knowledge before the technology could be fully adopted and successfully deployed. The fact that no more damaging incidents have occurred since the subway attack may mean that other potential sources of the technology, such as rogue states—which would transmit the tacit knowledge to the group in addition to delivering the weapon, have not been as forthcoming as was initially feared.

Although Aum Shinrikyo's experience did demonstrate that an underground group can amass the technical resources and expertise necessary to present a credible CB threat, subsequent events have changed the nature of the environment with respect to these weapons. While Aum "got away" with small CB operations and tests which allowed it to begin perfecting its abilities, increased sensitivity to these threats would make such testing far riskier today. Beyond simply testing, the risk inherent in the weapons themselves is also a strong disincentive for groups to even attempt to adopt them. Unlike assembling a bomb, where risk is confined to those within the potential blast radius, working with chemical and biological agents could put the entire terrorist organization "in harm's way." As a result, the potential costs associated with such research could not only cripple the technical resources of an organization but cripple it operationally as well. The experience of the Soviet biological warfare facility, run by a superpower with significant resources, is telling: in an accident in 1979, a plume of anthrax was released resulting in between 100 and 1,000 deaths. In light of this experience, the anthrax mailing incidents which occurred through the fall of 2001 represent a case in which understanding the technological aspects of terrorist activity are extremely important. As more details become available through investigation of the agents and perpetrators involved, it will be critical to understand the sources of the biological agents, the technology decision-making of the individual or group that released it, and how this most recent case can help improve future counter-terrorist policy.

Although other organizational characteristics also discourage the use of CB weapons, including the opinions of group members and the fragmented structure of most terrorist organizations, likely the most important barrier is the effort required to prepare and deploy a workable weapon. Most individuals drawn to terrorism want to take direct action rather than use slower, legitimate mechanisms to advance their political or religious agendas. Initiation of a multi-month to several-year research program to perfect a chemical weapon is incompatible with a group that may disintegrate unless it begins its operations immediately. This basic fact, when coupled with the risks inherent in the use of highly toxic and virulent agents, represents the most likely explanation for the limited use of these weapons by terrorists and a rationale to expect this limited use to continue in the future.

Implications for Anti-Terrorist Policy. Given the central role of technology in terrorist activities, it is relevant to ask whether this type of "technology-focused" analysis can suggest any novel strategies through which such threats might be countered. Although not originally framed in these terms, the technology studies literature does in fact contain insights that might be applicable as part of a comprehensive anti-terrorist and counter-terrorist policy. Because of the economic importance of technology diffusion in the economic realm, a great deal of effort has been devoted to devising strategies to *remove* roadblocks to effective technology use in commercial processes and product manufacture. In the case of terrorism, the policy should strive to do the opposite—ensure that any technological roadblocks that hinder a given terrorist group persist as long as possible and, if practical strategies exist, increase in number and difficulty.

Examining the two stages of technology adoption discussed in this analysis, several "pressure points" can be identified that might serve as sites where the internal decision and learning processes of terrorist groups could be influenced by external means. At the decision-making stage, the choice of a technology is made among known options (the group's technology awareness) in light of some judgment of the risks and benefits of pursuing it. As a result, any efforts that could either limit the technological awareness of an organization or shift its perception of the payoffs and costs of adoption decisions could influence the process. At the implementation stage, the key to successful technology adoption is bringing together the necessary tacit and explicit knowledge to effectively use a new weapon or tactical advance. Any actions that would interfere with this synthesis process could prevent a group from successfully completing a new technology acquisition.

The United States has long included some parts of such a "technology-focused" approach in its anti-terrorism policy. One component is the stance of "technology denial," which the West, and the U.S. particularly, has taken towards regimes like Iraq in an attempt to prevent them from developing accurate missile technology. Such denial includes limiting the spread of U.S. weapons that involve technologies that could be applied to undesired ends (applicable explicit knowledge) and pursuing diplomatic efforts to dissuade other countries from transferring sensitive information. Nuclear non-proliferation efforts have always included attempts to prevent the spread of the hardware involved in bomb and warhead construction. Some other nations, including Israel, have taken a more direct approach to these types of non-proliferation issues by damaging equipment during shipment (thereby destroying the explicit knowledge embodied in it), intimidating firms involved in transferring technology, and even going as far as assassinating members of the Iraqi atomic energy commission, thereby eliminating any tacit knowledge they possessed (Stern, 115). The sanctions that have been imposed on Iraq since the Gulf War have reportedly had an effect on the technological capabilities of the country. The aging of its technical workforce, the removal of opportunities for younger people to pursue training abroad, and the exodus of trained workers have led to significant reductions in the country's knowledge "stocks" and technical abilities.

Beyond such "traditional" policy strategies, a wide range of "technology-directed" actions might strike specifically at the technology adoption and deployment activities of different organizations. Possible actions, admittedly varying in their levels of diplomatic acceptability, could include:

- Pursuit of diplomatic, law enforcement, or military strategies to prevent known terrorist groups from training. Even small operations that increase the risk of such activities could have a significant effect by pushing a group's effective deployment of a technology far enough into the future that the group will disband before employing it, or by allowing time for the development of effective countermeasures to the threat. Attention should also be devoted to limiting the number of safe havens and states friendly to terrorism to reduce the number of areas available for training and tactical experimentation.

- Pursuit of diplomatic or covert strategies to interfere with the recruitment of competent technological workers into known terrorist groups. Such operations would restrict the passage of the tacit knowledge held by these individuals and prevent the accumulation of expertise to facilitate future technological adoption. Amnesties or incentives could be utilized to encourage knowledgeable individuals to leave groups, or direct operations could be undertaken to extract key personnel from a group.

- Efforts attempting to reduce the "market pull" effect forcing terrorist towards new technology could be beneficial. Such efforts could include reducing the emphasis and publicity given to new, high-technology threats—including the current high profile given to WMD threats. By giving inordinate attention to events, threats, and hoaxes involving new weapons, society encourages the adoption of newer, more destructive technologies.

- Pursuit of covert and publicly announced actions to undermine trust between extremist groups and potential technology sources. Sting operations and programs of infiltration or subterfuge could increase the risk of approaching external sources of information and technology.
- In the event a group is suspected to be "near" the effective acquisition or deployment of a dangerous innovation, increasing law enforcement pressure on that group could be used to interfere with the process. Such pressure could force the group to deploy the technology prematurely (and hence less effectively) or, by changing the perceived risk of the activity, cause the group to alter its priorities. Keeping pressure on an advancing group may also deprive it of the time to explore new technology or, once pursued, fully integrate it into its operations.
- In an effort to reduce the value or usefulness of readily available explicit knowledge, efforts could be made to "contaminate" sources of bomb-making information, for example, with incorrect and dangerous information. The public disclosure of these efforts would serve to increase the risk associated with using such information and could limit the effectiveness of the Internet as a source for such military data. Additional efforts could also be made specifically to assault known groups with misinformation by electronic or human means to hinder their research and development efforts.
- Traditional anti-terrorist operations to obtain intelligence and stop operations before they are initiated may also play an important part in affecting the technological capabilities of a group. If an organization is prevented from using a technology for long enough, the technology will eventually be lost as knowledgeable members of the group are captured or killed and new members cannot gain the experience necessary to master the technology.

Although such activities cannot, on their own, eliminate the threat posed by extremist groups to mainstream society, restricting the technological capabilities of these groups could partially blunt the severity of their attacks. In the case of weapons or tactics that pose the most serious threats, this blunting could prove to make the difference between terrorist strikes that result in hundreds to thousands of casualties and those that are limited to a very few. Even if such "technology-directed" strategies do not represent a comprehensive way of attacking the terrorist threat in its entirety, one may speculate that, if groups can be deprived of technologies or successfully punished for the methods and tactics they *seek* to obtain, other groups may be discouraged from making similar attempts.

KEY REFERENCES:

Clutterbuck, R. *Terrorism in an Unstable World*. London, Routledge, 1994.

Hoffman, B. *Inside Terrorism*. New York, Columbia University Press, 1998.

Hoffman, B. *Terrorism and Weapons of Mass Destruction: An Analysis of Trends and Motivations*, RAND Report P-8039, Santa Monica, CA, 1999 (1).

Hoffman, B. "Terrorism Trends and Prospects" in *Countering the New Terrorism*, RAND Report MR-989-AF, Santa Monica, CA, 1999 (2).

Hoffman, B. *Terrorist Targeting: Tactics, Trends, and Potentialities*, RAND Report P-7801, Santa Monica, CA, 1992.

Horchem, H. J. "West Germany's Red Army Anarchists" in *Contemporary Terrorism*. W. Gutteridge, ed. New York, Facts on File, 1986.

Mullins, W. C. *A Sourcebook on Domestic and International Terrorism: An Analysis of Issues, Organizations, Tactics, and Responses*. Springfield, IL, Charles C. Thomas, 1997.

Rapoport, D. C. "Sacred Terror: A Contemporary Example from Islam" in *Origins of Terrorism: Psychologies, Ideologies, Theologies, States of Mind*. Reich, W., ed. Washington, DC, Woodrow Wilson Center Press, 1998.

Stern, J. *The Ultimate Terrorist*. Cambridge, MA, Harvard University Press, 1999.

Wardlaw, G. *Political Terrorism: Theory, Tactics, and Counter-Measures*. Cambridge, UK, Cambridge University Press, 1989.

Wilkinson, P. "Terrorism: International Dimensions" in *Contemporary Terrorism*. W. Gutteridge, ed. New York, Facts on File, 1986.

Terror Training Manual: Military Studies in the Jihad Against the Tyrants

In the name of Allah, the merciful and compassionate

PRESENTATION

To those champions who avowed the truth day and night . . .

. . . And wrote with their blood and sufferings these phrases . . .

—*—The confrontation that we are calling for with the apostate regimes does not know Socratic debates . . . , Platonic ideals . . . , nor Aristotelian diplomacy. But it knows the dialogue of bullets, the ideals of assassination, bombing, and destruction, and the diplomacy of the cannon and machine-gun.

* * *   . . .

Islamic governments have never and will never be established through peaceful solutions and cooperative councils. They are established as they [always] have been

> by pen and gun

> > by word and bullet

> > > by tongue and teeth

Principles of Military Organization:

Military Organization has three main principles without which it cannot be established.

1. Military Organization commander and advisory council
2. The soldiers (individual members)
3. A clearly defined strategy

Military Organization Requirements:

The Military Organization dictates a number of requirements to assist it in confrontation and endurance. These are:
1. Forged documents and counterfeit currency
2. Apartments and hiding places
3. Communication means
4. Transportation means
5. Information
6. Arms and ammunition
7. Transport

Missions Required of the Military Organization:

The main mission for which the Military Organization is responsible is:

The overthrow of the godless regimes and their replacement with an Islamic regime. Other missions consist of the following:
1. Gathering information about the enemy, the land, the installations, and the neighbors.
2. Kidnaping enemy personnel, documents, secrets, and arms.
3. Assassinating enemy personnel as well as foreign tourists.
4. Freeing the brothers who are captured by the enemy.
5. Spreading rumors and writing statements that instigate people against the enemy.
6. Blasting and destroying the places of amusement, immorality, and sin; not a vital target.
7. Blasting and destroying the embassies and attacking vital economic centers
8. Blasting and destroying bridges leading into and out of the cities.

Importance of the Military Organization:

1. Removal of those personalities that block the call's path. [A different handwriting:] All types of military and civilian intellectuals and thinkers for the state.
2. Proper utilization of the individuals' unused capabilities.
3. Precision in performing tasks, and using collective views on completing a job from all aspects, not just one.
4. Controlling the work and not fragmenting it or deviating from it.
5. Achieving long-term goals such as the establishment of an Islamic state and short-term goals such as operations against enemy individuals and sectors.

6. Establishing the conditions for possible confrontation with the regressive regimes and their persistence.

7. Achieving discipline in secrecy and through tasks.

SECOND LESSON: NECESSARY QUALIFICATIONS AND CHARACTERISTICS FOR THE ORGANIZATION'S MEMBER

Necessary Qualifications for the Organization's members

1. Islam:

The member of the Organization must be Moslem. How can an unbeliever, someone from a revealed religion [Christian, Jew], a secular person, a communist, etc. protect Islam and Moslems and defend their goals and secrets when he does not believe in that religion [Islam]? The Israeli Army requires that a fighter be of the Jewish religion. Likewise, the command leadership in the Afghan and Russian armies requires any one with an officer's position to be a member of the communist party.

2. Commitment to the Organization's Ideology:

This commitment frees the Organization's members from conceptional problems.

3. Maturity:

The requirements of military work are numerous, and a minor cannot perform them. The nature of hard and continuous work in dangerous conditions requires a great deal of psychological, mental, and intellectual fitness, which are not usually found in a minor. . . .

4. Sacrifice:

He [the member] has to be willing to do the work and undergo martyrdom for the purpose of achieving the goal and establishing the religion of majestic Allah on earth.

5. Listening and Obedience:

In the military, this is known today as discipline. It is expressed by how the member obeys the orders given to him. That is what our religion urges. The Glorious says, "O, ye who believe! Obey Allah and obey the messenger and those charged with authority among you." . . .

6. Keeping Secrets and Concealing Information

[This secrecy should be used] even with the closest people, for deceiving the enemies is not easy. Allah says, "Even though their plots were such that as to shake the hills! [Koranic verse]." Allah's messenger—God bless and keep him—says, "Seek Allah's help in doing your affairs in secrecy."

It was said in the proverbs, "The hearts of freemen are the tombs of secrets" and "Moslems' secrecy is faithfulness, and talking about it is faithlessness." [Mohammed]—God bless and keep him—used to keep work secrets from the closest people, even from his wife A'isha—may Allah's grace be on her.

7. Free of Illness

The Military Organization's member must fulfill this important require-ment. Allah says, "There is no blame for those who are infirm, or ill, or who have no resources to spend."

8. Patience

[The member] should have plenty of patience for [enduring] afflictions if he is overcome by the enemies. He should not abandon this great path and sell himself and his religion to the enemies for his freedom. He should be patient in performing the work, even if it lasts a long time.

9. Tranquility and "Unflappability"

[The member] should have a calm personality that allows him to endure psychological traumas such as those involving bloodshed, murder, arrest, im-prisonment, and reverse psychological traumas such as killing one or all of his Organization's comrades. [He should be able] to carry out the work. . . .

12. Truthfulness and Counsel

The Commander of the faithful, Omar Ibn Al-Khattab—may Allah be pleased with him—asserted that this characteristic was vital in those who gather information and work as spies against the Moslems' enemies. He [Omar] sent a letter to Saad Ibn Abou Wakkas—may Allah be pleased with him—saying, "If you step foot on your enemies' land, get spies on them. Choose those whom you count on for their truthfulness and advice, whether Arabs or inhabitants of that land. Liars' accounts would not benefit you, even if some of them were true; the deceiver is a spy against you and not for you."

13. Ability to Observe and Analyze

The Israeli Mossad received news that some Palestinians were going to at-tack an Israeli El Al airplane. That plane was going to Rome with Golda Meir—Allah's curse upon her—the Prime Minister at the time, on board. The Palestinians had managed to use a clever trick that allowed them to wait for the arrival of the plane without being questioned by anyone. They had beaten a man who sold potatoes, kidnaped him, and hidden him. They made two holes in the top of that peddler's cart and placed two tubes next to the chimney through which two Russian-made "Strella" [PH] missiles could be launched. The Mossad officers traveled the airport back and forth looking for anything that would lead them to the Palestinians. One officer passed the potato cart twice without noticing anything. On his third time, he noticed three chimneys, but only one of them was working with smoke coming out of it. He quickly steered toward the cart and hit it hard. The cart overturned, and the Palestinians were captured.*. . .

THIRD LESSON: COUNTERFEIT CURRENCY AND FORGED DOCUMENTS

Financial Security Precautions:

1. Dividing operational funds into two parts: One part is to be invested in projects that offer financial return, and the other is to be saved and not spent except during operations.

2. Not placing operational funds [all] in one place.

3. Not telling the Organization members about the location of the funds.

4. Having proper protection while carrying large amounts of money.

5. Leaving the money with non-members and spending it as needed.

Forged Documents (Identity Cards, Records Books, Passports)

The following security precautions should be taken:

1. Keeping the passport in a safe place so it would not be seized by the security apparatus, and the brother it belongs to would have to negotiate its return (I'll give you your passport if you give me information).

2. All documents of the undercover brother, such as identity cards and passport, should be falsified.

3. When the undercover brother is traveling with a certain identity card or passport, he should know all pertinent [information] such as the name, profession, and place of residence.

4. The brother who has special work status (commander, communication link, . . .) should have more than one identity card and passport. He should learn the contents of each, the nature of the [indicated] profession, and the dialect of the residence area listed in the document.

5. The photograph of the brother in these documents should be without a beard. It is preferable that the brother's public photograph [on these documents] be also without a beard. If he already has one [document] showing a photograph with a beard, he should replace it.

6. When using an identity document in different names, no more than one such document should be carried at one time.

7. The validity of the falsified travel documents should always be confirmed.

---

*This story is found in the book A'n Tarik Al-Khida' "By Way of Deception Methods," by Victor Ostrovsky [PH]. The author claims that the Mossad wants to kill him for writing that book. However, I believe that the book was authorized by the Israeli Mossad.

8. All falsification matters should be carried out through the command and not haphazardly (procedure control).

9. Married brothers should not add their wives to their passports.

10. When a brother is carrying the forged passport of a certain country, he should not travel to that country. It is easy to detect forgery at the airport, and the dialect of the brother is different from that of the people from that country.

Security Precautions Related to the Organizations' Given Names:

1. The name given by the Organization [to the brother] should not be odd in comparison with other names used around him.

2. A brother should not have more than one name in the area where he lives (the undercover work place).

FOURTH LESSON: ORGANIZATION MILITARY BASES "APARTMENTS — HIDING PLACES"

Definition of Bases:

* These are apartments, hiding places, command centers, etc. in which secret operations are executed against the enemy.

These bases may be in cities, and are [then] called homes or apartments. They may be in mountainous, harsh terrain far from the enemy, and are [then] called hiding places or bases.

During the initial stages, the Military Organization usually uses apartments in cities as places for launching assigned missions, such as collecting information, observing members of the ruling regime, etc.

Hiding places and bases in mountains and harsh terrain are used at later stages, from which Jihad [holy war] groups are dispatched to execute assassination operations of enemy individuals, bomb their centers, and capture their weapons. In some Arab countries such as Egypt, where there are no mountains or harsh terrain, all stages of Jihad work would take place in cities. The opposite was true in Afghanistan, where initially Jihad work was in the cities, then the warriors shifted to mountains and harsh terrain. There, they started battling the Communists.

Security Precautions Related to Apartments:

1. Choosing the apartment carefully as far as the location, the size for the work necessary (meetings, storage, arms, fugitives, work preparation).

2. It is preferable to rent apartments on the ground floor to facilitate escape and digging of trenches.

3. Preparing secret locations in the apartment for securing documents, records, arms, and other important items.

4. Preparing ways of vacating the apartment in case of a surprise attack (stands, wooden ladders). . . .

6. Providing the necessary cover for the people who frequent the apartment (students, workers, employees, etc.).

7. Avoiding seclusion and isolation from the population and refraining from going to the apartment at suspicious times. . . .

10. Care should be exercised not to rent apartments that are known to the security apparatus [such as] those used for immoral or prior Jihad activities.

11. Avoiding police stations and government buildings. Apartments should not be rented near those places. . . .

13. It is preferable to rent apartments in newly developed areas where people do not know one another. Usually, in older quarters people know one another and strangers are easily identified, especially since these quarters have many informers.

14. Ensuring that there has been no surveillance prior to the members entering the apartment.

15. Agreement among those living in the apartment on special ways of knocking on the door and special signs prior to entry into the building's main gate to indicate to those who wish to enter that the place is safe and not being monitored. Such signs include hanging out a towel, opening a curtain, placing a cushion in a special way, etc.

16. If there is a telephone in the apartment, calls should be answered in an agreed-upon manner among those who use the apartment. That would prevent mistakes that would, otherwise, lead to revealing the names and nature of the occupants.

17. For apartments, replacing the locks and keys with new ones. As for the other entities (camps, shops, mosques), appropriate security precautions should be taken depending on the entity's importance and role in the work. . . .

19. In a newer apartment, avoid talking loud because prefabricated ceilings and walls [used in the apartments] do not have the same thickness as those in old ones. . . .

FIFTH LESSON:
MEANS OF COMMUNICATION AND TRANSPORTATION

In the name of Allah, the merciful and compassionate

Introduction:

It is well known that in undercover operations, communication is the mainstay of the movement for rapid accomplishment. However, it is a double-edged sword: It can be to our advantage if we use it well and it can be a knife dug into our back if we do not consider and take the necessary security measures.

Communication Means:

The Military Organization in any Islamic group can, with its modest capabilities, use the following means: 1. The telephone, 2. Meeting in-person, 3. Messenger, 4. Letters, 5. Some modern devices, such as the facsimile and wireless [communication].

Communication may be within the county, state, or even the country, in which case it is called local communication. When it extends expanded between countries, it is then called international communication.

Secret Communication Is Limited to the Following Types:

Common, standby, alarm

1. *Common Communication:* It is a communication between two members of the Organization without being monitored by the security apparatus opposing the Organization. The common communication should be done under a certain cover and after inspecting the surveillance situation [by the enemy].

2. *Standby Communication:* This replaces common communication when one of the two parties is unable to communicate with the other for some reason.

3. *Alarm Communication:* This is used when the opposing security apparatus discovers an undercover activity or some undercover members. Based on this communication, the activity is stopped for a while, all matters related to the activity are abandoned and the Organization's members are hidden from the security personnel.

Method of Communication Among Members of the Organization:

1. Communication about undercover activity should be done using a good cover; it should also be quick, explicit, and pertinent. That is, just for talking only.

2. Prior to contacting his members, the commander of the cell should agree with each of them separately (the cell members should never meet all in one place and should not know one another) on a manner and means of communication with each other. Likewise, the chief of the Organization should [use a similar technique] with the branch commanders.

3. A higher-ranking commander determines the type and method of communication with lower-ranking leaders.

First Means: The Telephone:

Because of significant technological advances, security measures for monitoring the telephone and broadcasting equipment have increased. Monitoring may be done by installing a secondary line or wireless broadcasting device on a telephone that relays the calls to a remote location. . . . That is why the Organization takes security measures among its members who use this means of communication (the telephone).

1. Communication should be carried out from public places. One should select telephones that are less suspicious to the security apparatus and are more difficult to monitor. It is preferable to use telephones in booths and on main streets.

2. Conversation should be coded or in general terms so as not to alert the person monitoring [the telephone]. . . .

4. Telephone numbers should be memorized and not recorded. If the brother has to write them, he should do so using a code so they do not appear as telephone numbers (figures from a shopping list, etc.)

5. The telephone caller and person called should mention some words or sentences prior to bringing up the intended subject. The brother who is calling may misdial one of the digits and actually call someone else. The person called may claim that the call is for him, and the calling brother may start telling him work-related issues and reveal many things because of a minor error.

6. In telephone conversations about undercover work, the voice should be changed and distorted. . . .

8. When a telephone [line] is identified [by the security apparatus], the command and all parties who were using it should be notified as soon as possible in order to take appropriate measures.

9. When the command is certain that a particular telephone [line] is being monitored, it can exploit it by providing information that misleads the enemy and benefits the work plan.

10. If the Organization manages to obtain jamming devices, it should use them immediately.

Second Means: Meeting in-person:

This is direct communication between the commander and a member of the Organization. During the meeting the following are accomplished:

1. Information exchange, 2. Giving orders and instructions, 3. Financing, 4. Member follow-up

Stages of the In-Person Meeting:
A. Before the meeting, B. The meeting [itself], C. After the meeting

A. *Before the Meeting:*
   The following measures should be taken:

1. Designating the meeting location, 2. Finding a proper cover for the meeting, 3. Specifying the meeting date and time, 4. Defining special signals between those who meet.

1. Identifying the meeting location: If the meeting location is stationary, the following matters should be observed:

i. The location should be far from police stations and security centers.

ii. Ease of transportation to the location.

iii. Selecting the location prior to the meeting and learning all its details. . . .

v. The availability of many roads leading to the meeting location. That would provide easy escape in case the location were raided by security personnel.

vi. The location should not be under suspicion (by the security [apparatus]). . . .

ix. When public transportation is used, one should alight at some distance from the meeting location and continue on foot. In the case of a private vehicle, one should park it far away or in a secure place so as to be able to maneuver it quickly at any time.

If the meeting location is not stationary, the following matters should be observed:

i. The meeting location should be at the intersection of a large number of main and side streets to facilitate entry, exit, and escape.

ii. The meeting location (such as a coffee shop) should not have members that might be dealing with the security apparatus.

iii. The meeting should not be held in a crowded place because that would allow the security personnel to hide and monitor those who meet.

iv. It is imperative to agree on an alternative location for the meeting in case meeting in the first is unfeasible. That holds whether the meeting place is stationary or not.

Those who meet in-person should do the following:

i. Verifying the security situation of the location before the meeting. . . .

iii. Not heading to the location directly.

iv. Clothing and appearance should be appropriate for the meeting location.

v. Verifying that private documents carried by the brother have appropriate cover.

vi. Prior to the meeting, designing a security plan that specifies what the security personnel would be told in case the location were raided by them, and what [the brothers] would resort to in dealing with the security personnel (fleeing, driving back, . . .).

2. *Finding a proper cover for the meeting:* [The cover]

    i. should blend well with the nature of the location.

    ii. In case they raid the place, the security personnel should believe the cover.

    iii. should not arouse the curiosity of those present.

    iv. should match the person's appearance and his financial and educational background.

    v. should have documents that support it.

    vi. provide reasons for the two parties' meeting (for example, one of the two parties should have proof that he is an architect. The other should have documents as proof that he is a land owner. The architect has produced a construction plan for the land). . . .

If the two individuals do not know one another, they should do the following:

    a. The initial sign for becoming acquainted may be that both of them wear a certain type of clothing or carry a certain item. These signs should be appropriate for the place, easily identified, and meet the purpose. The initial sign for becoming acquainted does not [fully] identify one person by another. It does that at a rate of 30%.

    b. Safety Signal: It is given by the individual sitting in the meeting location to inform the second individual that the place is safe. The second person would reply through signals to inform the first that he is not being monitored. The signals are agreed upon previously and should not cause suspicion.

    c. A second signal for getting acquainted is one which the arriving person uses while sitting down. That signal may be a certain clause, a word, a sentence, or a gesture agreed upon previously, and should not cause suspicion for those who hear it or see it. . . .

C. *After the Meeting:* The following measures should be taken:

    1. Not departing together, but each one separately.

    2. Not heading directly to the main road but through secondary ones.

    3. Not leaving anything in the meeting place that might indicate the identity or nature of those who met.

Meeting in-person has disadvantages, such as:

    1. Allowing the enemy to capture those who are meeting.

    2. Allowing them [the enemy] to take pictures of those who are meeting, record their conversation, and gather evidence against them.

3. Revealing the appearance of the commander to the other person. However, that may be avoided by taking the previously mentioned measures such as disguising himself well and changing his appearance (glasses, wig, etc.).

Third Means: The Messenger:

This is an intermediary between the sender and the receiver. The messenger should possess all characteristics mentioned in the first chapter regarding the Military Organization's member.

These are the security measures that a messenger should take:
1. Knowledge of the person to whom he will deliver the message.
2. Agreement on special signals, exact date, and specific time.
3. Selecting a public street or place that does not raise suspicion.
4. Going through a secondary road that does not have check points.
5. Using public transportation (train, bus, . . .) and disembarking before the main station. Likewise, embarking should not be done at the main station either, where there are a lot of security personnel and informants.
6. Complete knowledge of the location to which he is going.

Fourth Means: Letters:

This means (letters) may be used as a method of communication between members and the Organization provided that the following security measures are taken:
1. It is forbidden to write any secret information in the letter. If one must do so, the writing should be done in general terms.
2. The letter should not be mailed from a post office close to the sender's residence, but from a distant one.
3. The letter should not be sent directly to the receiver's address but to an inconspicuous location where there are many workers from your country. Afterwards, the letter will be forwarded to the intended receiver. (This is regarding the overseas-bound letter.)
4. The sender's name and address on the envelope should be fictitious. In case the letters and their contents are discovered, the security apparatus would not be able to determine his [the sender's] name and address. . . .

Transportation Means:

The members of the Organization may move from one location to another using one of the following means:

a. Public transportation, b. Private transportation

Security Measures That Should be Observed in Public Transportation:

1. One should select public transportation that is not subject to frequent checking along the way, such as crowded trains or public buses.

2. Boarding should be done at a secondary station, as main stations undergo more careful surveillance. Likewise, disembarkation should not be done at main stations. . . .

4. The existence of documents supporting the cover. . . .

6. The brother traveling on a "special mission" should not get involved in religious issues (advocating good and denouncing evil) or day-to-day matters (seat reservation, . . .).

7. The brother traveling on a mission should not arrive in the [destination] country at night because then travelers are few, and there are [search] parties and check points along the way. . . .

Security Measures That Should be Observed in Private Transportation:

Private transportation includes: cars, motorcycles

A. Cars and motorcycles used in overt activity:

1. One should possess the proper permit and not violate traffic rules in order to avoid trouble with the police.

2. The location of the vehicle should be secure so that the security apparatus would not confiscate it.

3. The vehicle make and model should be appropriate for the brother's cover.

4. The vehicle should not be used in special military operations unless the Organization has no other choice.

B. Cars and motorcycles used in covert activity:

1. Attention should be given to permits and [obeying] the traffic rules in order to avoid trouble and reveal their actual mission.

2. The vehicle should not be left in suspicious places (deserts, mountains, etc.). If it must be, then the work should be performed at suitable times when no one would keep close watch or follow it.

3. The vehicle should be purchased using forged documents so that getting to its owners would be prevented once it is discovered. . . .

5. While parking somewhere, one should be in a position to move quickly and flee in case of danger.

6. The car or motorcycle color should be changed before the operation and returned to the original after the operation.

7. The license plate number and county name should be falsified. Further, the digits should be numerous in order to prevent anyone from spotting and memorizing it.

8. The operation vehicle should not be taken to large gasoline stations so that it would not be detected by the security apparatus.

NINTH LESSON: SECURITY PLAN

Defining Security Plan:

This is a set of coordinated, cohesive, and integrated measures that are related to a certain activity and designed to confuse and surprise the enemy, and if uncovered, to minimize the work loss as much as possible.

Importance of the Security Plan:

The work will be successful if Allah grants that. The more solid is the security plan, the more successful [the work] and the fewer the losses. The less solid the security plan, the less successful [the work] and the greater the losses.

Specifications of the Security Policy: A number of conditions should be satisfied to help the security plan to succeed. These are: [It should be]

A. realistic and based on fact so it would be credible to the enemy before and after the work.
B. coordinated, integrated, cohesive, and accurate, without any gaps, to provide the enemy [the impression of] a continuous and linked chain of events.
C. simple so that the members can assimilate it.
D. creative.
E. flexible.
F. secretive.

The Method of Implementing the Security Plan: There should be a security plan for each activity that is subject to being uncovered by the enemy. For example, the brother who is charged with a certain mission might be arrested. It is, therefore, essential that a security plan be designed for him through which he will be able to deny any accusation. Likewise, for the group assigned a collective mission, there should be a security plan to which all members are committed. Each member would then find out, learn, and be trained in his role to ensure his assimilation of it.

A meeting held by those responsible for covert work. For that [meeting], great effort on our part should be exercised to ensure its safety. We shall discuss that meeting and what makes it secure from enemy spies.

The security plan for that meeting is divided into several stages:

A. Before the meeting, B. The meeting location, C. During the meeting, D. After the conclusion of meeting, E. In case security personnel storm the meeting place and capture one of the members.

A. *Before the meeting:* Here the meeting for covert work is divided into:

Meeting in Stationary Location: A meeting where more than three members gather to discuss a plan or prepare for an activity.

Mobile Meeting (Encounter): A meeting among a small number of members, not more than three, to inform [one another] of a certain issue.

Security Measures Necessary Prior to the Stationary Meeting:

1. Establishing a plan suitable for the members if any of them is arrested. It consists of:

Who is the owner of the apartment?
What was discussed in the meeting?
Who was with you?
What was agreed upon?

2. Specifying the timing of the meeting in such a way as not to raise suspicion of the members' movements.

3. Not allowing a long period of time between specifying the meeting time and the meeting itself.

4. Securing the meeting location and the routes leading to it by the following:

a. Ensuring the security status via telephone.

b. Assigning members to monitor the place before and during the meeting.

c. Planting a member close to the nearest enemy security point (police station, security administration) to communicate the first sight of security movement.

d. Posting an armed guard to stop any attack and to give those meeting a chance to escape.

5. Specifying what would happen in the event the police storm the place. . . .

Necessary Security Measures Prior to the Mobile Meeting: When a brother goes to a certain meeting (mobile meeting), he should review these things:

a. Is he sure that the enemy is not behind him nor at the meeting place?

b. Who will meet him?

c. Is there anything that might raise suspicion?

d. Is this the first appointment or the second (alternative, changed)?

e. Does he know the meeting place in detail?

f. Are his appearance and clothing suitable for the location where he will stand [meet]?

g. Is his weapon in good working condition?

h. What is the alternative for each action?

i. Not going directly to the person whom he would like to meet. Verifying the person's appearance and features.

B. *The Stationary Meeting Location:* It is necessary that it have special characteristics to confront any danger to the meeting members:

1. Location-wise, it should be in the middle of a group of houses, not at the beginning.

2. Having many routes leading to that location. That would assist entering and exiting in many ways. Consequently, it makes surrounding the place difficult and facilitates escaping from danger.

3. The location should not be close to suspicious locations ([where] individuals or establishments work with the security [apparatus]).

4. It is preferable that the apartment be on the ground floor and have a telephone.

The Mobile Meeting Location (Encounter):

1. The meeting location should be at the intersection of many roads where it is easy to come, go, and flee.

2. The meeting should be held far from places where it is believed some of whose elements deal with the security apparatus (coffee shops).

3. The place should not be crowded because that allows security personnel to go undetected.

4. It is necessary to have alternative locations and times. That would make it difficult for security personnel to monitor the place. . . .

C. *After the Conclusion of the Meeting:*

1. Departing singly or in pairs, depending on the number of members present.

2. Not heading directly onto main roads but to secondary ones.

3. Not speaking about what was discussed in the meeting, during or after departure.

4. Removing all observers after the members depart.

5. Not leaving anything that would lead [to the fact that] there was anyone there except the owner.

D. *Raiding and capturing one of the members:*
    1. Establishing a plan to repel the attack, which consists of the following:
        a. Who will engage the enemy with bullets?
        b. Who will flee with the important documents and who will burn the
rest?
        c. Not heading directly to other organization locations.
        d. Specifying the escape roads and streets.
        e. If the place is surrounded by barbed wire, make sure all members
have left.

In case an individual is caught, the following should be done:

Executing what was agreed upon with the brother in the security plan.

If the brother has important work position (commander, one who knows the arsenal locations, . . .), whatever is necessary should be done before the enemy discovers anything.

Instruct all members not to go to the meeting location.

Inform all members of the telephone number of that apartment in order to mislead the enemy.

An Example of a Security Plan for a Group Mission (assassinating an important person)[3]: Assassination is an operation of military means and basic security. Therefore, it is essential that the commanders who establish plans related to assassination give attention to two issues:

First Issue: The importance of establishing a careful, systematic, and solid security plan to hide the operation from the enemy until the time of its execution, which would minimize the losses in case the executing party is discovered.

Second Issue: The importance of establishing a tactical plan for the assassination operation that consists of the operational factors themselves (members, weapons, hiding places . . .) and factors of the operation (time, place). In this example, we shall explain in detail the part related to the security plan. The part related to operational tactics will be explained in the lesson on special operational tactics.

Security Plan for the Assassination Operation: The security plan must take into account the following matters:

---

3. It is possible to also say "kidnapping an important person." All security measures and arrangements in assassination and kidnapping are the same.

A. The Commander: The security apparatus should not know his whereabouts and movements. All security measures and arrangements related to members of the Military Organization (soldiers, commanders) apply to him.

B. The Members:

1. They are elements who are selected from various provinces and are suitable for the operation.

2. During the selection process, members should not know one another. They should not know the original planners of the operation. In case they do, the commander should be notified. He then should modify the plan.

3. They should be distributed as small groups (3 members) in apartments that are not known except to their proprietors. They should also be given field names.

4. During the selection process, consider whether their absence from their families and jobs would clearly attract attention. We also apply to them all security measures related to the Organization's individuals (soldiers).

C. *Method of Operating:*

1. The matters of arming and financing should not be known by anyone except the commander.

2. The apartments should not be rented under real names. They [the apartments] should undergo all security measures related to the Military Organization's camps.

3. Prior to executing an operation, falsified documents should be prepared for the participating individuals.

4. The documents related to the operation should be hidden in a secure place and burned immediately after the operation, and traces of the fire should be removed.

5. The means of communication between the operation commander and the participating brothers should be established.

6. Prior to the operation, apartments should be prepared to hide the brothers participating in it. These apartments should not be known except to the commander and his soldiers.

7. Reliable transportation means must be made available. It is essential that prior to the operation, these means are checked and properly maintained.

D. *Interrogation and Investigation:* Prior to executing an operation, the commander should instruct his soldiers on what to say if they are captured. He should explain that more than once, in order to ensure that they have assimilated it. They should, in turn, explain it back to the commander. The commander should also sit with each of them individually [and go over] the agreed-upon matters that would be brought up during the interrogation:

1. The one who conceived, planned, and executed this operation was a brother who has a record of those matters with the enemy.

2. During the interrogation, each brother would mention a story that suits his personal status and the province of his residence. The story should be agreed upon with the commander.

3. Each brother who is subjected to interrogation and torture, should state all that he agreed upon with the commander and not deviate from it. Co-ordination should be maintained with all brothers connected to the operation.

Note: The fictitious brother who the brothers say conceived, planned, trained, and executed the operation, should be sent away on a journey [outside the country].

TENTH LESSON: SPECIAL TACTICAL OPERATIONS

Definition of Special Operations:

These are operations using military means and basic security. Special operations are some of the tasks of groups specialized in intelligence and security.

Characteristics of Members That Specialize in the Special Operations:

1. Individual's physical and combat fitness (jumping, climbing, running, etc.).

2. Good training on the weapon of assassination, assault, kidnapping, and bombing (special operations).

3. Possessing cleverness, canniness, and deception.

4. Possessing intelligence, precision, and alertness.

5. Tranquility and calm personality (that allows coping with psychological traumas such as those of the operation of bloodshed, mass murder). Likewise, [the ability to withstand] reverse psychological traumas, such as killing one or all members of his group. [He should be able] to proceed with the work.

6. Special ability to keep secrets and not reveal them to anyone.

7. [Good] security sense during the interrogation.

8. Great ability to make quick decisions after altering the agreed-upon plan (proper actions in urgent situations).

9. Patience, ability to withstand, and religiousness.

10. Courage and boldness.

11. Unknown to the security apparatus.

Weapons of Special Operations:

1. Cold steel weapons (rope, knife, rod, . . .)

2. Poisons

3. Pistols and rifles

4. Explosives

We note that special operations include assassinations, bombing and demolition, assault, kidnapping hostages and confiscating documents, freeing prisoners.

Importance of Special Operations:

1. Boosting Islamic morale and lowering that of the enemy.

2. Preparing and training new members for future tasks.

3. A form of necessary punishment.

4. Mocking the regime's admiration among the population.

5. Removing the personalities that stand in the way of the [Islamic] Da'wa [Call].

6. Agitating [the population] regarding publicized matters.

7. Rejecting compliance with and submission to the regime's practices.

8. Giving legitimacy to the Jama'a [Islamic Group].

9. Spreading fear and terror through the regime's ranks.

10. Bringing new members to the Organization's ranks.

Disadvantages of Special Operations:

1. Restraining the [Islamic] Da'wa [Call] and preachers.

2. Revealing the structure of the Military Organization.

3. Financially draining the Military Organization.

4. Use of [operations] as propaganda against the Islamic Jama'a [Group].

5. Spreading fear and terror among the population.

6. The regime's safeguards and precautions against any other operation.

7. Special operations cannot cause the fall of the regime in power.

8. Increase in failed [operation] attempts causes an increase in the regime's credibility.

9. [Operations] cause the regime to assassinate the Jama'a [Islamic Group] leaders.

10. Boosting enemy morale and lowering that of the Organization's members in case of repeated failure.

11. Members of the Organization lose faith in themselves and their leaders in case of repeatedly failed special operations. The inverse is also true.

Necessary Characteristics of Special Operations:

A successful special operation requires the following:

1. A security plan for the operation (members, weapons, apartments, docu-

ments, etc.). This requirement has been explained in detail in the security plan [lesson]. Refer to it.

2. An operational tactical plan. This requirement will be explained in this lesson in detail.

Special Operation Tactical Plan:

A special operation must have stages. These stages are integrated and inseparable, otherwise, the operation would fail. These stages are:
1. Research (reconnaissance) stage.
2. Planning stage.
3. Execution stage.

1. Research (reconnaissance) stage:

In this stage, precise information about the target is collected. The target may be a person, a place, or . . .

For example, when attempting to assassinate an important target—a personality, it is necessary to gather all information related to that target, such as:
a. His name, age, residence, social status
b. His work
c. Time of his departure to work
d. Time of his return from work
e. The routes he takes
f. How he spends his free time
g. His friends and their addresses
h. The car he drives
i. His wife's work and whether he visits her there
j. His children and whether he goes to their school
k. Does he have a girlfriend? What is her address, and when does he visit her?
l. The physician who treats him
m. The stores where he shops
n. Places where he spends his vacations and holidays
o. His house entrances, exits, and the surrounding streets
p. Ways of sneaking into his house
q. Is he armed? How many guards does he have?

However, if the target is an important place, such as a military base, a ministry [building], it is necessary to know the following:

From the Outside:

1. How wide are the streets and in which direction do they run leading to the place?
2. Transportation means to the place
3. The area, physical layout, and setting of the place
4. Traffic signals and pedestrian areas
5. Security personnel centers and nearby government agencies
6. Nearby embassies and consulates
7. The economic characteristics of the area where the place is located
8. Traffic congestion times
9. Amount and location of lighting
10. Characteristics of the area of the place (residence, leveled, industrial, rural, lots of trees, . . .)

From the Inside:

1. Number of people who are inside
2. Number and location of guard posts
3. Number and names of the leaders
4. Number of floors and rooms
5. Telephone lines and the location of the switchboard
6. Individuals' times of entrances and exits
7. Inside parking
8. Electric box

2. *Planning Stage:*

After receiving information about the target, the operational plan is created. The commander who makes the operation's tactical plan should consider the following:

1. The type of required weapons
2. Number of required members and their training
3. An alternative to the original plan
4. Type of operation from a tactical perspective. Is it a silent or loud elimination operation?
5. Time specified for the execution of the operation
6. The target of the operation. Is it one individual or many?
7. Team meeting place prior to execution of the operation
8. Team meeting place after execution of the operation
9. Securing withdrawal of the team after the execution and routes of withdrawal
10. Difficulties that the team may encounter

Afterwards, the commander of the operation shares his plan with other group commanders. When the plan is discussed and modified, a final one is determined. Then the group commanders instruct their soldiers on their individual missions, and the members repeat their orders in order to ensure that they have assimilated them.

3. *Third Stage: Execution:*

In order to discover any unexpected element detrimental to the operation, it is necessary, prior to execution of the operation, to rehearse it in a place similar to that of the real operation. The rehearsal may take place shortly before the execution. It is then that the operation is executed in the place and time specified. After execution of the operation, a complete evaluation is made. At the end, a full report is given to the commanders of the Organization.

Important Recommendations for Commanders of Special Operations:

Before the Operation:

1. The operation should be appropriate to the participants' physical and mental abilities and capabilities.

2. The participants should be selected from volunteers, not draftees.

3. Roles should be distributed according to the members' physical and moral abilities.

4. The execution equipment should be brought to the place of the operation in a timely fashion and should be placed in a convenient location.

5. The members should be well disguised and placed in a location close to that of the operation.

6. Shortly before the operation, reconnaissance should be repeated in order to confirm that nothing new has occurred.

7. The operation members should not all be told about the operation until shortly before executing it in order to avoid leaking of its news.

8. Weapons should be tested prior to their use in the operation.

9. The place and time should not be unsuitable for the operation.

10. When using a pistol or rifle, a bullet should be already placed in the firing chamber.

After the Operation:

1. The operation should be completely evaluated as far as advantages and disadvantages. Also, each member of the operation should be evaluated according to his assigned role.

2. Each member who succeeded in his role should be rewarded, and each member who was weak or slackened in his role should be dismissed.

3. Hiding or sending abroad those who executed the operation.

4. Hiding the weapons used in the operation in a location difficult to find by the security apparatus.

5. Burning any documents, maps, or drawings related to the operation. Removal of all traces of burning them.

6. Defending members who participated in the operation in case they are captured, and taking care of their families.

7. The party that performed the operation should not be revealed.

8. No signs that might lead to the execution party should be left at the operation's location.

Examples of Types of Assassinations:

Elementary Operations: Crossing the Street:

1. The target is on his way to work via public transportation.

2. The moment he crosses the street to get to the bus stop or to the main thoroughfare, the assassins, "two people" riding a motorcycle, open fire on the target and get away quickly in the opposite direction of the traffic.

An Actual Example of an Assassination When the Target Is Crossing the Street:

This operation took place on 3/22/1948 AD in Egypt. Al-Khazander, a puppet judge who viewed the English presence in Egypt as legal, was the person assassinated. Al-Khazander had been issuing severe sentences against personnel in the covert branch of the Muslim Brotherhood [Al-Akhwan Al-Muslimin] who were involved in bombing operations. The "Al-Khazander Assassination" operation [occurred] during the Christmas bombings.

1. The choice fell to both Hassan Abdel Hafez and Mahmoud Saeid to assassinate Al-Khazander. They were from the covert branch of the Al-Akhwan Al-Muslimin, which at that time was headed by Abdel Rahman Al-Sandi.

2. Al-Khazander was surveyed for a period of days, and it was learned that he went to the court at Bab Al-Khalaq in Cairo and returned to Helwan via public transportation. They went ahead to the railroad station in Helwan, [and took] the train from Helwan to Bab Al-Khalaq and then other public transportation.

3. They made the plan as follows [we interpret the next paragraph to be the original plan and the following paragraph to be the actual events as they occurred]:

The assassins, Abdul Hafez and Mahmoud Saeid, were waiting for Al-Khazander when he was leaving his house, and Hassan assassinated him with a pistol while Mahmoud was standing guard and protecting him with a pistol and percussion bombs as he got away. They escaped to the home of Abdul Rahman Al-Sandi, the chief of the organization.

After Al-Khazander left his house, walking resolutely, Hassan Abdul Hafez approached him and fired several rounds which did not hit Al-Khazander. When Mahmoud Saeid saw that, he left his place, approached Al-Khazander, seized him, threw him to the ground, and emptied several rounds into him. He and his companion left [the victim] and departed.

Hassan Abdul Hafez and Mahmoud Saeid were caught because of several mistakes.

The Errors Which Hassan and Mahmoud Committed Were as Follows:
   1. There was no car or motorcycle with which to flee after executing the operation.
   2. They did not anticipate the possibility of a chase after the operation. They didn't notice that the operation was carried out near the Helwan Police Department.
   3. They had no training with the pistol, as evidenced by Hassan's inability to kill Al-Khazander in spite of his proximity to him.
   4. The agreement to meet after executing the operation at the home of the chief of the Covert Branch of the Brotherhood was a fatal error.
   5. After police cars began pursuing them, the brothers fled to the mountain [called] "Al-Muqattam" Mountain, which was not suitable for evading [pursuit].

The Second Operation: Blocking the Way of the Target's Car
   1. The target goes to work in his own automobile, which comes to get him in the morning and brings him back after work is over. A driver operates the car and the target's bodyguard sits beside the driver.
   2. The group of assassinations, composed of three or four people, wait for the target's car. The waiting place should allow the assassins' car freedom of movement at any time.
   3. The assassins' car departs upon sighting the target's car and proceeds slowly until it comes to a spot which would allow it to block the way in front of the target's car. It then immediately stops, blocking the target's car.
   4. At the instant the assassins' car stops, the personnel in charge of killing or kidnapping the target get out, kill the bodyguard and the driver, and then execute their mission.
   5. This operation requires the utmost speed within a short time to avoid any one pursuing the assassins' car or seeing any of the brothers.

Observations:
   1. It is best that one of the brothers participating in the assassination or kidnapping fire at the automobile's tires so that it can not evade or run away.

2. Most of the brothers participating in the operation should be very skilled drivers to avoid problems if the driver is wounded or killed.

An Actual Example of an Assassination by Blocking the Target's Path:

Members of the Egyptian Revolution Organization* decided to assassinate a high-ranking Israeli living in Cairo.

2. Surveillance of the target was carried out for a period of time. The exits and entrances to the theater of operations were studied. The time was set to execute the operation at eight a.m. 8/20/85, when the Israeli target would leave for work at the Israeli embassy in Cairo.

3. A car was purchased for use in the operation. Someone's identification was purchased indirectly, the photo was removed, and that of one of the organization's members was put [in its place.]

4. The organization members participating in the operation (there were four of them) rode in a car belonging to one of them. They put their weapons in the car (they had hidden their weapons in tennis racket covers). Before arriving at the theater of operations, they left that car and got into the operations vehicle, which was close to the site of the operation.

5. After riding in the car, it became apparent the car was not in good running order, and had leaked a lot of oil, so they decided to delay the operation.

6. While they were returning in the car in poor condition, they saw a man from the Israeli Mossad, and the operation leader decided to kill him. The Israeli Mossad man was riding in a car with two Israeli women with him.

7. The Assassins' car drove behind the Israeli target's car, which noticed the surveillance in the rear view mirror, but the driver of the assassins' car was able to choke off the Mossad man's car and he wasn't able to escape. They blocked his way and forced him over by the curb.

8. One of the four personnel got out of the car and emptied the magazine of his American rifle in the direction of the Mossad man. The second one got out on the other side and emptied his bullets, and the third did likewise. After executing the operation, they fled to the other car, and left the operations car on the street.

9. After a period of time, the police force came and found the car with traces of blood.

---

*The Egyptian Revolution Organization: An Organization, which followed Nasser ([and which he] Jamal Abdel Nasser deified), executed its first assassination in 1984 and the last in 1987. It undertook four assassinations of Jews or Americans in Cairo, and Egyptian Security as well as Israeli and American intelligence were not able to. . . .[The rest of this page is cut off.]

[It was not] known that the crime was committed by the organization until one of its members (the brother of the organization's leader) turned himself in to the American Embassy and disclosed all the secrets of the operation which the Egyptian Revolution Organization undertook.

Positive [Aspects]

1. The assassins killed an Israeli person they found on the way back.
2. The purchase of a car just for the operation and a counterfeit identification.
3. Concealing the weapons in tennis racket covers.
4. Choosing a good method to stop the Israeli Mossad man's car.

Negative [Aspects]

1. Failure to inspect the car prepared for the operation with sufficient time before the execution.
2. Undertaking the operation even though the car was malfunctioning, which could have broken down and failed to run after executing the operation.
3. Failure to remove the traces of blood found on the car.

The Third Operation: The Entrance to a Building:

1. The Assassins' car is parked in a location near to the target's building.
2. When the target gets out of the car or exits from the building, the assassins open fire upon him, the bodyguard, and the driver who is opening the car door for him.
3. Run away immediately or ride the car or motorcycle which is prepared for an immediate get away.

An Actual Example of an Assassination at the Entrance to a Building (Assassination Attempt on the Former Minister of the Interior, Hassan Abu Basha):

1. A group from the Islamic organization called "[Those who have] escaped the Fire" composed of three people waited for the previous Minister of the Interior, Hassan Abu Basha's car in a location near the entrance to the building.
2. When Abu Basha arrived, and as soon as he got out of the car, two of the brothers opened fire on him over the cabin of their vehicle (pick-up).
3. Abu Basha threw himself between his car and another car parked nearby as soon as they opened fire. As a result of this incident, the minister was paralyzed in half [of his body].
4. The brothers fled after the incident took place, and they took their car in the opposite direction of the flow of traffic.

Important Observations:

When the brothers went to the location near Abu Basha, they hadn't gone to kill him but to do reconnaissance (gather information on him).

1. One of the brothers was bearded while doing the reconnaissance.

2. The brothers were armed while gathering information about the minister.

3. There was no established plan for the assassination.

The Fourth Operation: While Going to or from Work:

1. The target is going to work in his own car, and he has a driver and a body-guard.

2. The assassins lie in wait for the target in a certain place while he is going to or from work.

3. When the assassins see the target's car approaching, they take their places.

4. The car's tires, the bodyguard, driver, and target are hit.

An Actual Example of an Assassination While the Target Is Going to Work (The Assassination of Rif'at El-Mahgoub):

1. The brothers began surveillance of all the Interior Minister—Abdul Halim Mousa's movements, from his departing his house until entering the ministry. The surveillance lasted several weeks.

2. Friday morning was set for the execution of the operation where the minister heads to work.

3. Exactly at ten in the morning the brothers were fully prepared. An observer was going to give a signal to the brothers when the minister's car departed from his house.

4. When the convoy reached the specified location of the operation (the operations stage), bullets were sprayed from all directions on the private car in front of him and on the escort vehicle.

5. The brothers approached the car after firing at the tires to confirm that the minister was dead. The brothers did not find the Minister of the Interior, but they did find Rif'at El-Mahgoub, Head of the People's Assembly, dead inside the car. [TN: Similar to our Speaker of the House].

6. This was an startling situation. The two convoys (the Interior Minister's convoy and that of the Head of the People's Assembly) were separated by only about seven minutes. After about seven minutes the Minister of the Interior arrived at the location of the incident.

7. The brothers who were participating in the operation (four brothers to execute the assassination and two to drive the motorcade) had only two motor-cycles (three people to each motorcycle), and after executing the operation,

one of the two motorcycles fled and the other broke down, and after a moment they left that motorcycle behind.

8. When the motorcycle broke down, one of the brothers fled on foot, carrying his weapon in the opposite direction of the cars. He stopped a taxi and threatened the driver with his weapon, and then rode with him. During the drive, a police officer (a general in the police force) stopped the car, supposing that the armed man was just a thief. He opened the door to arrest him, but the brother put the rifle to his chest and emptied a burst of rounds into it and the officer fell to the ground like a slain bull. It came to light afterwards, that this officer was one of the criminals who used to torture the brothers in some neighborhoods of Cairo.

Examples of Assassination Operations Using Explosives:

1. Blowing up a building or motorcade using a car bomb, whereby the driver of the car loaded with explosives blows up his [illegible — possibly car].

An Actual Example:

Some of the brothers in Egypt tried to blow up the motorcade of the former Minister of the Interior's vehicle (Z I B) by putting 200 kilograms of TNT in a pick-up truck. When the minister's car was seen, the brother approached in his car and blew up the car. However, it didn't cause an explosion in the car, and it was confirmed afterward that the explosives didn't go off because no catalyst was placed with the large quantity of explosives. The explosives ignited but they did not explode.

2. Throwing one or more bombs into a group of enemy personnel or into the target's car:

An Actual Example:

Personnel from the Covert Branch of the Muslim Brotherhood threw some bombs into [some] stores and bars on the evening of January 7, 1947 at 11:00 p.m.

3. Blowing up a location or car with a time bomb.

Some Palestinians were able to place a time bomb inside an aircraft's radio, and after the aircraft took off it blew up in the air.

It is also possible to explode a time bomb using the timer from a washing machine or any other device (a fan, etc.); at a specified time, the two wires make contact and the charge explodes.

PART VI

The Record of the 1990s

THE STATISTICAL RECORD kept by U.S. authorities shows that terrorism, in terms of the number of incidents recorded, peaked during 1987. Ronald Reagan's administration engaged in a high-profile war on terrorism, attempted to dissuade nations it termed state sponsors of terror, but also traded weapons for hostages in the notorious Iran-Contra affair. These measures did not stem the tide of international terror, which averaged more than six hundred incidents annually during the second Reagan administration. President George H. W. Bush presided over a quieter shadow struggle, and the average level of incidents fell by almost a third. The high point during the Bush years coincided with the Gulf War of 1990–1991, though at the time American authorities considered they had been effective in staving off major terrorist responses to the war against Iraq. There were no terrorist incidents at all in North America from 1990 through 1992, and the trendlines featured fewer Americans killed or wounded, and fewer attacks that seemed aimed at the United States or at Americans.

The trends in terms of numbers of incidents continued during William J. Clinton's presidency, with average rates falling to match those of the early 1970s. Latin America was the main theater of terrorist activity. Europe, where social and political struggles continued in Spain, Greece, the Balkans, and France (to a certain extent a consequence of an Islamic insurgency in Algeria), was a distant second. But there was a marked change in the character of attacks compared to the 1970s. Many of the events that concerned us in the 1970s were airplane hijackings (in which the planes themselves were used for transport, not as weapons of destruction) or individual shooting attacks. In contrast, the first attempt at a bombing attack against the World Trade Center in January 1993 caused more than a thousand casualties (though only five deaths). The Oklahoma City bombing in March 1995 inflicted 168 deaths. The tactic of bombing itself changed from one aimed at attacking property to one intended not only to destroy things but to harm people. Thus, even though terrorist incidents declined during Clinton's second term to less than 350 a year, concern over terrorism increased steadily along with a considerable rise in federal spending on efforts to counter those using terrorist tactics.

A series of horrible terrorist bombings played a major role in increasing the attention given to these matters. The events were of the same type as the September 11 incidents, though not quite as destructive as the attacks on New York City. They served notice that the earlier attempt on the World Trade Center and the Oklahoma City bombing formed part of a pattern. The only one of these incidents not involving the United States was the March 1995 nerve gas attack on the Tokyo subway system by the religious cult Aum Shinrikyo. Another event was the June 1996 truck bombing of the U.S. military barracks in Dhahran, Saudi Arabia. The bombing destroyed the barracks and killed 19 Americans and a number of Saudis while injuring 500 more. Even more horrendous were the simultaneous truck bombings of the American embassies at Dar es Salaam, Tanzania, and Nairobi, Kenya, on August 7, 1998. The destruction of the targets and collapse of surrounding buildings, in the manner of September 11, killed 301 people, of whom a dozen were Americans and another 32 embassy employees, and injured almost 5,100, seven of whom were American. The third relevant episode occurred on October 12, 2000, when a suicide boat attacked the U.S. destroyer *Cole*, which had stopped to refuel at the Red Sea port of Aden. Seventeen American sailors died in the explosion or subsequent flooding of parts of the ship.

This chapter contains details of these earlier attacks on Americans along with the results of official investigations of each of the incidents. The investigation reports show that U.S. authorities paid close attention to terrorist methods of operation and tactical practices through the 1990s. Basic security was emphasized, measures to reduce the impact of attacks were recommended, and specific means to improve defenses against terrorist attacks were identified. During the 1990s both the State Department and the U.S. military adopted new standard procedures for setting alerts against terrorist activity, in large part as a result of these experiences. The State Department also adopted an ambitious plan for construction of buildings that would be better protected against bombings and other attacks. Until September 11 progress remained relatively slow, for the programs were constantly underfunded by Congress, which has made a practice of keeping the foreign affairs budget low, with major cuts in administration requests year after year.

One consistent conclusion from the investigations of these different terrorist incidents is that the disasters *did not result from intelligence failures.* This is particularly evident in the case of the Khobar Barracks bombing, where military commanders were aware of a threat, had implemented or were implementing initiatives to improve defenses, and were prevented from adopting even more stringent measures by diplomatic or economic obstacles, or simply by the fact that ongoing improvements were not yet completed. In the other cases too, however, security measures were in place and practices were followed by responsible authorities. In all these situations, terrorists succeeded by doing the unexpected. The lesson is that specific warning is the exception and not the rule with respect to terrorism.

A point that needs to be made but is not brought out in the reports is that initial understandings of the source of an act of terrorism are often subject to modification. In the Khobar Barracks episode the most likely source of the act was Saudi dissidents, but this did not prevent authorities from attributing the attack to Iran. This evidence of Saudi unrest, in addition, revealed itself as early as 1995 and sheds important light on the goals of Osama bin Laden, one of which was to overthrow the current Saudi monarchy. It is also significant that the vast majority of the terrorists who flew to their deaths in the September 11 attacks were Saudi citizens, evidence that bin Laden has been able to build on Saudi domestic dissatisfaction. Bin Laden has been linked directly to the major attacks on the African embassies in 1998, as well as to the bombing of the *Cole* in 2000. In the latter case, however, dissident groups in Aden have also been suspected in the affair.

The Federal Bureau of Investigation reports in this section suggest the degree of involvement of that organization in investigations of the terrorist attacks. The FBI has strong expertise but has not been well known as a diplomatic force. In both the Saudi and Aden cases, friction developed between FBI investigators and the governments of those countries. The friction proved intense enough that FBI director Louis Freeh met officials of those countries in an effort to smooth difficulties. The FBI was not satisfied with the degree of its participation in the interrogation of suspects or its access to evidence. Given the character of these investigations taking place on foreign soil, the misgivings were probably unavoidable and should be expected to arise again in future inquiries of this kind. In Aden the FBI got into trouble with both the host government and the U.S. embassy, and ultimately pulled out its agent team. That effort was reoriented, and a fresh agent team was beginning a new round of work in Aden when September 11 came. Meanwhile FBI special agent John O'Neill, who headed the investigation team in Africa on the embassy attacks of

1998, among the most successful FBI inquiries, had retired and was entering his second month on the job as security director for the World Trade Center when he died in the attacks of September 11. The FBI had been given a free hand by the Kenyan and Tanzanian governments in its efforts to track down the perpetrators of the 1998 bombings in their capitals. With the cooperation of those authorities, as well as security services in such other nations as Pakistan, five suspects were apprehended, tried in New York, and found guilty of the embassy bombings.

The Protection of U.S. Forces Deployed Abroad

Report to the President from the Secretary of Defense, September 15, 1996

The attack on U.S. forces at Khobar Towers has dramatically underscored that for U.S. forces deployed overseas, terrorism is a fact of life. Every terrorist attack provides lessons on how to prevent further tragedies. However, the Khobar Towers attack should be seen as a watershed event pointing the way to a radically new mind-set and dramatic changes in the way we protect our forces deployed overseas from this growing threat. This report reviews the Khobar Towers attack, the context of our Persian Gulf force deployments, the force protection measures taken before and after the attack, and lessons learned for all of our military operations.

THE ATTACK AGAINST KHOBAR TOWERS ON JUNE 25TH

Khobar Towers is a compound built by the Saudi Government near Dhahran that housed the residential quarters of almost 3,000 U.S. military personnel of the 4404th Air Wing (Provisional), along with military personnel from the United Kingdom, France, and Saudi Arabia. U.S. military personnel first occupied this compound in 1991 during the Coalition force buildup before the Gulf War.

Shortly before 10:00 p.m. local time on Tuesday, June 25, 1996, a fuel truck parked next to the northern perimeter fence at the Khobar Towers complex. Air Force guards posted on top of the closest building, Building 131, immediately spotted the truck and suspected a bomb as its drivers fled the scene in a nearby car. The guards began to evacuate the building, but were unable to complete this task before a tremendous explosion occurred. The blast completely destroyed the northern face of the building, blew out windows from surrounding buildings, and was heard for miles. Nineteen American service members were killed and hundreds more were seriously injured. Many Saudis and other nationals were also injured.

The response of our forces at Khobar Towers to this tragedy reflected their thorough training and bravery. The buddy system worked, and every injured airman received on-the-spot first aid before being escorted to the clinics. Medical teams, both military and civilian, American and Saudi Arabian, performed commendably without rest for many hours and, in some cases, despite their own wounds.

Once the immediate steps were taken to care for the injured, search for survivors, and account for everyone, the command of the 4404th Air Wing began to reconstitute itself to carry out its Southern Watch mission. In less than three days, the skies over southern Iraq once again were being patrolled by the Coalition in full force. . . . The Department of Defense (DoD) knows neither who the perpetrators of this attack are, nor who sponsored them.

WHY ARE WE IN THE PERSIAN GULF?

The attack on Khobar Towers has raised questions about the need for our presence in the Arabian Gulf Region, and Saudi Arabia in particular.

Our security interests in Saudi Arabia date back to 1945 when President Franklin Roosevelt met with King Abdul Aziz on his way home from the Yalta Conference. The United States has had a military presence in Saudi Arabia since the early 1950s. During most of this time, our presence has been well under 1,000 uniformed personnel and civilian employees, in addition to their families, engaged in training and advising the Saudi Arabian military. The United States Military Training Mission to Saudi Arabia (USMTM) was established in 1953 to assist the regular Saudi military under the Ministry of Defense and Aviation. In 1965 a U.S. Army program manager's office (OPM/SANG) was established to help in the modernization of the Saudi Arabian National Guard.

Our presence in helping the Saudis modernize their military and absorb new equipment was welcomed and unobtrusive. The Kingdom was a benign environment in which tens of thousands of American civilians lived and worked, particularly since the oil boom of the 1970s. Since 1977, our military assistance, including the salaries and expenses of our uniformed personnel and civilian employees, has been fully funded by the Saudi Arabian Government.

Saudi Arabia has never hosted foreign military bases of any nation. While Saudi Arabia and its Gulf neighbors generally welcomed an American military presence in the region after Great Britain ended its security responsibilities east of Suez in the early 1970s, they preferred that presence to be "over the horizon." . . . The major exception before the Gulf War was during the Iran-Iraq war in the 1980s when American AWACs and tanker aircraft were deployed to Riyadh.

The Iraqi invasion of Kuwait on August 2, 1990, dramatically changed the security dynamics, and the U.S. presence, in the region. The United States, acting to protect its vital interests, led a coalition of Western and Islamic forces that deployed over half a million men and women to the Gulf to defend Saudi Arabia and the smaller Gulf states and to free Kuwait from Iraq's brutal occupation. Through Operations Desert Shield and Desert Storm they won an impressive victory, although the threats to the region from aggressor states were not completely destroyed.

The primary American interest that we acted decisively to protect in the Gulf War was access to the vast energy resources of the region, i.e., nearly two-thirds of the world's proven oil reserves upon which our own economy and those of the entire industrial world depend so heavily. This fact alone would have justified our actions in 1990–1991, but America also has other vital interests in the region. The security of Israel and Egypt and the Gulf states themselves was endangered by Iraq's aggression and desire to dominate the politics of the region. Coupled with the end of the Cold War, the Coalition victory allowed the United States to move forward on the Middle East peace process in a manner not previously possible. America also has vital interests in protecting U.S. citizens and property abroad, and in ensuring freedom of navigation through the air and sea lanes that connect Europe and the West with Africa, Asia, and the Indian Ocean, all of which pass through and alongside the Arabian Peninsula.

THE NATURE OF OUR CURRENT MISSION

When President Bush sought King Fahd's permission to deploy American forces to Saudi Arabia in 1990 for the build-up to Desert Shield/Desert Storm, he made a commitment that we would depart when our wartime mission was concluded. The United States sought no permanent bases or operational presence on the Arabian Peninsula, and that continues to be our policy.

However, the threat to U.S. vital interests in the region from Saddam Hussein's regime did not end with Desert Storm. . . . Saddam Hussein has remained in power in Baghdad and continues to ignore or obstruct the U.N. Security Council resolutions that defined the terms of the cease-fire, particularly the requirement to disclose and destroy all weapons of mass destruction (WMD), nuclear, chemical, and biological, and their long-range means of delivery. Consequently, at the invitation of the Gulf countries, a coalition of forces, primarily from the United States, Great Britain and France, has remained in the region to enforce the U.N. Resolutions. These forces include the 4404th Air Wing, the unit that occupied the Khobar Towers facility.

In the years since the Gulf War, Saddam Hussein's regime has undertaken overt acts threatening peace in the region. In 1992, in response to Iraqi repression of the Shia, the Coalition created Operation Southern Watch. In 1993, the Iraqi regime plotted to assassinate former President George Bush during a visit to Kuwait. In response, the United States launched cruise missile strikes against the Iraqi intelligence headquarters. In 1994, the Iraqi regime again moved forces toward the Kuwaiti border with an intent to launch another invasion. U.S. forces responded with a rapid buildup, using host nation bases, including those in Saudi Arabia, and the Iraqis turned back. . . . In August 1996, Saddam Hussein, again in violation of U.N. resolutions, attacked without provocation the Kurdish city of Irbil. He then declared the two No Fly Zones, established in the terms of the ceasefire and after Saddam's repression of the Kurds, null and void. The United States and the United Kingdom extended the southern No Fly Zone to 33 degrees parallel and launched a series of missile attacks against Iraqi air defenses. . . .

Our forward presence not only allows us to respond quickly, but to monitor Iraq's compliance with U.N. Security Council resolutions, with respect to both repression of the Kurds and direct military threats to the Gulf states. This forward presence includes:

Nearly 5,000 U.S. Air Force men and women in Operation Southern Watch who conduct combat air missions from Saudi Arabia and Kuwait, enforcing the No Fly Zone over southern Iraq that restricts Saddam Hussein's ability to oppress his people and threaten the peace and stability of the region. . . .

U.S. Army PATRIOT air defense batteries that have been deployed to protect our forces and major Saudi population centers at Dhahran and Riyadh since 1991 and regular rotations of battalion-sized armor units that exercise in Kuwait.

The U.S. Navy Middle East Force that has been greatly expanded from a few surface combatant ships to include the presence of an Aircraft Carrier Battle Group and a Marine Amphibious Ready Group throughout most of the year.

Robust military exercise programs with every Gulf state, unheard of before Desert Storm, that contribute to the operational readiness of all our military forces and help deter Iraq as well as Iran, which also has hegemonic ambitions coupled with a military modernization program that is out of all proportion to its defensive needs.

Prepositioned equipment—a full brigade's worth in Kuwait, another two brigades' worth afloat, and we are building up to a fourth brigade's worth in Qatar. This equipment allows us to insert a substantial deterrent force onto the Arabian Peninsula in a fraction of the time that it took us in 1990.

Maintaining the U.S. military presence in the Arabian Gulf has not been easy for our uniformed personnel who have served repeated tours of duty in a harsh environment. It places a serious strain on ships, aircraft, and other equipment operating at high tempo. While the cost of our presence has been greatly eased through generous Host Nation Support contributions from Saudi Arabia, Kuwait and the other Gulf countries, the monetary cost to the United States remains high. But this residual cost and the other sacrifices associated with our presence, are justified because they protect vital U.S. national interests at stake in the region.

Our experience clearly shows that an immediate and forceful response to Saddam Hussein's provocative actions has been effective in causing his regime to back off from threatening moves each time it has been foolish enough to try them. It is far more cost-effective to be in a position to deter Saddam Hussein than have to fight another war.

In addition, should deterrence fail, we are, without question, in a better position to defeat aggression than we were in the Summer of 1990, prior to Desert Shield. Then, it took more than four weeks to place meaningful combat power ashore. Today, we can do so in four to five days, using the combination of forward presence and measures that we have taken to improve our ability to deploy rapidly. We demonstrated this potential in October 1994 with great success, and we continue to exercise with the equipment for both training and deterrent purposes.

TERRORIST ATTACKS

The terrorist attacks on the OPM/SANG in Riyadh last November and on Khobar Towers in Dhahran last June were not only attacks on American citizens and forces, they were also an assault on our security strategy in the region.

Our military presence in the region is opposed by Iran and Iraq, obviously, but also by home-grown dissidents in some countries of the region. The opposition includes extremist groups who are not only coldblooded and fanatical, but also clever. They know that they cannot defeat us militarily, but they may believe they can defeat us politically, and they have chosen terror as the weapon to try to achieve this. They estimate that if they can cause enough casualties or threat of casualties to our forces, they can weaken support in the United States for our presence in the region, or weaken support in the host nations for a continued U.S. presence. They seek to drive a wedge between the U.S. security strategy in the Gulf and the American public, and between the United States and our regional allies.

Before the terrorist attacks, Saudi Arabia had long been seen as an oasis of calm and safety in the turbulent Middle East. . . . While U.S. military security practices around the world were tightened following the Beirut bombings in 1983, we felt little danger in Saudi Arabia. Our presence in Saudi Arabia after the Gulf War had been requested and agreed to by the Saudi Government. Indeed, our presence contributed significantly to our host's defense.

The location of a large number of our personnel and our major combat air operations in the Dhahran region reflected this sense of well-being. The air facilities were excellent and the Saudi Government provided good quality residences and office facilities in the nearby Khobar Towers complex. That complex had been built by the Saudi Government and was offered to the U.S. military for use during the Gulf War. It continued to be used by U.S. military personnel after Operation Southern Watch began.

The depth of feeling among strongly conservative Saudi elements that opposed inviting Western forces to the Kingdom in 1990 and remained opposed to our continued presence was slow to emerge clearly. There was evidence of anti-regime activity and a rise in anonymous threats against American interests, especially following the additional troop deployment in October 1994. Resentment over the costs of the Gulf War and the continued high costs of military modernization, and discontent over strains in the social fabric of the Kingdom, even from normally pro-Western Saudis, were recognized but not considered a threat to American military security. Since our personnel worked on Saudi military installations and lived in guarded compounds, any risks were seen as manageable by maintaining a low profile and following standard personal security practices. Force protection was actively pursued, but in the context of a stable and secure environment.

Following the November OPM/SANG bombing, that environment was re-evaluated, the threat level assessment was raised to "High" and extensive improvements were made in all our Arabian Gulf region facilities. In addition, we received a number of intelligence indications that new attacks were being contemplated against American forces and that Khobar Towers could be a target. What these indications lacked was warning of the specific kind of attack that occurred. However, they caused our commanders to put in place a wide variety of new security measures. At Khobar Towers alone, over 130 separate force protection enhancements were undertaken—barriers were raised and moved out, fences strengthened, entrances restricted, guard forces increased. The enhancements were aimed at a variety of potential threats, ranging from bombs to attempts to poison food and water supplies. The enhancements may well have saved hundreds of lives by preventing penetration by bombers into the center of the compound. The approach, however, was one of enhancing security of existing facilities despite their overall limitations, and this proved insufficient to protect our forces.

The climate of calm and safety in Saudi Arabia vanished with the November 1995 bombing of the OPM/SANG office in Riyadh and the highly sophisticated attack on Khobar Towers, which used a bomb now estimated at more than 20,000 pounds. It became clear that we needed to radically re-think the issue of force protection in the region, and that our conclusions from this effort would carry implications for the protection of our forces around the world.

RESPONSE TO THE KHOBAR TOWERS BOMBING: RELOCATE, RESTRUCTURE AND REFOCUS

Immediately following the Khobar Towers bombing attack, we undertook a fundamental re-evaluation of our force posture in the Arabian Gulf region. The guiding principles were: (1) We would continue to perform our missions; (2) Force protection would be a major consideration; and (3) Other tradeoffs could be made. Essentially, we looked at the mission tasks as if we were planning the operation from scratch within a very high threat environment. Consequently, we came to the conclusion that a far different force posture was appropriate. After extensive discussions with the senior Saudi leadership, I ordered a major realignment of our force posture in Saudi Arabia, an effort known as Operation Desert Focus. This new posture will greatly enhance force protection, while still permitting us to accomplish our missions. The effort, which is nearing completion, is two-pronged.

First, with the full cooperation and support of the Saudi Arabian Government, we began immediately to relocate our deployed air forces (the 4404th Air Wing) from the Saudi air bases located in urban concentrations at Riyadh and Dhahran to an isolated location at the uncompleted Prince Sultan Air Base near Al Kharj, where many Coalition forces were located during the Gulf War. While our personnel will be living in tents initially, we will be able to construct very effective defenses against terrorist attacks. This relocation effort, which will require over 1,400 truck loads to accomplish, is well underway. More than 500 tents, most of them air-conditioned, have been erected to house more than 4,000 troops and provide dining and recreation facilities, communications sites, and maintenance and operations facilities. The refueling tankers and reconnaissance aircraft from Riyadh were the first to arrive last month, and the move of the fighters and other aircraft from Dhahran is almost complete. More than 2,000 additional military personnel were deployed to Saudi Arabia temporarily to assist in this effort to provide security for the moves, erect facilities, and provide services at the base until permanent arrangements are in place. The Saudi Arabian Government has assumed responsibility for constructing permanent facilities. The isolated location and large size of the Prince Sultan Air Base allows for extensive perimeters and avoids intense concentrations of troops.

Some of the units in Saudi Arabia cannot be relocated without degrading their effectiveness. Our USMTM and OPM/SANG security assistance personnel who train and advise the Saudi military must be in close proximity to their Saudi counterparts in the capital and at various bases. Our PATRIOT missile battery crews must be located near the urban areas and air bases that they defend. While these units must continue to work where they are now, we are taking steps to improve their security by consolidating them and moving them to more secure housing areas, providing more guards and barriers, and taking other steps to enhance their protection and lessen the impact of any future attacks. . . .

At my request, the Department of State implemented an "authorized departure" of all U.S. Government dependents from Saudi Arabia in July 1996, which provides monetary entitlements to any families who wish to leave. In addition, DoD has withdrawn command sponsorship for dependents of most permanently assigned military members, which had the practical effect of an orderly, mandatory return. . . . Military members understand personal risk and accept it by the nature of their profession. That is not true of their dependents, especially children, and we cannot allow them to remain in harm's way.

In the future, nearly all permanent assignments in Saudi Arabia will be one-year unaccompanied tours. There are some assignments where the nature of the job requires longer tours for continuity and familiarization with the host government, and we have identified 59 billets that will be permitted to be accompanied by dependents. School-aged children will not be allowed under any circumstance under current conditions.

OTHER REGIONAL AND WORLDWIDE INITIATIVES

We also looked beyond Saudi Arabia, first to the other countries on the Arabian Peninsula where we have DoD personnel, both combatants and noncombatants alike. In Kuwait, we will move exposed Air Force personnel onto the Ali Al Salem Air Base where they will live temporarily in tents, as at Prince Sultan Air Base at Al Kharj in Saudi Arabia. In the United Arab Emirates (UAE), we have completed moving our Air Force personnel from an urban hotel onto a UAE air base where they will also live in temporary facilities. In both cases we have received strong support from the host countries.

The situation in each country in the Gulf is different in terms of dependent numbers, threat, and security exposure. We decided to reduce the number of family members in Kuwait through a program of accelerated attrition. In the future, there will be only about 30 billets designated for accompanied tours. In Bahrain we are looking at reducing our numbers through gradual attrition matching the normal rotation cycles of personnel. We have decided to leave the dependent status as is in the UAE, Qatar, Oman, and Yemen, affecting approximately 65 family members. . . .

I have incorporated many . . . recommendations and ideas from the CINCs in the force protection initiative the Department is undertaking. Each of the CINCs responded personally with detailed suggestions of additional force protection improvements that could be undertaken without compromising the mission. The CINCs suggestions fell into the following key categories:

- Establish location of forces as a critical factor in force protection considerations. Cross check with dependent security assessment.
- Tailor anti-terrorism training to increase situational awareness of deploying personnel.
- Provide more focused anti-terrorism intelligence to field units.
- Improve interchange with host nations on intelligence and security matters. . . .

Terrorists will always search out and strike at the weakest link in our chain of defenses. Our goal is to find and strengthen those weak spots and we are doing just that.

FORCE PROTECTION VS. MISSION

The relocation of our forces in Saudi Arabia and the change in personnel assignment policies are just two examples of the need to rethink fundamentally our approach to force protection around the world. Prior to the Khobar Towers bombing, our force protection measures focused on incremental fixes to existing arrangements, rather than consideration of radical changes in force posture. Incremental fixes in force protection can always be trumped by attacks of greater magnitude.

To stay ahead of the threat, we now see that we must always put force protection up front as a major consideration with other key mission goals as we plan operations, and that that parity must be maintained throughout the operation. Changes in threat level must trigger fundamental reconsiderations of force protection and cause commanders to reexamine this issue as if they were designing a new mission. Moreover, commanders must be empowered to do this.

The task of protecting our forces would be easy if we were willing to abandon or compromise our missions, but that is not an option. We have global interests and global responsibilities. Those require our forces to be deployed overseas to protect our national security interests. And our troops cannot successfully complete their tasks if they are required to live in bunkers 24 hours a day.

How then can we accomplish our missions without compromising their success or abandoning them altogether? The answer is that we will require tradeoffs in other areas, such as cost, convenience, and quality of life. This is a tough answer for our men and women in uniform who will live in less comfortable surroundings and spend more time avoiding and defending against terrorism, and it is a tough answer for them and their families, who must experience the loneliness of unaccompanied tours. We will have to compensate for these changes and greater hardships in order to continue to maintain the superb quality force we have today.

Putting force protection up front as a major consideration along with other mission objectives around the world will require a fundamental change in the mind-set with which we plan and carry out operations. It also requires structural changes in the Department. Many of the initial actions we are taking are directed only in part at the Southwest Asia theater. They all have global implications.

COMMISSIONING OF DOWNING ASSESSMENT

On June 28, three days after the Khobar Towers bombing, I issued a charter for an assessment of the facts and circumstances surrounding the tragedy and appointed General Wayne A. Downing, United States Army (Retired), to head the assessment effort. I asked General Downing to give me a fast, unvarnished and independent look at what happened there and offer ideas on how we can try to prevent such a tragedy in the future. The final report was delivered to me on August 30.

General Downing has given me that unvarnished and independent review of the Khobar Towers bombing and a tough critique of past practices and attitudes. His report confirms my belief that we must make a fundamental change in our mind-set. On the whole, I accept General Downing's recommendations and I believe we can take effective action to deal with each of the problems identified in his comprehensive report. His conclusions have by and large validated the initiatives we have already launched, and many of his recommendations already have been implemented through the changes we have made. Where his recommendations have identified additional changes that should be considered, we have a process underway either to implement them or to put them on a fast track to decision. General Downing's report is an important contribution to changing our entire approach to force protection and provides evidence of the need for changes in the way we do business. . . .

We have taken the following actions in response to the principal recommendations regarding force protection in the report.

ISSUE DOD-WIDE STANDARDS FOR PROVIDING FORCE PROTECTION

DoD has maintained a variety of directives and standards related to force protection. These documents have been of great use to organizations and have served us well. However, as General Downing has indicated, the diversity of these documents, and their "advisory" rather than "directive" nature, may have caused confusion. . . . To correct this situation, I have revised and am reissuing this day DoD Directive 2000.12, "DoD Combating Terrorism Program." . . . In applying this standard, commanders and managers must take account of the mission, the threat, and specific circumstances. The new directive also implements other new initiatives I have identified elsewhere in this report.

GIVE LOCAL COMMANDERS OPERATIONAL CONTROL WITH REGARD TO FORCE PROTECTION MATTERS

Under the traditional peacetime command and control arrangements, force protection is the responsibility of the CINC, through the service component commanders, to the local commanders in the field. In the U.S. Central Command (CENTCOM), whose area of responsibility includes Saudi Arabia, the service component commanders exercised operational control of deployed forces from their headquarters, including for force protection. But the Commander, Joint Task Force Southwest Asia (CJTF-SWA) exercised tactical control over forces in theater that are operating specific missions in support of Operation Southern Watch. Thus force protection responsibilities and tactical control were not in the same hands.

Following the attack on OPM/SANG in Riyadh last November, the Commander-in-Chief, U.S. Central Command (CINCCENT) gave additional responsibilities to the Commander, JTF-SWA, for coordination of force protection in the Kingdom of Saudi Arabia. Following the subsequent attack on Khobar Towers in June, CINCCENT has directed the Commander, CJTF-SWA, to assume full responsibility for force protection of all combatant forces deployed in support of Operation Southern Watch. With respect to force protection, CJTF-SWA now has authority and responsibility to establish policy, and . . . authority to implement and enforce the CINCCENT force protection policies and directives. Tactical control and force protection are now in the same hands. Service component commanders continue to maintain operational control of combatant forces deployed in support of JTF-SWA. . . .

The DoD directive I have issued establishing DoD-wide standards for providing force protection now requires that each CINC review the command arrangements for every Joint Task Force when it is established and periodically thereafter with regard to force protection responsibilities. The directive also requires that the CINCs report to me any decisions to vest operational control for force protection matters outside a Joint Task Force Commander and to detail the reasons why this decision has been made.

DESIGNATE THE CHAIRMAN OF THE JOINT CHIEFS OF STAFF AS THE PRINCIPAL ADVISOR AND THE SINGLE DOD-WIDE FOCAL POINT FOR FORCE PROTECTION ACTIVITIES. GENERAL DOWNING'S REPORT CORRECTLY RECOGNIZES THE NEED FOR A STRONGER CENTRALIZED APPROACH TO FORCE PROTECTION WITHIN DOD. THERE INDEED SHOULD BE A SINGLE INDIVIDUAL DESIGNATED AS RESPONSIBLE FOR ENSURING THAT OUR POLICIES WILL RESULT IN ADEQUATE FORCE PROTECTION MEASURES BEING TAKEN AND FOR AUDITING THE PERFORMANCE OF OUR UNITS.

Because force protection measures must be carried out by our uniformed military organizations, I have therefore designated the Chairman of the Joint Chiefs of Staff as the principal advisor and the single DoD-wide focal point for force protection activities. He will review and coordinate these activities in the context of broader national security policy matters with the Under Secretary of Defense for Policy. The Chairman will establish an appropriate force protection element within the Joint Staff to perform this function.

As the primary, high-level advocate for force protection, the Chairman will help ensure that this requirement is placed as a major consideration along with other mission goals as we plan military operations, and that focus on force protection is maintained throughout the operation. The Chairman will also ensure that adequate force protection is a top priority for every commander at every level within our military organization, and that commanders will be empowered to ensure that force protection measures respond to the unique situation on the ground. As the key military advisor to the President and the Secretary of Defense, the Chairman can also ensure that force protection receives a high priority in budgetary allocations. And as the representative of the joint forces, the Chairman is also in the position to ensure a joint and uniform approach to force protection throughout the Service components.

The instructions carrying out this recommendation are included in DoD Directive 2000.12 being issued today.

MOVE FORCE PROTECTION RESPONSIBILITIES FROM THE DEPARTMENT OF STATE TO THE DEPARTMENT OF DEFENSE WHERE POSSIBLE

In some cases, the Department of State, rather than the Department of Defense, is responsible for the security of military forces overseas, including force protection. This division of responsibilities can result in different standards of force protection, as highlighted by the bombing of the OPM/SANG in Riyadh, in November 1995.

Immediately following that event, I directed that the Chairman create a DoD Anti-Terrorism Task Force to assess DoD anti-terrorism worldwide and to provide a report with recommendations to improve anti-terrorism readiness. The Task Force highlighted the bifurcated responsibilities for security of DoD personnel. In particular, combatant forces were under the authority of the CINCCENT, but U.S. military personnel assigned to OPM/SANG and USMTM were under the control of the U.S. Ambassador for security matters. The final report and recommendations, completed just days before the bombing of Khobar Towers, called for a clarification of the division of responsibilities, including consideration of changes to the President's Letter to Chiefs of Mission. . . .

The Secretary of State and I have agreed that he should delegate force protection responsibility and authority to me for all DoD activities within the Arabian Peninsula. . . . The only DoD elements that will remain under the security responsibility of the Chief of Mission will be the integral elements of the country team (i.e. the Defense Attaché Office, the USMC Security Detachment, and the Security Assistance Offices that are located within or in close proximity to their respective U.S. Embassies, in Qatar, the UAE, Bahrain and Oman), those sensitive intelligence and counter-intelligence activities that are conducted under the direction and control of the Chief of Mission/Chief of Station, and any DoD personnel detailed to other U.S. Government agencies or departments. . . .

This arrangement balances the requirement for protecting DoD forces with the overall mission of the U.S. Government overseas. The Ambassador must be in charge of all activities that have a direct impact on the conduct of our nation's foreign policy. However, in those high threat instances where the number of DoD forces in country assigned to the embassy exceeds the country team's ability to provide for their security, the regional CINC will be charged with ensuring their safety from terrorist attack.

IMPROVE THE USE OF AVAILABLE INTELLIGENCE AND
INTELLIGENCE COLLECTION CAPABILITIES

Passive protective measures are always important, but the real key to better, more effective force protection against terrorism is to take active measures against the terrorists. This brings me to another major action we are taking in Saudi Arabia—improving our intelligence capabilities. We do not want to simply sit and wait for terrorists to act. We want to seek them out, find them, identify them, and do what we can to disrupt or preempt any planned operation. The key to this is better intelligence.

In Saudi Arabia, the U.S. intelligence community was providing 24-hour a day coverage of terrorist and terrorist related activity. All of the available intelligence was widely distributed in theater. This intelligence support for force protection was very good in some areas, sufficient in others, and lacking in at least one key area—that of providing tactical warning of impending attack.

There was a strong relationship between intelligence threat reporting and the theater security posture. The physical and personnel security enhancements that were in place at the time of the bombing were based on vulnerability analysis that came from general intelligence threat reporting. The linkage between intelligence reporting and the operational commander's action is critically important whether it involves intelligence threat information feeding physical security improvements or supporting target selection for precision weapons. In the case of the threat to U.S. forces in Saudi Arabia, the available intelligence clearly formed the basis for security planning and procedures. Intelligence reports drove the extensive security enhancements that were completed prior to the attack. We must not lose sight of the fact that U.S. forces in Saudi Arabia acted on the general threat intelligence available prior to the bombing and that information saved lives and injuries. We had intelligence and we acted on it, but we lacked the specificity necessary that would have made the critical difference in this incident. What was missing was the hard tactical warning of impending attack—the information we needed to thwart the operation before it reached fruition.

There is no doubt that we can always have better and more precise intelligence and we are continuously striving for that level of detail. I am reviewing the Department's ability to meet this long-term requirement and I have the active assistance of the Director of Central Intelligence in reviewing intelligence policies and capabilities to acquire better tactical threat information from all intelligence assets.

I am also taking steps to address General Downing's specific recommendations that we look at both how we make intelligence available and how we use it at small unit levels. I will work with CENTCOM and the Military Departments to implement those recommendations.

The goal is not only to have better intelligence collection, but to be better able to use it. We need to sort out the real and useful intelligence from the misinformation and disinformation that is also collected. One key to improved analysis at the Washington level is the Counter Terrorist Center, which is now receiving higher priority in the face of the higher threat. But even with improved analysis in Washington, we still have to make this intelligence available in a timely way to the forces threatened, and to combine national intelligence with the local intelligence being collected. Among the steps we are taking to improve intelligence in the Gulf region is augmentation of the Southern Watch fusion cell with counter-terrorism analysts. We developed the model for intelligence fusion cells in Bosnia. We are replicating this model now not only in the Gulf region, but around the world wherever our forces are deployed. A fusion cell combines, in a timely way, national strategic intelligence, which we gather around the world, with local or tactical intelligence. That allows us to quickly "fuse" together the global picture and the regional picture to help us see patterns, keep information from falling through the cracks, and to focus U.S. and our allies' intelligence services on the same pieces of information at the same time. Equally important, it emphasizes the timely delivery of useful information to the tactical commander. We also are leveraging technology to build the tools we need to manage information better over the long term.

General Downing rightly identified that we must commit ourselves to sustained in-depth, long-term analysis of trends, intentions, and capabilities of terrorists. This is a systemic issue, not just in terrorism analysis, that we must address across the board in our intelligence analysis and reporting. In recognition of this systemic problem, the Department developed an initiative earlier this year for the intelligence community that will make a career-long investment in selective intelligence analysis to provide the skills and expertise the community needs to sustain proficiency against hard target problems.

ESTABLISH A WORKABLE DIVISION OF RESPONSIBILITIES ON FORCE PROTECTION MATTERS BETWEEN THE UNITED STATES AND HOST NATIONS

General Downing correctly identified close and cooperative relationships with the host government as a key component of successful force protection programs in peacetime environments overseas. Without strong working relationships at all levels between U.S. and host nation officials, many force protection measures cannot be implemented.

Formal, structured relationships have their place and should be established where appropriate and possible. It is most important that those U.S. officials with responsibility for force protection, including all commanders responsible for activities in the field, work consciously to build personal relationships of trust and confidence with their foreign counterparts.

The Department is examining its personnel policies and practices to ensure that they support this important objective. For example, we are increasing tour length for additional key U.S. personnel in Saudi Arabia, including the commanders of the USAF Office of Special Investigations and Security Police allowing them to form deeper relationships with their counterparts.

RAISE THE FUNDING LEVEL AND PRIORITY FOR FORCE PROTECTION AND GET THE LATEST TECHNOLOGY INTO THE FIELD AND INTO THE DEPARTMENT OF DEFENSE

. . . With force protection now given a higher overall mission priority, we need to ensure force protection also is given a higher overall budget priority in the allocation of defense resources. To do so, we must be able to collect, consolidate and track our disparate expenditures for force protection, and measure our total expenditures against the requirements.

I have initiated a comprehensive review of future funding for force protection and I have designated force protection as a major issue for the FY 1998–2003 program review. All DoD components are scrubbing the latest budget estimates to ensure that no key projects related to force protection and anti-terrorism were omitted. . . .

I have designated the Under Secretary of Defense for Acquisition and Technology as responsible for anti-terrorism technology development and asked him to expedite the adoption of new advanced technologies to meet force protection needs. This effort includes working with our allies, especially Israel and Great Britain, who have extensive experience in countering terrorism. . . .

SUMMARY AND CONCLUSIONS

We live in an era of great hope. Our hopes are nurtured by the emergence of democracies around the globe, by the growth of global trade relationships and by expansion of global communications.

Terrorism hangs over this bright future like a dark cloud, threatening our hope for a future of freedom, democracy and cooperation among all nations. It is the antithesis of everything America stands for. It is an enemy of the fundamental principles of human rights—freedom of movement, freedom of expression and freedom of religion. Perpetrators and sponsors of terrorist acts reject the rule of law and basic human decency. They seek to impose their will on others through acts of violence. Terrorism is a tool of states, a vehicle of expression for organizations and even a way of life for individuals. We can expect the terrorists to continue to seek out vulnerabilities and attack. Terrorists normally prey on the weak, but even militaries have vulnerabilities and present targets with high publicity value.

America has global interests and responsibilities. Our national security strategy for protecting those interests and carrying out those interests requires deployment of our forces to the far reaches of the globe. When terrorists aim their attacks at U.S. military forces overseas, they are attacking our ability to protect and defend our vital interests in the world. Our military presence in many areas provides the crucial underpinning that has made progress towards democracy and economic growth possible. We have the ability to project power far from our borders and influence events on a scale unmatched by any other country or organization. But as General Downing points out in his report, terrorism provides less capable nations, or even organizations, the means to project a particularly insidious form of power, even across borders, and contest U.S. influence.

But terrorists cannot win unless we let them. Sacrificing our strategic interests in response to terrorist acts is an unacceptable alternative. We cannot be a great power and live in a risk-free world. Therefore we must gird ourselves for a relentless struggle in which there will be many silent victories and some noisy defeats. There will be future terrorist acts attempted against U.S. military forces. Some will have tragic consequences. No force protection approach can be perfect, but the responsibility of leaders is to use our nation's resources, skills, and creativity to minimize them. We must learn from the Khobar Towers tragedy, taking advantage of the U.S. military's tradition of strengthening itself out of adversity. The actions outlined in this report, the lessons articulated by General Downing and the ideas we have garnered from our military commanders around the world, will strengthen our defenses.

Senate Intelligence Committee Chairman Finds Khobar Towers Bombing "Not the Result of an Intelligence Failure"

Washington, D.C.—After a personal fact finding trip to Saudi Arabia and a comprehensive staff review of voluminous materials, U.S. Senator Arlen Specter (R-PA), Chairman of the Senate Select Committee on Intelligence, concludes there was no intelligence failure prior to the June 25 deadly bombing of the Khobar Towers complex. A . . . committee staff report . . . focused on the adequacy of intelligence information regarding the terrorist threat in Saudi Arabia.

"There was sufficient information available from the Intelligence Community which gave clear and continuous warning signals to our military commanders before the bombing occurred," Senator Specter said. "There was no failure of intelligence, but a failure to use intelligence."

Senator Specter traveled with committee staff to Dhahran, Riyadh and Jeddah, Saudi Arabia and other Middle East countries . . . to investigate the terrorist attack. In Saudi Arabia, Senator Specter met with senior Saudi officials and interviewed field commanders and military personnel who had a critical role in force protection and security.

The Committee staff reviewed raw and finished intelligence produced from late 1994 through June 1996. These products included reports from the Central Intelligence Agency, the Defense Intelligence Agency, the National Security Agency, the State Department and others. The staff also interviewed individuals in the Intelligence Community, the Defense Department, and the State Department. . . .

The Committee report determined that the U.S. Intelligence Community in Saudi Arabia gave its highest priority to the terrorist target and aggressively collected against a range of internal and external threats from Iran, Hizballah and others. From April 1995, through the time of the Khobar Towers bombing

Truck Bomb Attack of Al-Khobar Towers
Dhahran, Saudi Arabia, June 25, 1996
Department of State, Bureau of Diplomatic Security

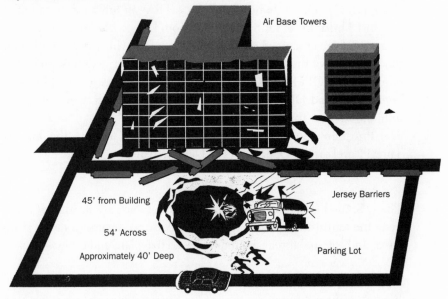

Air Base Towers

45' from Building

54' Across

Approximately 40' Deep

Jersey Barriers

Parking Lot

in June 1996, the analytic community published more than 100 products on the topic of terrorism on the Arabian peninsula.

As early as June 1995, U.S. officials in Saudi Arabia began briefing on a regular basis all U.S. diplomatic leaders and military commanders on intelligence threats and vulnerabilities concerning U.S. military installations and personnel in the Eastern Province. . . .

EXECUTIVE SUMMARY

In the wake of the June 25, 1996, deadly bombing at the Khobar Towers housing complex in Saudi Arabia, the Senate Select Committee on Intelligence staff undertook an inquiry to determine the adequacy of the intelligence concerning the terrorist threat situation in Saudi Arabia. The Committee staff reviewed the collection posture, the analytical products available and the dissemination of threat information.

Conclusion

- The Khobar Towers tragedy was not the result of an intelligence failure.

Threat Level

- Intelligence regarding the terrorist threat in Saudi Arabia was sufficient to prompt the Defense Intelligence Agency (DIA), in July 1995, to raise the Terrorist Threat Level for Saudi Arabia from Low to Medium.
- Reporting from enhanced intelligence efforts following the November 13, 1995 bombing of the Office of the Program Manager, Saudi Arabian National Guard (OPM-SANG), in which 5 Americans were killed by a car bomb, prompted DIA to raise the Threat Level to High, where it stayed until the Khobar Towers bombing.
- The threat in Saudi Arabia is now considered Critical—the highest Threat Level on the Department of Defense scale.

Collection

- The U.S. Intelligence Community in Saudi Arabia gave its highest priority to the terrorist target and aggressively collected against a range of internal and external threats including Iran, Hizballah, and others.

Analysis

- From April 1995 through the time of the Khobar Towers bombing in June 1996 the intelligence analytic community published more than 100 products on the topic of terrorism on the Arabian peninsula. Among these were several CounterTerrorism Center Threat Assessments and DIA Threat indicators.
- Among the most significant analytical products were the June 13, 1996 Department of State, Bureau of Intelligence and Research report and the June 17, 1996 *Military Intelligence Digest* article outlining numerous suspicious incidents that had occurred at Khobar Towers, which noted that "a pattern appears to be developing that warrants improved security efforts."
- The above warnings incorporated intelligence such as (1) ongoing Iranian and radical Islamic fundamentalist groups' attempts to target American servicemen in the Eastern province of Saudi Arabia for terrorist acts; (2) the heightened threat that accompanied the execution, carried out on May 31, of the four suspects in the November OPM-SANG attack; and (3) well before the Khobar attack, there was reporting that Khobar might be the target of a bombing attempt.

Vulnerability Assessments

- The Air Force Office of Special Investigations (AFOSI) conducted a vulnerability assessment of the Khobar Towers facility and published its findings in January 1996.
- This AFOSI assessment highlighted various weaknesses that could be exploited by terrorists, but emphasized the particular vulnerability of perimeter security given the proximity of the outside fence to many of the buildings as well as the lack of the protective coating Mylar on the windows of the Khobar Towers compound where Americans were housed.
- In fact, this weakness had already come to the attention of the base security personnel, who approached the Saudis with a request to move the perimeter 10 feet back. The request to move the fence, made initially in November 1995, was still pending in June 1996, but successive base commanders did not push hard enough for a meaningful movement of the fence for fear of offending host country sensibilities.
- The recommendation concerning Mylar was made part of a "five-year plan" for security enhancements on the compound and thus had been delayed indefinitely at the time of the June 25 attack.

Dissemination

- Analytical products, threat and vulnerability assessments, and valuable raw intelligence were readily available to senior military commanders in Saudi Arabia and their civilian counterparts at the Pentagon.
- Among the most significant were monthly briefings prepared and presented in Saudi Arabia beginning in April 1995 that informed senior military commanders of the three most vulnerable U.S. installations in Saudi Arabia; of the three, two have been attacked (OPM-SANG and Khobar Towers) and the third (the PX Commissary in Riyadh) has been closed.

SENATE SELECT COMMITTEE ON INTELLIGENCE STAFF REPORT ON THE KHOBAR TOWERS TERRORIST ATTACK

Scope, Objectives, and Methodology

The staff of the Senate Select Committee on Intelligence has conducted a preliminary inquiry into the United States Intelligence Community's collection, analysis and dissemination of intelligence concerning terrorist threats in Saudi Arabia prior to the June 25, 1996, bombing at the Khobar Towers housing complex in Dhahran, Saudi Arabia. . . .

During and immediately following the visit to Saudi Arabia and the Middle East, Committee staff interviewed field commanders and military personnel

who played a critical force protection and security role just prior to and imme-
diately after the blast. The staff also interviewed the FBI lead investigator on the
scene in Dhahran, as well as top ranking Intelligence Community personnel.
Finally, the staff accompanied Senator Specter to meetings with Saudi Crown
Prince Abdullah and Defense Minister Sultan while in Jeddah, as well as other
Middle East leaders with unique insight into terrorist activity in the region such
as Prime Minister Netanyahu of Israel, President Assad of Syria, and President
Arafat of the Palestinian Authority.

Since the Khobar blast, the Senate Select Committee on Intelligence has
held seven hearings focusing on terrorism, Saudi Arabia, and support to the
military in the region. The Committee received testimony from Secretary of
Defense William J. Perry, CIA Director John Deutch, FBI Director Louis
Freeh, numerous other Administration officials, academicians and other experts.

Background

On June 25, 1996, at approximately 10:00 p.m. local time, a massive explosion
shook the Khobar Towers housing compound in Dhahran, Saudi Arabia. The
blast killed 19 American military service personnel and at least one Saudi civilian, wounded more than 200 Americans and injured hundreds of other civilians. At the time, the Khobar Towers complex was home for the airmen of
the U.S. Air Force's 4404th Fighter Wing (Provisional). . . . The complex also
housed forces from the United Kingdom, France, and Saudi Arabia participating in the United Nations effort to enforce the "no-fly" zone in southern Iraq.

Before the explosion, American personnel at an observation post on the roof
of Building 131 at the northeast corner of the Khobar complex reported seeing a
fuel truck and a car approach the northwest end of the Khobar Towers compound from the north and turn east onto 31st Street just outside the perimeter
fence separating the compound from a public parking lot. The truck and the
car that it was following traveled along the perimeter fence toward the northeast
corner of the compound and then stopped. A car already in place and facing
the two approaching vehicles flashed its lights, presumably to signal to them
that their approach was "all clear." The two companion vehicles then continued to travel along the perimeter fence. When the vehicles reached a point adjacent to Building 131, they turned left, pointing away from the building, and
stopped. The fuel truck backed into the hedges along the perimeter fence directly in front of Building 131 as the third car idled and then departed. Two men
exited from the truck and hurried into the remaining car, which then sped
away.

Noting this suspicious activity, the U.S. personnel at the Building 131 observation post began an evacuation, but within three to four minutes the bomb

exploded, completely demolishing the front facade of this eight-story building. The explosion severely damaged five adjacent buildings and blew out windows throughout the compound. According to a recent report by the House National Security Committee, the size of the blast indicates that the truck carried between 3,000 and 5,000 pounds of explosives. In addition to the American casualties, hundreds of Saudi and third country nationals living in the complex and immediate vicinity were also wounded. U.S. intelligence experts and 4404th Wing leaders have concluded that Americans were the target of the terrorist attack.

The attack at Khobar Towers was the second major terrorist incident directed at U.S. interests, and U.S. military presence specifically, in Saudi Arabia in the past year. On November 13, 1995, a car bomb containing approximately 250 pounds of explosives detonated outside the headquarters of the Office of the Program Manager of the Saudi Arabian National Guard (OPM-SANG) in Riyadh. The building was used by American military forces as a training facility for Saudi military personnel. Five Americans died and 34 were wounded in this attack. Prior to this incident DIA categorized the threat to Americans in Saudi Arabia as medium. Six weeks after this incident, that threat level was raised to high.

Adequacy of Intelligence

Collection. Pursuant to Presidential Decision Directive 35 (PDD-35), terrorism targets in the Middle East are Tier 1 targets and receive the highest priority for collection. Thus, current Director of Central Intelligence John Deutch has placed from the beginning of his tenure the utmost urgency on collection against these targets.

Even prior to the issuance of PDD-35, however, the U.S. intelligence collection posture in Saudi Arabia had shifted focus. In late 1994, the U.S. Intelligence Community in Saudi Arabia began reporting an increase in threatening activity directed against Americans in the region. Much of this heightened activity was carried out by agents of Iran, either alone or in cooperation with elements of regional radical Islamic fundamentalists. During a visit to Saudi Arabia in December 1994, DCI James Woolsey raised with senior Saudi officials the CIA concern over Iranian intentions and activities in the region.

Upon his confirmation in May 1995, Deutch concentrated immediately upon the issue of antiterrorism and force protection as a top priority. Deutch visited Saudi Arabia on October 22, 1995, and raised with senior Saudi officials his "serious concerns" over Iranian intentions in the region as he emphasized the commitment of the United States to fighting the terrorist threat. Deutch also dispatched other senior CIA officials to Saudi Arabia for detailed discussions of how to address this problem. Intelligence was focused during this period on Iranian operatives in the Eastern Province who were attempting to gather intelligence on the Dhahran Air Base.

After the . . . attack on November 13, 1995, collection against terrorist targets in general intensified. Intelligence Community personnel interviewed in Saudi Arabia said that almost all of their time was devoted to counterterrorism and force protection issues and much of this . . . was driven by the requirements of the military commanders in the theater.

Analysis. By March 1995, the Intelligence Community had determined that Iranian operations in Saudi Arabia were no longer simply intelligence gathering activities but contained the potential for the execution of terrorist acts. It had been previously learned that weapons and explosives had been moved in and stored in apparent support of these acts.

From the period beginning in April 1995 through the time of the Khobar Towers bombing in June 1996, the Intelligence Community issued finished analysis that clearly highlighted the ongoing and increasing terrorist threat in Saudi Arabia. The CIA and DCI's Counter Terrorism Center (CTC) issued at least 41 different reports on terrorism on the Arabian peninsula. Ten of these were specific threat assessments and six were CTC commentaries focused on the threat to U.S. personnel in Saudi Arabia.

During the same period, the Defense Intelligence Agency produced more than 60 intelligence products on the terrorist threat in Saudi Arabia. Many of these were factual in nature, reporting on terrorist incidents such as the OPM-SANG bombing, but many others reflected the Intelligence Community's analytical judgment of higher threat levels. In July 1995, DIA raised the terrorist threat level for Saudi Arabia from Low to Medium. After the OPM-SANG attack, the threat level was raised again to High where it stayed until the Khobar Towers bombing. . . . Perhaps the most significant single DIA analytical product was a June 17, 1996 *Military Intelligence Digest* article outlining numerous suspicious incidents that had occurred at Khobar Towers. . . . This report followed only four days after the Department of State, Bureau of Intelligence and Research published "Saudi Arabia/Terrorism: US Targets?" focusing attention on the same series of incidents. . . .

Some officials prior to the June 25 bombing believed that the earlier events and planning for terrorist acts were actually leading up to a larger bombing campaign against U.S. forces in the Eastern province. These officials postulated after the June 25 attack that Khobar Towers was the likely end-game of the earlier bombing scheme.

Dissemination. The emphasis that the DCIs placed on providing intelligence for force protection was reflected by the U.S. intelligence officers in the field as well. As early as January 1995 intelligence officers briefed the commander of Joint Task Force/SouthWest Asia (JTF/SWA) and the commander of the Air Base in Dhahran of the serious threat posed to U.S. forces in the Eastern province.

These briefings continued throughout 1995. The incoming JTF/SWA commander, Major General Franklin, and his Deputy, Admiral Irwin, were briefed on March 16, 1995 along with General Keck, Commander of the 4404th Air Wing, on the most recent intelligence.[1] Follow up briefings were ordered for JTF/SWA command and security personnel to alert them to the threat. By April 5, . . . all senior military commanders in the region had received detailed briefings on the threat posed by the increased Iranian presence and activity in the area.

On April 20, . . . the senior U.S. intelligence official in Saudi Arabia briefed . . . top military commanders . . . on the Iranian plotting against U.S. military personnel in Saudi Arabia. Discussions were held on actions to be taken to beef up security awareness at various installations throughout Saudi Arabia. . . . The intelligence official provided his assessments on the "softest targets" in the kingdom (OPM-SANG, Khobar Towers, and the PX-Commissary in Riyadh).[2] A decision was then made to brief all . . . commanders . . . on a more regular basis on the serious terrorist threat to U.S. military personnel in the region. The military, based upon these threats, sent out a general threat advisory to remain in effect through June 15, 1996. The plan was apparently to supplement this . . . notice with the regular briefings.

On April 30, 1995, the briefings were expanded to include the "working level" commanders in the various units in Saudi Arabia. As part of these briefings, Major General Franklin put out an advisory to senior military commanders including the following:

> "Our facilities and access procedures should be reexamined to ensure we are doing the necessary things to minimize unauthorized individuals or vehicles from entering our compounds. Of special concern are unattended vehicles parked near entrances and exits or close to our work and living areas."

At the same time Major General Boice, Commander of the U.S. Military Training Mission, increased the threat posture for the troops under his command from "no security threat" to "threat alpha." On June 25, 1995 Security of-

---

1. On April 3, 1995, a U.S. intelligence cable noted that "U.S. military commanders here are very/very concerned about the Iranian efforts in Saudi Arabia."

2. After this briefing, the Commander of OPM-SANG, General Nash, approached the same intelligence official to express concern for physical security at the OPM-SANG facility and to specifically ask the official to pass along his concern to U.S. and Saudi intelligence and security officials, which he did.

ficers from across the Kingdom held the first monthly (and later weekly, after OPM-SANG) counter-intelligence/force protection meeting.

In sum, prior to the OPM-SANG bombing there was extensive information available to U.S. personnel in Saudi Arabia concerning the nature of the threat posed by Iranian and other terrorist groups. After the OPM-SANG bombing, more specific intelligence threat information became available. Notable among these are:

Well before the Khobar attack, there was reporting that Khobar might be the target of a bombing attempt;

There were a variety of reports in 1996 indicating that large quantities of explosive had been smuggled into the Eastern province of Saudi Arabia;

Threats from associates of those Saudi dissidents beheaded by the Saudi government on May 31, 1996 for their alleged role in the November 13, 1995 bombing of OPM-SANG;

A Department of State, Bureau of Intelligence and Research report on June 13, 1996 focusing attention on a series of incidents around the Khobar facility;

A June 17, 1996 Pentagon intelligence report highlighting the . . . incidents . . . concluding that a suspicious "pattern [of surveillance of the Khobar compound's perimeter and other similar events] seems to be developing that warrants improved security efforts;"

In addition, . . . commanders . . . were very familiar with the terrorism vulnerability assessment of the Khobar Towers compound conducted by the Air Force Office of Special Investigations (OSI) in January 1996. Included within the OSI vulnerability assessment is a "threat scenario," based upon a State Department threat warning system, that included:

an assessment that a "park and abandon" car bomb was a threat to the compound's security, and an additional assessment that moving back the perimeter fence would lessen the damage that would result from a "park and abandon" car bomb;[3]

---

3. Senator Specter and staff found the distance to be slightly less than 60 feet from the perimeter fence to the front of Building 131. This is significant because (a) the Defense Department had previously placed the distance at 80 feet; (b) according to the House National Security Committee in a recent study, the AFOSI report makes clear that targets closest to perimeter are most vulnerable; and (c) the AFOSI report concluded that "every effort should be made to maximize the distance between a given structure and a potential threat."

It is also significant because the military commanders apparently never asked the Saudis to move the fence back 400 feet, as DoD had previously claimed. The request was instead to move the fence back 10 feet, which the Saudis quite correctly deemed a purely cosmetic and de minimus action and did not take seriously.

a recommendation for the additional security measure of Mylar protective coating on the compound's windows to avoid shattering and fragmentation of glass; the Air Force made this recommendation part of a 5-year plan and thus delayed the addition of Mylar indefinitely.[4]

This intelligence and the vulnerability assessments were combined in three separate but related series of meetings. First, a monthly force protection meeting was convened, co-chaired by the Defense Attache and senior intelligence officer. These force protection meetings were made more frequent (once a week) following the OPM-SANG bombing. Second, regular political-military meetings were held at the U.S. Embassy, at which the threat intelligence and vulnerability assessments were discussed. Third, after the OPM-SANG bombing an Emergency Action Committee composed of the most senior military and intelligence officials in the region met regularly and discussed threat intelligence and vulnerability information as the major topic at each meeting.

As discussed above, senior military commanders in the region were fully briefed on the vulnerability and intelligence threat information. Further, General Shalikashvili, Chairman of the Joint Chiefs of Staff, was briefed at length on all intelligence and vulnerability assessments by the senior intelligence officer in Saudi Arabia in May 1996. This officer referred to his briefing of General Shalikashvili as "intense and to the point" concerning the threat and vulnerability information. Also, senior military commanders in the regions were quite familiar with the Long Commission Report of the Beirut bombing in 1983, which destroyed the U.S. Marine barracks, killing 241 Marines.[5]

THERE WAS NOT AN INTELLIGENCE FAILURE

Section 502 of the National Security Act of 1947 makes it incumbent upon the Director of Central Intelligence, as well as the heads of all departments, agencies, and other entities of the United States Government involved in intelligence activities to:

> keep the intelligence committees [House and Senate] fully and currently informed of all intelligence activities, . . . including any . . . *significant intelligence failure*; 50 *United States Code* §413a(1)(emphasis added)

---

4. According to tests conducted by military experts since the Khobar arrack, even if a bomb the size of OPM-SANG had been used (250 pounds) rather than the 3000–5000 pound device that a House National Security Committee report said was used at Khobar Towers, there would still have been 12 fatalities because the glass on the windows of Building 131 was not treated with Mylar to prevent shattering (as had been recommended by the OSI report).

5. The Secretary of Defense has recently testified that the military was not prepared for a bomb the size of the Khobar device because an explosive that large was unheard of in the region. This testimony is inconsistent with the fact that the U.S. Marine barracks in Beirut was destroyed by a 12,000 pound bomb in 1983, killing 241 U.S. Marines.

The totality of the threat information available to the Department of Defense, as well as the posture of the Intelligence Community at the time of the Khobar Towers bombing makes clear that an intelligence failure, either in collection, dissemination or analysis, did not occur. Military commanders in the region and in Washington received highly relevant threat information for a year and a half prior to the Khobar Towers bombing. Intelligence personnel in the region briefed this information exhaustively throughout the region, and the DCI Counterterrorism Center ensured that senior policymakers in Washington were made aware of the threat and vulnerability information.

CONCLUSION

Regarding the question of the adequacy of the collection, analysis and dissemination of intelligence concerning terrorist threats in Saudi Arabia to Defense Department officials in Washington and military commanders in the field prior to the June 25, 1996, bombing at the Khobar Towers housing complex, the available information leads the Committee staff to conclude that the U.S. Intelligence Community provided sufficient information not only to suggest active terrorist targeting of U.S. personnel and facilities, but also to predict probable terrorist targets. Further, having concluded that the DCI was fully cognizant of and attentive to the force protection issues in the Eastern Province prior to the June 25 attack, and that consecutive DCIs ensured that this force protection information was disseminated to proper Defense Department recipients, the Committee staff concludes that an intelligence failure did not occur. . . .

Embassy Bombings:

U.S. Response to Bombings in Kenya and Tanzania: A New Policy Direction?

Raphael F. Perl,
Foreign Affairs and National Defense Division,
September 1, 1998

SUMMARY

On August 20, 1998 the United States launched retaliatory and preemptive missile strikes against training bases and infrastructure in Afghanistan used by groups affiliated with radical extremist and terrorist financier Usama bin Laden. A "pharmaceutical" plant in Sudan, making a critical nerve gas component, was destroyed as well. This is the first time the U.S. has unreservedly acknowledged a preemptive military strike against a terrorist organization or network. This has led to speculation that faced with a growing number of major attacks on U.S. persons and property and mounting casualties, U.S. policymakers may be setting a new direction in counter-terrorism—a more proactive and global policy, less constrained when targeting terrorists, their bases, or infrastructure. Questions raised include: What is the nature and extent of any actual policy shift; what are its pros and cons; and what other policy options exist? Issues of special concern to Congress include: (1) U.S. domestic and overseas preparedness for terrorist attacks and retaliatory strikes; (2) the need for consultation with Congress over policy shifts which might result in an undeclared type of war; and (3) sustaining public and Congressional support for a long term policy which may prove costly in: (a) dollars; (b) initial up-front loss of human lives, and (c) potential restrictions on civil liberties. Whether to change the presidential ban on assassinations and whether to place Afghanistan on the "terrorism" list warrants attention as well. This short report is intended for Members and staffers who cover terrorism, as well as U.S. foreign and defense policy. It will be updated as events warrant. For more information, see CRS Issue Brief 95112, *Terrorism, the Future and U.S. Foreign Policy* and CRS Report 98-722F, *Terrorism: Middle East Groups and State Sponsors.*

BACKGROUND

On August 7, 1998, the U.S. Embassies in Kenya and Tanzania were bombed. At least 252 people died (including 12 U.S. citizens) and more than 5,000 were injured. Secretary of State Albright pledged to "use all means at our disposal to track down and punish" those responsible. On August 20, 1998, the United States launched missile strikes against training bases in Afghanistan used by groups affiliated with radical extremist and terrorist financier Usama bin Laden. U.S. officials have said there is convincing evidence he was a major player in the bombings. A pharmaceutical plant in Sudan, identified by U.S. intelligence as a precursor chemical weapons facility with connections to bin Laden, was hit as well.

The United States has bombed terrorist targets in the past in retaliation for anti-U.S. operations (Libya, in 1986 following the Berlin Disco bombing and Iraq in 1993 as a response to a plot to assassinate former President Bush) and an increasingly proactive law enforcement policy has resulted in bringing roughly 10 suspected terrorists to the U.S. for trial since 1993. However, this is the first time the U.S. has given such primary and public prominence to the *preemptive,* not just retaliatory, nature and motive of a military strike against a terrorist organization or network. This may be signaling a more proactive and global counter-terrorism policy, less constrained when targeting terrorists, their bases, or infrastructure.*

---

*The same day as the missile strike, the President signed an executive order E.O. 13099, [63 Fed. Reg. 45167] which would freeze any assets owned by bin Laden, specific associates, their self-proclaimed Islamic Army Organization, and prohibiting U.S. individuals and firms from doing business with them. Bin Laden's network of affiliated organizations pledged retaliation; the State Department issued an overseas travel advisory warning for U.S. citizens, and security has been heightened, particularly at embassies, airports and domestic federal installations and facilities. On August 25, 1998 it was reported a federal grand jury in New York had indicted bin Laden in June 1998 in connection with terrorist acts committed in the U.S. prior to the embassy bombings. A "retaliatory" bombing at a South African Planet Hollywood restaurant in Capetown on August 25, 1998 killed one and wounded 24 persons. For information on the role of Sudan and Afghanistan in support of international terrorism: See CRS Issue Brief 95112, *Terrorism, the Future, and U.S. Foreign Policy* by Raphael Perl, See also: *Terrorism: Middle Eastern Groups and State Sponsors,* by Kenneth Katzman, CRS Report No. 98-722 F.

IS THERE A POLICY SHIFT AND WHAT ARE ITS KEY ELEMENTS?

The proactive nature of the U.S. response, if official Administration statements are to be taken at face value, can readily be interpreted to signal a new direction in anti-terrorism policy. A series of press conferences, TV interviews and written explanations given by Administration officials reveal what appears to be a carefully orchestrated theme that goes well beyond what could be characterized as one-time, isolated-show-of-strength-statements. Defense Secretary William S. Cohen, in words similar to those of National Security Adviser Sandy Berger, characterized the response as "the long term, fundamental way in which the United States intends to combat the forces of terror" and noted that "we will not simply play passive defense." Secretary of State Albright stressed in TV interviews that: "We are involved in a long-term struggle. . . . This is unfortunately the war of the future . . ." and National Security Adviser Sandy Berger stressed in public media appearances that "You can't fight this enemy simply in defense. You also have to be prepared to go on the offense". In what some see as a warning to other terrorist groups who may seek weapons of mass destruction, President Clinton in his August 20th statement from Martha's Vineyard, gave as one of four reasons for ordering the attacks: "because they are seeking to develop chemical weapons and other dangerous weapons".

Statements aside, the fact remains that this is the first time the U.S. has: (1) launched and acknowledged a preemptive strike against a terrorist organization or network, (2) launched such a strike within the territory of a *state* which presumably is not conclusively, actively and directly to blame for the action triggering retaliation, (3) launched military strikes at multiple terrorist targets within the territory of more than one foreign nation, and (4) attacked a target where the avowed goal was not to attack a single individual terrorist, but an organizational infrastructure instead. Moreover, in the case of the facility in Sudan, the target was characterized as one that poses a longer term danger rather than an immediate threat.

Inherent in Administration statements and actions are allusions to a terrorism policy which, in response to immediate casualties and a global vision of higher levels of casualties is: (1) more global, less defensive, and more proactive; (2) more national security oriented and less traditional law enforcement oriented, (3) more likely to use military force and other proactive measures, (4) less likely to be constrained by national boundaries when sanctuary is offered terrorists or their infrastructure in instances where vital national security interests are at stake, and (5) generally more unilateral when other measures fail, particularly if other nations do not make an effort to subscribe to like-minded policies up front. A policy with such elements can be characterized as one shifting from a long term diplomatic, economic and law enforcement approach to one which more frequently relies on employment of military force and covert operations. Implied in such a policy shift is the belief that though terrorism increasingly poses a threat to *all* nations, all nations may not sign up with *equal* commitment in the battle against it and bear the full financial and retaliatory costs of engagement. In such an environment, the aggrieved nations with the most at stake must lead the battle and may need to take the strongest measures alone.

WHAT ARE THE PROS AND CONS OF SUCH A SHIFT?

Arguments in favor of a proactive deterrent policy. Such a policy: (1) shows strength and world leadership—*i.e.*, other nations are less inclined to support leaders that look weak and act ineffectively; (2) provides disincentives for other would be terrorists; (3) is more cost-effective by thwarting enemy actions rather than trying to harden all potential targets, waiting for the enemy to strike, and suffering damage; (4) may truly damage or disrupt the enemy—dry up his safe-havens—sources of funds and weapons and limit his ability to operate, and (5) provides governments unhappy with the U.S. response an incentive to pursue bilateral and multilateral diplomatic and law enforcement remedies to remain active players. *Arguments against a proactive military/covert operations oriented deterrent terrorism policy*: Such a policy: (1) undermines the rule of law, violating the sovereignty of nations with whom we are not at war; (2) could increase, rather than decrease, incidents of terrorism at least in the short run; (3) leaves allies and other nations feeling left out, or endangered—damaging future prospects for international cooperation; (4) may be characterized as anti-Islamic, and (5) may radicalize some elements of populations and aid terrorist recruitment; and (6) may result in regrettable and embarrassing consequences of mistaken targeting or loss of innocent life.

WHAT OTHER POLICY OPTIONS EXIST?

The U.S. government has employed a wide array of policy tools to combat international terrorism, from diplomacy, international cooperation and constructive engagement to economic sanctions, covert action, protective security measures and military force. Implementation of policy is often situation-driven and a military response is more likely in close time proximity to a terrorist attack when public world outrage is high and credible accountability can quickly be established. When combating non-state sponsors of terrorism like bin Laden's networks, direct *economic or political pressure* on sanctuary states and indirect pressure through neighboring states may be an effective policy tool in restricting activities and sanctuary locations as well creating a favorable climate for *legal approaches* such as criminal prosecution and extradition which is gaining prominence as an active tool in bringing terrorists to trial. Working with other victim states through the U.N. and the Organization of African Unity are options which would build on the March 1996 Sharm al-Sheikh peacemaker/ terrorism summit. *Enhanced intelligence targeting* of non-state "amorphous" groups and intelligence coordination and sharing among agencies, governments, and with the private security community is critical, but mechanisms to achieve such intelligence objectives must be in place. All agree that more effective human intelligence sources must be developed. In this regard, other nations such as Saudi Arabia and Kenya may be more effective in penetrating terrorist groups than the U.S. Another option is *not to overpersonalize conflicts* against terrorist organizations and networks. Publicly focusing on individuals like bin Laden (instead of on their networks or organizations) too often glamorizes such persons—drawing funding and recruits to their cause and misses the purpose of countermeasures—e.g. disabling terrorist capabilities.

Enhanced unilateral use of *covert operations*, though not without downsides, holds promise as an effective long-term policy alternative to high profile use of military force. A seeming industrial explosion at a factory believed to be producing nerve gas chemicals draws less formal criticism and political posturing by other nations than an openly announced missile attack. The dangers here are that the United States is not especially competent at secret-keeping and that counter-terror can be misequated to terrorism. Effective use of covert policy alternatives requires institutionalization of covert action capability tapping into the best that each agency has to offer. In a world where state sponsorship for terrorism is drying up, private funding becomes critical to the terrorist enterprise. Terrorist front businesses and banking accounts could increasingly become the target of creative covert operations. To support such efforts and effective law enforcement oriented approaches to curbing money flows, assisting personnel in other countries in tracing and stopping money flows to terrorists, their organizations and front companies may warrant consideration. So-called "grey" area or "black" area *information operations* which bring to light vulnerabilities in the personalities of key terrorist leaders (*i.e.* corruption, deviant sexual behavior, drug use), promote paranoia, and inter-organizational rivalries, warrant increased attention as well. One can assassinate a person physically only once; but "character assassination" in the media can be done daily. U.S. terrorism policy lacks a multifaceted information offensive aspect which is not merely reactive in nature.

ISSUES FOR CONGRESS

Issues of special concern to Congress include: (1) U.S. domestic and overseas preparedness for terrorist attacks and retaliatory strikes, (2) the need for consultation with Congress over policy shifts which might result in an undeclared type of war, and (3) sustaining public support for a long-term policy which may prove costly in: (a) dollars; (b) initial clearly seen loss of human lives, as well as (c) potential restrictions on civil liberties. Whether the Presidential ban on assassinations should be changed and whether Afghanistan should be placed on the "terrorism" list warrants consideration as well.*

An important issue brought to the forefront in the wake of the U.S. military response to the August 7, 1998 embassy bombings is that of *U.S. preparedness for domestic and overseas terrorist and retaliatory attacks.* There is no absolute preparedness; a determined terrorist can always find a soft target somewhere. Thus, advance intelligence is perhaps the most critical element of preparedness. Good working relationships with foreign intelligence services are important here. Other key elements of preparedness include: (1) the ability through law enforcement channels and covert means to actively thwart terrorist actions before they occur, (2) high profile physical security enhancement measures; (3) and the ability to limit loss of life and mass hysteria, confusion and panic in the face or wake of terrorist attacks. Particularly in situations involving weapons of mass destruction, effective mechanisms to minimize panic and ensure coordinated dissemination of critical life saving information is important, as is planing on practical matters such as how to dispose of bodies. Essential is the ability to maintain and promptly dispatch emergency teams to multiple disaster sites.

A central issue of concern is Administration *consultation with Congress over policy shifts which may result in an undeclared war.* To paraphrase a familiar congressional adage: We need to be there for the takeoffs if you expect us to support you on the crash landings. It can be argued that given the need for secrecy and surprise, and given the fact that the Administration's timing of the military response was dependent to large degree on the configuration of events

---

*A key question here is whether Afghanistan should be on the terrorism list in light of the Taliban's enhanced consolidation of control over the country and its harboring of bin Laden and associated terrorist groups, facilities, and individuals. Given the "wild west" nature of Afghanistan today, is it fair to hold Afghanistan liable as a viable country for state action? Also, would such action legitimize the Taliban government which so far only 3 nations have recognized? Many suggest that diplomatic initiatives and the threat of sanctions and further military retaliation against the Taliban's harboring known terrorists and supporting or countenancing terrorist training activity on their soil, will continue to prove to no avail. Should such assertions bear out, *then* a strong argument can be made that the Administration, pursuant to Section 6 (j) of the 1979 Export Administration Act (P.L. 96-72) must place Afghanistan on the Department of State's list of countries supporting terrorism. Imposed would be restrictions of foreign aid, and severe export controls on dual use and military items. See also CRS Report 98-722F, previously cited.

and the activities of terrorist operatives on the ground, the Administration made reasonable efforts to inform Congress in advance of the August *action* to be taken as well as the targets and rationale of the pending missile-strike-response. Notwithstanding Administration efforts to brief Congress on the attack, has the Administration been remiss in its failure to consult with and brief Congress on any new policy or major change in policy emphasis or direction? Questions for congressional inquiry might include: What is the policy; how exactly is it different; how does it fit in with other policy options; what consequences are foreseeable; how is it to be implemented; how is effectiveness to be measured; how is it to be coordinated; what funding, organizational mechanisms or legislative authority are required to implement it effectively, and how is international support for, and cooperation in, this strategy to be pursued?

In justifying the U.S. missile response under Article 51 of the U.N. Charter (self defense), the Clinton Administration has invoked *22 USC 22377 note (otherwise known as Section 324(4) of the Antiterrorism and Effective Death Penalty Act of 1996 P.L. 104-132)* which provides: "The Congress finds that. . . . The President should use all necessary means, including covert action and military force, to disrupt, dismantle, and destroy international infrastructure used by international terrorists, including overseas terrorist training facilities and safe-havens". Does 22 USC 22377, as passed by Congress in 1996, amount to the counter-terrorism analogue to the Vietnam era Gulf of Tonkin Resolution? Some analysts suggest that such authority is too broad and open-ended and may pave the way for a quagmire of unconventional violent exchanges, and consequently amendment of the statute may be warranted. Others, however, feel that such broad authority is essential to allow a president maximum flexibility to counter mounting terrorist threats and stress that potential for abuse can be checked through active congressional oversight and reporting to Congress. Another issue involving presidential authority is how the presidential *ban on assassinations* (E.O. 12233) fits into any policy shift and if it should be modified or rescinded.

A more proactive terrorism policy may prove costly in dollars [even in relatively quiet times] as well as in potential restrictions on civil liberties. Unresolved questions include: what is the potential dollar cost; and is the public prepared to accept the loss of lives and other consequences of such a "war of the future?" In this regard, should there be a more active federal role in public education? An informed, involved, and engaged public is critical to sustain an active anti-terrorism response. The American public will be more likely to accept casualties if they understand why they will be sustained and that sometimes it is cheaper to pay the cost up front.

Embassy Bombings:

Incident Report

Political Violence Against Americans, Department of State, 1998

AUGUST 7, 1998 — NAIROBI, KENYA

... At approximately 10:36 a.m., a truck bomb containing two terrorists approached the rear entrance to the U.S. Embassy. It is believed that the terrorists' goal was to drive the truck bomb into the underground parking garage of the U.S. Embassy and detonate the device. When the terrorists approached the rear entrance to the Embassy, they were challenged by local unarmed Embassy guards who refused to let the truck enter the underground parking garage. In an effort to scare off the guards, the passenger in the truck got out and threw flash/bang grenades at the guards while the driver fired on the guards with a handgun. None of the guards were harmed.

When the driver realized that they could not penetrate the dual security perimeter protecting the underground basement entrance, he detonated the truck bomb. The passenger who was outside the truck at the time of the explosion was injured, but was able to flee the scene. The explosion killed 291 people and injured nearly 5,000. Among the dead were 12 Americans and 32 Foreign Service nationals (FSNs) employed by the U.S. Embassy. Six Americans and 13 FSNs were injured. The majority of the deaths were caused by the collapse of the Ufundi Building located 2–3 meters from the blast site.

Bombing of U.S. Embassy
Nairobi, Kenya
August 7, 1999

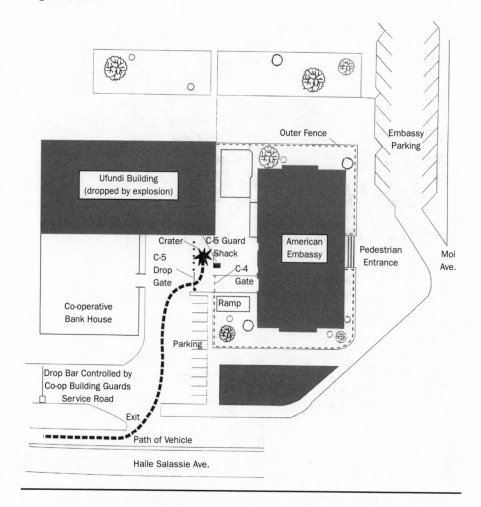

AUGUST 7, 1998 — DAR ES SALAAM, TANZANIA

Almost simultaneously to the bombing of the U.S. Embassy in Nairobi (see August 7, 1998—Nairobi, Kenya, above) at approximately 10:39 a.m., a truck bomb pulled up to the front entrance of the U.S. Embassy in Dar es Salaam. As the truck bomb approached the entrance to the U.S. Embassy, an Embassy water truck was blocking the entrance to the Embassy. The presence of the water truck coupled with access control procedures prevented the truck bomb from entering the compound. The driver then detonated the truck bomb, which was located 10–12 meters from the U.S. Embassy building. The explosion

Bombing of U.S. Embassy

Dar es Salaam, Tanzania
August 7, 1998

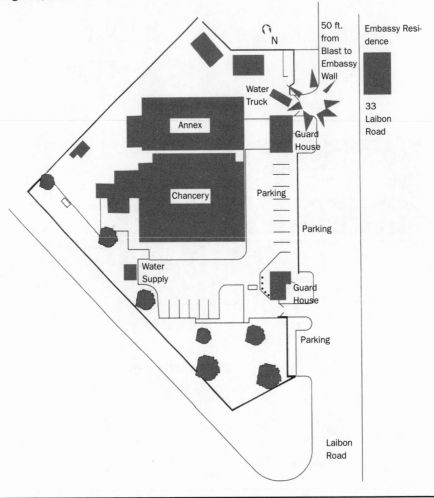

killed 10 people (no Americans) and injured 77 people, including one American.

Ensuring Public Safety and National Security Under the Rule of Law

Louis J. Freeh, Director, Federal Bureau of Investigation

FOREWORD

He who walks in the way of integrity
　　shall be in my service.
No one who practices deceit
　　can hold a post in my court.
No one who speaks falsely
　　can be among my advisors.
　　　　　　　　　　　　　—Psalm 101

Since its formation in 1908, the FBI has had just one central mission—to ensure domestic tranquility by protecting the American people from enemies both domestic and foreign, while honoring and defending the Constitution and the rule of law. This responsibility requires that we advise the American people of our accomplishments in ensuring their welfare and liberty; the manner in which we have utilized the resources provided by Congress; and the emergence of new threats and the FBI's plans to counteract them. In our democracy, agencies such as the FBI must inform the public that we serve and protect.

Since being sworn in as Director on September 1, 1993, the FBI and the Nation have experienced dramatic changes relating to crime, terrorism and national security. Transnational and cybercrime impact both our national and economic security. Economic espionage has transformed both the targets and strategies necessary to combat these new threats. Health care fraud, global economic crimes, Eurasian organized crime, Environmental crime, and hate crimes have been added to the FBI's enforcement priorities for public corruption, white collar crimes, traditional organized crime, violent crime and drug trafficking. Terrorism and the proliferation of weapons of mass destruction have significantly altered both our national security strategies and committed resources. Moreover, all of these changes have necessitated the critical need to enhance the FBI's relationships with our federal, state, local and foreign law enforcement and national security counterparts.

The expansion of the FBI's overseas presence, the design and implementation of vast new criminal justice and forensic services and more integrated operations with federal, state, local and foreign public safety and security agencies have been initiated to ensure the continued success of the FBI's mission as we enter a new century.

The occasion of the FBI's 90th Anniversary marked an opportunity to look back with pride and forward with confidence at the FBI's mission. Our 1998–2003 Strategic Plan outlines the FBI's current assessment of its challenges and objectives. This Report and Plan summarize the dedicated work, accomplishments, challenges and objectives of the extraordinary men and women of the FBI from 1993 to 2003. The five-year period encompassed by this Report chronicles the immense responsibilities of the FBI and the dedicated service and heroism of its 27,829 employees, past, present and future.

My continuing commitment for the FBI as we enter the new millennium is the same as when I took office. First, that the FBI maintain its Core Values of fidelity, bravery and integrity. Ninety years of changes in technology, jurisdiction and mission have only reinforced the critical requirement that FBI employees always tell the truth, promote justice, and act with fairness and compassion to protect the people and uphold the Constitution. Second, that the FBI maintain the resources and jurisdiction to ensure its competence. Third, that the FBI develop to the highest potential its cooperation and assistance with its federal, state, local and foreign law enforcement and national security counterparts. Our greatest successes will flow from the willingness to "share our toys" with our partners and avoid the dysfunctional turf-fighting that detracts from our mission. Finally, that the FBI remain free from inappropriate political interference and all attempts to politicize its work. "One of the cardinal rules enunciated at this time [1924, while the Honorable Harlan F. Stone was Attorney General of the United States] was that the Federal Bureau of Investigation should be completely divorced from the vagaries of political influence."

All of our past accomplishments and plans for the future depend on the FBI's commitment to these four basic principles. Having been associated with the FBI for the last quarter century of its history, I am completely confident that the FBI will carry out this commitment. The men and women of the FBI stand ready to serve with honor, "one Nation, under God, with liberty and justice for all."

Louis J. Freeh, Director

FBI LEADERSHIP IN NATIONAL SECURITY

Leadership in national security means many things:

—Devising new ways to protect the public from harm.

—Taking every possible step under existing laws to combat the worst crimes.

—Developing more effective techniques to prevent all types of national security offenses.

—Reacting with the utmost speed and efficiency to deal with new types of national security crimes.

Those who commit national security offenses are tearing at the fabric of our legal system, the Constitution, and our freedoms. Their ultimate aim is the destruction of our democracy.

One of my major priorities has been to seek increased funding for the FBI's counter-terrorism programs. The Congress has shown great foresight in strengthening this vital work. For example, the counter-terrorism budget for Fiscal Year 1996 was $97 million. The FY 1999 budget contains $301 million for counter-terrorism efforts.

One of the national security crimes that has become more prevalent in recent years that is most frightening to all Americans is terrorism.

Some terrorism now comes from abroad. Some terrorism is home-grown. But whatever its origin, terrorism is deadly and the FBI has no higher priority than to combat terrorism; to prevent it where possible; and where prevention fails, to apprehend the terrorists and to do everything within the law to work for conviction and the most severe sentences. Our goal is to prevent, detect and deter.

Bombings in Africa

One of the cases that best illustrates how the FBI reacts to acts of terrorism occurred in the wake of the August 1998 bombings of the United States Embassies in Nairobi, Kenya, and Dar es Salaam, Tanzania. Twelve Americans were among the more than 250 persons killed in Nairobi and 10 persons were killed in Tanzania. More than 5,000 were injured.

Within hours, the first contingent of FBI Special Agents was on its way to both cities to begin an intensive investigation. At the height of our work there, 471 FBI Agents, FBI Laboratory experts, and other FBI specialists worked tirelessly at the sites of both bombings. They collected evidence and worked closely with the very cooperative and committed law enforcement authorities of both nations.

I flew to East Africa to confer with FBI supervisors and personnel in both cities and to personally observe the progress of the investigations. I also met with leaders of Kenya and Tanzania, and we pledged our mutual cooperation to solve these dreadful crimes. Kenya and Tanzania gave us their complete support, for which the FBI and the United States are forever grateful.

One of my priorities has been to develop close ties between the FBI and its law enforcement counterparts in nations throughout the world—what I term "cop-to-cop" relationships that are essential to fight the new types of international crime that harm all law-abiding countries. This goal of close cooperation was of vital importance in the investigation of the Embassy bombings.

Within a short time, assistance from Kenya, Tanzania, Germany, and Pakistan helped the United States identify or detain suspects. Two persons were flown from East Africa to New York and both charged with murder. A third suspect was arrested in Texas.

On November 4, 1998, the major indictment in the case was returned in New York charging Usama Bin Laden, alleged head of the world-wide terrorist organization "al Qaeda," and Muhammad Atef, his military commander, with murder in the Embassy bombings. Mohamed Sadeek Odeh and Mohamed Rashed Daoud Al-'Owhali, who had been brought to New York from East Africa, were charged with murder. Wadih El Hage, who was arrested in Texas, was charged with conspiracy in the fatal bombings. The sixth defendant, Fazul Abdullah Mohammed, was charged with murder, and is a fugitive, along with Bin Laden and Atef.

In September 1998, German authorities arrested Mamdoud Mahmoud Salim on an international provisional arrest warrant coordinated through the FBI's Legal Attache office in Berlin. Salim, an Iraqi Kurd, was charged with conspiracy to murder U.S. citizens and use of weapons of mass destruction in the two Embassy bombings. In December 1998, Salim was extradited to the United States to face the charges.

In December 1998, five additional defendants were indicted on charges of bombing the U.S. Embassy in Tanzania and conspiring to kill American nationals outside of the United States. They are Mustafa Mohammed Fadhil, Khalfan Khamis Mohamed, Ahmed Khalfan Ghailani, Famid Mohammed Ally Msalam, and Sheikh Ahmed Salim Swedan. All are fugitives.

We seek to bring to justice every person who was involved in the bombings. We will accomplish this using all available legal means for as long as it takes.

This case clearly shows the priority that the FBI places on the struggle against terrorism, wherever it is aimed at harming Americans and other innocent victims.

Foreign Terrorists in U.S.

Terrorism can be carried out by U.S. citizens or by persons from other countries. At one time, with these crimes erupting in much of the world, many

Americans felt we were immune from terrorism with foreign links. All of that ended in 1993.

The type of terrorism which had previously occurred far from our shores was brought home in a shocking manner when in February a massive explosion occurred in the parking garage at the World Trade Center complex in New York City. Six persons were killed and more than 1,100 injured. The FBI led a coordinated law enforcement effort to determine who was responsible for this terrorist incident, and ultimately identified seven individuals, including Ramzi Ahmed Yousef. Six of the seven were convicted between 1994 and 1997 and are currently serving lengthy prison terms. One individual was indicted but remains a fugitive.

Following the World Trade Center bombing, Ramzi Ahmed Yousef surfaced in the Philippines where he and a group of co-conspirators plotted in 1995 to bomb U.S. commercial airliners in the Far East. Yousef was apprehended abroad in 1995 by FBI Agents and State Department Diplomatic Security Officers and ultimately convicted and sentenced to life in prison. Two co-conspirators were also found guilty in 1996.

A major terrorist incident was also prevented in 1993, when the FBI uncovered a plot to bomb a variety of government and critical infrastructure targets across the New York City area. The investigation culminated with multiple arrests. In 1994 and 1995, four defendants entered guilty pleas and ten defendants were convicted, including Sheik Omar Abdel Rahman. Sentences ranged from 15 years to life in prison.

In another major terrorist case in 1993, Mir Aimal Kasi, armed with an AK-47 assault rifle, shot five individuals as they were stopped at the entrance of CIA Headquarters in Langley, Virginia. Two CIA employees were killed and three were seriously wounded. A joint task force was established, consisting of FBI Agents and local detectives. For the next four years, an intensive investigation took place to locate and apprehend Kasi. Through careful coordination with other intelligence and law enforcement agencies, the FBI was able to locate and apprehend Kasi abroad in June, 1997. Kasi was returned to the United States and stood trial in state court for murder. He was later found guilty and sentenced to death.

In 1996, an explosive device contained in a truck detonated outside Building 131 at the Al Khobar Towers in Dhahran, Saudi Arabia, that housed U.S. military personnel. The explosion killed 19 U.S. servicemen and wounded 280. The FBI has conducted an intensive investigation, and has worked with Saudi law enforcement officials to identify and to apprehend those responsible. The FBI has a firm commitment to find and prosecute the bombers, no matter how long it may take.

Through the efforts of FBI Legal Attache offices over an 18-month period, Mohammed Rashid, wanted for the 1982 bombing of a U.S. commercial aircraft, was detained while exiting a Middle Eastern airport. He was returned to the United States in June 1998 to face murder charges. FBI Legal Attaches are Special Agents stationed at U.S. Embassies abroad who work with foreign law enforcement agencies on crime problems of common concern, including locating and apprehending fugitives charged with offenses in the United States.

Domestic Terrorism—Federal Building Bombing

The 1995 bombing of the Alfred P. Murrah Federal Building in Oklahoma City remains the worst terrorist attack ever to occur on American soil, killing 168 persons and wounding nearly 700 more.

It was a crime that shocked the nation and the world. The FBI immediately began one of the most intensive investigations in its history. Law enforcement cooperation played an unusually important part in the initial stages of the investigation: an alert Oklahoma State Police officer arrested one of the subjects on a traffic charge and he was held in custody as the FBI investigation unfolded.

FBI Agents and laboratory and evidence technicians combed the bombing site and Agents were able to link the person in custody to the bombing. The suspect, Timothy James McVeigh, was taken into custody by the FBI and the investigation stretched quickly over a number of states.

As the investigation expanded, the FBI also developed evidence against a second person, Terry Lynn Nichols, and he was also taken into federal custody.

For months, FBI Agents gathered evidence and conducted thousands of interviews as they worked closely with prosecutors from the Department of Justice. At the trial of McVeigh, the painstaking investigative work yielded great dividends for the law-abiding public and the rule of law: McVeigh was convicted of all 11 counts, including eight counts of first degree murder in the deaths of federal law enforcement officers who died in the blast at the federal building. McVeigh was then sentenced to death.

In a later trial, Nichols was also found guilty in the bombing and he received a sentence of life in prison.

In both cases, the evidence gathered in the grueling investigation held up under the sharpest challenges. The credibility and trustworthiness of FBI investigators and Laboratory scientists were unanimously confirmed by the jury and the courts.

UNABOMB Case

One of the FBI's longest violent crime investigations went on for 17 years before ending in the capture of a man wanted for a series of fatal bombings. It was called the UNABOMB case—a code name selected because some of the bombs were set off on university campuses and one was placed aboard an airliner. During the 17 years, beginning in 1978, the serial bomber, later identified as Theodore J. Kaczynski, mailed or placed sixteen improvised explosive devices—killing three persons and injuring 23 others. A crucial development in the case occurred in 1996 when the bomber sent a manuscript to *The New York Times* and *The Washington Post*, and both newspapers set a new standard of public service when they published it at the FBI's request. Publication set into motion a series of events that led to the bomber's capture. Kaczynski was living as a recluse near a small town in Montana. The FBI conducted a search of his cabin pursuant to a warrant, found evidence linking him to the bombings, and arrested him. After the beginning of his trial, Theodore Kaczynski agreed to an unconditional plea of guilty to all of the charged acts, as well as bombings for which he was not formally charged. He was sentenced in 1998 to life in prison without possibility of parole.

Other Terrorism Cases

Another major domestic case involved members of the terrorist group Aryan Nation who set themselves up as an organization called the New Order and conspired to carry out a series of murders, robberies, and weapons violations. Following a careful FBI investigation, six persons were arrested on conspiracy and weapons charges. All either pleaded guilty or were convicted at trial, and sentences of up to seven years in prison were imposed. The FBI investigation showed that the targets of the plot included the Southern Poverty Law Center, the Simon Wiesenthal Center in Los Angeles, the Anti-Defamation League of B'nai B'rith, Federal Reserve Chairman Alan Greenspan, and film director Steven Spielberg.

The FBI arrested members of the True Knights of the Ku Klux Klan before they could carry out a plot to bomb a natural gas processing and storage facility in Texas as a diversion to robbing an armored car. Three defendants received sentences ranging from 14 to 22 years in prison.

The FBI has worked closely with our law enforcement partners at home and abroad to bring terrorists to justice. Terrorist incidents are crimes against all humanity. Terrorists must be found, prosecuted and imprisoned. All law enforcement world-wide must cooperate in the fight against terrorists and in the efforts to prevent terrorist incidents wherever they may be planned. This cooperation is working. Between 1993 and 1998, ten individuals charged with terrorism were returned from abroad to the United States by the FBI working in coordination with other U.S. Government agencies and the countries in which those subjects were located.

New Terrorists

State-sponsored terrorism is no longer the only terrorism problem. There are new terrorists—loosely organized groups and ad hoc coalitions motivated by perceived injustices or ideologies, along with domestic groups and disgruntled individual American citizens. They have attacked the U.S. at home and abroad. Terrorists represent the very worst of criminals—they attack without regard to the lives of their victims, and they generate fear intended to intimidate nations and democracies. The growing and changing threat of terrorism in the United States has required a well-coordinated and decisive response from the federal law enforcement community. For example, the FBI established a Counterterrorism Center in 1996 after the Federal Building in Oklahoma City was bombed. Eighteen federal agencies maintain a presence in the Center. It was created to strengthen the FBI's ability to track potential terrorist threats, prevent attacks, and investigate events that do occur. The Center has provided invaluable assistance in recent terrorist incidents, including the attacks on the United States Embassies in Kenya and Tanzania.

Weapons of Mass Destruction

The threat of domestic terrorism, or international terrorism targeting U.S. interests, is a principal concern of the FBI and other government agencies. This concern is magnified when the terrorism involves a weapon of mass destruction (WMD). Recent national and international events have validated this point and illustrate the need for interagency preparedness.

In Washington, D.C., a container was found at the Anti-Defamation League that was believed to contain a chemical or biological agent. Fortunately, the contents proved harmless. In Buffalo, NY, Stuart Lee Von Adelman was the first person arrested and prosecuted for fraudulently obtaining radioactive material. He posed as a professor of physics and acquired Cadmium 109 and Sodium 22 from legitimate sources in Missouri and California.

In 1995, Larry Wayne Harris, an Ohio resident, obtained three vials of bubonic plague from a Maryland firm using a fraudulent Environmental Protection Agency (EPA) authorization. Harris was convicted of Fraud by Wire. Also in 1995, four Minnesota men who were members of a militia organization were arrested for possession of the chemical agent ricin which they were planning on using against law enforcement officials. They were the first people convicted under the Biological Weapons Anti-Terrorism Act. In 1997, Thomas C. Leahy was convicted in a similar ricin incident that targeted his family.

WMDs have also been used on a larger scale. The bombings in Oklahoma City, OK; the World Trade Center in New York, NY; and the U.S. Embassies in

Africa as well as the Tokyo subway sarin attack are tragic examples of terrorism on a large scale.

In 1995, to address events of this kind and bring organization to the federal government's response to a domestic WMD threat or incident, the President issued Presidential Decision Directive-39. PDD-39 established the FBI as the lead federal agency (LFA) in charge of the crisis management aspects of a domestic terrorism WMD threat or incident. The Federal Emergency Management Agency (FEMA) was tasked with LFA status in the area of consequence management.

To fulfill this responsibility, the FBI has implemented a program of interagency contingency planning, exercises, and a command control framework designed to coordinate federal resources and interface with responders from state and local agencies. This team approach recognizes each agency's role in a WMD incident or threat and is designed to take advantage of each agency's unique resources and abilities. Additionally, the concept ensures that federal assets will be available to augment state and local on-scene resources when the scope of an incident exceeds their capabilities.

The FBI is also actively engaged in WMD exercises at all levels. Recently, the FBI and the Department of Defense (DOD) hosted an interagency, national-level WMD field training exercise (FTX) during which the FBI established an interagency Joint Operations Center (JOC) and Joint Information Center (JIC). The FTX was very successful and validated the FBI's WMD response command and control plan. Additionally, the FBI has hosted and participated in numerous interagency WMD table top exercises (TTXs) and the Nunn-Lugar first responder exercises sponsored by the DOD.

Examples of this activity include six interagency regional training seminars hosted by the Milwaukee Field Division that focused on tracking potential terrorists and understanding WMD statutes. The Oklahoma City Field Division hosted a domestic preparedness conference attended by the governors and city officials from four states as well as representatives from DOD and FEMA.

Command, control and coordination requirements exist beyond the on-site federal response. The ability of local and state agencies to understand how the federal WMD response functions and how national resources will be made available to augment their assets during a WMD incident is crucial. To accomplish this and in response to a plea from local and state authorities, the Attorney General recently established the National Domestic Preparedness Office (NDPO). The NDPO, an interagency organization under direction of the FBI, will provide state and local agencies across the nation a single point-of-contact to coordinate training and readiness.

At the strategic level of command and control, the FBI recently activated the new Strategic Information Operations Center (SIOC). This 40,000 square foot, $20 million facility features the ability to manage several crisis situations simultaneously. A staff of up to 450 personnel may operate from SIOC, allowing the facility to meet the needs of all FBI operational divisions. SIOC operates on a 24-hour a day, 7-days a week basis providing support to FBI Headquarters executives and units, field offices and legal attaches throughout the world. SIOC's mission is operations coordination and information management, serving as the focal point for information flowing into and out of the FBI Headquarters and providing a single point of contact for operational reporting and requests for assistance Bureau wide. During a crisis, SIOC provides the facility, advanced technologies, communication links and trained staff to support the crisis managers and collaborative teams formed to deal with the situation. The SIOC has been designed to support simultaneous events which may have differing operational requirements and varying security levels. Information system resources can be quickly customized to support any event. Located on the fifth floor of the J. Edgar Hoover building, the SIOC facility is close to most of the principal Headquarters National Security Division and Criminal Investigative Division operational units, providing ready access as the situation warrants.

The FBI considers a WMD terrorism event an increasing possibility and is taking every step available to better prepare the FBI and the interagency community for this eventuality.

For the past several years the tactical response to a WMD situation has been the responsibility of the Critical Incident Response Group's (CIRG) Hostage Rescue Team. During 1998 this responsibility was expanded to include the 1,100 Bureau SWAT field Agents. Protective equipment has been procured and an aggressive training package is being developed.

The National Center for Analysis of Violent Crime (NCAVC) has the capability to analyze communicated threats regarding Weapons of Mass Destruction matters. CIRG defines WMD to include nuclear, biological, chemical and large conventional explosive devices for use in domestic terrorism. An agreement exists which details the responsibilities of the various governmental agencies involved in the handling of WMD matters. In preparation for response to WMD issues CIRG has hosted a seminar on the psychological makeup and motivation of groups that have used WMD tactics in the past. A seminar held at Quantico featured Dr. Gerrold Post, a former CIA Director of Psychological Services, and Dr. Ian Reader, who has studied first hand the Aum Shinrikyo organization and their use of sarin gas in 1995 in the Tokyo subway system. CIRG has hosted other seminars on religious/extremist groups that may use WMD tactics as part of their apocalyptic vision. CIRG is continually sensitive to changing trends and organizations which may represent potential threats to the U.S. government and may have the inclination and methodology to use WMD.

NCAVC's Pale Horse Research Project involves a behavioral study of offenders who have previously engaged in WMD threats and activities. CIRG has signed an agreement with the Department of Energy's Office of Nonproliferation and National Security to establish a data base on past WMD offenders and incidents.

Terrorism in the United States, 1998

Federal Bureau of Investigation

In accordance with U.S. counterterrorism policy, the FBI considers terrorists to be criminals. The FBI investigates terrorists in the United States under the following guidelines:

Domestic terrorism investigations are conducted in accordance with the *Attorney General's Guidelines on General Crimes, Racketeering Enterprise, and Domestic Security/Terrorism Investigations.* These guidelines set forth the predication threshold and limits for investigations of U.S. persons who reside in the United States, who are not acting on behalf of a foreign power, and who may be conducting criminal activities in support of terrorist objectives.

International terrorism investigations are conducted in accordance with the *Attorney General Guidelines for FBI Foreign Intelligence Collection and Foreign Counterintelligence Investigations.* These guidelines set forth the predication level and limits for investigating U.S. persons or foreign nationals in the United States who are targeting national security interests on behalf of a foreign power.

Although various Executive Orders, Presidential Decision Directives, and congressional statutes address the issue of terrorism, there is no single federal law specifically making terrorism a crime. Terrorists are arrested and convicted under existing criminal statutes. All suspected terrorists placed under arrest are provided access to legal counsel and normal judicial procedure, including Fifth Amendment guarantees. . . .

THE FBI DIVIDES TERRORIST-RELATED ACTIVITY INTO THREE CATEGORIES:

A terrorist *incident* is a violent act or an act dangerous to human life, in violation of the criminal laws of the United States, or of any state, to intimidate or coerce a government, the civilian population, or any segment thereof.

A *suspected terrorist incident* is a potential act of terrorism to which responsibility cannot be attributed at the time to a known or suspected group or individual.

A terrorism *prevention* is a documented instance in which a violent act by a known or suspected terrorist group or individual with the means and a proven propensity for violence is successfully interdicted through investigative activity.

TERRORISM IN THE UNITED STATES, 1998

The year 1998 demonstrated the wide range of terrorist threats confronting the United States. Terrorists in Colombia continued to target private American interests, kidnapping seven U.S. citizens throughout the year and carrying out 77 bombings against multinational oil pipelines, many of which are used by U.S. oil companies. On August 7, 1998, the U.S. embassies in Nairobi, Kenya, and Dar es Salaam, Tanzania, were attacked in nearly simultaneous truck bombings that left 224 persons dead, including 12 U.S. citizens (all victims of the Nairobi attack). The bombings also wounded over 4,500 persons.

In the United States, the FBI recorded five terrorist incidents in 1998. Within the same year, 12 planned acts of terrorism were prevented in the United States. There were no *suspected* incidents of terrorism in the United States during 1998.

Three of the terrorist incidents recorded in the United States occurred on the U.S. Commonwealth of Puerto Rico. None of the three attacks—the bombing of a superaqueduct project in Arecibo and separate pipe bombings at bank offices in Rio Piedras and Santa Isabel—caused any deaths. By contrast, the bombing of a women's clinic in Birmingham, Alabama, left an off-duty police officer dead and a clinic nurse seriously wounded. (Eric Robert Rudolph was later charged in this attack—as well as three previous bombings in Atlanta, Georgia.) The fifth incident, a large-scale arson at a ski resort in Vail, Colorado, caused an estimated 12 million dollars in damage, but resulted in no deaths or injuries. All of the terrorist incidents recorded in the United States during 1998 were attributed to domestic terrorists; there were no acts of international terrorism carried out in the United States in 1998.

Likewise, the 12 acts of terrorism prevented in the United States during the year were being planned by domestic extremists. Nine of these planned acts were prevented as a result of the arrest of several members of the white supremacist group The New Order, based in Illinois. The six men, who were arrested on weapons violations in February 1998, planned to conduct a crime spree that was to include bombings, assassinations, and robberies. Consistent with a steady increase in cases involving the use or threatened use of chemical and biological agents, two additional terrorist preventions involved the planned use of biological toxins. The final prevention involved a plan to detonate a bomb at an unspecified target in Washington, D.C.

The United States continued to pursue an aggressive policy toward terrorism in 1998. In January, international terrorist Ramzi Ahmed Yousef received a lengthy prison sentence for masterminding the February 26, 1993 World Trade Center bombing, as well as a foiled plot to bomb U.S. commercial aircraft transiting the Far East in 1995. A Yousef accomplice in the World Trade Center bombing was also sentenced in 1998. Eyad Mahmoud Ismail Najim, who drove the bomb-laden van into the parking garage of the World Trade Center, was sentenced to 240 years in prison and ordered to pay 10 million dollars in restitution and a 250-thousand dollar fine. An associate of the plotters, Mohammad Abouhalima, who drove his brother (Mahmud) to Kennedy International Airport after the 1993 World Trade Center bombing, was sentenced to eight years in prison. In addition, Ibrahim Ahmad Suleiman received a 10-month sentence for providing false statements to the grand jury investigating the bombing. In May, Abdul Hakim Murad, an accomplice in Ramzi Yousef's plot to bomb U.S. airliners, was sentenced to life plus 60 years in prison, without parole. In June, international terrorist Mohammed Rashid was rendered to the United States from overseas to stand trial on charges related to the detonation of a bomb on Pan Am Flight 830 in 1982, which killed one passenger and wounded 15 others.

In addition, a number of domestic terrorists and extremists were convicted and/or sentenced for their illicit activities throughout the year. These included Terry Lynn Nichols, who was sentenced to life in prison for his role in the Oklahoma City bombing, and 21 individuals convicted of charges related to the 1996 Montana Freemen siege.

In the immediate aftermath of the August 7 U.S. embassy bombings in East Africa, the FBI launched the largest extraterritorial investigation in its history. Two subjects, Mohammed Saddiq Odeh and Mohammed Rashed Daoud al-Owhali, were arrested in Kenya within 20 days of the bombings and, shortly thereafter, were rendered to the United States. Information obtained from these subjects, as well as information collected through other investigative leads, quickly focused investigative attention on terrorist financier Usama Bin Laden and his terrorist network *Al-Qaeda* (the base), as allegedly being behind the embassy bombings. On November 4, 1998, Bin Laden and several members of his network, including his military commander Muhammad Atef, as well as Odeh and al-Owhali, were named in an indictment unsealed in the Southern District of New York. Another subject, Mamdouh Mahmud Salim, who had been arrested in Germany in September 1998, was extradited to the United States on December 20. In addition, Wadih El-Hage, a naturalized American citizen who was living in Arlington, Texas, at the time of the bombings, was arrested by the FBI for making false statements during questioning. El-Hage is believed to be a key member of the *Al-Qaeda* network.

At year's end, four suspects (Odeh, al-Owhali, Salim, and El-Hage) were in custody in the Southern District of New York, awaiting trial for their roles in the embassy bombings. The FBI continues to work with other agencies in the U.S. Intelligence Community and foreign governments to identify and apprehend additional subjects involved in the bombing plot.

This edition of *Terrorism in the United States* chronicles significant terrorism-related events occurring within the United States during 1998. It also includes articles on issues relating to the terrorist threat facing the United States. These articles focus on the threat posed to the security of the United States by weapons of mass destruction, FBI efforts to bring to justice subjects who perpetrate crimes against U.S. interests overseas, protection of our nation's critical infrastructure, and steps being taken to safeguard U.S. military facilities and personnel.

In addition, this report provides statistical data relating to terrorism in the United States during the 1990s. (This data focuses only on activity taking place in the United States and Puerto Rico, and therefore, does not include figures related to the U.S. embassy bombings in East Africa or other international incidents involving U.S. targets.)

Terrorism in the United States, 1990–1998

	1990	1991	1992	1993	1994	1995	1996	1997	1998
Incidents	1	5	4	12	0	1	3	2	5
Suspected Incidents	1	1	0	2	1	1	0	2	0
Preventions	5	5	0	7	0	2	5	20	12

SIGNIFICANT EVENTS

January 8, 1998, Sentencing of Ramzi Ahmed Yousef and Unsealing of Indictment Naming Khalid Shaikh Mohammed in Airliners Plot

On January 8, 1998, Ramzi Ahmed Yousef—the mastermind of the 1993 bombing of the World Trade Center—was sentenced to 240 years in prison and ordered to pay a 4.5-million-dollar fine, as well as 250 thousand dollars in restitution for his role in the attack. Yousef was simultaneously sentenced to life plus 60 years in prison for his role in a plot to bomb U.S. commercial airliners transiting the Far East. The sentences are to run consecutively.

Also on January 8, an indictment charging Khalid Shaikh Mohammed with involvement in Yousef's plot to bomb U.S. airliners was unsealed in the Southern District of New York. At year's end, Shaikh Mohammed remained a fugitive. . . .

February 20, 1998, Sentencing of Alleged Japanese Red Army Member

On February 20, 1998, Tsutomu Shirosaki, an alleged member of the Japanese Red Army, was sentenced to 30 years in federal prison for a May 14, 1986 rocket attack on the U.S. Embassy compound in Jakarta, Indonesia. No one was injured in the attack. Shirosaki evaded capture for more than 10 years but was eventually apprehended and rendered to the United States in September 1996. On November 14, 1997, he was convicted on all counts related to the Embassy attack.

February 26, 1998, National Infrastructure Protection Center Established

The FBI established the National Infrastructure Protection Center (NIPC) at FBI headquarters on February 26, 1998. The NIPC integrates personnel from U.S. Government agencies with personnel from state and local public safety agencies and representatives from the private sector to prevent, deter, respond to, and investigate attacks on the nation's critical infrastructure. . . .

April 3, 1998, Sentencing of Eyad Mahmoud Ismail Najim

On April 3, 1998, Eyad Mahmoud Ismail Najim, a key figure in the February 26, 1993 World Trade Center bombing, was sentenced to 240 years in prison with no chance of parole. He also was ordered to pay 10 million dollars in restitution and a 250-thousand-dollar fine. Najim was found guilty of driving the explosive-laden van into the World Trade Center. . . .

May 15, 1998, Sentencing of Abdel Hakim Murad

On December 12, 1994, Ramzi Yousef—mastermind of the February 1993 World Trade Center bombing—placed a small explosive on Philippine Airlines Flight 434 en route from the Philippines to Tokyo, Japan. After Yousef departed the plane on a layover stop, the device exploded as the plane approached Japan. The blast killed a Japanese businessman but failed to down the aircraft.

Investigators later discovered that the explosion onboard Flight 434 was part of a much broader conspiracy against the United States. Yousef and three co-conspirators were testing a new bomb design for a plot to down several U.S. commercial aircraft transiting the Far East over a two-day period in 1995. On January 6, 1995, Yousef, Abdel Hakim Murad, and Wali Khan were mixing chemicals in a Manila (Philippines) apartment when a fire broke out. Responding police units arrested Murad at the scene when they found the explosives-making materials. Wali Khan was arrested days later, but Yousef successfully fled the Philippines and ultimately found his way to Pakistan. He was subsequently apprehended in Pakistan and rendered to the United States in February 1995.

On September 5, 1996, a jury in New York convicted Ramzi Yousef, Abdel Hakim Murad, and Wali Khan for conspiring to bomb U.S. commercial aircraft. On January 8, 1998, Yousef was sentenced for his roles in both the World Trade Center bombing and the plot to bomb the U.S. airliners. (Also on that date, an indictment for Khalid Shaikh Mohammed, the fourth named subject in the airliners plot, was unsealed in the Southern District of New York.) On May 15, 1998, a federal District Court in New York sentenced Abdel Hakim Murad to life in prison without parole, plus 60 years, for his role in the aircraft bombing conspiracy, as well as the death of the Japanese passenger killed on Flight 434. The judge also fined Murad 250,000 dollars.

By year's end, Wali Khan was awaiting sentencing, and Khalid Shaikh Mohammed remained a fugitive. . . .

June 4, 1998, Sentencing of Terry Lynn Nichols

On June 4, 1998, Terry Lynn Nichols was sentenced to life in prison for his role in the April 19, 1995 bombing of the Alfred P. Murrah Federal Building in Oklahoma City. Nichols also was sentenced to eight, six-year terms concurrently for his conviction on eight counts of involuntary manslaughter. U.S. District Court Judge Richard Matsch imposed the maximum sentence for the conspiracy and involuntary manslaughter charges of which Nichols was convicted on December 23, 1997. On August 14, 1997, Nichols' co-conspirator, Timothy McVeigh, was sentenced to death by lethal injection for masterminding and carrying out the bombing. On May 27, 1998, Michael Fortier, who had become a witness for the government, received a sentence of 12 years' imprisonment for failing to warn authorities of the impending plot.

July/November 1998, Conviction and Sentencing of New York Subway Plotters

In July 1997, officers from the New York City Police Department (NYPD) narrowly averted a bomb attack on the New York Subway system. Officers took two men—Gazi Abu Mezer and Lafi Khalil—into custody after a brief firefight in the subjects' apartment during which both men were wounded as they attempted to reach switches on pipe bombs they were constructing.

Subsequent investigation by the FBI/NYPD Joint Terrorism Task Force resulted in multiple charges being brought against the two subjects. On July 23, 1998, Gazi Abu Mezer was convicted on all counts related to the bombing plot, including conspiracy to use a weapon of mass destruction. Lafi Khalil was convicted of possessing a fraudulent alien registration card, but acquitted on more serious charges. On November 6, 1998, Lafi Khalil was sentenced to three years in federal prison and ordered deported at the conclusion of his incarceration. Sentencing for Abu Mezer was scheduled for early 1999. . . .

November/December 1998, Suspects Indicted for Attacks on U.S. Embassies in East Africa

On November 4, 1998, the U.S. District Court for the Southern District of New York returned indictments for six suspects in the August 7, 1998 bombing attacks on the U.S. embassies in Nairobi, Kenya, and Dar es Salaam, Tanzania. The indictment charged international terrorist Usama Bin Laden, his military commander Muhammad Atef, as well as Wadih El-Hage, Fazul Abdullah Mohammed, Mohammed Saddiq Odeh, and Mohammed Rashed Daoud al-Owhali with various counts related to the embassy bombings.

On December 16, five additional subjects, Mustafa Mohammed Fadhil, Khalfan Khamis Mohamed, Ahmed Khalfan Ghailani, Fahid Mohammed Ally Msalam, and Sheikh Ahmed Salim Swedan, were added to the indictment for their roles in the Dar es Salaam bombing. By the end of 1998, four of the subjects were in custody in the United States. Saddiq Odeh and Rashed Daoud al-Owhali were apprehended overseas within 20 days of the attacks and transported to the United States to stand trial. Wadih El-Hage, a U.S. citizen and a suspected member of Bin Laden's terrorist organization Al-Qaeda, was arrested and charged with perjury and providing false statements to a Special Agent of the FBI. Mamdouh Mahmud Salim was arrested in Germany and extradited to the United States in December. The four subjects are being held in the Southern District of New York pending trial.

RESPONDING TO THE WMD THREAT

Since the March 1995 sarin gas attacks on the Tokyo Subway by the Aum Shinrikyo doomsday cult, the United States continues to experience an increasing number of incidents involving the threatened use of chemical or biological agents. FBI investigations into these threats have revealed that domestic extremists are becoming increasingly interested in the potential misuse of chemical or biological agents, while international terrorists are interested as well, and in fact, as evidenced by the Tokyo Subway incident, have launched attacks overseas using such lethal agents.

Although the threatened release of lethal agents without actual dispersal generally is not life threatening, these cases do cause panic for those potentially exposed and for responding law enforcement and emergency personnel, and remain a serious criminal violation. Additionally, reacting to these threats diverts resources that could be dedicated to addressing true emergencies. Given the potentially dire consequences of an actual attack involving weapons of mass destruction (WMD), the FBI is coordinating efforts to ensure that the federal, state, and local personnel responsible for mobilizing a response are prepared to address threats, whether they be fabricated or actual attacks.

On October 16, 1998, the U.S. Attorney General and Director of the FBI announced the establishment of the National Domestic Preparedness Office (NDPO). Headed by the FBI, the NDPO is a multi-agency center made up of representatives from various federal agencies, including the Federal Emergency Management Agency, Department of Health and Human Services, Environmental Protection Agency, Department of Defense, National Guard Bureau, and Department of Energy, as well as state and local law enforcement and emergency response personnel. The NDPO is designed to serve as a central point of contact for agencies around the United States concerning WMD training issues. In this capacity, it will provide up-to-date WMD-related information and coordinate congressionally mandated WMD training initiatives. Recent trends reinforce the need for comprehensive and coordinated preparedness activities to address the threat of WMD attacks.

Rising Levels of WMD Threats

WMD cases—primarily those dealing with attempted procurement or threatened use of chemical, biological, and nuclear/radiological materials—have increased steadily since 1995, rising from 37 in 1996 to 74 in 1997, to 181 in 1998. Threatened release of biological agents, such as anthrax, has become the most prevalent component of this disturbing trend. Threatened use of biological agents accounted for more than half of the WMD cases in 1998. By mid-1998, anthrax—also known as *Bacillus anthracis*—had emerged as the agent of choice in WMD-related threats. Anthrax spores are found naturally in diseased sheep and cattle and can also exist in other organic materials, including soil. This bacterial pathogen may be grown and exploited for illicit purposes. Although technically difficult to weaponize, anthrax can be spread in the form of an aerosol which can be ingested through the nose and into the respiratory system. The spores are harmful only if inhaled, ingested, or when introduced into an open wound or the eyes.

Anthrax-related threats can have significant ramifications for targeted communities. As previously demonstrated, a fabricated WMD threat may be as effective as an actual attack in achieving the desired terrorist objectives of creating public fear, mass panic, and disruption:

- In April 1997, a suspicious package was sent to the Washington, D.C., headquarters of *B'nai B'rith*—a Jewish social service organization. Investigators found a shattered petri dish inside labeled with a misspelled variation of the word "anthrax" and "yersinia," the bacterium that causes bubonic plague. Although the substance contained in the petri dish was ultimately determined to be harmless, the emergency response resulted in crippling traffic problems in the Scott Circle area of the nation's capital and necessitated that workers in the building be temporarily quarantined while the package was transported and analyzed.

• In August 1998, a threat was received at the Finney State Office Building in Wichita, Kansas, resulting in the evacuation of a large number of government workers from the building. Because of concerns that some of the workers had come into contact with a biological substance, the FBI's Hazardous Materials Response Unit (HMRU) was deployed to the scene. Analysis revealed no biological agent present at the scene or in the collected evidence. Although interagency coordination resulted in a well-executed response, the incident still gained extensive media coverage, due in large part to copies of the threat letter that were mailed to newspapers and radio stations. The publicity generated by this hoax is suspected to have contributed significantly to a rash of copy-cat threats received around the country in the months following the incident.

• In late December 1998, nearly two dozen anthrax threats were reported in greater Los Angeles, California. The threats—transmitted by telephone or mail—were ultimately determined to be fabricated. As a result of these threats, however, a large number of people were temporarily quarantined at Los Angeles area social, educational, and business sites, including a nightclub, a department store, an office building, a courthouse, and a high school. Arrests have been made in two of these threat cases. Some of the perpetrators were found to be pranksters or those wishing to avoid legal responsibilities. Since the arrests, the rate of anthrax threats in the Los Angeles area has diminished dramatically. Following this rash of threats, the U.S. Government, led by the FBI, developed a comprehensive threat assessment process for such incidents. This process provides a real-time assessment of any WMD threat directly to first responders. These assessments, which come from FEMA, the Department of Defense, the Department of Energy, Health and Human Services, and the Environmental Protection Agency, have significantly enhanced the response to WMD incidents by providing local on-scene responders with the information needed to conduct a measured and safe response.

Close Calls

Since the early 1990s, the FBI has investigated a number of domestic extremist groups and associated individuals, as well as lone, unaffiliated individuals interested in procuring, or ready to employ, chemical or biological agents against perceived enemies or innocent civilians. . . .

International terrorists also have demonstrated an interest in chemical and biological materials. In fact, press reporting indicates that approximately a dozen international groups, all sharing anti-U.S. sentiment and some with a history of kidnapping and killing U.S. persons abroad, are attempting to use or procure these lethal materials for future attacks. Although there are currently no indications that international terrorists have plans to use these lethal materials in the United States, past attacks and plots—such as the bombing of the World Trade Center and the thwarted attempt by followers of Shaykh Omar Abdel Rahman to bomb various landmarks in New York—indicate an interest in causing mass civilian casualties. According to court testimony, Ramzi Ahmed Yousef—the convicted mastermind behind the World Trade Center bombing and a self-taught chemist—originally considered carrying out a cyanide gas attack against the complex. Cyanide was confiscated at the site where the bomb was assembled, but there is no indication that cyanide was contained in the bomb that was ultimately used in the attack on the building.

The Future

Currently, many chemicals and biological pathogens and toxins that are suitable for weaponization are not subject to export and treaty controls because they have legitimate commercial applications. Several terrorist attacks carried out during the past five years were facilitated by the commercial availability of these same materials. Timothy McVeigh, for example, procured ammonium nitrate for the bomb used in the Oklahoma City bombing at feed stores in the Midwest. There are also indications that international terrorists are procuring large volumes of cyanide and arsenic in commercial centers worldwide. Additionally, investigation has revealed that some domestic extremists are trained in the advanced sciences, while some international terrorists are simply procuring scientific expertise to meet their demands. In short, terrorist capabilities to produce exotic chemical and biological agents for their attacks currently exists, or is advanced enough to present a threat. However, this threat is still considered low in comparison to the threat from conventional terrorist tactics, such as bombings, shootings, and kidnappings, which remain the preferred method to carry out attacks.

Weapons of Mass Destruction (WMD), Investigations Opened 1997–1998

	1997	1998
Nuclear	25	29
Chemical	20	23
Biological	22	112
Missile	2	1
Unknown	5	16

EXTRATERRITORIAL INVESTIGATIONS

In 1998, the FBI continued to successfully assert extraterritorial jurisdiction in cases involving criminal acts of terrorism. Extraterritorial jurisdiction is the principle that allows the FBI to expand its investigative authority outside U.S. borders and deploy FBI personnel to work in conjunction with host government law enforcement agencies in order to effect timely arrests and prosecutions. The application of enforcement jurisdiction over terrorist incidents occurring anywhere in the world continues to be one of the strongest methods the U.S. Government has for responding to terrorism directed at U.S. interests abroad.

The so-called "long arm" legislation that allows the FBI to effectively respond to acts occurring outside the United States is embodied in several U.S. statutes. The most important of these statutes resulted from the cooperative efforts of the Executive Branch and the U.S. Congress over the last two decades. Historically, the U.S. Government exercised jurisdiction over individuals only when they were discovered on U.S. territory. Reacting to terrorist attacks against U.S. nationals abroad in the 1980s, and subsequent concerns that those responsible for the attacks would escape justice by fleeing to countries ideologically opposed to the United States and with whom we did not have extradition treaties, Congress enacted three landmark pieces of legislation.

The first was the Comprehensive Crime Control Act of 1984. Two years later, the Omnibus Diplomatic Security and Antiterrorist Act of 1986 was signed into law. These two pieces of legislation effectively expanded the federal jurisdiction of the United States to terrorist crimes, including hostage taking, homicide, conspiracy to commit homicide, or physical violence committed against a U.S. national or interest occurring anywhere in the world.

The third major piece of legislation to be enacted was the Antiterrorism and Effective Death Penalty Act of 1996. This act created additional methods for combating the specific problem of international terrorist infrastructures which have developed during the past decade. Specifically, the act grants the authority to designate foreign terrorist organizations, prohibits the providing of material support or resources to a foreign terrorist organization, and makes it a federal crime to participate in certain international terrorism activities.

Acting under the authority of these laws and Presidential Decision Directive 39, the FBI exercises jurisdiction over extraterritorial terrorist acts when a U.S. national is a victim or perpetrator of the offense, the U.S. Government is the victim of the offense, or the perpetrator is later found in the United States. Since the mid-1980s, the FBI has investigated more than 350 extraterritorial cases. Prior to conducting terrorism investigations outside U.S. borders, the FBI secures permission from the host country and coordinates the investigation with the U.S. Department of State.

More than 900 FBI Special Agents were sent overseas following the August 7, 1998 bombings of the U.S. embassies in Nairobi, Kenya, and Dar es Salaam, Tanzania, which resulted in the deaths of 12 Americans. This represented the largest overseas deployment in FBI history.

The results achieved from the on-site presence of FBI Special Agents were immediate. Mohammed Rashed Daoud Al-Owhali and Mohammed Saddiq Odeh were arrested in Kenya on August 27 and 28, 1998, respectively, and surrendered by Kenyan authorities to the United States to face charges arising from the embassy bombings. On September 17, 1998, Mamdouh Mahmud Salim was arrested in Germany and was later extradited to the United States to face similar charges arising from the twin bombings. This investigation further reinforced the belief that the cornerstone of successful international terrorism investigations is the ability to deploy federal law enforcement agents to the crime scene within hours of the incident.

As the above examples demonstrate, extraterritorial jurisdiction also allows terrorist suspects to be indicted and tried in the United States for violation of federal statutes outlawing terrorist acts. In the 1990s, several high-profile international terrorists, including Ramzi Ahmed Yousef, Omar Mohammad Ali Rezaq, and Tsutomu Shirosaki, were tried and convicted in the United States for acts of terrorism. The trend continued in 1998 when on June 3 Mohammed Rashid was arrested overseas and brought to the United States to stand trial for the August 11, 1982 bombing of Pan Am Flight 830. The bombing resulted in the death of a Japanese youth and injury to several other passengers. . . .

PROTECTING CRITICAL NATIONAL INFRASTRUCTURES

Revolutionary advances in our nation's computer software, hardware, and other information technologies have dramatically improved the capabilities and efficiency of these systems. At the same time, the rapid proliferation and integration of telecommunications and computer systems have connected the country's infrastructures to one another in a complex information network. While these changes have stimulated the growth of U.S. infrastructures, they also have made them increasingly interdependent and vulnerable to a new range of threats. Whether from foreign governments or transnational terrorists, in the twenty-first century the United States faces new types of terrorist threats to our national infrastructures.

To meet this challenge, in May 1998, President Clinton signed Presidential Decision Directive 63, formally establishing the National Infrastructure Protection Center (NIPC). The NIPC functions as an interagency warning and response center located at FBI Headquarters in Washington, D.C. Its mission is to deter, detect, and respond to unlawful acts involving computer and information technologies and other threats to critical U.S. infrastructures. The critical infrastructures—such as electric power, telecommunications, banking and finance, gas and oil, and transportation—are those which provide services so vital that their incapacity or destruction would have a debilitating impact on the defense or economic security of the United States.

While the threat of conventional, physical attacks on our critical infrastructures has always been a source of concern, electronic, information-based attacks constitute a relatively new and growing threat. Adversaries may use a number of software and hardware tools to launch such attacks. Software weapons include computer viruses, Trojan horses, and logic bombs. Advanced electronic hardware weapons include high-energy radio frequency (RF) weapons, electronic pulse weapons, and RF jamming equipment. Either set of tools (software or electronic hardware) can be used to degrade or destroy property and data, thereby denying crucial services to users of information systems.

Some foreign nations now include information warfare in their military planning and doctrine. To compensate for the United States' advantage in military power, certain nations believe they must focus their military efforts on offensive information operations—and they consider privately owned critical infrastructures to be the best targets. Even if a nation does not use such methods openly, the cyber tools and methods it develops may find their way into the hands of terrorists, with or without direct state involvement. While there is no evidence of state sponsored terrorist cyber attacks to date, the spread of cyber attack tools, like the proliferation of conventional weapons technology, may be unavoidable.

Terrorists are known to use information technology and the Internet to formulate plans, raise funds, spread propaganda, and communicate securely. For example, convicted terrorist Ramzi Yousef, the mastermind of the World Trade Center bombing, stored detailed plans to bomb U.S. commercial airliners in encrypted files on his laptop computer. Some groups have used cyber attacks to inflict damage on their enemies' information systems. A group calling itself the

"Black Tigers" conducted a successful "denial of service" attack on computer servers of Sri Lankan embassies. Italian sympathizers of the Mexican *Zapatista* rebels attacked the web pages of Mexican financial institutions. These examples illustrate the increasing ability and willingness of terrorists to use cyber tools and methods to plan and carry out attacks against government and civilian targets.

Fortunately, no nation or terrorist has yet launched a cyber attack serious enough to cause a national crisis. Nevertheless, U.S. dependence on information systems is increasing. As the means to exploit these dependencies become more widely available, and as the costs of carrying out an infrastructure attack decrease, the probability of a serious infrastructure attack increases.

The U.S. Government and the private sector need to prepare for possible infrastructure attacks preemptively by developing new institutional alliances, more robust security doctrines, and cutting-edge prevention and response capabilities. Together with its government and private sector partners, the NIPC is forging the analytical, information-sharing, investigative, and warning capabilities necessary to confront the terrorist threats of the twenty-first century.

CONCLUSION

The nearly simultaneous bombings of the U.S. embassies in Nairobi, Kenya, and Dar es Salaam, Tanzania, on August 7, 1998, vividly underscored the continuing threats to U.S. interests around the world. However, examples of terrorist violence were also all-too-evident in the United States during 1998. For the fourth consecutive year, terrorists carried out destructive attacks in the United States. Combined, attacks in 1998 resulted in one death and two serious injuries.

The United States continued to take a strong stand against terrorism in 1998. Ramzi Yousef . . . was sentenced to consecutive sentences of 240 years and life in prison for the World Trade Center bombing and airliner conspiracy. Several of Yousef's accomplices also received lengthy prison sentences in 1998. Another international terrorist, Mohammed Rashid, was rendered to the United States to stand trial for a 1982 attack on a U.S. commercial aircraft. In addition, by year's end, four suspects in the twin U.S. embassy bombings in East Africa were also in U.S. custody, awaiting trial.

The FBI, working closely with other law enforcement agencies, also succeeded in preventing 12 planned acts of terrorism from taking place in the United States. All of these conspiracies were being planned by domestic extremists. . . .

In 1998, the U.S. Government also continued to enhance the nation's counterterrorism capabilities with the establishment of the National Infrastructure

Protection Center (NIPC) in February and the National Domestic Preparedness Office (NDPO) in October. This greatly improves the ability of the intellience and law enforcement communities to prevent and respond to attacks on our nation's critical infrastructure and threats from weapons of mass destruction, respectively. Led by the FBI, but comprised of personnel from multiple agencies and disciplines, the NIPC and NDPO reflect the cooperation and combined sense of mission that has become a hallmark of our country's counterterrorism efforts.

The continued targeting of innocent victims, as well as U.S. Government and commercial interests, both in the United States and abroad by terrorists, requires such a concerted response.

USS Cole Bombing Attack:

Review of USS COLE (DDG-67) Attack Reports and Suggestions for Additional Recommended Actions, January 9, 2001

William S. Cohen, Secretary of Defense

Combating terrorism, including the protection of our forces serving around the world, has long been a primary concern of the Department of Defense. In the aftermath of the attack on Khobar Towers in June 1996, the Department established a formal combating terrorism program and took significant steps to improve force protection efforts worldwide. The Chairman of the Joint Chiefs of Staff was named the principal advisor and focal point for the Secretary of Defense on all anti-terrorism and force protection issues, and the Combatant Commanders were given expanded responsibility for force protection of all DoD activities within their geographic areas of responsibility. . . .

The attack on USS COLE (DDG-67) on October 12, 2000, visibly reinforced the fact that our forces are always at risk of terrorist attack. Immediately after the attack, we took additional steps to improve force protection worldwide. Now we must review all of our policies and procedures in light of that attack, and take every step possible to improve our responses to the threat of terrorism. Our goal must be continued vigilance to identify potential vulnerabilities and to appropriately strengthen our defenses.

By separate cover, I am forwarding for your review and advice a copy of the report submitted by General Crouch and Admiral Gehman regarding the attack on USS COLE (DoD USS COLE Commission). In addition, I will also forward to you for your review the Navy's Manual of the Judge Advocate General investigation into the attack as soon as that report is available. The report submitted by General Crouch and Admiral Gehman provides a view . . . focused on the challenges for in-transit units. Consistent with your responsibility as my principal military advisor . . . I request your advice concerning implementation of the USS COLE Commission recommendations, and any additional actions the Department should now take. . . .

I am very proud of the determination and dedication that the military has brought to the fight against terrorism, and I am confident that we will continue to find new ways to defend our interests and our engagement in a dangerous world.

USS Cole Bombing Attack:

Executive Summary, Department of Defense

USS Cole Commission Report, January 9, 2001

Since the attack on Khobar Towers in June 1996, the Department of Defense (DoD) has made significant improvements in protecting its service members, mainly in deterring, disrupting and mitigating terrorist attacks on *installations*. The attack on USS COLE (DDG 67), in the port of Aden, Yemen, on 12 October 2000, demonstrated a seam in the fabric of efforts to protect our forces, namely in-transit forces. Our review was focused on finding ways to improve the US policies and practices for deterring, disrupting and mitigating terrorist attack on US forces in transit.

1. OVERSEAS PRESENCE SINCE THE END OF THE COLD WAR

Our review was based on the premise that worldwide presence and continuous transit of ships, aircraft and units of the United States military support the . . . National Security Strategy . . . and are in the nation's best interest. The US military is conducting overseas operations in a new post-Cold War world environment characterized by unconventional and transnational threats. Operating in this new world exposes US forces to terrorist attacks and requires a major effort in force protection. This . . . will require more resources and . . . better use of existing resources for protecting transiting units. The net result of our recommendations is a form of operational risk management applied at both the national and operational levels. . . . We determined that the "fulcrum" of this balance is usually the Unified Commander-in-Chief's (CINC) Service Component Commander; therefore, a significant number of our recommendations are designed to improve that commander's . . . antiterrorism/force protection (AT/FP) capabilities.

We organized our findings at both the national and operational levels into the five functional areas of organization, antiterrorism/force protection, intelligence, logistics and training. . . .

2. NATIONAL LEVEL POLICIES AND PRACTICES

2.a. Organization

Unity of effort among the offices and agencies in the DoD providing resources, policy, oversight and direction is critical to truly gain the initiative over a very adaptive, persistent, patient and tenacious terrorist. This unity of effort extends . . . to . . . coordination of engagement activities across . . . agencies, including developing the security capabilities of host nations to help protect US forces. . . .

2.b. Antiterrorism/Force Protection

In force protection, we identified seven national level policy and procedural improvements to better support . . . transiting units. . . . Five of the seven . . . address additional resources and two address procedural changes. They are covered in the findings.

2.c. Intelligence

Intelligence priorities and resources have shifted from Cold War focus to new and emerging threats only at the margins. We, like other commissions before us, recommend the reprioritization of resources for collection and analysis, including human intelligence and signal intelligence, against the terrorist. Intelligence production must be refocused . . . to mitigate the terrorist threat. Furthermore, an increase in counterintelligence (CI) resources dedicated to combating terrorism and development of clearer CI assessment standards is required. . . .

2.e. Training

We believe most firmly that the US military must create an integrated system of training that produces a unit that is clearly and visibly ready, alert and capable. To achieve this level of . . . proficiency, AT/FP training must be elevated to the same priority as primary mission training. The level of competence . . . must be the same level for which primary combat skills are executed; and we must develop . . . credible deterrence standards; deterrence specific tactics, techniques and procedures; and defensive equipment packages.

3. OPERATIONAL LEVEL LESSONS LEARNED

The links between national policies/resources and individual transiting units are the geographic Unified CINCs and their Component Commanders. Transiting units do not have time or resources to focus on a series of locations while in transit, requiring these units to rely on others to support their efforts to deter, disrupt and mitigate terrorist attacks. We think it is the Component Commander who . . . is capable of controlling the resources to fight the fight and tailor specific AT/FP measures to protect transiting units. . . .

3.a. Antiterrorism/Force Protection

First, we must get out of the purely defensive mode by . . . applying . . . techniques and assets to detect and deter terrorists. Second, transfer of transiting units between and within theaters must be better coordinated. Third, a discrete operation risk management model should be adopted and utilized in AT/FP planning and execution.

3.b. Intelligence

Independent transiting units must be better trained . . . to provide appropriate requests for information to . . . intelligence organizations to be responsive to the transiter's AT/FP requirements. . . .

3.d. Training

Predeployment training regimes must include deterrence tactics, techniques and procedures; deterrence AT/FP measures specific to the area of operation; and equipment rehearsals.

The AT/FP training provided to unit commanding officers and force protection officers and the tools necessary to sustain an AT/FP training program needs increased attention.

In summary, we found Component Commanders are the fulcrum of a balance with the benefits of engagement on one side and the associated risks/costs on the other side. Our review suggests there is much we can do to help the field commander reach the proper balance. Taken as a whole, the Commission's recommendations are intended to enhance the tools available to commanders in making this balance.

UNCLASSIFIED FINDINGS AND RECOMMENDATIONS SUMMARY

Organizational

Finding: Combating terrorism is so important that it demands complete unity of effort at the level of the Office of the Secretary of Defense.

- *Recommendation: Secretary of Defense develop an organization that more cohesively aligns policy and resources within DoD to combat terrorism and designate an Assistant Secretary of Defense (ASD) to oversee these functions. . . .*

Finding: DoD needs to spearhead an interagency, coordinated approach to developing non-military host nation security efforts in order to enhance force protection for transiting US forces.

- *Recommendation: Secretary of Defense coordinate with Secretary of State to develop . . . shared responsibility to enhance host nation security capabilities that result in increased security for transiting US forces.*

ANTITERRORISM/FORCE PROTECTION (AT/FP)

Finding: Service manning policies and procedures that establish requirements for full-time Force Protection Officers and staff billets at the Service Component level and above will reduce the vulnerability of in-transit forces to terrorist attacks.

- *Recommendation: Secretary of Defense direct the Services to provide Component Commanders with full-time force protection officers and staffs. . . .*

Finding: Component Commanders need the resources to provide in-transit units with temporary security augmentation of various kinds.

- *Recommendation: Secretary of Defense direct the Services to . . . adequately augment units transiting through higher-threat areas.*

Finding: Service AT/FP programs must be . . . manned and funded to support threat and physical vulnerability assessments of ports, airfields and inland movement routes that may be used by transiting forces.

- *Recommendation: Secretary of Defense direct the Chairman of the Joint Chiefs of Staff, the CINCs and the Services to identify and resource manning and funding requirements to perform quality assessments of routes and sites used by transiting forces in support of Component Commanders.*

Finding: The Chairman of the Joint Chiefs of Staff Combating Terrorism Readiness Initiative Fund is a responsive and relevant program. . . .

- *Recommendations: The Chairman of the Joint Chiefs of Staff Combating Terrorism Readiness Initiative Fund should be increased to cover the period prior to which a Service program can fund the remaining life-cycle costs.*

- *Secretary of Defense direct the Services to establish a formal link to the . . . Initiative Fund to ensure that initiatives receive a commitment for follow-on programming.*

Finding: More responsive application of . . . military equipment, commercial technologies, and aggressive research and development can enhance the . . . posture of transiting forces.

- *Recommendation: Secretary of Defense direct the Services to initiate a major unified effort to identify near-term AT/FP equipment and technology requirements, field existing solutions from either military or commercial sources, and develop new technologies for remaining requirements.*

Finding: The Geographic Commander in Chief should have the sole authority for assigning the threat level for a country within his area of responsibility.

- *Recommendations: Secretary of Defense direct that the Geographic CINCs be solely responsible for establishing the threat level within the appropriate area of responsibility with input from DIA.*
- *Secretary of Defense coordinate with Secretary of State, where possible, to minimize conflicting threat levels between the Department of Defense and the Department of State.*
- *Secretary of Defense designate an office or agency responsible for setting the threat level for Canada, Mexico, Russia, and the United States. . . .*

Finding: The CJCS Standing Rules of Engagement for US forces are adequate against the terrorist threat.

- *Recommendation: Make no changes to the SROE.*

Finding: We need to shift transiting units from an entirely reactive posture to a posture that more effectively deters terrorist attacks.

- *Recommendation: Secretary of Defense direct the CINCs and Services to have Component Commanders identify proactive techniques and assets to deter terrorists.*

Finding: The amount of AT/FP emphasis that units in-transit receive prior to or during transfer between CINCs can be improved.

- *Recommendation: Secretary of Defense direct the CINCs and Services to have Component Commanders ensure unit situational awareness by providing AT/FP briefings to transiting units prior to entry into higher threat level areas. . . .*

Finding: Using operational risk management standards as a tool to measure engagement activities against risk to in-transit forces will enable commanders to determine whether to suspend or continue engagement activities. . . .

Finding: Incident response must be an integral element of AT/FP planning.

- *Recommendation: Secretary of Defense direct the Geographic CINCs to identify theater rapid incident response team requirements and integrate their utilization in contingency planning for in-transit units, and the Services to organize, train, and equip such forces.*

INTELLIGENCE

Finding: In-transit units require intelligence support tailored to the terrorist threat in their immediate area of operations. This support must be dedicated from a higher echelon (tailored production and analysis).

- *Recommendation: Secretary of Defense reprioritize intelligence production to ensure that in-transit units are given tailored, focused intelligence support for independent missions. . . .*

Finding: DoD does not allocate sufficient resources or all-source intelligence analysis and collection in support of combating terrorism.

- *Recommendations: Secretary of Defense reprioritize all-source intelligence collection and analysis personnel and resources so that sufficient emphasis is applied to combating terrorism. Analytical expertise must be imbedded, from the national, CINC, and Component Command levels, to the joint task force level.*
- *Secretary of Defense reprioritize terrorism-related human intelligence and signals intelligence resources.*
- *Secretary of Defense reprioritize resources for the development of language skills that support combating terrorism analysis and collection.*

Finding: Service counterintelligence programs are integral to force protection and must be adequately manned and funded to meet the dynamic demands of supporting in-transit forces.

- *Recommendation: Secretary of Defense ensure DoD counterintelligence organizations are adequately staffed and funded to meet counterintelligence force protection requirements.*

Finding: Clearer DoD standards for threat and vulnerability assessments must be developed at the joint level and be common across Services and commands.

- *Recommendations: Secretary of Defense standardize counterintelligence assessments and increase counterintelligence resources.*
- *Secretary of Defense [set standards] for the conduct of threat and vulnerability assessments for combating terrorism.*
- *Secretary of Defense direct the production of a DoD-standard Counterintelligence Collection Manual for combating terrorism.*

LOGISTICS

Finding: While classifying the diplomatic clearance and logistics requirement process may improve the operational security of transiting units, it is not practical due to the commercial nature of the process.

- *Recommendation: None. Implementing proactive AT/FP measures identified in this report mitigate the effect of public knowledge of US military ship and aircraft visits. . . .*

Finding: Local providers of goods, services, and transportation must be employed and evaluated in ways that enhance the AT/FP posture of the in-transit unit.

- *Recommendation: Secretary of Defense direct the Defense Logistics Agency and the Services to incorporate AT/FP concerns into the entire fabric of logistics support. . . .*

TRAINING

Finding: Better force protection is achieved if forces in transit are trained to demonstrate preparedness to deter acts of terrorism.

- *Recommendations: Secretary of Defense direct the Services to develop and resource credible deterrence standards, deterrence-specific tactics, techniques, and procedures and defensive equipment packages for all forms of transiting forces.*
- *Secretary of Defense direct the Services to ensure that pre-deployment training regimes include deterrence tactics, techniques, and procedures and AT/FP measures specific to the area of operation and equipment rehearsals.*

Finding: DoD must better support commanders' ability to sustain their antiterrorism/force protection program and training regimens.

- *Recommendations: Secretary of Defense direct the Chairman of the Joint Chiefs of Staff to publish a single source document that categorizes all of the existing AT/FP training literature, plans and tactics, techniques, and procedures for use by the Services (on both classified and unclassified versions) (short term).*

- *Secretary of Defense direct the Chairman of the Joint Chiefs of Staff to consolidate and develop a single repository for all AT/FP lessons learned. This database should be accessible to unit commanders in the classified and unclassified mode (long term).*
- *Secretary of Defense direct the Chairman of the Joint Chiefs of Staff to continually update training tools, capture lessons and trends and aid Commanders in sustaining meaningful AT/FP training programs. . . .*

USS Cole Bombing Attack:

Lost Patrol: The Attack on the *Cole*

Admiral Harold W. Gehman Jr., U.S. Navy (Retired)

. . . The likelihood of someone challenging the United States to a great sea bat-tle is fairly small. Someone challenging the United States to a tank battle prob-ably is not going to happen in the next ten years. Somebody challenging the United States to a tactical air superiority battle anytime soon probably also is unlikely. But the United States is going to be challenged. The questions are, How? and Where?

What happened to the USS *Cole* (DDG-67)—or to our airmen at Khobar Towers in 1996 or our two East African embassies in 1998—is more likely than a great naval or tank battle to be the challenge we are going to face. Recently, I served as cocommissioner of the ten-week review on the attack on the *Cole*, and our experiences and recommendations might offer some perspective.

First, our charter specifically forbade us from looking at accountability is-sues, so we did not. We also did not look at why the *Cole* was in Yemen. That is important because our review took as a given that the United States is going to remain engaged around the world. That is what naval professionals do—con-duct U.S. policy around the world by a program of active engagement. That is what the *Cole* was doing. The U.S. National Security Strategy and U.S. Na-tional Military Strategy say we are going to be engaged actively around the world. And we are not likely—if you listen to our leaders—to back down from that policy because of terrorist activities. Therefore, the answer to Why Yemen? is because it is there.

We did look at Department of Defense (DoD) policies and practices as they apply to small, transiting units such the *Cole* and aircraft. For example, what is done for the single U.S. Air Force C-141 and its crew when they stop in Nairobi for fuel? Who is protecting them? Who is doing their threat analysis? Who is providing them intelligence? We also found that individual engagement activities such as small humanitarian demining teams act just like the *Cole*. They have all the same characteristics. They are like the lost patrols of the world. They are out there by themselves without much oversight.

What we were to look at is whether DoD—and all its entities—was doing what needed to be done to make that kind of engagement activity safe. Therefore, the crew or the captain of the *Cole* was not a party to our inquiry. The parties to our inquiry were people such as the Chief of Naval Operations, the Commander-in-Chief, Central Command, the Director of the Defense Intelligence Agency, the Chairman of the Joint Chiefs of Staff, and the Secretary of Defense.

We thought it important to start by putting our report in its cultural and historical context. In addition to engagement activities, we discussed terrorism, surprises, sovereignty, and what the commanding officer could be expected to do. DoD has done a lot since the terrorist attack on the Air Force barracks at Khobar Towers. Money has been spent, and people have been trained. But the effort largely has been aimed at fixed installations; the *Cole* and her situation were not very well addressed.

We looked at whether terrorism is a crime or an act of war. The Secretary of Defense and the President said, "This cowardly criminal act will not go unpunished." Was it cowardly? The guys who attacked the *Cole* died for their cause.

Is it criminal or war? The attackers were members of an armed force doing their duty. Their goal is to get U.S. presence in the Middle East reduced or to get us out of there entirely. They are trying to remove us from the battlefield and they are attacking uniformed members of our armed forces in the performance of their duties. Does this sound like war?

The trouble is that U.S. national policy defines a terrorist attack as a cowardly crime. When members of the uniformed military think about cowardly criminals, we tend to think of people who steal from the post exchange and things like that. So somehow we have to get our people in uniform to realize that national policy calls terrorism a crime because it fits into the international context much better that way—if we call it a crime, most nations of the world will support activities to fight it. Even the Syrians will arrest people for terrorist crimes. But to translate this activity into terms our people in uniform will pay attention to, we have to use words such as *war*. If we say you are at war and these people are trying to kill you, then everybody in the military knows what to do. So we discussed this issue in our report.

You need to look at the patterns of terrorist activity, and we did this in our report, to come to any judgment about the *Cole* and DoD's role in either supporting her or leaving her hanging out there. When you examine the attacks on the Marine barracks at Beirut, the World Trade Center in New York, the federal office building at Oklahoma City, Khobar Towers, the two East Africa embassies, and the *Cole*, there are some striking similarities. They all were truck bombs. The *Cole* was attackd by a truck bomb. It had an outboard motor, but it was a truck bomb. All these attacks were in daylight.

There is another similarity. They were all different. In every case the terrorists changed their pattern just a little bit; they found a seam or a way to get at us for which we were not prepared. This has enormous implications for the intelligence and training communities.

So what is the next attack going to look like? It is going to be a truck bomb in daylight, and it is going to be applied in some new and different way. The bottom line of our review of the case of the *Cole* was to give the Secretary of Defense 30 findings and 50-some recommendations by which we felt the United States could continue to do its engagement activities but mitigate the risk.

I will summarize briefly what we told the Secretary of Defense. First, we found no tactically actionable intelligence predicting this attack. Nevertheless, we came up with a series of recommendations that the intelligence community must do if we are to continue with these kinds of engagement activities. Some are classified, and many of them have serious resource implications. I will address a couple of them.

We believe that units such as the *Cole* or that Air Force C-141 refueling in Nairobi require tailored overwatch. Someone has to be responsible for watching out for them, like we do for other kinds of special missions in the U.S. military. That is not being done. If you go to the theater joint intelligence centers and examine their workload and their priorities, which we did, you will find they are related to war plans, contingency plans, and the Cold War. The transiting unit does not get much attention. We—like General Wayne Downing after Khobar Towers; Admiral William Crowe after the East Africa bombings; and Admiral Robert Long after the Beirut barracks—concluded that the U.S. intelligence organizations need to shift more assets and resources to analytical resources supporting antiterrorism.

The intelligence community has shifted some resources from its Cold War missions to its post-Cold War missions, but only at the margins. That is particularly true for analytical support. We also found that our counterintelligence assets really have not shifted to fighting terrorism. We have not thought that this is a serious threat that is not going away. In fact, we found that counterintelligence assets actually have moved away from fighting terrorism recently to the protection of technology, à la Los Alamos and things like that.

In the area of training, the *Cole* and her crew met or exceeded all the DoD and Navy antiterrorism and force-protection training requirements. In fact, the *Cole* received a letter of commendation from Second Fleet for her training performance. Nevertheless, the product of this training was not a vigilant, alert, deterrence-oriented team. So we have to assume the problem was the training regime. When we examined it in detail, we found serious flaws.

First, in the U.S. Navy, force protection/antiterrorism is not a primary mission. It is a noncombat operation. It is in the second order of training priorities, after antiair, strike, and submarine warfare and all these other things. Force protection/antiterrorism does not get the support, the energy, the resources, the time, the observer-trainers, or a thinking opposition force. We simply do not produce the antiterrorism posture we need. So we recommended it be elevated in priority.

Training for uncertainty creates a problem. This is a cultural problem. Our trainers will tell you that you train for certainty; you educate for uncertainty. When we train, we want people to do things the same way every time. Whether fighting fires or launching airplanes, it does not make a difference—you do it the same way every time. But how do you train people to recognize the unusual? The next terrorist attack is going to be different from the last one. How do you train people to recognize the unexpected? That is a requirement the current system is not meeting.

We recommended shifting the entire training regime to train people to recognize uncertainty, to recognize the unusual, to recognize when something is wrong, and to be able to take quick action. That is the easy part.

The harder part is to train people to a level where their performance can be construed as a deterrence function. In the U.S. doctrine for fighting terrorism, there are three pillars: detect, disrupt, and deter. In the case of the *Cole*, the threat was not detected. Maybe the *Cole*'s crew could have disrupted the attack had it been detected, maybe not. Deterrence, however, is enormously important. Terrorists are willing to die to succeed, but they are not willing to die for failure. If you can deter them, they will seek another enemy. We have tons of intelligence documenting cases where terrorists have collected intelligence, planned, gotten in position to conduct an attack, and then decided not to execute it because the target was judged too tough. Deterrence works.

The U.S. Navy training regime does not teach deterrence. It does not require people to have a game face. It does not require the posting of guards who look like guards, who look like they are ready to do things, who are equipped with the right stuff. In the case of the *Cole*, topside security watches were equipped with shotguns. That is not a deterrent to a guy coming in a boat from 200 yards away. You have to look and act like you are serious. You have to have the right posture—a game face. This is not easy to do. The training to achieve this level of sophistication is rigorous.

As part of a sophisticated deterrent training program, you must have a solid understanding of the rules of engagement. Our report found that the standing rules of engagement—the Joint Chiefs of Staff rules of engagement—themselves were adequate.

Finally, under the training area, we found that in some high-threat areas the threat is so severe that no one should expect the average unit to be able to counter it alone, and some temporary augmentation would be useful. There are cases in the Department of Defense where services do this; they temporarily augment units for transits through dangerous areas. The U.S. Navy has a history of doing this. During the Tanker War, the Navy put Stinger surface-to-air missile teams on the decks of transiting ships as a temporary augmentation measure.

Force protection is the third area we spent a lot of time examining. We recommended that the department implement 20-some things to address force protection issues. I will not go through them all, but I will highlight a couple to demonstrate what we measured.

Essentially, the bottom line of our force protection recommendations was to raise the cost of doing business in high-threat areas. We said, if you are going to go into these very nasty areas, you need to do these 10-15 things. Some will require spending money. Some will require host-nation agreements. A lot of our diplomats do not want to have to hammer out such agreements because they fear aggravating the host nation. In our report we raised the cost of doing this kind of engagement activity to the point where if you cannot get that agreement with the host nation, then you do not visit that nation.

Another of our recommendations dealt with the need for fully manned force protection positions. We found throughout DoD and all the services the widespread practice of having force protection be a collateral duty. This is true at the one-, two-, three-star level staffs and fleet commander staffs. Force protection positions need to be full-time.

We need to do better manning of counterintelligence organizations; these are the people who really sort out where the threats are. We need to fix the threat-level system. If you followed the congressional hearings having to do with the attack on the *Cole* you know that even experts confuse threat levels with threat conditions. As soon as you get into a discussion about whether the threat level was lower in Djibouti than it was in Aden, immediately you confuse threat conditions and threat levels. We do it to ourselves. We have a very complex system that nobody can figure out.

Three different agencies—the State Department, the Defense Intelligence Agency, and the theater commander-in-chief (CinC)—set threat levels. That is a terrible situation. It is awfully confusing. Then there is the name: threat condition, threat con. It is a completely different system. So we recommended changing the name of the threat con system. Threat levels refer to what the bad guy is doing. Whereas, the measures of threat conditions—for example, the *Cole* was in Threat Con Bravo in Aden—refer to things we are doing. So why not change the name of measures that refer to our actions as alert conditions? The threat level refers to the other guy; what we are doing should not have the word "threat" in it.

We recommended that higher authority direct the threat condition measures that transiting units should undertake. Right now, we have this ridiculous process in which a transiting unit submits a message to its higher authority that says, "I'm going to do the following measures for my threat condition." The higher authority then either approves or disapproves the proposed plan. The guy submitting his plan is clueless. He never has been there, does not know the local host-nation people, does not know what to expect from the host-nation security forces, and does not know what the last guy before him did.

Now, of course, immediately we took flak for this recommendation: "Oh, the commanding officer is king, and we should never take away the commanding officer's prerogative to do whatever he wants to do." Hogwash.

We also recommended threat conditions be classified. We should not advertise to the bad guys what we are doing. In addition, we made strong recommendations about procedures for reporting into a new operating area.

Rules of engagement is another area that deserves special attention. Essentially, if you are a U.S. military commander, there are two ways you can open fire. One is in reaction to a hostile attack. The other is in reaction to hostile intent. Hostile attack is not applicable to terrorism. When the guy has completed his attack, there is no point in shooting anybody; the attack is over.

So that leaves us with hostile intent. We believe that the current rules of engagement are adequate if you have a way to determine hostile intent. But as someone comes toward you, how do you determine that this guy is a terrorist with hostile intent and you should shoot him? There are ways to do it. You can build barriers and warning zones and keep-out zones and inspection points and things like that. We already do that on the land side; why can't we do it on the water side? If you cannot negotiate these types of conditions with the host nation, then you have to evaluate whether you should do that engagement activity.

The second rule of engagement caveat we raised is very important to serving military professionals. We told the Secretary of Defense and the Chairman of the Joint Chiefs that the higher the threat level the lower the threshold for declaring hostile intent. For the CinC, this means that if you are keeping areas at very high threat levels, then you should support the commanding officer who fires a warning shot. Well, this did not go down very well, because this is another cost of doing business that the system may not be able to stand up to. In other words, the establishment says, "Oh, no, no. If a commanding officer or one of his guys fires a warning shot in a foreign country, he better damn well be firing at real terrorists."

We said, "Well, you can't have it both ways." We found that keeping threat levels extraordinarily high for long periods of time is numbing. The result is that the forces kind of went to sleep.

In the area of logistics much was made in the press about why the port visit was unclassified. Well, you cannot do logistics with commercial companies and keep it classified, but there are actions you can undertake to turn this to your advantage. You can use contracting to increase your force protection. You can contract with host-nation people to do things you cannot do because of sovereignty issues. Host-nation people can carry guns; they can control the local nationals; they can control traffic; they can manage separation zones. You can write into the contract that the contractor has to provide interpreters. You can write it into the contract that the contractor has to put some kind of obvious marker on all the boats designated to come alongside, so you can tell the good guys from the bad guys.

The final area I will address has to do with organizational matters. We found that organizations in Washington, D.C., are not well placed to fight terrorism and to provide force protection for units such as the *Cole*. In DoD, there is no unity of effort. There are six or seven vertical stovepipes that deal with intelligence, counterintelligence, counterterrorism, force protection, antiterrorism, consequence management, etc. Then horizontally they are not even organized the same. You go into one of them and you will find that the intelligence guy has policy responsibility, oversight responsibility, and budgetary responsibility. You go to the force protection guy and he has one of these responsibilities, but not two. We recommended to the Secretary of Defense that he appoint someone at the Assistant Secretary of Defense level to do something about this issue. Interestingly, the 2001 Authorization Act requires the Secretary of Defense to do that. By the filing of our report in January, the Secretary had chosen not to.

We found the interagency coordination process for engagement activities to be unsatisfactory. DoD has a very aggressive, well-managed engagement activity around the world. The other departments do not. We strongly recommended an interagency coordination process that would facilitate the coordination of our activities, because there were questions about what the embassy did and what the DoD attaché did, and things like that.

Finally, it is in DoD's best interests that host-nation security forces help our military units. In most places, host-nation security forces does not mean the navy, air force, or army; it usually means coast guards, internal security forces, customs, or something like that. And DoD cannot easily work with those kinds of activities, except on an exception or waiver basis. If that is the responsibility of the State Department, it needs funding for it. It is in our nation's best interest that these activities be robust. So we recommended that these activities be streamlined, so that DoD can help State in ports, airports, and things like that.

Our commission's findings are designed to permit the U.S. military to continue to do its mission and mitigate the risk. They call for a training program and an equipping program that will help the U.S. military recognize the next threat. We were not permitted or asked to address accountability issues; we did not. We coordinated our report with the Navy JAG Manual investigation. I have read every word of it, including all the endorsements. We coordinated our report with the FBI as to who-done-it. I know all about it. One must take all three reports together to evaluate fairly accountability and responsibility.

The bottom line is that the terrorist threat is not going away. It will be the weapon of choice of our future adversaries. The U.S. military is going to continue active engagement programs. Therefore, we are going to bump into these guys on a regular basis. We have to get out of the purely defensive posture of building bigger sandbags. We must have an active force-protection stance. We hope our report will help save lives.

Admiral Gehman served as coleader of the USS *Cole* (DDG-67) commission. He was Commander-in-Chief, U.S. Joint Forces Command, when he retired from active duty in 2000. This article was adapted from Admiral Gehman's 23 January address at West 2001, the annual AFCEA-Naval Institute cosponsored symposium and exhibition in San Diego.

USS Cole Bombing Attack:

Terrorist Attack on the USS Cole: Background and Issues for Congress

Raphael F. Perl and Ronald O'Rourke, Foreign Affairs, Defense, and Trade Division

SUMMARY

On October 12, 2000, the U.S. Navy destroyer Cole was attacked by a small boat laden with explosives during a brief refueling stop in the harbor of Aden, Yemen. The suicide terrorist attack killed 17 members of the ship's crew, wounded 39 others, and seriously damaged the ship. Evidence developed to date suggests that it may have been carried out by Islamic militants with possible connections to the terrorist network led by Usama bin Ladin.

The FBI, Defense Department, and Navy launched investigations to determine culpability for the attack and to review procedures. A broad DoD review of accountability was conducted by a special panel. On January 9, 2001, the panel issued its report which avoided assigning blame but found significant shortcomings in security against terrorist attacks, including inadequate training and intelligence. On January 23, 2001, Senate Armed Services Committee Chairman, John Warner, announced intentions for the Committee to hold its own investigation. Issues for Congress include the adequacy of (1) procedures by U.S. forces to protect against terrorist attacks; (2) intelligence related to potential terrorist attacks; and (3) U.S. anti-terrorism policy and response. This report will be updated if major new developments warrant.

BACKGROUND

On October 12, 2000, the U.S. Navy destroyer Cole was attacked by a small boat laden with explosives during a brief refueling stop in the harbor of Aden,

Yemen. The suicide terrorist attack killed 17 members of the ship's crew, wounded 39 others, and seriously damaged the ship.* The attack has been widely characterized as a "boat bomb" adaptation of the truck-bomb tactic used to attack the U.S. Marine Corps barracks in Beirut in 1983 and the Khobar Towers U.S. military residence in Saudi Arabia in 1996.

The FBI, in conjunction with Yemeni law-enforcement officials, is leading an investigation to determine who is responsible for the attack. At least six suspects are in custody in Yemen. Evidence developed to date suggests that it may have been carried out by Islamic militants with possible connections to the terrorist network led by Usama bin Ladin. In addition to the FBI-led investigation, Secretary of Defense William Cohen has formed a special panel headed by retired General William W. Crouch, former Vice Chief of Staff of the Army, and retired Admiral Harold W. Gehman, Jr, former commander-in-chief of U.S. Joint Forces Command. The panel, in a report released January 9, 2001, avoided assigning blame but found significant shortcomings in security throughout the region and recommended improvements in training and intelligence designed to thwart terrorist attacks. A Navy investigation, the results of which were released by the Commander of the Atlantic Fleet on January 19, 2001, concluded that many of the procedures in the ship's security plan had not been followed, but that even if they had been followed, the incident could not have been prevented. Consequently, no single individual should be disciplined for the incident, i.e. blame must be distributed at a number of administrative levels. Members and staff have also held classified meetings on the attack with Administration officials.

ISSUES FOR CONGRESS

The attack on the Cole raises potential issues for Congress concerning (1) procedures used by the Cole and other U.S. forces overseas to protect against terrorist attacks; (2) intelligence collection, analysis, and dissemination as it relates to potential terrorist attacks; and (3) U.S. anti-terrorism policy and how the U.S. should respond to this attack. These issues are discussed below.

Force-Protection Procedures

Before it arrived at Aden for its brief refueling stop, the Cole, like all visiting U.S. ships, was required to file a force-protection plan for the visit. This plan was approved by higher U.S. military authorities, and was implemented during the ship's visit. In accordance with the plan, the Cole at the time of the attack

---

*The Cole (DDG-67) is an Aegis-equipped Arleigh Burke (DDG-51) class destroyer. It was one of four DDG-51s procured in FY1991 at an average cost of about $789 million per ship. This is equivalent to about $924 million in FY2001 dollars. The ship entered service in 1996. The cost to repair the ship has been preliminarily estimated at about $243 million.

was operating under threat condition Bravo, which is a heightened state of readiness against potential terrorist attack. (The lowest condition of heightened readiness is Alpha; Bravo is higher; Charlie is higher still, and Delta is the highest.) This threat condition includes steps that are specifically intended to provide protection against attack by small boats.

Members of the House and Senate Armed Services committees and other observers have raised several issues concerning the force-protection procedures being used by the Cole and by other U.S. military forces and bases in the region, including the following:

- What were the elements of the Cole's force-protection plan and how were these elements determined?
- Did the Cole effectively implement all the elements of this plan? If not, why not? If so, does this indicate that the plan was not adequate for defending against this type of attack?
- Was the force-protection plan, including the use of threat condition Bravo, appropriate in light of the terrorist threat information that was available to military officials in the days leading up to the ship's visit? Was the ship's threat condition consistent with the very high threat condition being maintained at that time by the U.S. embassy in Yemen?
- What changes, if any, should be made in force-protection policies for ships and other U.S. military forces and bases overseas, particularly in the Middle East and Persian Gulf region? Given the need for Navy ships to periodically refuel and receive other services from local sources, as well as the potential difficulty of identifying hostile craft in often-crowded harbors, how much can be done to reduce the risk of future attacks like this one? What can be done to protect against more sophisticated terrorist tactics for attacking ships, such as using midget or personal submarines, scuba divers with limpet mines, or command-detonated harbor mines? Should the Navy reduce its use of ports for refueling stops and instead rely more on at-sea tanker refuelings? How many additional tankers, at what cost, might be needed to implement such a change, and how would this affect the Navy's ability to use such stops to contribute to U.S. engagement with other countries?

In addition to these issues, members of the House and Senate Armed Services committees at the hearings also raised an underlying question on whether the Cole's refueling stop was necessary from an operational (as opposed to political/diplomatic) point of view.*

---

*Defense Department officials testified that the refueling stop was necessary operationally because the Cole was making a 3,300-mile transit from the Mediterranean (where it previously

Intelligence Collection, Analysis, and Dissemination

Members of the Armed Services and Intelligence committees as well as other observers have raised several questions relating to the role of intelligence collection, analysis and dissemination in the Cole attack and in preventing other terrorist attacks against the United States. In some cases, these questions have been spurred by press reports about the existence of information and analyses from the U.S. Intelligence Community that, some argue, might have helped prevent the attack had it been given greater consideration or been disseminated more quickly. The details of these claims are currently under investigation by the Executive Branch and Committees in Congress. Questions include the following:

- Does the United States have sufficient intelligence collection capacity, particularly in the form of human intelligence (as opposed to intelligence gathering by satellites or other technical means), for learning about potential terrorist attacks, particularly in the Middle East or Persian Gulf? Does the attack on the Cole represent a U.S. intelligence failure, or does it instead reflect the significant challenges of learning about all such attacks soon enough to head them off?
- In the days and weeks prior to the attack on the Cole, was all the available intelligence information about potential terrorist attacks in the Middle East and Persian Gulf given proper weight in U.S. assessments of the terrorist threat in that region? Were reports providing information and analyses of potential terrorist attacks in the region disseminated on a timely basis to U.S. military and civilian officials in the region who have responsibility for providing advice or making decisions about ship refueling stops or other military operations?
- Was there adequate coordination, prior to the attack on the Cole, between the Defense Department [including the National Security Agency], the State Department, and the U.S. Central Command (the regional U.S. military command for the Middle East and Persian Gulf) in sharing and using available intelligence information and analyses on potential terrorist attacks?

---

refueled) to the Persian Gulf. Defense Department officials argue that it would be impractical to have enough tankers so that one could always be assigned to combat ships engaged in solitary transits. Since the end of the Cold War, though, the Navy has become more comfortable with the idea of breaking forward-deployed battle groups into small sub-formations, including solitary ships, to take better advantage of the modular flexibility of naval forces for responding to specific needs overseas. The policy issue might thus be as follows: Are the refueling-related risks created by (possibly-more-frequent) solitary transits combined with the 50-percent fuel policy properly balanced against the benefits of moving ships in this manner and preserving their projected tactical mobility upon arrival at the intended area of operation?

- What actions, if any, should be taken to improve U.S. intelligence collection and analysis, particularly as it relates to potential terrorist attacks on U.S. assets in the Middle East and Persian Gulf or elsewhere?

U.S. Anti-terrorism Policy and Potential Response

Beyond these more specific issues, the attack on the Cole poses several additional potential issues relating to U.S. anti-terrorism policy in general. Some of these issues highlight dilemmas and concerns inherent in policies designed to prevent or mitigate terrorist acts. These issues include the following:

Why Was Yemen Chosen for Refueling?

U.S. Navy ships began making refueling stops in Aden in January 1999. Since then, Navy ships have stopped there 27 times to refuel, twice to make port visits, and once to take on supplies. Members of the Armed Services Committees and other observers have asked why the U.S. Central Command decided in 1998 to begin using Yemen for refueling stops rather than continuing to use nearby Djibouti on the Horn of Africa (which U.S. Navy ships had used for refueling for several years)—and why Central Command continued to use Yemen this year for refuelings when an April 2000 State Department report on worldwide terrorism characterized Yemen as a haven for terrorists but did not mention Djibouti. Members and others have asked whether the risk of a terrorist attack against a U.S. ship in Yemen was properly balanced against the political/diplomatic goals of improving relations with Yemen and encouraging its development toward a stable, pro-Western, democratic country that does not support terrorism and cooperates with U.S. efforts to contain Iraq. In response, General Tommy R. Franks, the current Commander-in-Chief of U.S. Central Command, stated the following regarding the process that led his predecessor, General Anthony C. Zinni, to the decision to use Yemen for refueling stops:

> The decision to go into Aden for refueling was based on operational as well as geostrategic factors and included an assessment of the terrorist and conventional threats in the region. As you know, the Horn of Africa was in great turmoil in 1998. We had continuing instability in Somalia, the embassy bombings in Kenya and Tanzania, an ongoing war between Ethiopia and Eritrea, and an internal war in Sudan. . . . As of December 1998, 14 of the 20 countries in the USCENTCOM AOR [U.S. Central Command area of responsibility] were characterized as "High Threat" countries.

> Djibouti, which had been the Navy refueling stop in the Southern Red Sea for over a decade, began to deteriorate as a useful port because of the Eritrea-Ethiopia war. This war caused increased force-protection concerns for our ships, as well as congestion in the port resulting in operational delays.

The judgment at this time was that USCENTCOM needed to look for more refueling options, and Aden, Yemen was seen as a viable alternative. At the time the refueling contract was signed, the addition brought the number of ports available in the USCENTCOM AOR to 13. Selection of which of these ports to use for a specific refueling operation involves careful evaluation of the threat and operational requirements.

The terrorism threat is endemic in the AOR, and USCENTCOM takes extensive measures to protect our forces. . . . The threat situation was monitored regularly in Yemen and throughout the AOR. The intelligence community and USCENTCOM consider this AOR a High Threat environment, and our assessments of the regional threat and the threat in Yemen were consistent in their evaluation. We had conducted a number of threat assessments in the port, and throughout the area. However, leading up to the attack on USS Cole on 12 October, we received no specific threat information for Yemen or for the port of Aden that would cause us to change our assessment. Had such warning been received, action would have been taken by the operating forces in response to the warning.

Anticipating New Modes of Terrorist Attack

Truck bombs have been used to attack U.S. targets for at least 17 years. Did U.S. intelligence and counter-terrorism agencies anticipate or consider sufficiently plausible the possible use of the maritime equivalent of a truck bomb against a U.S. Navy ship in a harbor? If not, what changes, if any, should be made to improve the ability of U.S. intelligence and counter-terrorism agencies to identify and give sufficient prominence to modes of terrorist attack that have not been previously used? Should U.S. officials reach out more to non-governmental organizations and individuals for help in this regard?

Protecting Against Threats Posed by Persons with Legitimate Access

What is the best way to defend against terrorist attacks by persons with legitimate access to U.S. installations or forces? The Cole was refueled by a private Yemeni ship supply company that had advance information on the ship's itinerary. Although it now appears that the attack may have been carried out by persons with no connection to this firm, the attack still raises questions about the security implications of relying on private foreign companies to refuel U.S. Navy ships. What steps can be taken to reduce the risk posed by relying on such firms? Should, for example, the State Department's Anti-Terrorism Assistance program (ATA) be enhanced so that it can better assist foreign governments, when needed, in personnel screening and security procedures?

The Role of the FBI in Overseas Counter-terrorism Investigations

Some observers have asked whether (or under what circumstances) it is appropriate for the FBI, traditionally a domestic U.S. law-enforcement agency, to take a *de facto* lead role in overseas investigations of terrorist attacks. Although the FBI's investigative skills are critical to such investigations, some observers argue that other skills outside the FBI's area of specialization, including having an in-depth understanding of foreign countries and cultures and the diplomatic ability to ensure host nation cooperation, are equally important components of such investigations. Clearly, small nations may feel overwhelmed by large numbers of FBI agents and the political sensitivities of their insistence on questioning local witnesses/suspects. Conferees on the FY2001 Foreign Operations Appropriations bill (H.R. 4811) made $4 million for counter-terrorism training in Yemen contingent on FBI certification that Yemen is fully cooperating in the Cole investigation.

Insuring Coordination of Any Retaliatory Response

An important challenge facing U.S. counter-terrorism officials is to ensure that U.S. actions for military/economic retaliation for terrorist attacks are adequately planned. The need for maintaining secrecy in planning military actions can discourage interagency coordination, which in turn can create a potential for making a planning mistake. Some observers argue that the U.S. cruise missile attack on what some believe was a legitimate pharmaceutical factory in Sudan in response to the 1998 embassy bombings in East Africa was a mistake caused in part by lack of interagency coordination that deprived decisionmakers of important data which might have influenced the target-selection process. If it is determined that the attack was linked to Bin Ladin, a major issue is how the U.S. responds and prevents further attacks from a network that is believed responsible for several anti-U.S. attacks since 1992. The U.S. retaliatory attack on Afghanistan in August 1998, a response to the East Africa Embassy bombings, did little to damage Bin Ladin's network or his ability to plan attacks.

PART VII

United States Responses

THE UNITED STATES has engaged in an escalating effort to counter terrorist organizations, and especially Osama bin Laden's Al Qaeda, at least since the summer of 1998. These efforts have included diplomatic approaches, attempts to isolate the terrorists, intelligence sharing to improve knowledge of the networks carrying out these activities, massive dragnets apprehending individuals hoped to have knowledge of the New York or Washington attacks, increased security measures at home and abroad, national and international measures to affect the financing of terrorists, and, since October 7, 2001, a formal military campaign in Afghanistan and elsewhere. The documentary record of these actions is so far limited. What appears in this section reflects activities already in progress as of the September 11 incidents, measures taken immediately afterward, and general statements of policy or doctrine governing the employment of means of force. The administration of President George W. Bush, having declared war on terrorism, is seeking to carry out that conflict behind closed doors. With a secrecy policy justified in terms of denying knowledge to the adversaries, the Bush administration is simultaneously avoiding legislative oversight and public accountability while arrogating to itself unprecedented executive powers without debate.

In terms of diplomatic maneuvers, since the Nixon administration a range of initiatives have been designed to isolate terrorist organizations and dilute their sources of support. These have included campaigns at the United Nations to tighten international treaties restricting terrorist activities, bilateral approaches to individual nations, and multilateral efforts to create groups of states willing to act in common or enforce common standards of security practice, evidence in legal cases, extradition, or other measures affecting terrorism. The UN General Assembly passed resolutions aimed at countering terrorism in 1972, 1976, 1977, 1979, 1981, 1983, 1985, 1987, 1989, 1991, 1994, 1995, 1996, 1997, 1998, and, most recently, after the attacks of September 2001. Clearly the UN action has become almost an annual exercise. Its focus has changed over the years, from Middle East violence early on, to protection from hijacking, to linkages with drug trafficking and other criminal activity, to the protection of nuclear plants and shipments, to today's across-the-board concerns, which have also involved the UN's Security Council. United Nations involvement is likely to strengthen multilateral cooperation through such bodies as the International Atomic Energy Agency and Interpol.

The 1994 UN resolution included a Declaration on Measures to Eliminate International Terrorism, strengthened in 1996, which among other things specified that seeking asylum could not be used as a device to avoid prosecution for terrorist acts elsewhere. Also within the UN framework, the Clinton administration pressed for an International Convention for the Suppression of Terrorist Bombings, which was opened for signature on December 15, 1997. The United States signed this treaty, which ensures that all states criminalize the delivery or detonation of explosives against "places of public use" and certain other facilities, but it has not yet taken effect. This creation of arrangements for dealing with international terrorists has also been a focus of much bilateral diplomatic activity, in particular on rules for extradition and encouraging states to extradite terrorist suspects. Congressional legislation has given the U.S. government authority to use economic sanctions against states that harbor terrorists. These measures played a role in the decision by Libya to permit the prosecution by a Scottish court of Libyan nationals implicated in the 1989 bombing of Pan American Airlines Flight 103. Two Libyan intelligence officers were convicted on these charges early in 2001. For several years during the 1990s, the annual *Patterns of Global Terrorism* reports listed terror suspects whom the United States had apprehended abroad or who had been remanded to U.S. custody.

In another multilateral initiative, the Clinton administration encouraged action by the Organization of American States (OAS), which led to conferences at Buenos Aires in August 1995, and Lima, Peru, in April 1996, following previous OAS actions in 1994 and 1990–1991. At Buenos Aires, in particular, where a bloody bombing of a Jewish community center had roused ire, diplomats considered the nexus between human rights and the need for rapid extradition. The Lima conference agreed to study the need for a new inter-American convention on terrorism. A further conference held in Argentina in November 1998 adopted a commitment against terrorism plus specific guidelines on notification and response to terror incidents, along with cooperation to eliminate terrorist fund-raising.

With the Group of 7 industrialized countries as well as the Group of 8 (the seven plus Russia), the United States secured further concrete provisions at a December 1995 meeting at Ottawa. Aside from exhorting nations to sign on to existing international conventions on terrorism, the G-8 declared an intention to strengthen measures designed to prevent the use of weapons of mass destruction, entry controls to catch terrorists at borders (these seem not to have been very effective in the United States shortly before September 11), extradition, transportation security, and again, terrorist funding. The 1995 declaration also included an attempt to increase intelligence sharing and security and police cooperation among the members. The G-7 summit six months later, which took place soon after the Khobar Barracks bombing (see Part VI), ended with a reaffirmation of the Ottawa declaration. The participants endorsed two dozen specific measures designed to improve security, prosecute and punish terrorists, tighten border controls, and prevent terrorist fund-raising. Conferences of both groups of developed countries in the years since have returned to these subjects.

Efforts to restrict terrorism have had both domestic and international consequences. An essential framework in U.S. law was created by the Omnibus Diplomatic Security and Antiterrorism Act of 1986 (Public Law 99-399). This statute already provided for some problems seen as exotic today, with regulations on international nuclear terrorism. At the behest of the Clinton administration, ten years later the 104th Congress passed the Antiterrorism and Effective Death Penalty Act. This 1996 law tightened some previous restrictions, codified legislation that has been passed in bits and pieces elsewhere, and provided authority for the U.S. government to engage in some of the intelligence sharing, border security, extradition, and other international arrangements that the Clinton administration had been negotiating. The act included provisions on implementation of international conventions on trafficking in plastic explosives; strictures on nuclear, biological, and chemical weapons; and increased criminal penalties for terrorist acts. The act also made it illegal for American individuals or institutions to render financial or material support to terrorist organizations, and required banks and other U.S. financial institutions to block the accounts of those groups. In October 1997, Secretary of State Madeleine Albright designated thirty foreign terrorist organizations to be covered by the restrictions. That list included the Japanese group responsible for the Tokyo subway attack; Egyptian, Algerian, and Filipino groups now thought to be associated with Al Qaeda; certain Latin American and South Asian groups; and a large number of Palestinian groups. Al Qaeda itself was not on the list.

Bilateral diplomacy through the past four administrations has included so many matters related to terrorism that simply listing the nations and issues would consume a great deal of space. It is more useful to note the general areas in which the United States has approached other nations: arrangements for extradition of suspected or accused terrorists; security cooperation; arrangements to restrict international financial transactions; intelligence sharing; and joint operations. For example, the Clinton administration arranged with Kenya and Tanzania to permit FBI investigative teams to work in those countries following the 1998 embassy bombings (see Part VI for details on all the incidents mentioned here), and later with both those nations and Pakistan to extradite suspects to the United States. Similarly, Clinton officials persuaded Canada to allow Americans to question suspects in the Khobar Barracks attack, and in incidents planned for the millennium but foiled in the event. Some of these suspects were also extradited to the United States. Clinton diplomacy led to intelligence sharing with the Philippines and Jordan, which provided important information to American analysts of terrorism as well as arrests (and convictions) in other cases. Diplomacy had some success with Yemen in achieving access for FBI teams in the wake of the explosive boat attack on the destroyer *Cole* in 2000, and with Saudi Arabia for FBI access after Khobar Barracks. The latter instances of investigative cooperation were less fruitful, with U.S. special agents unhappy with restrictions placed on them by the host countries.

After the September 11 bombings, the administration of President George W. Bush has made a variety of diplomatic arrangements designed to facilitate its war on terrorism. These include foreign aid agreements with Pakistan, Tadjikistan, and other countries to permit the entry of U.S. forces. The United States enlisted the North Atlantic Treaty Organization (NATO) in support of this effort and arranged with member states such as the United Kingdom, France, Germany, and Italy for commitments of troops to the Afghan front and for additional security measures at home. At last report more than 250 suspects had been apprehended in these countries, Spain, Pakistan, the Sudan, and elsewhere at the request of the United States or based on investigations conducted by these countries whose results have been shared with Washington. Bilateral exchanges with Saudi Arabia have resulted in permission to use the base at Al Kharj for staging forces into Afghanistan. Soon after September 11 the Saudis promised cooperation with American investigations of the attacks on New York and Washington, and, more reluctantly, new restrictions on international financial transactions. The Saudi attitude has cooled since indications developed that many of the Islamic militants involved in the attacks were Saudi citizens. Other Persian Gulf states, such as the United Arab Emirates, which has emerged as a center for the financing of the terrorist networks, have responded to American bids for cooperation to varying degrees.

After the September 11 attacks, President George W. Bush sought a congressional resolution authorizing the use of force (although not an actual declaration of war). Under a tight veil of secrecy, the Bush administration moved military forces to South Asia, the Persian Gulf, and the Indian Ocean. Led by the U.S. Central Command, under Army General Tommy R. Franks, naval forces surged into the littoral waters. The Navy unloaded the normal air group from its carrier *Kitty Hawk* so that the ship could be used entirely by the helicopters necessary to move ground troops. Two other aircraft carrier battle groups provided airpower. Two Marine amphibious units, each of which is built around an eight-hundred-man battalion of Marine infantry reinforced with tanks, artillery, engineers, special scout units, and organic helicopters, to a total of about thirteen hundred personnel, provided the seaborne component of the forces. Additional warships were sent to the African coast and the Persian Gulf to permit a sort of quarantine that might prevent evacuation by sea of the terrorist forces originally situated in Afghanistan.

As of September 11, Afghanistan was ruled by the Taliban, an Islamic fundamentalist group which was not a terrorist organization but which had fought a civil war in that country since 1992. In fact Afghanistan had been mired in war since the 1970s, when a monarchy of more than two centuries' standing was overthrown. Thereafter followed a succession of civil wars. The Taliban struggled against a coalition of tribal and religious-based Afghan groups in the fourth of these civil wars. The coalition they fought had won the second of the Afghan civil wars in the 1980s with the help of the American CIA, the Saudi and Pakistani intelligence services, and others, defeating Russian forces. In the third war the CIA had dropped out of the picture, and the Afghans defeated the residual forces of the Afghan Communist government. But they lost the support of former Pakistani backers, who turned to the nascent Taliban, a group not satisfied with the religious purity of daily life in the land. The coalition had always been a disparate one, unable to agree on much more than fighting the Russians; and faced with the Taliban challenge, much of its power disintegrated in a wave of defections. In 1995 the Taliban captured the Afghan capital Kabul. Progressively they beat back the coalition remnants, who now call themselves the Northern Alliance. In power the Taliban opened their doors to the arrival of Osama bin Laden and his Al Qaeda who, unlike Taliban as a whole, were terrorists. When the Taliban refused to hand over bin Laden to Americans after the September 11 attacks, their government and control of Afghanistan became the initial target of the Bush administration's war.

The problem for General Franks and his superiors was to forge links with the Northern Alliance, mobilize other tribal groups in the west and south of Afghanistan to make up for the narrow ethnic composition of Northern Alliance forces, and apply American military power that was remote from the theater of operations. For example, as Afghanistan is a landlocked country, aircraft and helicopters from the U.S. fleet in the Indian Ocean had to fly over Pakistan even to cross the the the Afghan border. Hence the need for U.S. bilateral diplomatic action. With promises of foreign aid, favorable trade terms, and other assistance, the administration was able to arrange with the surrounding countries—Pakistan, Tadjikistan, Uzbekistan, and China—for access to bases and permission to operate. That is where General Franks began the military buildup for what was called Operation "Enduring Freedom."

Into Tadjikistan the Central Command deployed a battalion of the 10th Mountain Division and other units to create a base to project power into Afghanistan. From there Army Special Forces linked up with the Northern Alliance and began funneling supplies and assisting them with training and military advice. Beginning on October 7, 2001, U.S. aircraft bombed targets in Afghanistan, clearing the way for bombing to blunt Taliban forces blocking a Northern Alliance advance from its perch in the northeast of the country. That ground advance began in November, successively capturing Taliban positions at the cities of Mazar-i-Sharif, Kabul, and Kandahar, the cradle of the Taliban. By mid-December the Taliban had been forced out of its bases and shorn of its ability to fight as a conventional military force. Afghan forces of a new Eastern Alliance were engaging directly with Al Qaeda jihadists in a series of mountain cave positions along the Pakistani border. Leaders of both Taliban and Al Qaeda remained at large. A probable consequence will be a campaign of guerrilla warfare.

American and allied military operations have assumed a pattern that shows signs of becoming a standard for this war. Daily air activity, ranging from forty to eighty-odd flights, relied on fighter-bombers and heavy bomber aircraft. The navy carried the brunt of the air mission in the early weeks, with air force heavy bombers for a Sunday punch. Due to the political sensitivity of U.S. bases in Saudi Arabia, it was difficult to mount strikes with air force jets located there, but at this writing diplomacy is building the foundation for basing air force fighter-bombers in forward locations in Tadjikistan and Uzbekistan. The air force's B-52 and B-1 heavy bombers fly shuttle bombing missions from the United States, landing at the island of Diego Garcia in the Indian Ocean, refueling there, and striking again as they return home; B-2 "Stealth" bombers leave from and return to their base in the United States. The crash of a B-1 bomber due to mechanical failure off Diego Garcia on December 12 was the first U.S. aircraft loss of the war (several helicopters succumbed to damage from ground fire or in-flight problems). Her crew were saved. American warships as well as those of the British Royal Navy fired a small number of cruise missiles, but this did not form a major feature of the air campaign.

Regular forces on the ground were used to hold a series of forward bases, first in Tadjikistan. When Northern Alliance troops overran Kabul and Mazar-i-Sharif, numbers of U.S. Special Forces, including their psychological warfare and civil affairs units, moved ahead to help in the cleared territory. The United Kingdom, France, and Germany all sent special operations forces to assist in this effort, and British troops were the first contingent at the former air base of Bagram, north of Kabul. British Special Air Service (SAS) troops worked with Special Forces in a series of lightning raids on promising targets, the first of which was in late October against a house near Kandahar used by Taliban leader Mullah Muhammed Omar. As the Afghan coalition bands began their efforts to clear the caves held by Al Qaeda and the Taliban, American and allied special operations forces provided teams to coordinate air strikes for them, and small units for important assault missions. Approximately a hundred Special Forces and British SAS commandos are reported to have been engaged in the siege of the Al Qaeda cave complex at Tora Bora. Later reinforced, the elite troops fought as combat units, not advisers. One of the readings in this section excerpts the 1992 edition of the Joint Chiefs of Staff manual governing special operations and conveys a very good idea of just how the role of Special Forces is seen and the manner in which their operations are planned.

The document is missing an indication of the organization of the Special Forces. Since April 1987 all the armed services' capabilities for unconventional warfare have been embodied into a single formation, the U.S. Special Operations Command (USSOC), its headquarters located at the same base as Central Command. In all, the USSOC has about 46,000 soldiers, sailors, and airmen, roughly 21,000 of whom are on active duty. The army provides the largest part of the command, 30,000, with its own Special Forces headquartered at Fort Bragg, North Carolina. Of five active duty and two reserve Special Forces groups, each specializes in one geographic or linguistic area of the world. At the working level the Special Forces, commonly called Green Berets, are experienced troops cross-trained with additional skills and formed into teams with an independent capability. When they train foreign military forces, like the 7th Group's work in Colombia with the strike battalions of the anti-drug war, the detachments are called mobile training teams. The 1st Special Forces Group, working the Far East from Okinawa, recently sent mobile training teams to the Philippines to help against terrorist bands thought to be associated with Al Qaeda. The 5th Special Forces Group, ironically the same unit that served in South Vietnam during the war there, has done some of this work with the Northern Alliance. Scout missions behind the lines are a Special Forces métier. The helicopter that crashed in Pakistan in November, wounding two Americans, had been engaged in such an operation. Green Beret teams also have the ability to lead or advise large irregular forces, which may very well figure in Afghanistan.

For bigger attack missions the army has three 660-man battalions in its 75th Ranger Regiment, and perhaps 450 elite commandos in Special Forces Operational Detachment Delta. Air support is provided by the 160th Special Operations Aviation Regiment. Both the 5th Group and the 160th Aviation Regiment have home bases at Fort Campbell, Kentucky. The 96th Civil Affairs Battalion is helping reconstitute Afghan government services. This 300-man unit is USSOC's only active-duty civic action unit; 97 percent of American capability in this area resides in the reserve forces. Parts of the 4th Psychological Operations Group are also working in Operation Enduring Freedom.

The Naval Special Warfare Command has roughly half its 5,500 personnel on active duty, in special boat squadrons, swimmer delivery teams, and six Seal teams. Team Six has long had the specific mission of countering terrorism. But Seal teams are likely to have a large role in the navy's effort to stop and inspect ships on the high seas to prevent the escape by sea of Al Qaeda militants. As of this writing, at least two such maritime inspections have already been conducted. The air force Special Operations Command also has about half its 10,000-person complement on active duty in nine fixed-wing and five helicopter squadrons. These types of aircraft range from lumbering C-130 transports modified for stealth and low-altitude penetration, to similar big planes equipped as aerial artillery platforms, to special mission helicopters. The command has been in action supporting scout missions and raids in Afghanistan. Though not normally assigned to the USSOC, the Marine Corps has its unconventional warfare capability in units it terms Force Reconnaissance Battalions, detachments of which may form part of the expeditionary units afloat. One of the Marine expeditionary units in Enduring Freedom has Force Reconnaissance elements attached.

A measure of the secrecy shrouding the war on terrorism in Afghanistan, aside from the poor press relations of which media have complained, is that virtually no information has been given to the public on the size or shape of the U.S. military deployment for Operation Enduring Freedom. Judging from the forces known to have been committed, at this point the large majority of men and women engaged are from the navy, accounting for the crews of warships. A reasonable guess might be about eight thousand in ground and air forces and about eighteen thousand at sea. Depending on how ample the logistics support deployed with them, the total may come to between thirty thousand and forty thousand Americans. Several thousand allied troops are also involved, either with the Americans or as part of international peacekeeping forces sent into Afghanistan.

The cave offensive in the south of the country is beyond the reach of troops from the bases along the Tadjik border. General Franks therefore used the Marine forces (15th Marine Expeditionary Unit) aboard ship in the Indian Ocean to open Forward Operating Base Rhino in the desert southwest of Kandahar. Forces moved through here are the main participants in the direct action against Al Qaeda. The Marines first confined themselves to defending the base, but after reinforcement from the second available Marine expeditionary unit (26th), some of these troops fanned out into the countryside in an effort to block the withdrawal of Taliban troops from Kandahar, and Al Qaeda fighters from the mountain caves. A company-sized force took over the airport at Kandahar in mid-December. At the Tora Bora cave complex, American troops coordinated air support for Afghans of a new Eastern Shura coalition while some Americans and British SAS troops provided elite strike teams for the assaults. As many as several hundred Americans and British were engaged at the height of the fighting and afterward, when American searches of the conquered caves began to complement those of Eastern Shura forces. Tora Bora was declared secured on December 17, 2001, ending the most intense phase of the Afghan campaign.

While a number of Al Qaeda and Taliban fighters were captured in battle at Tora Bora, Kandahar, Marar-i-Sharif, and elsewhere, almost all senior Taliban and Qaeda figures eluded their pursuers. This included both the key leaders, Osama bin Laden and Mullah Omar. U.S. activity after December became a kind of grand-scale hide-and-seek campaign. Troops of the 101st Airborne Division were brought in to replace Marine units on the ground, while the former Camp Rhino was closed and the U.S. base moved to the airport at Kandahar. From there U.S. forces, primarily Marines and Special Forces, radiated out into the countryside and conducted strikes at places thought to harbor enemy leaders, or at former Al Qaeda training camps. Bombing responded to reports of enemy movements, or was used as a form of demolition for equipment and targets discovered by troops searching captured bases. Al Qaeda and Taliban prisoners were held at Kandahar, aboard U.S. warships in the Indian Ocean, or moved to a new prison compound built at Guantanamo Bay, Cuba. At this writing seventeen American soldiers, sailors, or airmen have died in the anti-terrorism campaign. Surviving leaders of Al Qaeda and other organizations are doubtless attempting to resuscitate their networks. A Pan Am 103–style aircraft bombing, and an alleged plot in Singapore were averted by the alert actions of bystanders or security forces.

In terms of presidential decisions, this dispatch of American forces into a war situation no doubt rests upon a directive issued from the White House. The Bush administration has continued the practice that has existed since the 1947 creation of the National Security Council (NSC) of ordering major initiatives by presidential directive. Terrorism has been no exception. Beginning in the Reagan administration, with a national security directive on managing terrorist incidents in April 1982, a series of presidential choices in these matters have been consecrated by official documents. Reagan issued at least four other directives on the subject, ending with the establishment of a "national program for combating terrorism" in January 1986. The Clinton administration also issued at least two presidential decision directives (PDDs) on terrorism, most importantly PDD-39 in June 1995. That order underlay much of the diplomatic activity summarized earlier in this section, and stated, "It is the policy of the United States to deter, defeat and respond vigorously to all terrorist attacks on our territory and against our citizens, or facilities, whether they occur domestically, in international waters or airspace or on foreign territory." As with many of the succession of orders issued in this area, the PDD provides for reducing vulnerabilities to terrorism, for deterring attacks, and for responding to terrorist incidents. A 1998 Clinton PDD established a national coordinator for counterterrorism, security, and infrastructure protection. Because much of the vital operative language in these directives remains classified, they have not been reproduced in this collection.

Another arrow in the White House quiver is the presidential finding. Under the laws governing intelligence activity, a presidential finding is required to authorize any U.S. covert operation above a certain size, and given certain other characteristics. Bill Clinton approved a presidential finding for an operation to stop Osama bin Laden following the embassy bombings in Africa in 1998 (see Part VI). Cruise missile attacks on Al Qaeda training camps in Afghanistan and a factory in the Sudan on August 21, 1998, were carried out under this authority. At least two further CIA attempts to neutralize bin Laden are reported to have been carried out. Both failed. Clinton reportedly later approved another order of this type. President George W. Bush issued his own presidential finding in conjunction with approval of the Enduring Freedom military operation. All presidential findings are secret and none is available for public view.

There has been much talk in the context of the effort against Osama bin Laden of the pros and cons of assassination. This is a matter for presidential findings and also of the executive orders which presidents can issue. After President Gerald Ford revealed in 1975 that the CIA had been involved in earlier assassination attempts, he issued an executive order prohibiting this practice, a stricture reaffirmed by President Jimmy Carter. In December 1981, President Ronald Reagan approved a fresh executive order (EO 12333) which provided that "No person employed by or acting on behalf of the United States government shall engage in, or conspire to engage in, assassination." The Reagan order broadened the prohibition in two respects, by covering all U.S. agents and assets (in addition to government personnel), and by ruling out the targeting of persons other than heads of state. That stricture has continued to this day.

The assassination prohibition proved controversial during the Reagan years, notably at the time the United States bombed the home of Libyan leader

Muammar Qaddhafi in 1986, and again in the Bush administration, in conjunction with Manuel Noriega of Panama and Saddam Hussein of Iraq. Experts have differed over the extent to which it is properly applicable. One of the documents included here is a memorandum of law prepared by the Judge Advocate General of the United States Army in 1989 which minimizes the effect of the prohibition. It should be noted that at the time the army was looking toward operations in Panama and wanted as free a hand as possible. The Bush presidential finding of 2001 is widely reported to have loosened the assassination prohibition.

Beyond assassination, the use of executive orders has been a major tool for presidents facing the question of what to do about terrorism. From the mid-1990s, Bill Clinton used the device to freeze the assets of a variety of groups, beginning in January 1995 with terrorists deemed to threaten the Middle East peace process. On August 20, 1998, he amended that directive to include Osama bin Laden and several additional terrorists or organizations. On July 4, 1999, President Clinton signed a further executive order aimed at the Taliban. This order, as well as the Treasury Department's 1999 annual report on the freezing of terrorist assets, is included here. Reporting on the difficulty of cutting terrorists off from their money has noted little success for efforts against bin Laden, but the 1999 Treasury document shows that by that time the United States had already succeeded in blocking $23.7 million worth of bin Laden assets.

President George W. Bush followed with his own executive order on terrorist assets on September 24, 2001. That document is also reproduced here. Although his list of terrorist entities has since been expanded twice, Bush's order aimed at further strengthening the drive to dry up the money flow to extremist organizations. The Bush administration went on to make blocking funds a key feature of its bilateral diplomacy. It has had considerable success on money questions with the United Kingdom and a good deal of success in Europe, but the outlook is not as certain in the Middle East (particularly Saudi Arabia) or Asia. The money drive is also hampered by the fact that a significant portion of terrorist funds are believed to move outside the banking system, by informal arrangement with speculators and money changers.

Bush's most controversial executive order provided for military tribunals to try persons who are not U.S. citizens. Issued on November 13, the order established a system circumventing many standards considered basic to justice—doing away with appeals, juries, the right to confront accusers, rules of evidence, unanimous votes in capital cases—and can be applied to persons who have simply harbored others thought to be preparing acts that might aim to cause "adverse effects." These amorphous effects are not the same as physical damage; they can be anything that impacts the U.S. economy, national security, or foreign policy. This wide-ranging order has itself already had adverse effects, since European nations are bound by international agreement to avoid extradition to countries that impose the death penalty. Spain and France have protested specific cases to the United States, and the Bush executive order may ultimately lead to a reduction in police and intelligence cooperation, with negative effects on the overall struggle to stop terrorism.

In summary, the American response to terrorism long predates September 11 and has involved many different tools and techniques. A more detailed examination of existing law would show that measures necessary to prosecute terrorists are already on the books. Indeed, defendants have been tried and found guilty in a number of prominent cases, including the 1993 World Trade Center bombing, the Oklahoma City bombing, the African embassy bombings, and others. Conspirators in plots that never came off have also been prosecuted, as in the millennium affair. Tribunals abroad have convicted defendants in cases like that of Pan Am 103. The United States has created an international diplomatic framework for cooperation against terrorists and is pursuing military operations against the prominent terrorist network Al Qaeda. An active effort to stymie money flow to terrorists is in progress. The element missing from current strategy is not legal, diplomatic, military, intelligence, law enforcement, or financial, but a program to dry up the sea in which the terrorist fish swim and from which they draw recruits—that is, actions to reduce the credibility of terrorist charges about American aims and intentions, and to improve the living conditions that make desperate people into volunteers. The contest for hearts and minds is the most crucial one, and that is where America falls short.

Executive Order on Terrorist Financing, September 24, 2001

President George W. Bush

. . . The President has directed the first strike on the global terror network today by issuing *an Executive Order* to starve terrorists of their support funds.

The Order expands the Treasury Department's power to target the support structure of terrorist organizations, freeze the U.S. assets and block the U.S. transactions of terrorists and those that support them, and increases our ability to block U.S. assets of, and deny access to U.S. markets to, foreign banks who refuse to cooperate with U.S. authorities to identify and freeze terrorist assets abroad.

DISRUPTING THE FINANCIAL INFRASTRUCTURE OF TERRORISM

- Targets all individuals and institutions linked to global terrorism.
- Allows the Treasury Department to freeze U.S. assets and block U.S. transactions of any person or institution associated with terrorists or terrorist organizations.
- Names specific individuals and organizations whose assets and transactions are to be blocked.
- Identifies charitable organizations that secretly funnel money to al-Qaeda.
- Provides donors information about charitable groups who fund terrorist organizations.
- States the President's intent to punish those financial institutions at home and abroad that continue to provide resources and/or services to terrorist organizations.

AUTHORITIES BROADENED

The new Executive Order broadens existing authority in three principal ways:

- It expands the coverage of existing Executive Orders from terrorism in the Middle East to global terrorism;
- The Order expands the class of targeted groups to include all those who are "associated with" designated terrorist groups; and
- Establishes our ability to block the U.S. assets of, and deny access to U.S. markets to, those foreign banks that refuse to freeze terrorist assets.

BLOCKING TERRORIST ASSETS

- The Order prohibits U.S. transactions with those terrorist organizations, leaders, and corporate and charitable fronts listed in the Annex.
- Eleven terrorist organizations are listed in the Order, including organizations that make up the al-Qaeda network.
- A dozen terrorist leaders are listed, including Osama bin Ladin and his chief lieutenants, three charitable organizations, and one corporate front organization are identified as well.
- The Order authorizes the Secretary of State and the Secretary of the Treasury to make additional terrorist designations in the coming weeks and months.

OTHER ACTIONS IN WAR ON TERRORIST FINANCING

This Executive Order is part of a broader strategy that we have developed for suppressing terrorist financing:

- A Foreign Terrorist Asset Tracking Center (FTAT) is up and running. The FTAT is a multi-agency task force that will identify the network of terrorist funding and freeze assets before new acts of terrorism take place.
- The President, the Secretary of the Treasury, the Secretary of State and others are working with our allies around the world to tackle the financial underpinnings of terrorism. We are working through the G-8 and the United Nations. Already, several of our allies, including Switzerland and Britain, have frozen accounts of suspected terrorists.

EXECUTIVE ORDER 13224 OF SEPTEMBER 23, 2001
BLOCKING PROPERTY AND PROHIBITING TRANSACTIONS WITH PERSONS WHO COMMIT, THREATEN TO COMMIT, OR SUPPORT TERRORISM

By the authority vested in me as President by the Constitution and the laws of the United States of America, including the International Emergency Economic Powers Act (50 U.S.C. 1701 et seq.) (IEEPA), the National Emergencies Act (50 U.S.C. 1601 et seq.), section 5 of the United Nations Participation Act of 1945, as amended (22 U.S.C. 287c) (UNPA), and section 301 of title 3, United States Code, and in view of United Nations Security Council Resolution (UNSCR) 1214 of December 8, 1998, UNSCR 1267 of October 15, 1999, UNSCR 1333 of December 19, 2000, and the multilateral sanctions contained therein, and UNSCR 1363 of July 30, 2001, establishing a mechanism to monitor the implementation of UNSCR 1333,

I, GEORGE W. BUSH, President of the United States of America, find that grave acts of terrorism and threats of terrorism committed by foreign terrorists, including the terrorist attacks in New York, Pennsylvania, and the Pentagon committed on September 11, 2001, acts recognized and condemned in UNSCR 1368 of September 12, 2001, and UNSCR 1269 of October 19, 1999, and the continuing and immediate threat of further attacks on United States nationals or the United States constitute an unusual and extraordinary threat to the national security, foreign policy, and economy of the United States, and in furtherance of my proclamation of September 14, 2001, Declaration of National Emergency by Reason of Certain Terrorist Attacks, hereby declare a national emergency to deal with that threat. I also find that because of the pervasiveness and expansiveness of the financial foundation of foreign terrorists, financial sanctions may be appropriate for those foreign persons that support or otherwise associate with these foreign terrorists. I also find that a need exists for further consultation and cooperation with, and sharing of information by, United States and foreign financial institutions as an additional tool to enable the United States to combat the financing of terrorism.

I hereby order:

Section 1. Except to the extent required by section 203(b) of IEEPA (50 U.S.C. 1702(b)), or provided in regulations, orders, directives, or licenses that may be issued pursuant to this order, and notwithstanding any contract entered into or any license or permit granted prior to the effective date of this order, all property and interests in property of the following persons that are in the United States or that hereafter come within the United States, or that hereafter come within the possession or control of United States persons are blocked:

(a) foreign persons listed in the Annex to this order;

(b) foreign persons determined by the Secretary of State, in consultation with the Secretary of the Treasury and the Attorney General, to have committed, or to pose a significant risk of committing, acts of terrorism that threaten the security of U.S. nationals or the national security, foreign policy, or economy of the United States;

(c) persons determined by the Secretary of the Treasury, in consultation with the Secretary of State and the Attorney General, to be owned or controlled by, or to act for or on behalf of those persons listed in the Annex to this order or those persons determined to be subject to subsection 1(b), 1(c), or 1(d)(i) of this order;

(d) except as provided in section 5 of this order and after such consultation, if any, with foreign authorities as the Secretary of State, in consultation with the Secretary of the Treasury and the Attorney General, deems appropriate in the exercise of his discretion, persons determined by the Secretary of the Treasury, in consultation with the Secretary of State and the Attorney General;

(i) to assist in, sponsor, or provide financial, material, or technological support for, or financial or other services to or in support of, such acts of terrorism or those persons listed in the Annex to this order or determined to be subject to this order; or

(ii) to be otherwise associated with those persons listed in the Annex to this order or those persons determined to be subject to subsection 1(b), 1(c), or 1(d)(i) of this order.

Sec. 2. Except to the extent required by section 203(b) of IEEPA (50 U.S.C. 1702(b)), or provided in regulations, orders, directives, or licenses that may be issued pursuant to this order, and notwithstanding any contract entered into or any license or permit granted prior to the effective date:

(a) any transaction or dealing by United States persons or within the United States in property or interests in property blocked pursuant to this order is prohibited, including but not limited to the making or receiving of any contribution of funds, goods, or services to or for the benefit of those persons listed in the Annex to this order or determined to be subject to this order;

(b) any transaction by any United States person or within the United States that evades or avoids, or has the purpose of evading or avoiding, or attempts to violate, any of the prohibitions set forth in this order is prohibited; and

(c) any conspiracy formed to violate any of the prohibitions set forth in this order is prohibited.

Sec. 3. For purposes of this order:

(a) the term "person" means an individual or entity;

(b) the term "entity" means a partnership, association, corporation, or other organization, group, or subgroup;

(c) the term "United States person" means any United States citizen, permanent resident alien, entity organized under the laws of the United States (including foreign branches), or any person in the United States; and

(d) the term "terrorism" means an activity that—

(i) involves a violent act or an act dangerous to human life, property, or infrastructure; and

(ii) appears to be intended—

(A) to intimidate or coerce a civilian population;

(B) to influence the policy of a government by intimidation or coercion; or

(C) to affect the conduct of a government by mass destruction, assassination, kidnapping, or hostage-taking.

Sec. 4. I hereby determine that the making of donations of the type specified in section 203(b)(2) of IEEPA (50 U.S.C. 1702(b)(2)) by United States persons to persons determined to be subject to this order would seriously impair my ability to deal with the national emergency declared in this order, and would endanger Armed Forces of the United States that are in a situation where imminent involvement in hostilities is clearly indicated by the circumstances, and hereby prohibit such donations as provided by section 1 of this order. Furthermore, I hereby determine that the Trade Sanctions Reform and Export Enhancement Act of 2000 (title IX, Public Law 106–387) shall not affect the imposition or the continuation of the imposition of any unilateral agricultural sanction or unilateral medical sanction on any person determined to be subject to this order because imminent involvement of the Armed Forces of the United States in hostilities is clearly indicated by the circumstances.

Sec. 5. With respect to those persons designated pursuant to subsection 1(d) of this order, the Secretary of the Treasury, in the exercise of his discretion and in consultation with the Secretary of State and the Attorney General, may take such other actions than the complete blocking of property or interests in property as the President is authorized to take under IEEPA and UNPA if the Secretary of the Treasury, in consultation with the Secretary of State and the Attorney General, deems such other actions to be consistent with the national interests of the United States, considering such factors as he deems appropriate.

Sec. 6. The Secretary of State, the Secretary of the Treasury, and other appropriate agencies shall make all relevant efforts to cooperate and coordinate with other countries, including through technical assistance, as well as bilateral and multilateral agreements and arrangements, to achieve the objectives of this order, including the prevention and suppression of acts of terrorism, the denial of financing and financial services to terrorists and terrorist organizations, and the sharing of intelligence about funding activities in support of terrorism.

Sec. 7. The Secretary of the Treasury, in consultation with the Secretary of State and the Attorney General, is hereby authorized to take such actions, including the promulgation of rules and regulations, and to employ all powers granted to the President by IEEPA and UNPA as may be necessary to carry out the purposes of this order. The Secretary of the Treasury may redelegate any of these functions to other officers and agencies of the United States Government. All agencies of the United States Government are hereby directed to take all appropriate measures within their authority to carry out the provisions of this order.

Sec. 8. Nothing in this order is intended to affect the continued effectiveness of any rules, regulations, orders, licenses, or other forms of administrative action issued, taken, or continued in effect heretofore or hereafter under 31 C.F.R. chapter V, except as expressly terminated, modified, or suspended by or pursuant to this order.

Sec. 9. Nothing contained in this order is intended to create, nor does it create, any right, benefit, or privilege, substantive or procedural, enforceable at law by a party against the United States, its agencies, officers, employees or any other person.

Sec. 10. For those persons listed in the Annex to this order or determined to be subject to this order who might have a constitutional presence in the United States, I find that because of the ability to transfer funds or assets instantaneously, prior notice to such persons of measures to be taken pursuant to this order would render these measures ineffectual. I therefore determine that for these measures to be effective in addressing the national emergency declared in this order, there need be no prior notice of a listing or determination made pursuant to this order.

Sec. 11. (a) This order is effective at 12:01 a.m. eastern daylight time on September 24, 2001.

(b) This order shall be transmitted to the Congress and published in the Federal Register.

GEORGE W. BUSH

Annex

Al Qaida/Islamic Army
Abu Sayyaf Group
Armed Islamic Group (GIA)
Harakat ul-Mujahidin (HUM)
Al-Jihad (Egyptian Islamic Jihad)
Islamic Movement of Uzbekistan (IMU)
Asbat al-Ansar
Salafist Group for Call and Combat (GSPC)
Libyan Islamic Fighting Group
Al-Itihaad al-Islamiya (AIAI)
Islamic Army of Aden
Usama bin Laden
Muhammad Atif (aka, Subhi Abu Sitta, Abu Hafs Al Masri)
Sayf al-Adl
Shaykh Sai'id (aka, Mustafa Muhammad Ahmad)
Abu Hafs the Mauritanian (aka, Mahfouz Ould al-Walid, Khalid Al-Shanqiti)
Ibn Al-Shaykh al-Libi
Abu Zubaydah (aka, Zayn al-Abidin Muhammad Husayn, Tariq)
Abd al-Hadi al-Iraqi (aka, Abu Abdallah)
Ayman al-Zawahiri
Thirwat Salah Shihata
Tariq Anwar al-Sayyid Ahmad (aka, Fathi, Amr al-Fatih)
Muhammad Salah (aka, Nasr Fahmi Nasr Hasanayn)
Makhtab Al-Khidamat/Al Kifah
Wafa Humanitarian Organization
Al Rashid Trust
Mamoun Darkazanli Import-Export Company

Blocking Property and Prohibiting Transactions with the Taliban, Executive Order 13129, July 4, 1999

By the authority vested in me as President by the Constitution and the laws of the United States of America, including the International Emergency Economic Powers Act (50 U.S.C. 1701 et seq.)("IEEPA"), the National Emergencies Act (50 U.S.C. 1601 et seq.), and section 301 of title 3, United States Code,

I, WILLIAM J. CLINTON, President of the United States of America, find that the actions and policies of the Taliban in Afghanistan, in allowing territory under its control in Afghanistan to be used as a safe haven and base of operations for Usama bin Ladin and the Al-Qaida organization who have committed and threaten to continue to commit acts of violence against the United States and its nationals, constitute an unusual and extraordinary threat to the national security and foreign policy of the United States, and hereby declare a national emergency to deal with that threat.

I hereby order:

Section 1. Except to the extent provided in section 203(b) of IEEPA (50 U.S.C. 1702(b)) and in regulations, orders, directives, or licenses that may be issued pursuant to this order, and notwithstanding any contract entered into or any license or permit granted prior to the effective date:

(a) all property and interests in property of the Taliban; and

(b) all property and interests in property of persons determined by the Secretary of the Treasury, in consultation with the Secretary of State and the Attorney General:

(i) to be owned or controlled by, or to act for or on behalf of, the Taliban; or

(ii) to provide financial, material, or technological support for, or services in support of, any of the foregoing, that are in the United States, that hereafter come within the United States, or that are or hereafter come within the possession or control of United States persons, are blocked.

Sec. 2. Except to the extent provided in section 203(b) of IEEPA (50 U.S.C. 1702(b)) and in regulations, orders, directives, or licenses that may be issued pursuant to this order, and notwithstanding any contract entered into or any license or permit granted prior to the effective date:

(a) any transaction or dealing by United States persons or within the United States in property or interests in property blocked pursuant to this order is prohibited, including the making or receiving of any contribution of funds, goods, or services to or for the benefit of the Taliban or persons designated pursuant to this order;

(b) the exportation, reexportation, sale, or supply, directly or indirectly, from the United States, or by a United States person, wherever located, of any goods, software, technology (including technical data), or services to the territory of Afghanistan controlled by the Taliban or to the Taliban or persons designated pursuant to this order is prohibited;

(c) the importation into the United States of any goods, software, technology, or services owned or controlled by the Taliban or persons designated pursuant to this order or from the territory of Afghanistan controlled by the Taliban is prohibited;

(d) any transaction by any United States person or within the United States that evades or avoids, or has the purpose of evading or avoiding, or attempts to violate, any of the prohibitions set forth in this order is prohibited; and

(e) any conspiracy formed to violate any of the prohibitions set forth in this order is prohibited.

Sec. 3. The Secretary of the Treasury, in consultation with the Secretary of State, is hereby directed to authorize commercial sales of agricultural commodities and products, medicine, and medical equipment for civilian end use in the territory of Afghanistan controlled by the Taliban under appropriate safeguards to prevent diversion to military, paramilitary, or terrorist end users or end use or to political end use.

Sec. 4. For the purposes of this order:

(a) the term "person" means an individual or entity;

(b) the term "entity" means a partnership, association, corporation, or other organization, group, or subgroup;

(c) the term "the Taliban" means the political/military entity headquartered in Kandahar, Afghanistan that as of the date of this order exercises de facto control over the territory of Afghanistan described in paragraph (d) of this section, its agencies and instrumentalities, and the Taliban leaders listed in the Annex to this order or designated by the Secretary of State in consultation with the Secretary of the Treasury and the Attorney General. The Taliban is also known as the "Taleban," "Islamic Movement of Taliban," "the Taliban Islamic Movement," "Talibano Islami Tahrik," and "Tahrike Islami'a Taliban";

(d) the term "territory of Afghanistan controlled by the Taliban" means the territory referred to as the "Islamic Emirate of Afghanistan," known in Pashtun as "de Afghanistan Islami Emarat" or in Dari as "Emarat Islami-e Afghanistan," including the following provinces of the country of Afghanistan: Kandahar, Farah, Helmund, Nimruz, Herat, Badghis, Ghowr, Oruzghon, Zabol, Paktiha, Ghazni, Nangarhar, Lowgar, Vardan, Faryab, Jowlan, Balkh, and Paktika. The Secretary of State, in consultation with the Secretary of the Treasury, is hereby authorized to modify the description of the term "territory of Afghanistan controlled by the Taliban";

(e) the term "United States person" means any United States citizen, permanent resident alien, entity organized under the laws of the United States (including foreign branches), or any person in the United States.

Sec. 5. The Secretary of the Treasury, in consultation with the Secretary of State and the Attorney General, is hereby authorized to take such actions, including the promulgation of rules and regulations, and to employ all powers granted to me by IEEPA as may be necessary to carry out the purposes of this order. The Secretary of the Treasury may redelegate any of these functions to other officers and agencies of the United States Government. All agencies of the United States Government are hereby directed to take all appropriate measures within their authority to carry out the provisions of this order.

Sec. 6. Nothing contained in this order shall create any right or benefit, substantive or procedural, enforceable by any party against the United States, its agencies or instrumentalities, its officers or employees, or any other person.

Sec. 7. (a) This order is effective at 12:01 a.m. Eastern Daylight Time on July 6, 1999.

(b) This order shall be transmitted to the Congress and published in the Federal Register.

WILLIAM J. CLINTON

Report to Congress on the Declaration of a National Emergency and the Issuance of an Executive Order with Respect to the Afghan Taliban

The White House
Office of the Press Secretary

Text of a letter from the President to the Speaker of the House of Representatives and the President of the Senate

July 4, 1999

Dear Mr. Speaker: (Dear Mr. President:)

Pursuant to section 204(b) of the International Emergency Economic Powers Act, 50 U.S.C. 1703(b) and section 301 of the National Emergencies Act, 50 U.S.C. 1631, I hereby report that I have exercised my statutory authority to declare a National emergency with respect to the threat to the United States posed by the actions and policies of the Afghan Taliban and have issued an executive order to deal with this threat.

The actions and policies of the Afghan Taliban pose an unusual and extraordinary threat to the national security and foreign policy of the United States. The Taliban continues to provide safe haven to Usama bin Ladin allowing him and the Al-Qaida organization to operate from Taiban-controlled territory a network of terrorist training camps and to use Afghanistan as a base from which to sponsor terrorist operations against the United States.

Usama bin Ladin and the Al-Qaida organization have been involved in at least two separate attacks against the United States. On August 7, 1998, the U.S. embassies in Nairobi, Kenya, and in Dar es Salaam, Tanzania, were attacked using powerful explosive truck bombs. The following people have been indicted for criminal activity against the United States in connection with Usama bin Ladin and/or the Al-Qaida organization: Usama bin Ladin, his military commander Muhammed Atef, Wadih El Hage, Fazul Abdullah Mohammed, Mohammed Sadeek Odeh, Mohamed Rashed Daoud Al-Owhali, Mustafa Mohammed Fadhil, Khalfan Khamis Mohamed, Ahmed Khalfan Ghailani, Fahid Mohommed Ally Msalam, Sheikh Ahmed Salim Swedan, Mamdouh Mahmud Salim, Ali Mohammed, Ayman Al-Zawahiri, and Khaled Al Fawwaz. In addition, bin Ladin and his network are currently planning additional attacks against U.S. interests and nationals.

Since at least 1998 and up to the date of the Executive order, the Taliban has continued to provide bin Ladin with safe haven and security, allowing him the necessary freedom to operate. Repeated efforts by the United States to persuade the Taliban to expel bin Ladin to a third country where he can be brought to justice for his crimes have failed. The United States has also attempted to apply pressure on the Taliban both directly and through frontline states in a position to influence Taliban behavior. Despite these efforts, the Taliban has not only continued, but has also deepened its support for, and its relationship with, Usama bin Ladin and associated terrorist networks.

Accordingly, I have concluded that the actions and policies of the Taliban pose an unusual and extraordinary threat to the national security and foreign policy of the United States. I have, therefore, exercised my statutory authority and issued an Executive order which, except to the extent provided for in section 203 (b) of IEEPA (50 U.S.C. 1072(b)) and regulations, orders, directives or licenses that may be issued pursuant to this order, and notwithstanding any contract entered into or any license or permit granted prior to the effective date:

— blocks all property and interests in property of the Taliban, including the Taliban leaders listed in the annex to the order that are in the United States or that are or hereafter come within the possession or control of United States persons;
— prohibits any transaction or dealing by United States persons or within the United States in property or interests in property blocked pursuant to the order, including the making or receiving of any contribution of funds, goods, or services to or for the benefit of the Taliban;
— prohibits the exportation, re-exportation, sale, or supply, directly or indirectly, from the United States, or by a United States person, wherever located, of any goods, software, technology (including technical data), or services to the territory of Afghanistan under the control of the Taliban or to the Taliban; and

—prohibits the importation into the United States of any goods, software, technology, or services owned or controlled by the Taliban or from the territory of Afghanistan under the control of the Taliban.

The Secretary of the Treasury, in consultation with the Secretary of State, is directed to authorize commercial sales of agricultural commodities and products, medicine and medical equipment, for civilian end use in the territory of Afghanistan controlled by the Taliban under appropriate safeguards to prevent diversion to military, paramilitary, or terrorist end-users or end-use or to political end-use. This order and subsequent licenses will likewise allow humanitarian, diplomatic, and journalistic activities to continue.

I have designated in the Executive order, Mullah Mohammad Omar, the leader of the Taliban, and I have authorized the Secretary of State to designate additional persons as Taliban leaders in consultation with the Secretary of the Treasury and the Attorney General.

The Secretary of the Treasury is further authorized to designate persons or entities, in consultation with the Secretary of State and the Attorney General, that are owned or controlled, or are acting for or on behalf of the Taliban or that provide financial, material, or technical support to the Taliban. The Secretary of the Treasury is also authorized to issue regulations in the exercise of my authorities under the International Emergency Economic Powers Act to implement these measures in consultation with the Secretary of State and the Attorney General. All Federal agencies are directed to take actions within their authority to carry out the provisions of the Executive order.

The measures taken in this order will immediately demonstrate to the Taliban the seriousness of our concern over its support for terrorists and terrorist networks, and increase the international isolation of the Taliban. The blocking of the Taliban's property and the other prohibitions imposed under this executive order will further limit the Taliban's ability to facilitate and support terrorists and terrorist networks. It is particularly important for the United States to demonstrate to the Taliban the necessity of conforming to accepted norms of international behavior.

I am enclosing a copy of the Executive order I have issued. This order is effective at 12:01 a.m. Eastern Daylight Time on July 6, 1999.

Sincerely,

William J. Clinton

Terrorist Assets Report, 1998

Department of the Treasury

SUMMARY

More than $3.4 billion of assets of seven state sponsors of terrorism are located within U.S. jurisdiction. Of that amount, more than $3.3 billion are blocked by the U.S. Department of the Treasury pursuant to economic sanctions imposed by the United States against six of the terrorist countries. In addition, approximately $675,000 in assets of international terrorist organizations which were identified and blocked within the United States in 1995, remain blocked in 1998. Approximately $23.6 million in funds are currently blocked based upon an interest of Usama Bin Ladin.

BACKGROUND

Section 304 of Public Law 102–138, as amended by Public Law 103–236 (22 U.S.C. 2656g), requires the Secretary of the Treasury, in consultation with the Attorney General and appropriate investigative agencies, to provide annual reports to the Congress concerning the nature and extent of assets held in the United States by terrorist countries and organizations engaged in international terrorism. . . . The current report . . . was prepared by the Department of the Treasury's office of Foreign Assets Control ("OFAC"), which has the responsibility for administering and enforcing economic sanctions programs mandated by the President pursuant to his declaration of a national emergency with respect to particular foreign countries and non-state parties. Almost ninety-nine percent of the identified U.S.-based assets of state sponsors of terrorism and all blocked assets of international terrorist organizations are under the sanctions controls of OFAC.

More than a dozen Federal agencies and offices were polled in developing the report. They included:

Department of State Joint Chiefs of Staff
Department of Justice U.S. Customs Service
Federal Bureau of Investigation Internal Revenue Service
U.S. Secret Service Department of Defense
Intelligence Community Office of Foreign Assets Control
Bureau of Alcohol, Tobacco and Firearms
Committee on Foreign Investment in the United States (CFIUS)
Financial Crimes Enforcement Network (U.S. Treasury)

State Sponsors of Terrorism: State sponsors of terrorism are those countries designated by the Secretary of State under Section 40(d) of the Arms Export Control Act. . . . States currently listed as sponsors of terrorism are: Cuba, Iran, Iraq, Libya, North Korea, Sudan, and Syria, however blockings are only available for the first six countries, and not for Syria. . . .

Information concerning the known holdings in the United States of the seven state sponsors of terrorism is reported below in Part I. It should be noted that, with the exception of Syria, the totals represent amounts frozen under United States sanctions programs which, in most cases, block all property in which the target is believed to have any interest. In some instances the interest may be partial, or fall short of undisputed title to the property. Determinations concerning these interests are made based on all relevant information before OFAC. Many of the assets are also the subject of other claims, sometimes by multiple parties. Blocked assets may not be attached, however, by any claimant unless authorized by OFAC consistent with U.S. policy.

International Terrorist Organizations: Section 304 of Public Law 102–138 also requires the Secretary of the Treasury to report to the Congress annually on those assets of international terrorist organizations that are held within the United States. For purposes of this report, Treasury has used three documents to establish a baseline for determining which groups may fall within the definition of "international terrorist organization." . . .

The first baseline document . . . is the list of Foreign Terrorist Organizations ("FTOs") designated by the Secretary of State on October 8, 1997 pursuant to the Antiterrorism Act, which became effective on April 24, 1996. The Antiterrorism Act authorizes the Secretary of State, in consultation with the Departments of the Treasury and Justice, to designate certain organizations as foreign terrorist organizations. Thirty groups worldwide were designated by the Secretary of State as Foreign Terrorist Organizations. . . .

The second baseline document . . . is Executive Order 12947, which became effective on January 24, 1995, and which blocks assets in the United States or within the possession or control of U.S. persons of terrorists who threaten to disrupt the Middle East Peace Process. Twelve Middle East terrorist groups were identified in the Executive order. Accompanying and subsequent notices of the groups and individuals who comprise the "List of Specially Designated Terrorists Who Threaten To Disrupt the Middle East Peace Process" . . . are discussed in more detail in Part II, which addresses international terrorists organizations, assets in the United States, and are included as individual attachments.

The third baseline document . . . is Executive order 13099, which became effective on August 25, 1998, and amended Executive Order 12947 by blocking the assets of three additional terrorists and one organization. Specifically, this order identifies Usama bin Muhammad bin Awad bin Ladin, the Islamic Army (and its aliases), Abu Hafs al-Masri, and Rifa' i Ahmad Taha Musa as the individuals and organization added to the Annex of E.O. 12947.

PART I — KNOWN ASSETS OF STATE SPONSORS OF TERRORISM

The following information describes the nature and extent of assets within United States jurisdiction that belong to countries identified as state sponsors of terrorism. These countries and the gross amounts of their reported U.S.-based assets are (in millions): Cuba—$170.6; Iran—$22.5; Iraq—$2,200.2; Libya—$951.3; North Korea—$26.3; Sudan—$17.3; and Syria—$51.0. The total of their gross assets within U.S. jurisdiction is $3.439 billion dollars.

The assets reported for Iran in Exhibit A are diplomatic properties remaining blocked since the 1979–81 hostage crisis. A variety of other obligations to Iran may ultimately be determined to exist, depending on the outcome of cases before the Iran-U.S. Claims Tribunal.

Almost ninety-nine percent of the known assets within U.S. jurisdiction of state sponsors of terrorism are blocked by the Department of the Treasury. However, not all of the blocked assets are literally within the United States. Substantial amounts, identified further below, are in foreign branches of U.S. banks. They are blocked because, under U.S. law, those bank branches are subject to United States jurisdiction. Consequently, those assets are not blocked at institutions within the United States. . . .

Exhibit A: Known Assets of State Sponsors of Terrorism
(amounts in millions of U.S. dollars)

Country	Amount	Explanation
Cuba	$170.6	Government of Cuba's blocked assets. Primarily bank accounts. Source: OFAC, Treasury.
	(0.0)	(Blocked in U.S. banks' foreign branches.)
	$170.6	*Net Blocked Cuban Assets in U.S.*
Iran	$22.5	Government of Iran's diplomatic properties remaining blocked since the 1979–1981 hostage crisis. Primarily real estate. Source: OFAC, Treasury.

Country	Amount	Explanation
Iraq	$2,200.2	Government of Iraq's blocked assets. Primarily bank deposits. Source: OFAC, Treasury.
	($540.5)	(Blocked in U.S. banks, foreign branches.)
	($211.0)	(Loan to the United Nations in compliance with UNSCR 778.)
	$1,448.7	*Net Blocked Iraqi Assets in U.S.*
Libya	$951.3	Government of Libya's blocked assets. Primarily bank deposits. Source: OFAC, Treasury.
	($1.1)	(Blocked in U.S. banks' foreign branches.)
	$950.2	*Net Blocked Libyan Assets in U.S.*
North Korea	$26.3	North Korea's blocked bank deposits. Source: OFAC, Treasury.
	($2.8)	(Blocked in U.S. banks' foreign branches.)
	$23.5	*Net Blocked North Korean Assets in U.S.*
Sudan	$17.3	Sudan's blocked bank deposits. Source: OFAC, Treasury.
	(0.4)	(Blocked in U.S. banks' foreign branches.)
	$16.9	*Net Blocked Sudan Assets in U.S.*
Syria	$51.0	Total liabilities of U.S. banking and non-banking institutions to Syrian institutions. Source: Treasury Bulletin, December 1998.
TOTALS:	$3,439.2	Total state sponsor assets within U.S. jurisdiction.
	($51.0)	(Unencumbered assets of Syria.)
	$3,388.2	Total blocked state sponsor assets within U.S. jurisdiction.
	($544.8)	(Total blocked in U.S. banks' foreign branches.)
	($211.0)	(UNSCR 778 loan [Iraq].)
	$2,632.4	*Total blocked state sponsor assets within the United States.*

PART II — ASSETS OF INTERNATIONAL TERRORIST ORGANIZATIONS

On January 23, 1995, President Clinton declared a national emergency . . . and signed Executive Order 12947, "Prohibiting Transactions With Terrorists Who Threaten To Disrupt the Middle East Peace Process." Twelve Middle East terrorist organizations were named in the annex to the Order. The Order prohibits transfers, including "charitable contributions," of funds, goods, or services to any organizations or individuals designated under its authority; and it blocks all property in the United States or within the possession or control of a U.S. person in which there is an interest of any designated terrorist. . . .

The Order also blocks the property and interests in property of persons found by the Secretary of State, in coordination with the Secretary of the Treasury and the Attorney General, (1) to have committed, or to pose a significant risk of committing acts of violence that have the purpose or effect of disrupting the Middle East Peace, or (2) to be assisting in, sponsoring or providing financial, material, or technological support for, or services in support of, terrorist activities.

On August 20, 1998, President Clinton signed Executive Order 13099, "Prohibiting Transactions With Terrorists Who Threaten To Disrupt the Middle East Peace Process" . . . to amend E.O. 12947 by adding three individuals and one organization to the annex of E.O. 12947:

Usama bin Muhammad bin Awad bin Ladin

Islamic Army (and its aliases)

Abu Hafs al-Masri

Rifa' i Ahmad Taha Musa

Executive Order 13099 was issued under the same authority as E.O. 12947.

. . . *Blockings under E.O. 12947 and E.O. 13099.* Total current blockings by OFAC under the terrorism Executive orders are $24.4 million. These blockings involve assets of individuals added to the list of Specially Designated Terrorists subsequent to the publication of the first SDT list in January 1995. Accounts of agents acting on behalf of the terrorist organization HAMAS are blocked in U.S. banks; and $200,000 of their U.S. real estate holdings are blocked. On June 9, 1998, the Department of Justice seized both the real estate holdings and the bank accounts of an SDT under an asset forfeiture statute. The matter is still pending in the Northern District of Illinois.

Furthermore, a bank account belonging to Ramadan Abdullah SHALLAH, the head of the terrorist organization Palestinian Islamic Jihad (PIJ), has been blocked; and a related organization's account over which SHALLAH has held signature authority has been blocked. In addition, approximately $23.6 million in funds are currently blocked based upon an interest of Usama Bin Ladin.

The following chart (Exhibit B) details the assets of international terrorist organizations that have been blocked pursuant to E.O. 12947 and E.O. 13099. . . .

Exhibit B: Blocked Assets Under the SDT Program

SDT Organization	Description	Amount
Hamas	Bank Accounts	$196,116.26
	Credit/Debit Cards	$671.83
	Real Estate	$460,000.00
	Total (Hamas)	$656,788.09
Palestinian Islamic Jihad	Bank Accounts	$18,293.31
Usama bin Ladin		$23,685,731.30
Total blocked assets of SDTs		$24,360,812.70

FTO Blockings under the Antiterrorism Act. To date, the Treasury Department has not blocked any financial transactions under the Antiterrorism Act. All blockings of foreign terrorist assets to date have occurred in the SDT program under the authority of IEEPA and Executive Orders 12947 and 13099. The Treasury Department continues to work closely with other agencies in seeking information concerning possible assets within the jurisdiction of the United States in which there may be an interest of any of the 30 FTOs.

Intelligence Authorization Act for Fiscal Year 2002

Senate Select Committee on Intelligence

. . . We are at a point where continuing global instability and uncertainty forces us to refocus our attention on the importance of our intelligence apparatus. Transnational threats such as international terrorism, global crime syndicates, international drug trafficking, and the proliferation of weapons of mass destruction and their delivery systems pose significant risk to this nation's interests. Yet these threats cannot be defeated solely with traditional military force. Our Intelligence Community is our first line of defense. . . .

The five-year plan for correcting deficiencies in human intelligence should enable this critical component of the Intelligence Community to meet the increasingly complex and growing set of collection requirements. The Central Intelligence Agency (CIA) will need to hire case officers capable of dealing with the explosion of technology, both as collection tools and as potential threats. These individuals must be able to operate effectively in the many places around the world where U.S. interests are threatened. To do that, the CIA must place even greater emphasis on the diversity of the new recruits. Finally, the human intelligence system must be integrated more closely with our other collection agencies.

As we do a better job of collecting intelligence, we also must enhance our ability to understand this information. The percentage of the intelligence budget devoted to analysis and processing has been declining steadily since 1990. While collection systems are becoming more and more capable, our investment in analysis continued to decline. The disparity threatens to overwhelm our ability to analyze and use the information collected. To address this problem, the Committee has added funds to finance promising all-source analysis initiatives across the Community. The amount authorized is a down payment on a five-year spending profile to rebuild the Community's all-source analytical capability. . . .

COUNTERTERRORISM

The Committee notes that recent assessments of U.S. terrorism and structures for countering terrorism point to the need for increased attention to the Intelligence Community response to the problem of terrorism. The National Commission on Terrorism ("Bremer Commission") focused specifically on terrorism, while the U.S. Commission on National Security/21st Century set terrorism within a larger context of redefining concepts of national security. The Advisory Panel to Assess Domestic Response Capabilities for Terrorism Involving Weapons of Mass Destruction focused on domestic, catastrophic attacks, and acknowledged the blurred lines between domestic and international terrorism.

All three reports recognize the fundamental importance of intelligence in any strategy to combat and respond to terrorism. But all three reports also make clear that any effort to improve the government-wide approach to the terrorism problem must take into account every facet of the issue—detection, prevention, consequence management, crisis management, and law enforcement, diplomatic and military responses. A counterterrorism intelligence program must be designed within this larger context. Further, in addition to enhancement of the central coordinating authority for terrorism policy, we also must have a centralized authority for managing the intelligence component of that policy. The Director of Central Intelligence needs to perform that role for the United States Government.

Oversight of the intelligence component of the U.S. response to terrorism is the responsibility of this Committee and is among its highest priorities. The Committee believes a number of issues are of particular importance, and they are noted below.

The Relationship Between Intelligence and Law Enforcement: The relationship between law enforcement and intelligence that has developed, largely on an ad hoc basis over the last decade, is better than it ever has been. However, the Committee believes that a statutory framework may be necessary to institutionalize and rationalize the relationships among the agencies. Many observers have noted that while law enforcement is, theoretically, only one of a set of "tools" to respond to terrorism, it has often taken a preeminent, and sometimes exclusive, role. The Bremer Commission recognized this, highlighting the "pros and cons of the law enforcement approach" in its treatment of the Pan Am 103 prosecution efforts. One of the other tools is intelligence, and it is important to create a framework within which these issues can be addressed.

Sharing of Information Among Government Agencies: Effective sharing of information between and among the various components of the government-wide effort to combat terrorism is also essential, and is presently hindered by cultural, bureaucratic, resource, training and, in some cases, legal obstacles. The Bremer Commission noted that "[t]he law enforcement community is neither fully exploiting the growing amount of information it collects during the course of terrorism investigations nor distributing that information effectively to analysis and policymakers."

The Committee commends the Intelligence Community for aggressive, effective and creative intelligence efforts against the terrorism target. But there is room for improvement. The Committee remains concerned that, in the commendable rush to engage against the imminent threat associated with international terrorism, the Intelligence Community has adopted a crisis mentality. Ad hoc approaches to coordination and interaction among the agencies created during crisis situations become the norm after the crisis is over. International terrorism is not, however, in the view of the Committee, a "crisis," with its connotation of a short-lived phenomenon. International terrorism is a "condition" with which we will have to deal on a long-term basis. The Committee strongly encourages the Intelligence Community to orient itself accordingly by implementing policies—under the control of the Director of Central Intelligence—for regulating the various roles of the elements of the Intelligence Community that participate in the fight against terrorism.

Financial Intelligence Related to International Terrorism: The Committee believes that intelligence related to the finances of foreign terrorist organizations can play a valuable role in efforts to combat international terrorism. Such intelligence can allow for a better understanding of the form, structure and capabilities of individual terrorist groups, and the relationships within and among such organizations. Such intelligence can also contribute to active efforts to disrupt terrorist organizations, including, but not limited to, law enforcement and regulatory mechanisms.

The Committee endorses, in principle, efforts to develop elements within the Intelligence Community designed to exploit effectively financial intelligence. One effort within the Department of Treasury's Office of Foreign Assets Control, is the "Foreign Terrorist Asset Tracking Center " (FTATC), which shows promise as a vehicle to address this need. However, the Committee is concerned that FTATC, to the extent it will function as an element of the Intelligence Community, has not been coordinated adequately with the Director of Central Intelligence nor reviewed by this Committee.

Accordingly, the Committee directs the Director of Central Intelligence and the Secretary of the Treasury to prepare jointly a report assessing the feasibility and advisability of establishing an element of the federal government to provide for effective and efficient analysis and dissemination of foreign intelligence related to the financial capabilities and resources of international terrorist organizations. The report should include an assessment of the FTATC as a vehicle for addressing such a need and, if appropriate, a plan for its continued development.

National Virtual Translation Center: The Committee is concerned that intelligence in general, and intelligence related to terrorism in particular, is increasingly reliant on the ability of the Intelligence Community to quickly, accurately and efficiently translate information in a large number of languages. Many of the languages for which translation capabilities are limited within the United States Government are the languages that are of critical importance in our counterterrorism efforts. The Committee believes that this problem can be alleviated by applying cutting-edge, Internet-like technology to create a "National Virtual Translation Center". Such a center would link secure locations maintained by the Intelligence Community throughout the country and would apply digital technology to network, store, retrieve, and catalogue the audio and textual information. Foreign intelligence could be collected technically in one location, translated in a second location, and provided to an Intelligence Community analyst in a third location.

The Committee notes that the CIA, FBI, NSA and other intelligence agencies have applied new technology to this problem. The Committee believes that these efforts should be coordinated so that the solution can be applied on a Community-wide basis. Accordingly, the Committee directs the Director of Central Intelligence, in consultation with the Director of the FBI, and other heads of departments and agencies within the Intelligence Community, to prepare and submit to the intelligence committees by June 1, 2002, a report concerning the feasibility and structure of a National Virtual Translation Center, including recommendations regarding the establishment of such a center and the funding necessary to do so. . . .

Intelligence Authorization Act for Fiscal Year 2002

House Permanent Select Committee on Intelligence

... These provisions, along with others in this bill, are intended to highlight for the new Administration the critical need for intelligence, the critical state in which the Intelligence Community finds itself, and to emphasize that the Administration must broadly address the shortfalls and needs of the Community, lest we continue to suffer attacks such as those inflicted on September 11, 2001 — or worse!

TERRORISM THREAT ANALYSIS

In the wake of the USS Cole bombing, senior Defense intelligence officials were directed to devise and initiate sweeping structural and procedural changes to strengthen the Defense Intelligence Agency's (DIA) counterterrorism analysis and threat warning efforts. The focus of this task was to improve long-term threat analysis, reduce duplication of effort, more precisely apply all-source intelligence, expand the base of source information to include location and disposition of U.S. forces, and sharpen the focus of threat warning intelligence to those forces. The result was the formation of a new terrorism analysis center within the DIA.

Although the Committee applauded the innovative thinking of Defense Department officials with respect to the development of this center, the Committee was concerned that the initiative was moving forward without the resolution of significant implementation issues, particularly those involving information sharing of sensitive source data, and how such data might be reported — and more importantly protected in such a way as to be effective. Further, the Committee questioned the rationale for such a capability within DoD, since the CIA's existing center was designed to provide the all-source analysis needed by the Defense Department. The Committee has determined to support both capabilities, but in a much more community-wide sense.

The events of September 11, 2001, highlighted why and how the Intelligence Community, as a whole, must respond to the myriad national security requirements, especially to the war on terrorism. The Committee believes there can no longer be any cultural, bureaucratic or other artificial barriers to impede the flow and analysis of information related to countering this threat. Information must be ubiquitous and available to all-source analysts. The artificial, but existing barriers to true information sharing must be overcome. Security issues must be resolved such that source identifying information that needs protecting is protected and information that is needed to piece together terrorist activities be made available. Additionally, all technological impediments, such as on-line accesses to databases, must be immediately overcome. Existing data mining tools must be put to full use and additional tools must be developed. Most importantly, the concepts of the two centers must be adopted as a community-wide inter-agency approach. The war against terrorism necessarily crosses all boundaries. The Intelligence Community must, therefore, support all of its customers equally well—from the President, to the "soldier," to those in law enforcement. Thus, the Committee has supported a new construct; one that leverages all the concepts of the military and civilian analytical functions, and that is Intelligence Community-wide in composition and in service.

FOCUSING ON PEOPLE AS LONG-TERM INTELLIGENCE NEEDS

Congress has provided an initial response to the horrific terrorist attacks suffered by the United States on September 11. Emergency funds and grants of authority to the President have been provided. Additional responses will be necessary in the weeks ahead as the international effort against terrorism proceeds and as assessments are made about the performance of those federal agencies charged with safeguarding national security in the period before and during the September 11 attacks. . . .

This Committee . . . has been concerned for some time that intelligence agencies were not well positioned to respond to the national security challenges of the 21st century, including terrorism. Despite a succession of congressionally-provided funding increases to spur investment in all areas of intelligence, including human intelligence, the Committee is not satisfied that the Intelligence Community is moving quickly enough. There is a shortage of intelligence officers with the linguistic, operational, and analytic skills, as well as foreign area expertise and cultural background to discharge effectively the foreign intelligence mission.

Although a start has been made in increasing the ranks of officers, the Committee is not convinced that there is an Intelligence Community-wide strategy for ensuring that recruited persons have the diverse mix of skills and background necessary to enhance mission effectiveness. . . .

SECTION 403 — GUIDELINES FOR RECRUITMENT OF CERTAIN FOREIGN ASSETS

Section 403 addresses the CIA's 1995 guidelines on recruitment of foreign assets and sources. The Committee believes that the 1995 CIA guidelines on the handling of cases involving foreign assets and sources with human rights concerns have had the unintended consequence of deterring the effective recruitment of potentially high-value assets. The Committee has long been concerned that a culture of "risk aversion" has hindered decision-making across the Intelligence Community, and especially within the CIA. In the instance of the 1995 guidelines, we are concerned that excessive caution and a burdensome vetting process have undermined the CIA's ability to recruit assets. The Committee is concerned that the guidelines have had a negative impact on the recruitment of sources against terrorist organizations and other hard targets as well. Admittedly, in the past, there have been recruitments that have proved to be inappropriate. Since 1995, CIA's well-intended effort to address human rights concerns may have significantly limited the U.S. Government's access to foreign assets and sources.

Far too often, Committee members have learned of field officers who have been deterred from recruiting promising assets or who have lost potential assets to competing intelligence services, because of a slow and overly litigious vetting process. Legal and bureaucratic concerns must not be ignored, but neither should they dictate the asset recruitment process. New guidelines must rebalance the equation between potential gain and risk. Clearly, there is a certain class of individuals who, because of their unreliability, instability, or nature of past misconduct, should be avoided. A new balance must be struck that recognizes concerns about egregious human rights behavior, but provides the much needed flexibility to seize upon opportunities as they present themselves. The Committee looks to the Director of Central Intelligence to promulgate new guidelines that restore equilibrium to the asset vetting process, satisfactorily address legal questions in a time-urgent manner, thereby expediting recruitment of foreign assets and sources, and provide confidence to personnel in the field that their best judgment will be supported. . . .

Memorandum of Law: Assassination

Office of the Judge Advocate General

1. *Summary*. Executive Order 12333 prohibits assassination as a matter of national policy. This memorandum addresses the question of whether the use of military force in peacetime against a known terrorist or terrorist organization would constitute an act of assassination in violation of that order or the international legal obligations of the United States. It concludes that the employment of military force against a terrorist or terrorist organization to protect U. S. citizens or the national security of the United States is a legitimate exercise of the international legal right of self defense and does not constitute assassination.

2. *Interim Opinion*. This opinion is an interim opinion intended to address the issue of assassination only within the limited scope set forth above. It will be incorporated into a larger opinion examining the definition of assassination as the term may apply at all levels of conflict.

3. *Defining Assassination*. Executive Order 12333 is the successor to an Executive Order renouncing assassination first promulgated in the Ford Administration. This prohibition, contained in the Executive Order on intelligence activities, has been repromulgated by each successive administration. However, the term "assassination" has not been defined in any of these Executive Orders. While none are entirely satisfactory, the following definitions were considered in the formulation of this opinion.

a. *Assassination in Peacetime*. *Webster's Ninth New Collegiate Dictionary* (1984) defines *assassination* as

1. To murder by sudden or secret attack, usually for impersonal reasons; 2. to injure or destroy unexpectedly and treacherously.

Under the synonym *kill*, this source states:

Assassinate applies to deliberate killing openly or secretly, often for political motives.

The Oxford Companion to Law (1980) defines *assassination* as

The murder of a person by lying in wait for him and then killing him, particularly the murder of prominent people from (sic.) political motives, e.g., the assassination of President Kennedy.

Black's Law Dictionary (4th ed., 1951) does not contain a definition of assassination, but provides the following definition of *murder*.

The unlawful killing of a human being by another with malice aforethought, either express or implied.

Black's continues by explaining the distinction between *murder* and *homicide* by defining the latter as

. . . The act of a human being in taking away the life of another human being. . . . Homicide is not necessarily a crime. It is a necessary ingredient of the crime of murder, but there are cases in which homicide may be committed without criminal intent and without criminal consequences, as, where it is done . . . in *self-defense* . . . [emphasis supplied].

A recent law review article defines *assassination* as "the intentional killing of an internationally protected person." Brandenburg, "The Legality of Assassination as an Aspect of Foreign Policy," *Virginia Journal of International Law* 27, 3 (Spring 1987), p. 655; though limiting it to a class of individuals such as diplomats and other statesmen, who are protected by the Convention on the Prevention and Punishment of Crimes Against Internationally Protected Persons, Including Diplomatic Agents (28 U.S.T. 1975, T.I.A.S. No. 8532, 1035 U.N.T.S. 167 [1973]).

Historical analyses of assassination contain similar definitions. For example, one defines *assassination* as

. . . the sudden, surprising, treacherous killing of a public figure, who has responsibilities to the public, by someone who kills in the belief that he is acting in his own private or the public interest. McConnell, *The History of Assassination* (1969), p. 12.

Another analysis defines *assassination* as

. . . those killings or murders, usually directed against individuals in public life, motiated by political rather than by personal relationships. Havens, Leiden, and Schmitt, *Assassination and Terrorism: Their Modern Dimensions* (1975), p. 4.

On the other hand, other scholars have declined to define the term. See, for example, Bell, *Assassins!* (1979), p. 22; and Ford, *Political Murder* (1985), pp. 1, 46, 196, 301–307.

While assassination generally may be regarded as an act of murder for political purposes, its victims are not necessarily limited to persons of public office or prominence. The murder of a private citizen, if carried out for political purposes, may constitute an act of assassination. For example, the 1978 "poisoned-tip umbrella" killing of Bulgarian defector Georgi Markov by Bulgarian State Security agents on the streets of London would fall into the category of an act of murder carried out for political purposes, and would constitute an act of assassination. On the other hand, the murder of Leon Klinghoffer by the terrorist Abul Abbas during the 1985 hijacking by Abbas of the Italian cruiseship *Achille Lauro*, though an act of murder for political purposes, would not constitute an act of assassination. The distinction appears not to lie entirely in the purpose for the act and its intended victim, but also under certain circumstances in its covert nature. In contrast, while each was overt, the killing of Presidents Abraham Lincoln and John F. Kennedy generally are regarded as assassination because they were carried out for political purposes.

In peacetime, the citizens of a nation—whether private individuals or public figures—are entitled to immunity from intentional acts of violence by citizens, agents, or military forces of another nation. Article 2(4) of the Charter of the United Nations provides that all Member States

> shall refrain in their international relations from the threat or use of force against the territorial integrity or political independence of any state, or in any manner inconsistent with the Purposes of the United Nations.

Peacetime assassination, then, would seem to encompass the murder of a private individual or public figure for political purposes, and in some cases (as cited above) also require that the act constitute a covert activity, particularly when the intended victim is a private citizen.

b. *Assassination in Wartime.* Assassination in wartime takes on a different meaning. As Clausewitz noted, war is a "continuation of political activity by other means." Clausewitz, *On War* (Howard and Paret, eds. [1976]), p. 87. In wartime the role of the military includes the legalized killing (as opposed to murder) of the enemy, whether lawful combatants or unprivileged belligerents, and may include in either category civilians who take part in the hostilities. See Grotius, *The Law of War and Peace* (1646), Bk. III, Sec. XVIII(2); Oppenheim, *International Law II* (H. Lauterpacht, ed., 1952), pp. 332, 346; and Berriedale, *Wheaton's International Law* 2 (1944), p. 171.

The term *assassination* when applied to wartime military activities against enemy combatants does not preclude acts of violence involving a surprise attack. Combatants are liable to attack at any time or place, regardless of their activity when attacked. Spaight, *War Rights on Land* (1911), pp. 86, 88; U. S. Army Field Manual 27-10, *The Law of Land Warfare* (1956), para. 31. Nor is a distinction made between combat and combat service support personnel with regard to the right to be attacked as combatants; combatants are subject to attack if they are participating directly in hostilities through fire, maneuver, and assault, providing logistic support, or functioning as a staff planner. An individual combatant's vulnerability to lawful targeting (as opposed to assassination) is not dependent upon his or her military duties, or proximity to combat as such. Nor does the prohibition on *assassination* limit means that otherwise would be lawful; no distinction is made between an attack accomplished by aircraft, artillery, infantry assault, ambush, landmine or boobytrap, a single shot by a sniper, or a commando attack. All are lawful means for attacking the enemy, and the choice of one *vis-a-vis* another has no bearing on the legality of the attack. Likewise, the death of noncombatants ancillary to the lawful attack of a military target is neither assassination nor otherwise unlawful.

The scope of assassination in the U. S. military context was first outlined in U. S. Army General Orders No. 100 (1863); paragraph 148 states

> *Assassination.* The law of war does not allow proclaiming either an individual belonging to the hostile army, or a citizen, or a subject of the hostile government, an outlaw, who may be slain without trial by any captor, any more than the modern law of peace allows such international outlawry; on the contrary, it abhors such outrage. . . .

This provision, consistent with the earlier writings of Hugo Grotius (Cf. Bk. III, Sec. XXXVIII(4)), has been continued to this day in U. S. Army Field Manual 27-10, *The Law of Land Warfare*, which provides (paragraph 31):

> (Article 23b, Hague Regulations, 1907) is construed as prohibiting assassination, proscription, or outlawry of an enemy, or putting a price upon an enemy's head, as well as offering a reward for an enemy "dead or alive." It does not, however, preclude attacks on individual soldiers or officers of the enemy whether in the zone of hostilities, occupied territory, or elsewhere.

Thus, for example, neither of the following would constitute an act of assassination, even though the term has been applied loosely (and inaccurately) to each:

> 18 November 1941: Commando raid by No. 11 Scottish Commando at Bedda Littoria, Libya, to kill German Field Marshal Erwin Rommel.

> 18 April 1943: USAAF P-38s down Japanese aircraft carrying Admiral Osoruku Yamamoto over Bouganville.

Other military or law of war definitions of assassination are beyond the scope of this memorandum. Terrorists are not lawful combatants, and are not protected by the law of war. But the distinction between assassination in peacetime and hostilities is noted, as the employment of military force against a legitimate target (whether an enemy combatant; unprivileged belligerent or terrorist) in self defense is lawful killing rather than assassination.

4. *Self defense.* Article 51 of the Charter of the United Nations recognizes the inherent right of self-defense of nations. While invocation of the right of self defense generally is thought of in terms of a response to armed attack by conventional forces, historically the United States has resorted to the use of military force in peacetime where another nation has failed to discharge its international responsibilities in protecting U. S. citizens from acts of violence originating in or launched from its sovereign territory, or has been culpable in aiding and abetting international criminal activities. For example:

- 1804–1805: Marine First Lieutenant Presley O'Bannon led an expedition into Libya to capture or kill the Barbary pirates.
- 1916: General "Blackjack" Pershing led a year-long campaign into Mexico to capture or kill the Mexican bandit Pancho Villa following his attack on Columbus, New Mexico.
- 1928–1932: U. S. Marines conducted a campaign to capture or kill the Nicaraguan bandit leader Augusto Cesar Sandino.
- 1967: U. S. Army personnel assisted the Bolivian Army in its campaign to capture or kill Ernesto "Che" Guevara.
- 1985: U. S. Naval forces were used to force an EgyptAir airliner to land at Sigonella, Sicily, in an attempt to capture or kill the *Achille Lauro* hijackers.
- 1986: U. S. Naval and air forces attacked terrorist-related targets in Libya in response to Libya's continued employment of terrorism as a foreign policy means.

Hence there is historical precedent for the use of military force to capture or kill individuals whose activities constitute a direct threat to U. S. citizens or U. S. national security.

While the Charter of the United Nations recognizes the right of self defense, the Charter endeavored to narrow the scope of the right by establishing certain procedural steps to be taken prior to the exercise of this right. However, these procedural steps do not preclude unilateral action against an immediate threat. Moreover strict compliance with the procedures established in the UN Charter have been modified over the years through the practice of nations due to the frequent inability of the Security Council to act. Furthermore, as previously noted, the procedures established by the Charter of the United Nations suffer in that they contemplate overt attack by conventional forces only. Stated another way, an attractiveness of terrorism for those nations that support terrorist organizations is that it not only provides those nations plausible deniability for their illegal activities, but permits the use of violence below a threshold at which a victim nation normally would be expected to respond.

The United States recognizes three forms of self defense:

a. Against an actual use of force, or hostile act;

b. Preemptive self defense against an imminent use of force;

c. Self defense against a continuing threat.

The last, while perhaps the most difficult to grasp, has been exercised on several occasions within the past decade. It formed the basis for the U. S. Navy air strike against Syrian antiaircraft positions in Lebanon on 4 December 1983, following Syrian missile launches at Navy F-14 TARPS flights supporting the multinational peacekeeping force in Beirut the preceding day; it also was the basis for the air strikes against terrorist-related targets in Libya on the evening of 14-15 April 1986. This right of self defense would be appropriate to the attack of terrorist leaders or terrorist infrastructure that through their actions pose a continuing threat to U. S. citizens or the national security of the United States.

5. *Conclusion.* Whether an individual terrorist or terrorist organization constitutes a threat to the national security of the United States, or to individual citizens of the United States, that warrants a military response, is a command decision that can and should be made only by the President after consultation with appropriate Cabinet members, the National Security Council, and the Intelligence Committees of the Congress. As with other acts of self defense, it is an option that should be exercised only after there has been a reasonable exhaustion of other means to limit the threat. It is noted, however, that the terrorist individuals or organizations envisaged as appropriate to necessitate or warrant an armed response by U. S. military forces are well financed, highly organized paramilitary structures engaged full time in the illegal use of force. The purpose of Executive Order 12333 and its predecessors was to preclude unilateral actions by individual agents or agencies against selected foreign public officials, as allegedly had occurred prior to the promulgation of this prohibition. A national decision to employ military force in self defense against a legitimate terrorist threat would not be unlike that employed in response to an overt conventional threat; only the nature of the threat has changed, rather than the international legal right to respond to the threat. Whether the threat is by conventional force or by terrorists, a military response in defense of the national security of the United States would not constitute assassination.

6. *Coordination.* This opinion has been coordinated with the Offices of the Judge Advocates General of the Navy and Air Force; General Counsel, Department of the Army; General Counsel, Department of Defense; Legal Adviser, Department of State; and General Counsel, Central Intelligence Agency, who concur in its content and conclusion.

Doctrine for Joint Special Operations, October 28, 1992

Joint Chiefs of Staff

1. This publication has been prepared under the direction of the Chairman of the Joint Chiefs of Staff. It sets forth principles and military guidance to govern the joint activities and employment of the Armed Forces of the United States. . . .

8. The lead agent for this publication is the United States Special Operations Command.

9. The Joint Staff doctrine sponsor for this publication is the Director for Operations (J-3).

For the Chairman of the Joint Chiefs of Staff:

H. L. SHEFFIELD
Captain, USN
Secretary, Joint Staff

PREFACE

1. *Purpose.* This publication establishes the basic doctrine for the joint employment of SOF [see glossary, page 433, for acronyms used in text]. The principles, fundamentals, guidelines, and conceptual framework described herein are provided to facilitate interoperability with conventional military forces and between Service SOF and to establish a baseline for the development of joint tactics, techniques, and procedures. . . .

2. *Scope and Application.* This publication provides guidance for the planning and execution of joint SO in peacetime military operations, military hostilities short of war, and war. . . . Further, it provides commanders information

necessary to identify, nominate, and select objectives and missions appropriate for SOF. . . .

CHAPTER I: INTRODUCTION

1. *Purpose.* This publication describes SO missions and forces, characteristics, and capabilities across the operational continuum. . . . Further, it provides guidance for appropriate SOF mission selection and subsequent planning, preparation, and support to ensure full, effective employment of SOF in pursuit of national security policy.

2. *General*

  a. *Joint Doctrine*

    (1) Doctrine is a statement of the fundamental principles that guide the employment of military forces or elements thereof in support of national objectives. It is authoritative (vice directive) in nature and requires judgment in its application. Joint doctrine guides the employment of forces of two or more Services in coordinated action toward a common objective. Joint doctrine is promulgated by the Chairman of the Joint Chiefs of Staff.

    (2) The doctrine herein is authoritative guidance for the Services and combatant commands when active, reserve, or National Guard forces are employed in coordinated SO. Service doctrine will be consistent with joint doctrine. . . .

  b. *Joint Tactics, Techniques, and Procedures.* . . . This document provides broad doctrinal guidance for strategic and operational joint employment of SOF. . . .

    (1) *Tactics.* The term tactics refers to the employment of units in combat or to the ordered arrangement and maneuver of units or their elements in relation to each other or to the enemy in order to use their full potential. . . . tactics are the theoretical methods by which doctrinal principles are achieved. . . .

    (2) *Techniques.* Techniques provide the detail of tactics and refer to the basic methods of using people and equipment to carry out a tactical task. For example, to exercise the principle of maneuver, SOF may employ the tactic of infiltrating by night. . . .

    (3) *Procedures.* Procedures are the lowest level of detail and are used to standardize or make routine the performance of critical or recurring activities. . . .

3. *Special Operations.* SO are a form of warfare characterized by a unique set of objectives, weapons, and forces. A mission, under a certain set of environmental constraints, may require the application of SO skills and techniques. Change one or more of those characteristics, and the mission may no longer fit the category of SO. For example, the Grenada operation was designed to rescue

a large number of American citizens and publicly demonstrate US resolve. As such, it required a visible, conventional operation on a relatively large scale, with SO in support and targeted at specific objectives. Conversely, had the goals been to recover a small number of detained personnel and to limit US presence, SO might have been selected as the preferred option. SO are not bound by any specific environment. They are described by the transitory characteristics and the constraints placed upon a given mission.

a. Employment of conventional forces usually involves movement of large operational units and requires extensive support structures. Such force movement and employment generally are observable and traceable to the United States. However, the capabilities of SOF primarily are a function of individual and small unit proficiency in a multitude of specialized, often unconventional, combat skills applied with adaptability, improvisation, innovation, and self-reliance. The small size, unique capabilities, and often self-sufficient (for short periods) nature of SOF operational units provide the United States with feasible and appropriate military responses that do not entail the degree of political liability or risk of escalation normally associated with employment of necessarily larger, or more visible, conventional forces.

b. SOF are not a substitute for strong conventional forces but a necessary adjunct to existing conventional capabilities. Depending upon requirements, SOF can operate independently or in conjunction with conventional forces. SOF can complement and reinforce conventional forces so that they can achieve an objective that might not otherwise be attainable. The special skills and low visibility capabilities inherent in SOF also provide an adaptable military response in situations or crises requiring tailored, precisely focused use of force.

c. SOF can be quickly task-organized and rapidly deployed to provide . . . crisis response capability. Often, SOF may be the force of choice . . . to provide a capability that falls between diplomatic initiatives and the overt commitment of conventional force. . . . An imprecise understanding of SOF capabilities or the improper employment or support of SOF at any level of command can result in mission failure, attendant political costs, and possible loss of the entire force. . . .

4. *Characteristics of Special Operations.* SO are marked by certain characteristics that cumulatively distinguish them from conventional operations. They:

a. Are principally offensive, usually of high physical and political risk, and directed at high-value, critical, and often perishable targets. They offer the potential for high returns, but rarely a second chance should a first mission fail.

b. Are often principally politico-military in nature and subject to oversight at the national level. Frequently demand operator-level detailed planning and rapid coordination with other commands, Services, and Government agencies.

c. Often require responsive joint ground, air, and maritime operations and the C_2 architecture permanently resident in the existing SOF structure.

d. May frequently be covert or clandestine.

e. Are frequently prosecuted when the use of conventional forces is either inappropriate or infeasible for either military or political reasons.

f. Rely on surprise, security, and audacity and frequently employ deception to achieve success.

g. Are often conducted at great distances from established support bases, requiring sophisticated communications and means of infiltration, exfiltration, and support to penetrate and recover from hostile, denied, or politically sensitive areas.

h. May require patient, long-term commitment in a given operational area to achieve national goals. . . . Often, the training and organization of indigenous forces are required to attain these objectives.

i. Frequently require discriminate and precise use of force; a mix of high and low technology weapons and equipment; and often rapid development, acquisition, and employment of weapons and equipment not standard for other DOD forces.

j. Are primarily conducted by specially recruited, selected, and trained personnel, organized into small units tailored for specific missions or environments. . . .

k. Require detailed intelligence, thorough planning, decentralized execution, and rigorous detailed rehearsal.

5. *Characteristics of Special Operations Forces.* The demands of SO require forces with attributes that distinguish them from conventional forces. Commanders must be familiar with these characteristics to ensure that missions selected for SOF are compatible with their capabilities.

a. Personnel may undergo lengthy selection processes or extensive mission-specific training programs above basic military skill training to achieve entry-level SO skills.

b. Units are small and necessarily maintain high personal and professional levels of maturity and experience, usually in more than one principal field. The complex SO selection and long leadtime objective and subjective maturation process make any rapid replacement of personnel or capabilities very difficult.

c. SOF are often organized jointly and routinely plan, execute, command, and control operations from a joint perspective.

d. Area orientation is often required and includes the capability to execute all foreseeable operations in the full range of the area's environmental conditions. Detailed area orientation, including mastery of language and culture, requires long-term, dedicated training and may be applicable to air, ground, and maritime SOF units, depending upon mission assignment.

e. To develop and maintain skills, SOF should train and exercise under conditions resembling the operational environment in which they intend to operate. . . .

7. *Special Operations Objectives.* SO missions may be conducted across the entire operational continuum and may be focused on strategic, operational, or tactical objectives.

a. Strategic objectives are directed toward the attainment of national goals. The NCA designates these objectives and sanctions the military means to achieve them. In pursuit of these objectives, SOF may be employed directly by the NCA or combatant commanders. The British Special Operations Executive operation to destroy the German heavy water production at Vemork, Norway, in 1943 (and hence nullify the German capability to manufacture atomic weapons) and the US raid to rescue the prisoners of war at Son Tay, North Vietnam, in 1970, are examples of SO with strategic implications.

b. Operational objectives are established by theater commanders or their component commanders based on the theater campaign plan. Achieving operational objectives leads directly to military success within a theater of war or to the success of a major operation. SOF are normally employed in pursuit of operational objectives by a theater commander, the commander of a subordinate unified command, the commanders of JTF, or by the commander of a Service or functional component command. The employment of OSS operational detachments to organize behind-the-lines resistance in France and Burma in World War II, as well as the German neutralization of the Belgian fortress of Eban [sic] Emael by a surprise attack in force in 1940, are examples of SO with operational implications.

c. Tactical objectives drive the employment of forces in individual battles and engagements. The appropriate commander will assign SOF tactical objectives and operating areas within the context of a larger operation or campaign. They may also be assigned tactical objectives in support of conventional force operations. However, conventional force commanders should recognize that SOF are of finite size and should not be used simply as a substitute for inadequate conventional force availability. Assignment of SOF is normally for a specified period of time or for a specific task or tasks. Ranger operations to seize the airfield at Point Salines, Grenada, in 1983, as well as the Navy's Underwater Demolition Teams' efforts in clearing boat lanes for amphibious assaults in all theaters in World War II, are examples of such tactical support to conventional operations.

8. *The Operational Continuum.* Military operations are conducted within a

continuum consisting of three general states: peacetime military operations, hostilities short of war, and war. This model of a continuum assists the combatant commander to articulate strategic situations within a theater that are described by a variety of political, economic, and military conditions. . . . in actual circumstances there may be no precise distinctions where a particular state ends and another begins. The continuum model gives the NCA and JFC the ability to describe any strategic situation in clear terms. . . .

a. In many situations, the role of SOF is to support conventional operations. In others, when the application of conventional military force is not feasible or appropriate, and particularly when the situation calls for a subtle, indirect, or low visibility approach, SO may offer the most viable military option. . . .

b. Peacetime military operations are a nonhostile state wherein political, economic, psychological, and military measures, short of US combat operations or active support to warring parties, are employed to achieve national objectives. . . .

(1) Peacetime military operations routinely take place in a permissive environment where HN military and law enforcement agencies have the control, intent, and capability to assist friendly operations. US military forces may provide HA or train indigenous personnel to assist host-nation development of military/paramilitary infrastructure and capability. Here, the military instrument is applied for its preventive or deterrent effect to remove the underlying causes of armed conflict or war.

(2) Like all military forces, SOF are a deterrent. Regular demonstrations of their readiness and capabilities in combined exercises with friends and allies worldwide contribute to deterrence and provide a subtle, low-visibility means of extending US influence. Likewise, SOF also contribute to the attainment of peacetime military objectives and may promote regional stability by advising, training, and assisting friends and allies. Such peacetime activities could be characterized by SOF participation in US humanitarian and security assistance programs. When confrontation and tension occur involving the clear threat or use of armed force, a situation exists that is a potential point of transition to a state of conflict.

c. Hostilities short of war are armed struggles or clashes between organized parties within a nation or between nations to achieve limited political or military objectives. Although regular forces are often involved, irregular forces frequently predominate. These operations are often protracted, confined to a restricted geographic area, and constrained in weaponry and level of violence. Within this state, military power in response to threats may be exercised in an indirect manner while supportive of other elements of national power. Limited objectives may be achieved by the short, focused, and direct application of force. Depending upon environment, the full range of SOF capabilities may be applicable.

d. War is sustained armed conflict between nations or organized groups within a nation involving regular and irregular forces in a series of connected battles and campaigns to achieve vital national objectives. War may be limited, with some self-imposed restraints on resources or objectives. Or, it may be general, with the total resources of a nation or nations employed and the national survival of the belligerents at stake. . . .

(1) Regardless of the level of violence or scope of military involvement in peacetime military operations, hostilities short of war, or war, principal strategic objectives always remain political. In war, nonmilitary instruments of power frequently support the military in its goal of defeating the enemy. Such defeat need not necessarily come from the annihilation of the enemy's military force, but may come from the destruction of the enemy's ability or will to continue. This destruction may be achieved by selectively attacking a limited set of critical military, political, economic, and/or social targets, forcing a cessation of hostilities and, thereby, avoiding total or protracted war.

(2) In war, SO are normally conducted in support of conventional warfighting within the framework of the theater campaign. Autonomous SO directed toward strategic objectives may also be conducted, under the direct control of either the NCA or combatant commanders. . . .

9. *Low Intensity Conflict*

a. LIC is an environment in which political rather than military considerations predominate. . . . activities are normally focused on counterinsurgency and include nation building tasks. Advice, training, and assistance also may be focused on combatting terrorism and countering drug trafficking. Similar activities to facilitate national and regional security may also be conducted. These activities frequently require SOF to be sufficiently flexible and politically adroit to meet the nonmilitary objectives of many of these programs.

b. Certain SOF are well suited to participate in military advisory and assistance activities by virtue of their military skills, area orientation, cultural awareness, and mastery of languages. SOF are particularly capable and experienced in training indigenous forces in many of the small unit tactical skills applicable to insurgency and counterinsurgency. Training of indigenous forces is especially applicable in a coalition warfare environment, as in Operations DESERT SHIELD and DESERT STORM. . . .

d. In addition to supporting friendly and allied or coalition governments, the United States may also choose to support insurgencies or armed resistance movements against either hostile regimes or occupying powers. The military aspect of such missions is classic UW for which certain SOF are specifically trained, organized, and equipped. When directed by appropriate authority,

SOF may support these activities either directly or indirectly through other, nonmilitary, government agencies.

CHAPTER II: FORCES AND MISSIONS

1. *Special Operations Forces*

. . . b. Under certain circumstances, conventional forces may provide the capabilities required to conduct a specific special operation. However, designated SOF are principally structured to be the force of choice under most circumstances. They possess unique capabilities designed to address those missions, regardless of where they are conducted in the operational continuum.

(1) *US Army.* Active and Reserve component forces include Special Forces, Ranger, Special Operations Aviation, PSYOP and CA units.

(2) *US Navy.* Active and Reserve component forces include SEAL and SDV teams and SBUs.

(3) *US Air Force.* Active and Reserve component forces include:

(a) Fixed-wing and vertical-lift aircraft and aircrews to conduct infiltration, exfiltration, and resupply; aerial fire support; and aerial refueling

(b) Composite special tactics teams composed of combat control and pararescue forces, weather, communications, and other combat support units.

(4) *Other Forces.* Although not designated as core SOF, certain general purpose forces may receive enhanced training and be specially equipped and organized to conduct missions related to SO. These training enhancements are principally designed to improve the primary combat capabilities of the conventional force and, thereby, to SUPPORT SO on a nondedicated, mission-specific basis. . . .

2. *Missions.* The five principal missions of SO are UW, DA, SR, FID, and CT. While SOF provide unique, versatile, and flexible forces designed primarily to meet these missions, conventional forces may be required for support, depending upon mission circumstances. However, the inherent capabilities of SOF also make them suitable for employment in a range of collateral . . . activities, such as HA, counterdrug, and personnel recovery operations, among others. All of these missions can be conducted and are especially applicable in a coalition warfare environment, where SOF capabilities make them especially useful in this type of short term and/or limited scope operational arrangement of forces.

3. *Unconventional Warfare*

a. UW includes guerrilla warfare and other low visibility, covert, or clandestine operations, as well as subversion, sabotage, intelligence collection, and E&E.

(1) GW consists of military and paramilitary operations conducted by irregular, predominantly indigenous forces in enemy-held or hostile territory. It

is the overt military aspect of an insurgency or other armed resistance movement. Guerrilla forces primarily employ raid and ambush tactics against enemy
vulnerabilities. In the latter stages of a successful insurgency, guerrilla forces
may directly oppose selected, vulnerable enemy forces while avoiding enemy
concentrations of strength.

(2) Subversion is an activity designed to undermine the military, economic, psychological, or political strength or morale of a regime or nation. All
elements of the resistance organization contribute to the subversive effort, but
the clandestine nature of subversion dictates that the underground elements
perform the bulk of the activity.

(3) Sabotage is conducted from within the enemy's infrastructure in
areas presumed to be safe from attack. It is designed to degrade or obstruct the
warmaking capability of a country by damaging, destroying, or diverting war
material, facilities, utilities, and resources. Sabotage may be the most effective
or only means of attacking specific targets that lie beyond the capabilities of
conventional weapon systems. . . . Once accomplished, these incursions can
further result in the enemy spending excessive resources to guard against future
attack.

(4) In UW, the intelligence function must collect, develop, and report
information concerning the capabilities, intentions, and activities of the established government or occupying power and its external sponsors. In this context, intelligence activities have both offensive and defensive purposes and
range well beyond military issues, including social, economic, and political information that may be used to identify threats, operational objectives, and necessary supporting operations.

(5) E&E is an activity that assists military personnel and other selected
persons to:

(a) Move from an enemy-held, hostile, or sensitive area to areas
under friendly control,

(b) Avoid capture if unable to return to an area of friendly control,

(c) Once captured, escape. . . .

b. UW is the military and paramilitary aspect of an insurgency or other
armed resistance movement and may often become a protracted politico-military activity. From the US perspective, UW may be the conduct of indirect or
proxy warfare against a hostile power for the purpose of achieving US national
interests in peacetime; UW may be employed when conventional military involvement is impractical or undesirable; or UW may be a complement to conventional operations in war. The focus of UW is primarily on existing or
potential insurgent, secessionist, or other resistance movements. SOF provide
advice, training, and assistance to existing indigenous resistance organizations.
The intent of UW operations is to exploit a hostile power's . . . vulnerabilities . . . to accomplish US strategic or operational objectives.

c. When UW is conducted independently during military operations short of war or war, its primary focus is on political and psychological objectives. A successful effort to organize and mobilize a segment of the civil population may culminate in military action. Strategic UW objectives may include:

(1) Undermining the domestic and international legitimacy of the target authority.

(2) Neutralizing the target authority's power and shifting that power to the resistance organization.

(3) Destroying the confidence and will of the target authority's leadership.

(4) Isolating the target authority from international diplomatic and material support while obtaining such support for the resistance organization.

(5) Obtaining the support or neutrality of the various segments of the society.

d. When UW operations support conventional military operations, the focus shifts to primarily military objectives. However, the political and psychological implications remain. UW operations delay and disrupt hostile military activities, interdict LOC, deny the hostile power unrestricted use of key areas, divert . . . attention and resources from the main battle area, and interdict hostile warfighting capabilities. Properly integrated . . . operations can extend the depth of air, sea, or ground battles, complement conventional military operations, and provide . . . the windows of opportunity needed to seize the initiative through offensive action.

e. During war, SOF may directly support the resistance movement by infiltrating operational elements into denied or politically sensitive areas. They organize, train, equip, and advise or direct the indigenous resistance organization. In situations short of war, when direct US military involvement is inappropriate or infeasible, SOF may instead provide indirect support from an external location.

f. UW may be conducted by all designated SOF, but it is principally the responsibility of Army SF. Augmentation other than SOF, will usually be provided as the situation dictates by PSYOP and CA units, as well as other selected conventional combat, combat support, and combat service support forces.

4. *Direct Action*

a. In the conduct of DA operations, units may employ raid, ambush, or direct assault tactics; emplace munitions and other devices; conduct standoff attacks by fire from air, ground, or maritime platforms; provide terminal guidance for precision-guided munitions; and conduct independent sabotage.

b. DA operations are normally limited in scope and duration and usually incorporate a planned withdrawal from the immediate objective area. SOF may conduct these missions unilaterally or in support of conventional operations. DA operations are designed to achieve specific, well-defined, and often time-sensitive results of strategic, operational, or critical tactical significance. They frequently occur beyond the reach of tactical weapon systems and selective strike capabilities of conventional forces. . . .

e. DA missions to locate, recover, and restore to friendly control persons held captive, isolated, or threatened in sensitive, denied, or contested areas may be conducted when the priority of the operation is sufficiently high to warrant planning and conducting a special operation. . . . SOF recovery missions are often characterized by detailed planning, rehearsal, and thorough intelligence analysis. They routinely employ unconventional tactics and techniques, clandestine search, indigenous assistance, and the frequent use of ground combat elements. . . .

5. *Special Reconnaissance*

a. SR complements national and theater intelligence collection assets and systems by obtaining specific, well-defined, and time-sensitive information of strategic or operational significance. It may complement other collection methods where there are constraints of weather, terrain-masking, hostile countermeasures and/or other systems availability. SR is a human intelligence function that places US or US-controlled "eyes on target" in hostile, denied, or politically sensitive territory when authorized. SOF may conduct these missions unilaterally or in support of conventional operations. SOF may use advanced reconnaissance and surveillance techniques and equipment and/or sophisticated clandestine collection methods and may employ indigenous assets. . . .

6. *Foreign Internal Defense*

a. The primary role of SOF in this US Government interagency activity is to train, advise, and otherwise assist host nation military and paramilitary forces with the goal of the host nation being able, unilaterally, to assume responsibility to eliminate internal instability. . . .

c. FID is not exclusively a SO mission. Rather, it is a joint and interagency activity in which SOF participate. SO FID requirements may be unilateral in the absence of any other US military effort, may support other ongoing military or civilian assistance efforts, or may support the employment of conventional military forces. . . .

7. *Counterterrorism.* The primary mission of SOF in CT is to apply highly specialized capabilities to preempt or resolve terrorist incidents abroad.

a. Certain SOF are specifically organized, trained, equipped, and tasked to perform CT as a primary mission. CT missions may also be performed by other SOF or selected conventional US Armed Forces under extremely urgent and in extremis circumstances when principal NCA-designated SOF are not readily available. . . .

b. SOF conduct CT operations that include aspects of UW, DA, and SR missions to effect:

(1) Hostage rescue.

(2) Recovery of sensitive materiel from terrorist organizations.

(3) Attack on the terrorist infrastructure.

c. Because of the very low profile of most terrorist organizations, identifying targets for CT missions can be extremely difficult. Although a preemptive strike against terrorists may be preferred, CT missions must often be conducted after the terrorists have initiated a terrorist act.

d. Additionally, as a subset of FID, designated SOF units may also train selected host nation forces to perform CT missions. The level of SO force participation in this program is determined by US and host nation policy and legal considerations.

8. *Collateral Special Operations Activities.* The inherent capabilities of all military forces may periodically be applied to accomplish missions other than those for which the forces are principally organized, trained, and equipped. However, commanders should exercise care in allocating forces against nonprimary missions to preclude overcommitment of those forces and the attendant reduction in their ability to meet principal tasks. Collateral activities in which SOF, by virtue of their inherent capabilities, may selectively be tasked to participate include: SA, HA, antiterrorism and other security activities, counterdrug operations, personnel recovery, and special activities.

a. *Security Assistance.* SA is a group of programs authorized by the Foreign Assistance Act, the Arms Export Control Act, or other related US statutes. The US Government sells defense articles and services, including training, to eligible foreign countries and international organizations that further US national security objectives. The primary SOF role in SA is to provide MTT and other forms of training assistance. Personnel providing SA services (including mobile training assistance) are prohibited by law from performing combatant duties.

b. *Humanitarian Assistance.* HA programs employ military personnel but are principally designed to promote nonmilitary objectives within a foreign civilian community. These objectives may include disaster relief; medical, veterinary, and dental aid; rudimentary construction; water and sanitation assistance; expedient communications; and support to and/or resettlement of displaced civilians (refugees or evacuees). Although HA does not fall solely under the purview of SO, certain SOF are well-suited to assist US Government-sponsored HA activities in remote areas, especially in a conflict environment. . . .

c. *Antiterrorism and Other Security Activities.* These activities ensure that the physical security of important persons, facilities, and events meets acceptable standards. Responding to requests from the Services and other government agencies, SOF can provide training and advice on how to reduce vulnerability to terrorism and other hostile threats. SOF anticipate hostile activity and evaluate the adequacy of existing physical security systems, using their expertise in conducting operations similar to those that potentially threaten the persons and activities requesting their assistance. When directed, SOF can augment existing security forces to protect important persons and events. . . .

d. *Counterdrug.* CD measures are interagency activities taken to disrupt, interdict, and destroy illicit drug activities. As a general rule under the Posse Comitatus Act (18 USC 1385), DOD personnel and equipment may not be used in a domestic law enforcement capacity. In 1981, Congress enacted an exception that authorized specific DOD assistance in drug interdiction and drug eradication operations (10 USC 371-380). Designated civilian agencies of the US Government normally lead US CD activities within a host nation. The primary SOF role is to support US and host nation CD efforts abroad by advising, training, and assisting host nation military, paramilitary and, when specifically authorized, police operations targeted at the sources of narcotics and the LOC for narcotics movement. . . .

f. *Special Activities.* Special activities are governed by Executive Order 12333 and require a Presidential finding and congressional oversight. These are activities conducted abroad in support of national foreign policy objectives. They are conducted in such a manner that US Government participation is neither apparent nor publicly acknowledged. Whether supporting or conducting a special activity, SOF may perform any of their primary wartime missions, subject to the limitations imposed on special activities. Such activities are highly compartmented and centrally managed and controlled.

9. *Coalition Warfare and SOF.* SOF must be prepared to conduct SO under conditions of coalition warfare. SOF may be required to execute unilateral operations or apply their unique characteristics to provide liaison to coalition partners and, by so doing, facilitate interoperability between US and allied forces. As evidenced during operations DESERT SHIELD and DESERT STORM, the role that SOF played in support of the campaign objectives by training, working, and going into combat with the majority of the coalition nations was one of the keys to campaign success. SOF unique capabilities in language training, their regional orientation and forward deployment, and focus on independent small unit actions make them one of the principal forces of choice to complement and support coalition warfare objectives.

CHAPTER III: ORGANIZATION AND COMMAND AND CONTROL

1. *General.* SO require a responsive and unified C2 structure. Layering of headquarters within the SO chain of command decreases responsiveness, creates an opportunity for a security compromise, and is unnecessary. Normally, OPCON is exercised directly by a unified, subordinate unified, joint force, or Service or functional component commander without intervening levels of command. In rare instances, circumstances may require OPCON be exercised by a JSOTF commander reporting directly to the NCA through the Chairman of the Joint Chiefs of Staff. . . .

f. *Deconfliction and Coordination*

(1) Deconfliction and coordination with conventional forces are always critical concerns for SO commanders. Areas of interest routinely include target deconfliction, C4, frequency allocation, intelligence collection efforts, surface or airspace deconfliction, fire support coordination, and coordination of logistic and other theater support. Historically, SOF have been employed in advance of conventional operations. This coordination is important in the transition from special to conventional follow-on operations and ensures that the timing and tempo of the overall unified campaign is maintained.

(2) SOF must be interoperable with conventional forces that either host or support their activities. This is especially true during time-critical contingency operations. For example, if SOF are operating from naval surface vessels during forced entry operations, they must be prepared to function compatibly with the host vessel in the areas of weapons, communications equipment, and shipboard logistics. Likewise, the host conventional force commander must tailor his own operations and command arrangements so as not to inhibit the operation of SOF, since that commander may not be in the SOF operational chain of command.

(3) During extended operations involving both SOF and conventional forces, joint control and deconfliction measures take on added significance. A tested method of achieving these measures is for the unified, subordinate unified, or JTF commander, as appropriate, to establish a JSOA.

(a) Coordinating and deconflicting SO with other joint operations will be critical. SO will often involve air operations that transit theater airspace control areas and the air defense area. SO ground forces often operate in areas affected by friendly conventional force surface and air attacks on enemy targets throughout the area of operations. Therefore, it is extremely important that SO be deconflicted with all other joint force operations. This requires close coordination between the JSOTF and JTF. (Additional guidance is provided in Joint Pub 3-09, "Doctrine for Joint Fire Support" and Joint Pub 3-52, "Doctrine for Airspace Control in a Combat Zone.") SOF operations in enemy territory must be coordinated to prevent double targeting or fratricide.

(b) Joint deconfliction is further enhanced by the exchange of liaison elements between the staffs of appropriate conventional and SO forces (see Joint Pub 5-00.2, "Joint Task Force (JTF) Planning Guidance and Procedures" for details on liaison elements). The staffs may coordinate fire support, overflight, aerial refueling, targeting, deception, PSYOP, CA, and other theater operational issues based on ongoing or projected SO missions. . . .

4. *Command Relationships.* . . . Various organizational structures may be established for employment of SOF. Certain arrangements might be more commonly used during war or extended operations while others may be better suited for peacetime or contingencies of relatively short duration. However, the choice of organization for employment of SOF should depend upon specific objectives, security requirements, and the operational environment. Therein lies the flexibility of SOF. . . .

CHAPTER IV: PLANNING FOR JOINT SPECIAL OPERATIONS

1. *General.* Planning for SO can be either deliberate or time-sensitive, using crisis action procedures. . . . Experience has repeatedly demonstrated that SO planners must be brought into the planning process at the beginning, and that those who will execute the mission must be involved in that process. Likewise, political considerations usually figure prominently in the planning of SO. Changes in political objectives or constraints may cause operational characteristics to change rapidly and significantly. . . .

2. *Strategic Planning and Force Allocation.* The national security strategy of the United States seeks to assure and protect national interests that encompass much more than the pure military defense of the nation and its allies. In general, peacetime national policy is to prevent and deter aggression and acts of intimidation or terrorism that may hinder US political, economic, social, or military freedom of action or security. SOF play significant roles in this primarily political environment by offering uniquely trained and equipped units that can be tailored flexibly to execute a range of overt and low-visibility options designed to contain or resolve crises. . . .

3. *Deployment Planning.* . . . Principal goals of this process are to identify, resource, and phase those forces required to deploy in-theater. Additionally, plans must address transportation alternatives and ability to conduct in-theater reception of forces. Theater Service components must be informed of SOF deployments into their theaters, since Service components are responsible for logistic support to their respective Service SOF.

a. Selection of those SOF to deploy and, later, operate in support of an OPLAN or CONPLAN must be based on a clear concept of what is to be accomplished on land, at sea, and in the air. This concept must be developed from an unambiguous understanding of the mission capabilities resident in SOF, a comparison of SOF capabilities with those of other assigned and/or supporting forces, and a knowledge of the targets and operating areas in the theater against which SOF could be employed to enhance the theater commander's campaign. Special and conventional operations must be linked coherently to ensure the success of the overall theater strategy and campaign plan.

b. General war plans routinely deal in vast numbers of personnel and support equipment, SOF included, designed to support large operations. However, certain crises could require rapid deployment of smaller forces, including SOF, either directly to the crisis location, or to an intermediate or remote staging base. In the first instance, the long-range insertion of SOF into an objective area requires that the deployment be planned as an integral part of the operation as opposed to mere transportation. In the second case, political and military considerations may warrant further specialized deployment planning. In either instance, the introduction of SOF into a theater must be planned commensurate with the specific strategic, operational, and tactical objectives and the attendant political environment. . . .

6. *Deliberate Mission Planning and Targeting*

a. Detailed mission planning, based on specific detailed, comprehensive, and accurate tactical intelligence is vital to successful mission execution and also to the very survival of the operational element. Based on the SOC commander's mission guidance, subordinate SOF commanders conduct their own deliberate mission planning. The objective of this process is to develop a comprehensive plan that provides for flexible execution. SO force commanders cannot tie themselves to a rigid plan. They must anticipate the unexpected and remain flexible enough to modify their plans, as required, to achieve their higher commander's intent.

b. Deliberate SOF targeting and mission planning may require days or weeks to prepare for commitment into remote or denied territory. The operational and selected support elements must gain a thorough knowledge of the operational area. Personnel must understand the geographic, political, social, psychological, economic, climatic, and military situation in the target area. For some missions, they must also know the culture, language, customs, and ethnic and religious affiliations and antagonisms of the target audience that could affect mission execution. This level of area orientation is achieved either through intensive study before employment, or, better yet, by having previously lived in the intended area of operations.

c. SO in permissive environments . . . may be less complex and, therefore, require considerably less planning and preparation time. The same is true for certain short-duration SO activities directed against less sophisticated threats in a semipermissive environment. . . . Under these conditions, there is less re-quirement for elaborate infiltration, resupply, or exfiltration planning. . . .

d. Regardless of the mission or operational environment, three principles of SO planning remain important:

(1) Specific targets or mission assignments for SOF should always con-tribute substantially to the strategic or campaign plan being executed. Limited resources and the extensive planning required dictate that a commander selec-tively employ SOF for high priority operations. Further, the sensitivity of many SOF missions may force the NCA to place specific political, legal, time-of-day, geographic, or force size constraints upon the employing and supporting force.

(2) SOF missions are complete packages—insertion, resupply, fire and maneuver support, extraction—to be thoroughly planned before committing the force. The nature of the target, enemy situation, and environmental charac-teristics of the operational area are key planning factors. They will dictate the size and capabilities of the assigned force, the nature of tactical operations, methods of insertion and extraction, length of force exposure, logistic require-ments, and size and composition of the command and support structure. Al-though operational planning must focus on the objective, limiting intelligence and environmental information to the target area will not meet SOF require-ments.

(3) SO rarely can be repeated if they at first fail, since SO targets nor-mally are perishable either from a military or political viewpoint. Therefore, thorough, detailed, and, whenever possible, repeated rehearsal is critical. These rehearsals should be conducted with the exact force to be committed and under the same time and distance constraints in an environment whose terrain and weather conditions closely approximate the operational area. A by-product of such rehearsal is that the operational element absorbs alternative courses of action and is better able to adapt to changed circumstances during the mission. Commanders should recognize and plan for such preparation time.

7. *Time-Sensitive Mission Planning and Targeting*

a. Clearly, there will be those crises, especially in peacetime, that do not lend themselves to deliberate planning. Targets and objectives may be clear, but time may become a critical factor and impose constraints on planning and other mission preparation not experienced during deliberate planning. This is significant because the success of any SO largely depends on the quality of mis-sion preparation.

b. If time is insufficient for normal planning, the SOF commander must determine minimum essential preparation tasks and modify normal proce-dures to accomplish those tasks in the time available.

8. *Criteria for Evaluating SO Options.* To avoid misapplication of SOF,

commanders should evaluate SOF employment potential for appropriateness, feasibility, and supportability at the commencement of planning.

a. *Appropriateness*. Missions must be especially suitable for SOF capabilities and compatible with national policies.

(1) *Suitability for SOF Capabilities.* . . .

(2) *Compatibility with National Policy.* . . .

b. *Feasibility*. Successful execution of SO missions requires complete planning of all phases of the operation: infiltration, movement to the objective, actions at the objective, withdrawal, and extraction. . . . SOF are not structured for attrition or force-on-force warfare. Planning cannot ignore the vulnerability of SOF units operating in hostile territory. Feasibility assessments should also compare the skill levels required for successful execution, current training levels of SOF units to be tasked, and the time required for planning and attainment of necessary levels of individual and unit proficiency to meet the specific mission at hand.

c. *Supportability*. Resources and capability should be adequate to support the individual SO being considered and, when applicable, the entire SOF operation plan. Support involves aiding, protecting, complementing, and sustaining employed SOF. . . . Even though the target may be vulnerable to SOF, deficiencies in supportability may affect the scale of the contemplated SO or may entirely invalidate the feasibility of employing SOF.

9. *Operational Security*. OPSEC is used by SOF to deny information of intelligence value to hostile, or even friendly, agencies that could cause direct or indirect mission compromise. OPSEC is critical during SOF employments throughout the operational continuum.

a. The initial planning step for SO must determine the level of OPSEC protection required. . . . Requisite security measures, including deception and . . . protection, must be implemented immediately. During initial OPSEC planning phase, SO tactics, capabilities, personnel movements, and logistics should be protected in all phases of the operation including the post-execution phase.

b. The need for OPSEC must be properly balanced against the need for coordinated planning, execution, and deconfliction of these activities with conventional operations. Compartmentation of and special access to certain information may be necessary, however, commanders must balance the need for secrecy against the need for coordination. Key planners from all disciplines (i.e., intelligence, deception, PSYOP, medical, fire support, C4 systems, logistics, and conventional liaison) should be involved with the SO planners in all phases of planning. The keystone of SO is whomever will EXECUTE the mission must PLAN the mission.

10. *Military Deception Initiatives*

a. SOF should be capable of planning and conducting military deception operations. Similarly, military deception or perception management efforts may use actual SO and the threats SOF present to support the theater campaign. Theater deception or military deception initiatives that use or support SOF should not inadvertently heighten enemy awareness of SOF operations.

b. Most SO rely on secrecy and an unalerted enemy for mission success. However, the execution of some SO missions may reveal the presence of SOF to the enemy owing to distinct operating signatures.

c. Military deception initiatives should be manifested in concert with a cohesive OPSEC and PSYOP plan focusing on the culture, social organizations, intelligence collection and communications infrastructure of the targeted force. . . .

(1) If the objective is to preserve secrecy of SOF activities, deception may be used to support OPSEC. Such deception initiatives may be diversionary operations to focus enemy attention away from actual objectives, or more likely, deception efforts may be informational programs designed to mislead target audiences and cover activities to deny recognition of SOF.

(2) If the objective is to influence the adversary, OPSEC would be part of the deception effort. Actions may include deceptive feints, displays, and ruses; intrusive or deceptive communications; or exploitation of terrain and weather to mislead the opposition.

CHAPTER V: PREPARATION AND SUPPORT OF JOINT SPECIAL OPERATIONS FORCES

. . . 5. *Intelligence Support of SOF.* Intelligence must assist commanders in identifying special operations objectives that will further overall objectives. All other aspects of military operations depend on the determination of relevant, clear, and attainable objectives. In the process of identifying and nominating military objectives, the J-2 should understand the command's responsibilities, commander's mission and intent, the means available, and the characteristics of the theater or joint operations area. Intelligence should provide the commander with an understanding of the enemy in terms of enemy goals, objectives, strengths, weaknesses, values, and critical vulnerabilities. The J-2 then nominates as objectives those commander's ends and intent. Once objectives are determined, intelligence must continuously review them to see if they remain relevant to the commander's intent.

a. *General.* Timely, detailed, tailored, and fused all-source intelligence is vital in determining SO objectives, identifying relevant targets, and mission planning and execution. The US intelligence community includes numerous agencies that support various echelons of the command structure. Those agencies differ in purpose and the degree to which they support tactical mission requirements of individual operational elements. Just as intelligence requirements for different conventional forces vary, so do some of the intelligence requirements for SOF. In fact, SOF intelligence requirements are similar to those of conventional forces, although the degree of detail is frequently greater. However, the nature of many SOF objectives and methodologies require intelligence support different from that needed in conventional operations. SOF often require intelligence to avoid enemy forces, as opposed to information that would allow conventional forces to directly engage the enemy. A large percentage of such intelligence data is available within the US intelligence community and/or open source material. However, many "target-specific" items require more research, analysis, graphics, photos, and textual elaboration than normally needed for conventional mission planning. If target-specific intelligence is not available, analogies or estimates drawn from similar targets in the same region must be provided.

(1) The mechanics (procedural and technological) of providing suitable SO intelligence support must be flexible enough to satisfy both the time-sensitive (combat or crisis) and deliberate (peacetime or routine) mission planning processes. Intelligence requirements and OPSEC should be considered carefully to ensure that adequate intelligence can be acquired without compromising the mission. Adaptive or emergent targeting offers the most rigorous and critical conditions for conducting effective SO intelligence support. The system's ability to meet urgent, short-notice requirements is critical. Adaptive or time-sensitive requirements should also be used by the SO peacetime or routine intelligence support organization in order to facilitate periodic readiness exercises and effective transition to actual combat or crisis support. By continuous tasking during peace to support the SO mission planning process, the system's capability to effectively support SOF in wartime will be refined. An efficient, deliberate intelligence planning structure can meet accelerated requirements during crisis.

(2) The primary nonorganic sources for SO intelligence are the Service combat intelligence and production organizations, the theater CINC, J-2s, NSA, and DIA. SOF requirements must be identified and prioritized within overall national and theater intelligence requirements and capabilities. In conjunction with DIA, the theater CINC J-2s ensure that SO intelligence requirements are identified, understood, validated, and satisfied. For this arrangement to work, SOF commanders must develop and communicate these requirements to the intelligence community at the inception of a mission to ensure determination of relevant objectives and operations, and effective planning can begin. This will allow the intelligence community maximum time to respond, especially during time-sensitive operations. Optimum support is achieved through

constant interaction and feedback between commanders and intelligence and operations personnel.

(3) Interface through the theater SOC to theater and national intelligence systems and assets is critical for SOF success. SOF mission accomplishment may hinge on target or intelligence updates provided by other government agencies. A JSOTF, when formed, must have these same interfaces. . . .

b. *Targeting*. Targeting is the intelligence function of evaluating the enemy's intent and capabilities with respect to the commander's mission and objectives and identifying and nominating critical enemy activities, situations, capabilities or resources that are vulnerable to military operations. . . . SO targeting, like conventional targeting, combines intelligence and operations. It represents the integration of intelligence threat information, the target system, and target characteristics with operations data on friendly force posture, capabilities, weapons effects, objectives, rules of engagement, and doctrine. Targeting matches objectives and guidance with inputs from intelligence and operations to identify the forces necessary to achieve the objectives. SOF are limited in size and, therefore, must be judiciously applied against high-value, high-risk, or intelligence-critical targets whose destruction, elimination, degradation, or surveillance would have significant positive and lasting effects on achieving US national objectives or on a theater campaign plan. A coherent SOF targeting doctrine must encompass the full range of SOF mission characteristics. . . .

c. *Counterintelligence*. CI is a critical force protection asset that offers the commander varied support including operations, investigations, collection, and threat analysis. The commander should be well informed on the capability and effectiveness of host nation intelligence and security services.

(1) *Early Deployment*. Commanders and their planning staffs should consider the advance deployment of CI teams to establish liaison with host nation security forces and the US Country Team when possible. CI teams should be identified in deployment lists and operational orders.

(2) *Command and Control*. Upon execution of the operational plan, command and control of the supporting service CI elements will be assigned to the theater component commander. . . .

(3) *Threat Analysis*. CI analysis may be conducted at the theater (Joint Intelligence Centers) or national (DIA, CIA, or Services) level. Threat information available to the commander includes the intelligence threat, by either human or technical collection means, posed by foreign intelligence services and other adversarial organizations. . . .

8. *Public Affairs Support of SOF*. The political sensitivity of many SO, especially in peacetime, mandates that thorough and accurate PA guidance be de-

veloped during the operational planning stage and approved for use in advance of most operations. PA planning must integrate accurate representation of the mission to domestic audiences with the overall PSYOP operations effort and strategic and tactical OPSEC programs. The commander having operational authority should develop proposed PA guidance, coordinating with supporting commands and government agencies, as appropriate, and forward that guidance to the Assistant Secretary of Defense (Public Affairs) for approval.

9. *Legal Support of SOF.* SO frequently involve a unique set of complex issues. There are Federal laws and Executive Orders, Federal agency publications and directives, and theater ROE that may affect SO. These guidelines become especially critical during sensitive peacetime operations when international and domestic laws, treaty provisions, and political agreements may affect mission planning and execution. Commanders should seek legal review during planning and execution of SO.

10. *Environmental Support of SOF.* Environmental support services (weather and oceanography) are critical to the success of SO missions. From initial planning through execution, environmental intelligence should be included in the decision making process. Unique local conditions may expedite a particular course of action or make it impossible. Oceanographic surveys provide data on currents, surfs, tides, reefs, and dangerous marine animals. An examination of general climatology and specific weather forecasts for the operations area will provide the commander with the data necessary to choose the best windows of opportunity to execute, support, and sustain specific missions. Potentially, the execution decision may turn on exploiting certain adverse weather conditions to provide cover for operations while avoiding those environmental conditions that will hamper operations. Such decisions often require finesse and judgment. For example, many SOF aircraft are designed to operate at low level, at night, and in adverse weather (fog or moderate rain). However, heavier rain or sandstorms, for example, may exceed avionics operating limits. Since SO may be conducted over very great distances or extended periods of time, environmental planning and projection become critical components in the operational decision; a focus on just the target or terminal areas is too narrow. Support to the JFSOCC (SOC or JSOTF) may be provided on a continuing basis by specially trained and organized USAF or USN elements. The USAF Special Operations Weather Teams provide environmental support predominantly to AFSOF and ARSOF. NMET provide environmental services principally to NAVSOF. Support from the NMET includes weather and oceanography as well as maps and charts. Provision of selected maps and charts to AFSOF and ARSOF is routinely provided via intelligence channels (see paragraph 5 above).

11. *Space Support of SOF.* Space-based support to military operations is

continuing to improve. SO commanders and planners should be aware of potential space support for their operations and how best to obtain it. A sampling of space-based capabilities includes:

   a. Guidance, navigation, and air and maritime traffic control.

   b. Global communications.

   c. Global intelligence collection.

   d. Surveillance and warning.

   e. Meteorological support.

   f. Imagery for mapping and targeting.

   g. EW.

Abbreviations Used in the Text Above:

AFSOF, Air Force Special Operations Forces
ARSOF, Army Special Operations Forces
C2, Command and Control
C4, Command, Control, Communications, and Computers
CA, Civil Affairs
CONPLAN, Concept Plan
DIA, Defense Intelligence Agency
E&E, Evasion and Escape
EW, Early Warning or Electronic Warfare
HA, Humanitarian Assistance
HN, Host Nation
J-2, Intelligence Directorate of a Joint Staff
JFC, Joint Force Commander
JFSOCC, Joint Force Special Operations Component Commander
JSOA, Joint Special Operations Area
JSOTF, Joint Special Operations Task Force
JTF, Joint Task Force
LOC, Line of Communications
MTT, Mobile Training Team
NAVSOF, Naval Special Operations Forces
NCA, National Command Authorities
NMET, Naval Mobile Environmental Team
NSA, National Security Agency
OPCON, Operational Control
OPLAN, Operation Plan
PSYOP, Psychological Operations
ROE, Rules of Engagement
SBU, Special Boat Unit
SDV, Submerged Delivery Vehicle
SEAL, Sea-Air-Land Team
SOC, Special Operations Command
UW, Unconventional Warfare

For Further Reading

THE LITERATURE on terrorism has been driven by a crisis syndrome. Horrific events are followed by an outpouring of commentary. Threats perceived at the moment have also generated spates of books and articles. In between, far less attention has typically been devoted to the subject. Probably the high points in the evolution of the literature are the 1980s, when Lebanon disintegrated into a miasma of political movements, splinter groups, and terrorist activists, and the present. The earlier period was characterized by a great number of collections of papers from conferences, and monographs on facets of the larger subject that crossed over into political history, such as books on the origins and development of the Palestinian Liberation Organization, accounts of Israeli hit teams, or the huge literature on the Iran-Contra affair. For a more focused study of the American attempt to cope with these events, see David C. Martin and John Walcott, *Best Laid Plans: The Inside Story of America's War on Terrorism* (New York: Random House, 1988). In view of the current debate on assassination as a tool in foreign policy, it is worth recalling the 1986 bombing of Libya. On this see Seymour Hersh, "Target Qaddhafi" (*New York Times Magazine*, February 22, 1987).

The 1980s did produce one of the very few books that engages terrorism on a broad philosophical level and places responses to terrorism in the context of the need to answer terrorist demands with political programs in addition to force. That is Richard E. Rubenstein's *Alchemists of Revolution: Terrorism in the Modern World* (New York: Basic Books, 1987).

In the several years prior to September 11, 2001, experts saw the emergent terrorist threat in terms of the use of weapons of mass destruction, including chemical, biological, or nuclear weapons. Writing on the general subject of terrorism was dominated during that period by discussions of this aspect. In fact, a survey of foreign affairs and international security journals for the last two years reveals frequent articles on terrorists and mass destruction, and almost nothing on the overall problem. Many of these treatments began with an assumption that terrorists would acquire their exotic weapons (chemicals and biologicals first) from the former Soviet Union. For an inside account of the former Soviet chemical and biological weapons program, see Ken Alibek with Stephen Handelman, *Biohazard* (New York: Random House, 1999). A broader account that takes up the Alibek story but covers Russian and other foreign biological weapons programs is in Tom Mangold and Jeff Goldberg, *Plague Wars: The Terrifying Reality of Biological Warfare* (New York: St. Martin's Press, 1999). The most recent treatment of this subject is in Judith Miller, Stephen Engelberg, and William Broad, *Germs: Biological Weapons and America's Secret War* (New York: Simon and Schuster, 2001). The only actual use of any of these kinds of weapons to date is Aum Shinrikyo's 1995 sarin nerve-gas attack on the Tokyo subway. An account of this incident is in Haruki Murakami, *Underground* (New York: Vintage International, 2001).

On the theoretical problem of terrorist acquisition of nuclear weapons, the best treatment is that of former Clinton administration National Security Council staffer Jessica Stern in *The Ultimate Terrorists* (Cambridge, Mass.: Harvard University Press, 1999).

Behind worries over exotic weapons, a close second in recent analytical concern has been the possibility that terrorists will attack computer systems. This is a variant of the general discourse on cyberwar and has a limited specific literature. Periodicals abound with treatments of this subject.

The Bush administration's creation of an assistant for Homeland Defense within the White House has been prefigured in congressional reports and in the specialist literature. The 21st Century defense panel headed by Gary Hart and Warren Rudman had as one of its recommendations the creation of a cabinet-level department for this purpose. For a representative example of writings on this subject, see Terence Kelly, "An Organizational Framework for Homeland Defense" (*Parameters*, Autumn 2001, pp. 105–116).

For an approach to the general problem of terrorism from a legal and national point of view, see former senior Justice Department official Philip B. Heymann's *Terrorism and America: A Commonsense Strategy for a Democratic Society* (Cambridge, Mass.: MIT Press, 2000). A more security-oriented approach, which includes the cyberwar issue mentioned above, is in the RAND Corporation study *Countering the New Terrorism* by Ian O. Lesser, Bruce Hoffman, John Arquilla, David Ronfeldt, and Michelle Zanini, published in 1999. Hoffman and another RAND analyst, Brian M. Jenkins, are among the most experienced observers of terrorism, and any of their writings are worth attention. The view of a former CIA Counterterrorism Center official is in Paul R. Pillar's *Terrorism and U.S. Foreign Policy* (Washington, D.C.: Brookings Institution Press, 2001).

A few useful articles in the scholarly literature deserve mention. See Peter Chalk's "The Evolving Dynamic of Terrorism in the 1990s" (*Australian Journal of International Affairs*, 1999, No. 2, pp. 151–168) for a broad overview. An important critique of terrorism studies is in David W. Brannan, Philip F. Esler, and N. T. Anders Strindberg, "Talking to 'Terrorists': Towards an Independent Analytical Framework for the Study of Violent Substate Activism" (*Studies in Conflict & Terrorism*, No. 24, 2001, pp. 3–24). A broad effort to apply risk-management techniques to terrorism is in Richard Falkenrath, "Analytic Models and Policy Prescription: Understanding Recent Innovation in U.S. Counterterrorism" (*Studies in Conflict and Terrorism*, No. 24, 2001, pp. 159–181). Journals in the special field include the one just noted as well as *Low Intensity Conflict and Law Enforcement*. Some of the best writing on the subject appears in foreign journals of international affairs or strategic studies, especially those from India and Russia, no doubt motivated by the troubles in Kashmir and Chechnya.

INFORMATION RESOURCES CENTER
ASIS INTERNATIONAL
1625 PRINCE STREET
ALEXANDRIA, VA 22314
(703) 519-6200

DEMCO